Sappho and the Virgin Mary

Between Men ~ Between Women
Lesbian and Gay Studies
Lillian Faderman and Larry Gross, Editors

Sappho and the Virgin Mary

Same-Sex Love and the English Literary Imagination

Ruth Vanita

Columbia University Press

New York

Columbia University Press
Publishers Since 1893
New York   Chichester, West Sussex
Copyright © 1996 Columbia University Press
All rights reserved

Library of Congress Cataloging-in-Publication Data
Vanita, Ruth.
Sappho and the Virgin Mary : same-sex love and the English
literary imagination / Ruth Vanita.
p.   cm. — (Between men~Between women)
Includes bibliographical references (p.) and index.
ISBN 0–231–10550–9 (cloth). — ISBN 0–231–10551–7 (pbk.)
1. English literature—History and criticism. 2. Homosexuality
and literature—Great Britain—History. 3. Lesbians' writings,
English—History and criticism. 4. Mary, Blessed Virgin, Saint—In
literature. 5. Lesbians in literature. 6. Sappho—In literature.
7. Women in literature. 8. Love in literature.   I. Title.
II. Series.
PR408.H65V36   1996
820.9'353—dc20   96–17768
CIP

Casebound editions of Columbia University Press books are printed on permanent
and durable acid-free paper.
Printed in the United States of America
c 10 9 8 7 6 5 4 3 2 1

Contents

Acknowledgments

This book was written at Cornell University during a 1994–1995 fellowship at the Society for the Humanities. I am grateful to Professor Dominick La Capra, to the staff of the society, and to my colleagues there for the conducive work environment they created, to the students and staff of Telluride House whose generosity relieved me of the pressures of housekeeping and greatly facilitated my work, and to the wonderfully helpful staff of the Olin Library. I would also like to thank Miranda House for granting me a year's leave and the English Department, Delhi University, for permitting me to take up my new position there a year after I was appointed. Ann Miller and Susan Pensak of Columbia University Press have been uniformly helpful and accommodating; the readers' reports on the first draft were very useful to me in the process of revision. Part of chapter 8 appeared as "Throwing Caution to the Winds: Homoerotic Patterns in *The Waves*," in Eileen Barrett and Patricia Cramer, eds., *Re:Reading, Re:Writing, Re:Teaching Virginia Woolf* (New York: Pace University Press, 1995), and part of chapter 9 as "Love Unspeakable: The Uses of Allusion in *Flush*" in Vara Neverow-Turk and Mark Hussey, eds., *Virginia Woolf: Themes and Variations* (New York: Pace University Press, 1993). Some of the material was presented at the Woolf Society Conference, 1993, and at the Society for the Humanities in 1994 and I benefited from the discussions that followed. I also learned a lot from discussions with students of the course "Biography as Homoerotic Fiction" that I offered at Cornell in 1994.

Acknowledgments

Personal debts are much harder to describe; this listing is an entirely inadequate attempt. Frances and Brij Raj Singh, Chris Cuomo, Mary Katzenstein, Sabu George, Archana Prasad, Alaka and Kaushik Basu made New York City and Ithaca a home away from home, a blend of the best in American and Indian traditions of friendship; Asha George, Eileen Barrett, Patty Ruppelt, Suparna Bhaskaran, and Sujata Gupta provided invaluable emotional support over that miracle of modern technology, the telephone.

The Woolf material in the last three chapters is reworked from my doctoral dissertation. I am grateful for the guidance of my supervisor Professor Harish Trivedi of the English Department, Delhi University, and the support of my friends Kiran Kaushik, Prabha Dixit, Archana Varma, and Ravi Mehta.

My parents' encouragement and unshakable belief in me have been, as always, a crucial source of strength throughout the project. Apart from them, my greatest debt is to those who took time off from their own busy writing schedules to read the manuscript at various stages of its development. Chris Cuomo, Indrani Chatterjee, and Sumit Guha went through the draft manuscript in its entirety and offered very useful perspectives from their own disciplines. Indrani also copied extracts for me from the Michael Field papers at the British Library. My continuing discussions with Chris—on everything ranging from lesbian philosophy to animals, carried on everywhere, from the freeway to the cafeteria—enriched the book and made it vastly more fun to write than it would have been otherwise. Peter Kulchyski's comments on the introductory chapters and chapter 7 were particularly insightful. Mary Katzenstein, Bruce Robbins, and Suparna Bhaskaran made helpful comments on the introduction. I would like to thank my sister Anna and her friend Raveesh for unraveling the mysteries of the computer, especially those of the indexing program, and my friend Saleem Kidwai for helping me send material from Delhi to New York.

Finally, I am greatly indebted to Leela Gandhi, who went through the near-final draft with a toothcomb and advised me how to edit it and improve it stylistically, thereby considerably enhancing its readability. Furthermore, as an imaginative presence, she inspired more of this book than she knew.

Miranda House, Delhi University
December 1995

Sappho and the Virgin Mary

Introduction: Imagined Ancestries

> Yet one had ancestors in literature, as well as in one's
> own race, nearer perhaps in type and temperament,
> many of them, and certainly with an influence of which
> one was more absolutely conscious.
>
> —Oscar Wilde

> To realise the nineteenth century, one must realise
> every century that has preceded it and that has
> contributed to its making.
>
> —Oscar Wilde

This book began as a study of Virginia Woolf as a Sapphic writer in dialogue with her contemporaries and ancestors. Tracing her literary ancestry back through the Aestheticists to the Romantics, I began to realize that Sapphic writers did not operate within a tradition of their own, but were integrated with and constitutive of mainstream traditions. Sapphic love was not always silenced, invisibilized, or exoticized by the English literary imagination but was rather one of its central components. Love between women creators has functioned as an enabling element in the writings of both male and female authors at least since Romanticism.

After Freud and Lacan criticism has tended to assume that writers perforce operate in a phallocentric universe and with heterosexist biases. Pre-Freudian Romantic thinkers conceptualized the aesthetic imaginary differently. Walter Pater's readings of Leonardo da Vinci's Marian paintings as Sapphic pointed me in the direction of this difference. This book became an initial exploration of the significance in English literary texts of the following:

1. the female nonbiological ancestor as creator;
2. an erotic aesthetic that celebrates joy not geared to production and reproduction;
3. the love between female literary and mythological ancestors.

English literature since Romanticism draws many of its dominant ideals of human relations and creativity from models of love between women creators. One ideal, which I will call the Marian, eroticizes the mother-daughter relationship and gives rise to triangles in which the primary energy is between two women. Another, which I will call the Sapphic, develops passionate dialogue between women as a paradigm for lyric intensity and sublimity. Both models involve ideas of a community, of learning, teaching, writing, and study as activities occurring among women. These models are not mutually exclusive or exhaustive. Selecting, imagining, and relating to such ancestries entails remaking notions of gender. I will explore these remakings as undertaken by Romantic, Aestheticist, and Bloomsbury writers, in the context of the anarchist feminist worldviews that I see connecting them.

What follows is an attempt to respond to Terry Castle's call to "focus on presence instead of absence, plenitude instead of scarcity."[1] Implicitly, I shall contest de Lauretis's idea that "public forms of fantasy" regarding women's desire for women are unavailable and suppressed and that "Western cultures" hegemonically represent "lesbianism as phallic pretension or male identification."[2] I also follow Paula Bennett in her attempt to right the bias of most critical discourses on sexuality, including dominant queer theory discourses, that invisibilize the clitoris in favor of phallicism and/or anality.[3]

Heterosexist structures, are, for my purpose, the more important material condition than class, since "classes" are much more shifting and fluid over time, even within the same generation, for groups as well as for individuals, than are forms of organization of sexuality. Furthermore, my concern is not only with sexuality but also with erotic and affective preferences that are not, in my view, completely determined by "class." In all known societies heterosexual intercourse and reproduction have been, in different ways, privileged over homosexual intercourse. Insofar as I deal with written texts, my area of scrutiny is automatically limited to the *educated classes*. I prefer this term, used by Virginia Woolf, to terms like *bourgeois* since it is more exact and also cuts across different income categories and social backgrounds. In the nineteenth century, for instance, many self-educated working men and informally educated middle-class and working women were writers and readers of literary texts. As far as the essentialist/constructionist debate relates to homosexuality, I operate within the framework carefully mapped out by John Boswell in his essay "Categories, Experience, and Sexuality."[4] Following Boswell's reading of Kinsey's scale, I use the term *homoerotically inclined* rather than *homosexual* or *gay* for periods when these terms were not in use.[5]

Judy Grahn has suggested that homoerotically inclined people live not on the "fringe" or "margin" of mainstream culture but on the edge of its continuing transformation, pioneering and influencing that culture's myths, values, interactions, and movements.[6] This suggestion may be extended to argue that homoerotically inspired discontent with the major institutions of heterosexuality is often close to the heart of the most powerful literature and art. While many cultural critics today argue that what is canonical is decided by the politics of the academy, I agree with Woolf that it is by the consensus of common readers over a period of time that the canon (as distinct from syllabi) is built and changed and with T. S. Eliot, who argues that the uncommon readers who are also writers help build this canon by their interaction with it.[7] Clear-cut lines cannot be drawn between academic and nonacademic readers, for a person who reads as a specialist in one field may simultaneously read in other fields as a nonspecialist. Expertise, influence, and the lack of them constantly overlap and change during the lifetime of a reader or a generation of readers. If the power of literature consists in its ability to disturb, to question, and to engage with rather than to escape from discontent, pain, and grief, then homoerotic experience, which is the experience of a daring time in life for the majority (in the nineteenth century it was virtually an adolescent rite of passage) and of a lifetime for a daring minority, provides one of the most accessible sources of and metaphors for such disturbing energy.

Writers do not necessarily imagine literary ancestors as additional or even alternative "fathers" and "mothers."[8] Rather, they choose intellectual, emotional, spiritual ancestors, and their project is thus in opposition to the heterosexual family's insistence on the primacy of biological ties, of "blood" over "water." The rebellion intrinsic to this project cuts at the roots of the institutions of heterosexual marriage, the patriarchal family, and race, all of which are premised on the idea of the blood tie or blood line.[9] The Romantic search for alternative forms of family and community based on intellectual and emotional affinities across and within gender, class, and occasionally even race (Pantisocracy, Shelley's and Byron's experimental households, the Wordsworth-Coleridge brief but intensely creative communal life) involved looking for models in their own time as well as in the past. Solitude in companionship, or what Woolf was to term "aloneness together," was developed by them as an image of the ideal life, in contrast to the suffocating domesticity of conventional family life. This ideal, close to that of the cloister, is distinct from the Protestant idea of the soul alone with an all-seeing god in a purely private, and usually interior, space.

When a writer searching for a literary ancestor imagines her or him not as parent but as teacher, older friend, saint, or inspiring muse, the search comes to be compelling for readers who are not themselves writers. Childhood and youthful rebellion against parents, omnipresent in Victorian biography, autobiography, and novels, suggests a refusal to accept as definitive the biological parents' insistence that generating, giving birth, or even physical rearing is the most important part of the "making" of a human being. The child's perception that the emotional and intellectual rearing has been less than adequate if not actually damaging is almost always accompanied by the choice of another person—uncle, aunt, neighbor, teacher, friend, or dead writer—as the one responsible for "making" him or her.[10] Often dismissed as a crush or a youthful phase, this urge to find other ancestors frequently becomes muted when the young adult is subsumed into marriage and parenthood and develops a stake in biological ancestry, wishing to assert claims over his or her children. However, the often fond memory of that early choice makes for an imaginative stake in the more determined pursuit of it by others, whether these others are writers or homoerotically inclined persons. This would partly explain, for instance, the enthusiastic celebration of the Ladies of Llangollen by male and female writers alike (Anna Seward, Wordsworth, Byron) and also by a range of other persons with very different class backgrounds and political persuasions.

Romantic assertion of nonbiological ancestry is crucially linked to the idea that lovers of their own sex search for immortality not through children but through the text. Several recent commentators have explored the effects on late Victorian writers of the Platonic argument that homoerotic love is innately given to producing texts and conversely that all texts spring from homoerotic love and of its Renaissance restatements by such poets as Shakespeare and Barnefield. I suggest that these late Victorian writers were equally affected by Marian endorsement of a similar idea via different arguments and images and by accounts of Sappho's life and work that constituted an enactment of it. Victorian feminist, lesbian, and male homoerotic discourses drew on these ideas; these discourses developed simultaneously and were closely connected. Several homosexual men contributed crucially to the making of Victorian feminism, as several feminists and lesbians contributed to the making of Victorian homoerotic arguments.

Historians of Victorian feminism such as Philippa Levine acknowledge and explore the importance of marital and familial alliances between radical men and feminist women, as also of friendships and collaborations between single and married feminist women, but almost completely elide the importance of relationships between homoerotically inclined men and women.[11] Gay male historians err in the opposite direction by almost totally neglecting the importance of lesbians in homosexual networks. The group of influential English middle-class families that Noel Annan describes as an "intellectual aristocracy" was also a network of homoerotically inclined persons, men and women, married and single, many of whom were conscious of their preferences as life defining.

Construction of literary ancestries in critical discourse has tended toward gender segregation. Perhaps the most influential paradigm for male writers' relation to their male forebears as anxiety-ridden sons to dominant fathers was set up by Harold Bloom.[12] Virginia Woolf's remark that "if we are women, we think back through our mothers" was one starting point for feminist inquiry into women writers' relation to their female forebears, seen in terms not of anxiety but of recovery and reclaiming.[13] While women writers' relation to male literary ancestors has never been totally neglected, male writers' relation to female literary forebears has scarcely been considered in any serious way. One reason for this may be the general acceptance, from both feminist and antifeminist points of view, that dominant Western traditions have constructed the figure of the writer as definitively male.

From a feminist point of view this assumption is supported by Woolf's argument that there were no major women writers in the Western canon before the nineteenth century, no woman Shakespeare (she underrates the importance of Sappho), because women were violently deprived of the material opportunities, the economic and social wherewithal—money, independent space, freedom, mobility, solitude, intellectual community—that could have enabled them to write. From a psychoanalytic point of view, that may be read as either misogynist or feminist, Freud supported the same assumption when he argued that man creates artifacts, perhaps from womb envy, while woman lacks the urge to create artifacts since she is driven by penis envy to produce children.[14]

Later variants of these two approaches tend to agree in suggesting that canonical Western literature and art, being male produced, are male dominated, and represent women as objects of transaction, victims of violence, or reified objects of worship. Eve Sedgwick's reading of canonical Western literature as a series of transactions between men is one kind of feminist version of this approach.[15] These readings of the Western canon acquire some plausibility only if the canon is assumed to date from the Renaissance. A very different picture emerges if medieval ideas and images of writing are read as the ancestors of modern texts.

A feature shared by the thought of Marx, Freud, Lacan, Foucault, and most of their followers is a determined Protestant bias that reads Western culture as heir to the Judaic, to the classical Greek and Roman, and to the Renaissance, erasing at least a millennium of what was once known as "the dark ages" and is today, scarcely less condescendingly, termed the "premodern." This bias is built into the English language through such terms as the *Reformation* and the negative associations of such terms as *feudal* and *medieval*. Despite the pathbreaking work being done today by numerous medieval historians and literary and art critics, the insights acquired do not adequately inform the paradigms of what is called critical theory. It is too easily assumed both that the medieval wiped out the classical past and, more important, that the Reformation wiped out the cultural influences of the medieval past, especially in Protestant countries. How else would it be possible for Foucault's *History of Sexuality* to be taken seriously even though it blithely skips more than a millennium?[16] The same kind of leap is performed by Camille Paglia, enabling her to claim that the Western ideal of beauty is an adolescent boy, thus overlooking centuries of art that centrally glorified the Virgin and the female saints in far from boyish forms and often assimilated male and neuter figures (angels) to what might be called a girlish form. Others, like Sedgwick, simply begin with the Renaissance, as if English literature dates from Shakespeare. Ironically, the Romantic poets, the supposed progenitors of Bardolatry, were consistently engaged with medieval literary ancestors.

This privileging of the Reformation and the Renaissance implicitly privileges a heterosexual marriage-centered view of Western history and literature. Research such as that of John Boswell on celibacy and same-sex love in premodern Europe, and of feminist historians on female saints like St. Anne and on matriliny in medieval Christian worship, ritual, and iconography, has shown how Protestantism valorized marriage and the patriarchal family at the cost of celibacy, matriliny, and same-sex community. Janice Raymond demonstrates how the Reformation was preceded by satires on monks and nuns, often accusing the latter of hating men and practicing lesbianism.[17] Thus, in Erasmus's colloquy "The Virgin Averse to Matrimony," the male speaker, while persuading a young woman to give up her plan of entering a convent, accuses nuns of doing more "than becomes Maids to do" because "there are more among 'em that imitate Sappho in Manners, than are like her in Wit."[18] The dissolution of convents, Raymond argues, "smashed devotion to the mother goddess, Mary, and her incarnations in groups of nuns living together."[19] Nuns were abused for wanting to escape the natural duties of wifehood and motherhood and were, in many instances, violently dragged out of convents and raped or forced into marriage. Their collective property was appropriated to the use of men. She also makes a connection between these attacks on same-sex community and those that followed Catholic Emancipation in England in the nineteenth century.[20] Romantic and Aestheticist attraction to medieval ideas and images, as also the attraction of many homoerotically inclined Victorian writers, both men and women, to Catholicism, may be read as connected with their attempts to construct alternatives to the dominant fiction that marriage and work produce happiness while singleness and contemplation spell misery or morbidity.

The ubiquitousness of the Protestant bias makes for its invisibility. How, otherwise, could Freud's contention that the Oedipus myth is the most definitive, appealing, or influential Western myth be accepted by so many thinkers who differ on so many other questions? Writing as a Jew in a Protestant country, Freud, as I shall demonstrate in my exegesis of his *Leonardo da Vinci and a Memory of His Childhood*, erases the Marian myth that dominated the Western imagination for centuries and has far from lost its grip even today. Between the two myths who could doubt that the latter is better known, more often rewritten, and exercises a far more pervasive, more unbroken, influence on Western literary texts? The Marian myth is also a continuously evolving one, both in its mediation by popular devotion versus papal authority and in its innumerable local variations and entwinements with saints' legends.

On the basis of the Oedipal myth Freud concluded that the little boy wants to kill his father and marry his mother, whereas the little girl wants either the opposite or wants a child as penis substitute. He finally and famously confessed, however, that he did not know what women wanted. Without disputing the infinite variety of human desires or claiming that all or even the more important are contained in this or in any one myth, I would suggest that the Marian myth, in its hold over both women's and men's imaginations, suggests some possible answers to what they want. An immaculately conceived virgin Mary suggests that women want autonomous creativity, power and gentleness, women's community, sympathetic friendship with men, the joy and pain of love, and, most important, no father and no tying-in of childbirth with heterosexual marriage.[21] Conversely, an immaculately conceived virgin Christ suggests that what men want is, very simply, the same, his relation to the sexes being one of same-sex community (the twelve apostles) and sympathetic nonjudgmental friendship with women. It is important that the Marian syndrome came into being in response to popular demand over centuries; it was shaped by devotees' aspirations. Thus, while Christ's perpetual virginity was always taken for granted, the dogma of Mary's perpetual virginity evolved over time. Explanations were devised for the Biblical references to the "brethren of Jesus." In order to get rid of these other children of Mary, the phrase was interpreted as referring to Jesus's cousins rather than siblings, thus freeing Mary from heterosexual intercourse and childbearing. The popular demand for the immaculate conception of Mary suggests a drive for equality between the definitive male and female myths. Christ's immaculate conception was always taken for granted. Conferring the same status on Mary meant conferring on her the same status of sinlessness. I would also argue that, in both cases, it frees the central figure from the father's presence. The heavenly father may be present in the mind, but the earthly mother (both Christ's and Mary's) is ever present. Christ and Mary are free from earthly fathers and free from earthly children. The implications of such freedom become far clearer in the case of the ever proliferating saints' legends.

Evidence for this convergence, this drive toward equality and sameness, is available in the use of the same images for both. I shall be examining the legacy of these images—both Mary and Christ are termed phoenixes and doves, both are associated with the sun, moon, and stars, with trees, plants, and flowers, especially the rose and the lily, with gems, especially the pearl, and with fountains, wells, springs, rivers of life. Both open the gates to paradise, the new Eden, and both act as paths, gateways, mediators. I shall extend Paula Bennett's brilliant argument for the primacy of clitoral imagery in the language of flowers and gems in women poets' writing to suggest that this imagery of simultaneously diffusive and concentrated, continuing rather than goal-oriented, clitoral rather than phallic eroticism is found also in male poets' writings and is drawn from Marian traditions.

Most feminist and gay and lesbian theorists have accepted, in one form or other, Freud's insistence on the centrality of the penis to the male and the female imagination and/or Lacan's reading of this theory, whereby not the penis but the symbolic phallus, which nobody has but everybody wants, stands for the symbolic order, especially for language and the law. This acceptance compels such theorists as de Lauretis, for instance, to invent a theory of fetishism as an explanation of lesbian desire and many other feminist critics to insist on the woman-affirming quality of vaginal and uterine imagery in texts. The latter insistence only reinforces the bind of woman = heterosex = reproductive motherhood.[22] The story told by Freud and Lacan is only one possible story of several contesting stories within Western literary traditions, both dominant and marginal.[23] In nineteenth-century England the interplay of Sapphic and Marian myths posits continuing clitoral joy and romantic same-sex love and friendship as possibilities for both women and men. This interplay exists not only in marginal texts but also in canonical texts that were influential literary models in their own time or soon after and continue to be so today.

I am not suggesting that this is the only possible or even the dominant way in which the Marian myth was read at the time. Despite important work by feminist medieval historians, Marina Warner's reading of Mary as an ultimately misogynist male construct that combines the "impossible" demands for virginity and motherhood would seem to be the dominant feminist reading today. Conversely, Kristeva's reading glorifies biological motherhood in precisely the way that I would argue the Mary figure may contradict.[24] Variants of both kinds of reading were widely available in nineteenth-century English literary texts. But I suggest that the fascinating "impossibility" of Mary's virgin motherhood constitutes precisely its attraction for those constructing antimarriage and antireproduction narratives in the nineteenth century and that they drew on old traditions of reading this figure. Mary, flying in the face of biology and heterosexual normativity, is the exemplary figure for the odd lives of male and female saints who choose same-sex community over marriage, the "miracle" of creativity over reproduction. Those inclined to same-sex love in the nineteenth century were also making a choice that seemed impossible. Pater, Wilde, and others termed same-sex love "the love of things impossible."[25] This "impossibility" may breed despair in a text; it may also allow claims for special miraculous destiny, similar to the claims made for Mary and the saints. It does not seem to me accidental that a liturgy to the Virgin is part of every ceremony of same-sex union unearthed by John Boswell; she is called upon to bless these unions along with Christ and other saints but is not invoked in the same way in het-

erosexual marriage services. Emmanuel Cooper has pointed out that in
several Renaissance paintings she is at the center of a cluster of male
angels who are apparently more interested in one another than in her.[26]
And, in the nineteenth century, homosexual men were referred to as
"Maryannes"—the combined names of Mary and of the mother who
immaculately conceived her.[27]

The persistence, indeed the constitutive nature, of gender segregation in one of the most influential discourses in gay studies today, that of
Foucault, is evident in that he writes a history of sexuality with a detailed
examination of Greek ideas of sexuality yet nowhere considers Sappho's
writings about love between women. When he comes up against
Aristophanes' speech in Plato's *Symposium*, which treats love between
women on the same plane as love between men or love between men and
women, he hastily goes into avoidance and arbitrarily proposes that we:
"restrict[ing] ourselves to the parts of the speech that concern male love"
(2:232). He habitually refers to "the child" as "he" (1:27, 98) and mentions
women's sexuality only in relation to men's. Such practices render his history defective even as a history of male sexuality.[28]

Gender segregation and avoidance of sex between women are also
constitutive of the split between sex and love in the discourse of Foucault
and his followers, sex being implicitly identified with men and love with
women. This makes it possible for Sedgwick to distinguish between male
homosexual and homosocial desire but to collapse the two in the case of
women. She argues that women who vote for a woman candidate or
breast-feed female babies are "pursuing congruent and closely related
activities" to those of women who are sexually involved with or in love
with women.[29] Such a framework leaves out of account the questions:
What happens when a man loves a man in a text—as distinct from simply
desiring him homosocially or homosexually? What happens when a
woman loves a woman—as distinct from working for women's rights?
Which men and which women support such loving, and which men and
which women hate and punish it? Sedgwick's model excludes the possibility and the fact of violently and viciously homophobic women—the
women who actively participated in torturing early nineteenth-century
male sodomists in the pillory or the women said to have danced in the
streets at Wilde's conviction.[30] The constitution of all women as victims
and objects of transaction involves denying them full agency—as lovers
and as haters. Sedgwick's formulation of the two men–one woman triangle as central to canonical texts excludes all-women triangles, which I
find present in several canonical and noncanonical texts. Furthermore,
she does not allow for the possibility that in a triangle between two men
lovers and the woman lover of one of them the woman may have heterosexual privilege and power. Here, the male rival's hatred of her may not
be merely misogyny but may also be related to his underprivileged situation, just as in a woman-woman-man triangle the woman lover's hatred of

the male rival may not be merely male hating but may also be related to her underprivileged situation.[31]

In privileging "desire" over "love" Foucault and Sedgwick follow the emphasis of nineteenth-century sexologists. But homoerotically inclined persons who were contemporaries of those sexologists typically defended themselves from negative labeling by insisting on their "love," even when they were fully conscious of and unashamed of their desire. Edward Carpenter is an example. His use of the word *love* in a treatise like *Love's Coming of Age* was intended to stress the equal dignity of homosexual with heterosexual feeling. G. L. Dickinson, Cambridge don, mentor of E. M. Forster, remarked in his sexually explicit autobiography, written in 1921 and unpublished in his lifetime, that "casuists and medical men" were unlikely to "have anything important to say" about his "love" for men: "For emotion, which to me is the determining fact, lies outside their province, and usually outside their competence."[32]

If, as G. J. Barker-Benfield argues, sex and money were becoming in the nineteenth century the only measures of Western man's identity, Romantic and Aestheticist insistence on love and art as measures of identity is an important form of oppositional resistance.[33] Feminist criticism has tended to read Romanticism as inspired by a "male," even misogynist, desire to transcend the body, to reinforce mind-body dualism, to construct the individual, especially the creative individual (artist-seer), as a man capable of such transcendence and of imperialist dominance and thus to write humanism as male centered. The figures seen as most representative of this kind of Romanticism are thinkers like Kant and poets like Wordsworth and the later Coleridge. While such a trend no doubt exists within Romanticism, or as one of many Romanticisms, it is contested by an equally and often more powerful trend toward dissolving mind-body dualism in a non-Christian pantheism. The Shelleys, Keats, Byron, and the young Blake, Wordsworth, Coleridge are the figures most representative of this trend. Their writings tend to privilege the small, the powerless, the everyday, as important and joy giving and to construct the individual, especially the creative individual, as nonadult male, as a woman, a child, an elderly person, a disabled person. These texts write humanism as springing from the embodied, emotional-mental experience of ordinary human beings and therefore as antiimperialist and antidominance.[34] The effects of the trend are all-pervasive around the turn of the century and continue to gather power later; they develop an anarchist feminist worldview both in prose and in poetical texts. This kind of Romanticism constitutes the ancestry of feminism, is inseparable from it through the nineteenth century, and continues to be so in important ways even today. If Romanticism has its descendants, with whom this study is centrally concerned, it also has its ancestors, one of whom, I shall argue, is Sappho. The ideas with which it works are not new and do not spring out of a vacuum.

As the literary movement that insisted upon subjectivity, that said "I" in many different ways, Romanticism was impelled by an internal logic to the dissolution of gender categories. Witness the strategy that ungenders "I" and "you" and that replaces male or female human being by ungendered human or nonhuman being in so many Romantic lyrics.[35] For, as Monique Wittig points out, "Gender is ontologically a total impossibility. For when one becomes a locutor, when one says 'I' and, in so doing, reappropriates language as a whole, proceeding from oneself alone, with the tremendous power to use all language, it is then and there, according to linguists and philosophers, that the supreme act of subjectivity, the advent of subjectivity into consciousness, occurs."[36] One effective way in which the categories can be dissolved is suggested by Wittig's experiments in her fictions—she imagines a dialogue wholly between women, so that *woman* (without the word being used) comes to be synonymous with *human being* instead of suggesting the complementary of *man*. The Romantics are early experimenters in warring against what Wittig calls "the straight mind."

I will begin by outlining the significant resonances of the Marian and the Sapphic myths in nineteenth-century England and will proceed to demonstrate how Romantic, Aestheticist, and later writers in these traditions constructed an ancestry by drawing not only on Hellenic models, but on medieval and Renaissance models. Pursuing a dual strategy, these writers reinterpreted those models that were accepted by the literary establishment as undoubtedly "great." However, they simultaneously engaged in the oppositional reinterpretation of times, spaces, and figures whose "greatness" was in doubt or was viewed with suspicion.

The duality of their strategies indicates how they were constantly in interaction with dominant tendencies of their times rather than in simple opposition to them. Thus if in a mainstream fiction like Tennyson's *The Princess* the stress falls on the attraction to that which is different from oneself (oak and vine), the writing of same-sex love too stresses differences within an overall model of similarity. The primary difference that emerges here is the age difference. In a further complication the stress on age difference goes against the trend of the Victorian novel where the ideal marriage normally precludes a vast difference in age. Thus Esther Summerson in *Bleak House* is attracted to Walter rather than to her guardian (for whom she has a deep affection) because Walter is a young man, and the novel ratifies this age-based attraction as "natural." The fictions of same-sex love however, eroticize age difference. The teacher-student relationship is modeled on that of the eros-eromenos and on that of Shakespeare and his fair youth. For women it drew on the model of the Virgin Mary and her mother and also on such living models as the Ladies of Llangollen, between whom there was an eighteen-year age gap, and, later, Katherine Bradley and Edith Cooper, very well-known in literary circles, who were aunt and niece and between whom there was a seventeen-year age gap. The teacher-student, mother-daughter image recurs in the writings of women such as Virginia Woolf and Radclyffe Hall. The transgressiveness of homoeroticism is heightened and/or mitigated by the incestuous or affective associations of tenderness between mother and daughter. This model anticipates Freud's insight that the mother is the first love object for all babies (implicitly, then, love for a woman is the primary experience of all women).

While elaborating Perry Meisel's contention that Walter Pater is Virginia Woolf's "absent father," I shall also look for Pater's absent mothers.[37] Beginning with the presence of these Sapphic and Marian mothers in his critical writings, I will follow something like his own suggestive trajectory rather than linear chronology. In chapters 4 and 5 I will examine how the writing of female homoeroticism in Pater's essays and in Simeon Solomon's paintings and his *A Vision of Love Revealed in Sleep* laid the ground for the debate between Symonds's Ruskin-influenced "manly" and martial model of male homosexuality and Wilde's and Carpenter's anarchist and open-ended models. The latter can be traced back to Shelley's development of a discourse of love as likeness and his delineation of women-dominated love triangles.

In chapter 6 I will elaborate a reading of nineteenth-century English literature as framed by two pairs of women lovers who became literary monuments in their times—the Ladies of Llangollen and Michael Field. This chapter will examine two women–one man triangles in texts by early and late Romantic women writers—Jane Austen, the Ladies of Llangollen, and Field, reading these as narratives of the search for a "likeness." The Romantics, as the "chosen ancestors" of the Aestheticists, will be examined for their engagement in a discourse of "likeness" opposed to the Miltonic model but drawing on Shakespearean ideas of likeness.

Chapter 7 looks at mythmaking around love between women in novels by Meredith and Forster. These myths, which privilege the inner life or the life of the spirit over the outer life, are incorporated and questioned in lesser-known texts such as Hope Mirrlees's Sapphic novel *Madeleine: One of Love's Jansenists* and some of Lytton Strachey's papers presented to the Apostles. The last three chapters return to Virginia Woolf with whom I started, to suggest that her literary ancestry provided her with more than one model, both male and female, of creativity that is more than simply reproductive. Woolf's fictions and critical writings stand at a turning point because they are often fractured by a gender-segregated feminism at odds with an ungendering homoeroticism. Built around Marian notions of nurturing, creating, the search for love and for an ancestry, and the marginalization of marriage and reproduction, they are also Sapphic in their romantic lyrical intensity. Loss, anguish, and yearning constitute their emotional fabric—she suggested that they might be called "elegies" rather than novels. I will connect this elegiac quality and the texts' privileging of moments of intensity with Romantic and

Aestheticist Sapphism and will examine how Woolf's fictions and feminist essays interact with these ancestors and with her contemporaries.

The last chapter also looks at the ways in which animals function as tropes for homoerotic love in early twentieth-century texts. The love between human and animal, inherently nonreproductive and radically creative as well as transgressive of anthropocentricity, is a trope in twentieth-century gay writing, inherited from Romantic writing, which was influenced in this respect not only by antinomian and dissenting traditions but, very importantly, by translated Indian texts. I shall look at this trope as it comes full circle in the poetry of Vikram Seth and Suniti Namjoshi, inheritors and transformers of all these multifarious, mutually enriching traditions.

It is important to add that I am by no means suggesting that these are the only or even the primary literary ancestries or that they cancel out other sorts of literary ancestry. I am merely trying to add a strand, which I hope is significant, to the web woven by generations of scholars and commentators.

1

The Marian Model

Mary, Mary, quite contrary,
How does your garden grow?
With silver bells and cockle shells
And pretty maids all in a row

The only things that one can use in fiction are the
things that one has ceased to use in fact.

—Oscar Wilde

I like the Roman Catholic religion. I say it is an attempt
at art. . . . We burst into a service of little girls in white
veils this morning which touched me greatly. It seems
to me simply the desire to create gone slightly
crooked, and no God in it at all.

—Virginia Woolf

The growth and development of Mariology, on the basis of very scant biblical evidence, is one of the most fascinating chapters of Western culture. It has been argued convincingly by many historians that it helps constitute a space in which alternatives for women in premodern Europe developed.[1] It is generally accepted that almost from its beginnings Mary worship evolved, as it does today, in tension with papal authority.[2] The cult of Mary was developed by priests, nuns, and laypeople, especially women. Papal authority reacted to the cult by incorporating some of its elements into dogma while resisting and denouncing other elements.[3] This selective incorporation of Mariological ideas generally occurred several centuries after their acceptance by ordinary Catholics.

Within Catholicism, both before and after the Reformation, Mary becomes a site for contesting the empowerment of women. Making concessions to Marian cults may function as a safety valve from the point of view of papal authority, in order to deflect other demands for women's freedom and power within the church; however, it would be simplistic to reduce the many uses of Mary simply to a variant of "the opium of the people." I suggest that ideas of Mary and of the saints (I emphasize the plurality of ideas and legends, often mutually contradictory) were often empowering not only within Catholicism but for Protestants as well, especially at the level of suggestion. Luther had singled out these ideas for special attack, but they survived in an underground way, in opposition to

Protestantism's relentlessly male-dominated theology. In nineteenth-century England Marian models were received from many sources and rewritten in many ways. Romantic challenges to eighteenth-century British insularity entailed a revival of interest in Italy, Greece, France, and, most important, Ireland, all cultures in which Mary worship had an important place. When the literal becomes suggestive and symbolic, as it almost always does in Romantic texts, its radical potential often surfaces.

Walter L. Arnstein remarks that "most significant nineteenth-century Englishmen had either a close friend or relative who became a convert to the Roman Catholic faith."[4] Converting to Catholicism meant joining an oppressed minority in England.[5] Although the 1829 Catholic Emancipation Act opened Parliament and most state offices to Catholics, the continuing hostility to Catholicism is suggested by the widespread hysterical reactions to conversion. For instance, when the liberal marquess of Ripon converted in 1874, the *Times* stated that "to become a Roman Catholic and remain a thorough Englishman are—it cannot be disguised—almost incompatible conditions."[6] Roman Catholicism was stigmatized as "un-English" on the grounds that it was idolatrous and encouraged the "perversions" of celibacy, same-sex community, and "effeminate" ritualism. Idolatry was explicitly denounced as pagan and linked to the heathen religions of the colonies such as India, the pre-Christian empires of Greece and Rome, and rebellious Ireland. The active and "manly" work ethos of Protestant Victorian England was posed against the contemplative ideal of pagan civilizations. As Peter B. Neckles points out, "Anti-asceticism remained a feature of one element of Orthodox spirituality up to the eve of the Oxford Movement and beyond."[7] In 1807 the High Churchman Thomas Le Mesurier castigated the Roman Church for the "peculiar and extraordinary honour which she ascribes to virginity." Robert Southey, in his 1824 *Book of the Church*, denounced the medieval pilgrims who had reverenced St. Simeon Stylites on his pillar. Significantly, Southey sees the Syrian St. Simeon as more like a pagan than a Christian, claiming that he "vied with the yoguees in India in the folly and perseverance with which he inflicted voluntary tortures upon himself."[8]

Diatribes against Catholic idolatry centered on the worship of the Virgin, because the worship of a feminine deity was perceived as the element most alien to English Protestantism, especially in its dissenting, puritan, low church, and evangelical incarnations. The Roman Catholic leadership reacted defensively, insisting on the subordination of Mary to her son and condemning the excesses of popular devotion.[9] This reaction failed to stem the Protestant onslaught, based on the not unreasonable grounds that popular practice was as much if not more indicative of the nature of Catholicism as was papal pronouncement. In any case, by the nineteenth century enough Mary worship had been incorporated into dogma to offend the average Protestant. Anglican bishops, at the first

Lambeth Conference in 1867, denounced the exaltation of the Virgin as mediator and the practice of praying to her, claiming that "the jealous God" would disapprove of "his honour" being given "to another."[10]

The debate was not always conducted in such decorous terms; its general tone was hysterically misogynist. In the course of the virulent campaign against the endowment of the Royal College of St. Patrick at Maynooth, Ireland, hate-filled anti-Catholic propaganda proliferated. A typical example is the address of Rev. W. Chalmers at a public meeting in Covent Garden on April 14, 1845, where he denounced the worship of the Virgin Mary and the saints as "idolatrous" and related a horrific story of a statue of the Virgin being used during the Inquisition as an instrument of torture and murder.[11] The Roman Church itself was denounced as a whorish female, the Scarlet Woman, and the female pronoun constantly used in connection with it. Typical is a sermon preached by the curate of St. Mary's (!) Parish Church at Walthamstow on November 5, 1850. The sermon connects the salvation of the British government from the Guy Fawkes's plot with the imagined anti-Christian and antinational machinations of popery, and skillfully combines colorful misogynist imagery with antipagan language in an extended diatribe that begins: "Does not Papal Rome, as well as did Pagan Rome, *abound in images*? and wherever her influence extends; wherever temples are erected for her worship, *there* are images, and *there* are prostrate worshippers. Rome is, in very truth, 'the mother'—the fruitful parent—of 'harlots and abominations of the earth'" (emphasis in the original).[12] Temples, although referring to Roman religion, would also suggest Hinduism to a Victorian. The ritualistic practices of the high church Tractarians, influenced by Catholicism, aroused similar outrage. Lord Shaftesbury, visiting St. Alban's Church in Holborn in 1866, described its rituals as "the worship of Jupiter and Juno."[13] Such practices were seen, E. R. Norman says, "as essentially un-English and unmanly."[14]

The 1850 papal proclamation of a Roman Catholic hierarchy in England, with Cardinal Wiseman being appointed archbishop of Westminster, aroused indignation precisely because it was seen as setting up a hierarchy alternative to that of the British state and empire. When she read it Queen Victoria asked, "Am I Queen of England or am I not?"[15] Other commentators explicitly connected it with the alternative hierachies set up by pretentious subjects such as Hindus, whose caste hierarchy exalted Brahmins above Britishers, and Muslim potentates, whose royal and noble hierarchies countered the British ones. Thus *Punch* satirically commented on the papal proclamation: "The Hindoo Government has sent over Hoki Poki to commence the functions as Brahmin of Battersea. . . . The Mirzam of Moolrah has sent over Bow wow to commence his sittings at Marylebone as Mufti of Middlesex, and Rusti Khan goes to Westminster Hall, to take his place in the Court of Chancery, as Cadi of Chelsea."[16] To many Victorian Englishmen, Italians appeared geographically, racially, and culturally closer to Arabs, Turks, and Asians than to Northern Europeans, a disjunction to be explored in Forster's novels. The Roman Church stood for everything that was anathema to John Bull as represented by *Punch*—it was homosexual, womanly, pagan, and nonwhite.

A connection was constantly established between celibacy, same-sex community, and homosexuality, overtly in such anonymous publications as *The Confessional Unmasked*, sent by the Protestant Evangelical Mission and Electoral Union in 1865 to all members of Parliament, which claimed that Roman Catholic priests aimed to "convert an Eden into a Sodom,"[17] and implicitly in innumerable attacks by such respectable writers as Charles Kingsley, the proponent of "muscular Christianity," whose writings, including his novel *Yeast*, were intended to denounce Tractarianism's "unmanly" tendencies.[18] The evangelical *Record* claimed that Roman Catholics were always in search of rich "perverts" as potential converts.[19] Since monasteries continued to be illegal in England even after the 1829 act, the pitifully few nunneries were the targets of most attacks against celibate same-sex community.[20] Protestant women were perceived as more susceptible than men to the seductions of Catholicism, and the confessional was felt to constitute a threat to male authority in the Englishman's castle, his home. In popular cartoons, pamphlets, and paintings, and also in the works of such writers as Elizabeth Barrett Browning, nuns were stereotyped as frustrated victims of male oppression.[21] That there was not much difference between the tone of anonymous pamphlets and that of newspapers is suggested by one of the former calling for "the *suppression* of these dens of infamy [nunneries]," while the *Morning Advertiser*, supporting the demand for inspection of nunneries, termed a nunnery "but another sort of lunatic asylum."[22]

The campaign for inspection of convents by a parliamentary committee was orchestrated for over a decade by M.P. Charles Newdegate, a Conservative imperialist violently opposed to women's suffrage. Following his success in 1870, the committee belied his hopes by portraying convents as more victims than villains, but the campaign had done its damage, drawing on and regenerating a widespread fervor of anti-Catholic feeling that erupted at times into violent riots. Nuns were repeatedly denounced as "unnatural" and their vocation as "contrary to the voice of nature and to the ordinance of God."[23] Even the absurd 1869 case of a nun, Mary Saurin, who sued the convent that had expelled her, and insisted that she "would rather die than leave the convent of my own free will," became grist to the mill for demonstrating how wifehood and motherhood were preferable to celibacy and sisterhood.[24]

The success of Newdegate's campaign finally aroused protest from nuns whose reactions interestingly draw a parallel between the convent and the family, suggesting that the latter is more oppressive to women. A letter to the *Daily News* from "a Nun" asked, "Why not have a committee to investigate the condition of English families?"[25] The October 1870 issue of the *Dublin Review* elaborated this argument, and a pamphlet by Father Peter Gallwey outlined protest tactics similar to those later employed by British suffragettes and by the Gandhi-led freedom movement in India. He suggested that nuns should pray, fast, refuse to appear before the committee unless forcibly carried there by the police and, once there, should keep silent even at the risk of being jailed.[26] The Liberal M.P. Henry Winterbotham observed in 1870 that there might be good reasons for Catholicism's appeal to Englishwomen and that the House of Commons could hardly complain about women converting until "we give to women a higher, and I will add, a more manly education—until we open to them larger spheres of usefulness and activity."[27]

Despite or perhaps because of the heady mix of misogyny, racism, and homophobia in "No-Popery" vituperative, Victorian middle- and working-class attitudes to Catholicism, as D. G. Paz points out, remained radically ambivalent.[28] Not only were most Protestants connected by family or friendship links to Catholics; the conversions of some of the most charismatic public figures of the time, such as Newman, could not fail to have ambiguous effects. More important, I would argue, the legacy of European and English literature and art was saturated with ideas connected with Mary and the saints. England had been one of the centers of Mariology in medieval times, earning the name of "Our Lady's Dowry," and the traces were everywhere.[29] Romantic, Aestheticist, and pre-Raphaelite revival of interest in medieval themes brought to the surface an involvement with the idea of Mary that had never entirely disappeared from English literature. The Oxford movement, which stressed the connections between Anglicanism and Catholicism, further foregrounded the idea. The conflict between popular Mariolatry and the religious establishment that was being fought out in Catholicism was temporarily defused in the papal declaration of the immaculate conception as dogma in 1854. This battle had been decisively lost within Protestantism at the Reformation, when the male leadership's attacks had centered on precisely such nonbiblical traditions as those on which Marian cults were based.

Yet it is possible to argue that the idea of Mary herself continued to be present, emblazoned as it was in religious art in England, not all of which was destroyed by iconoclasts, and also in the form of the many Marys of ballad, folksong, nursery rhyme, and everyday life.[30] "Mary" and its variants remained very popular first names; the three most recurrent names in the British royal family were Mary, Elizabeth, Anne, the main names of the Marian holy kinship. Leigh Hunt, in his extended essay "Specimens of British Poetesses" had remarked that the name Anne "predominates" in the list of English women writers and "the name that prevails next, is Mary; and then Elizabeth."[31] More suggestively, Pater remarked on "the use of certain names, as expressing summarily, this name for you and that for me—Helen, Gretchen, Mary—a hundred associations . . . which, through a very wide and full experience, they have the power of bringing with them . . . such names are but revealing instances of the whole significance, power, and use of language in general."[32] The predominance continues among women writers of the nineteenth century and among heroines of novels as well.

Eric Trudgill has traced the growth of Madonna cults in Victorian England, noting that "even the most frigid Evangelicals were prepared to countenance its use."[33] The vitality of this symbol for the English imagination is evidenced by the range of uses to which it is put by different writers—from its domestication as angelic and sexless wife, mother, daughter by such writers as Patmore and Tennyson, heterosexual prettification by some of the pre-Raphaelites, radicalization in advocacy of heterosexual "free love" by such feminist writers as Grant Allen, to its empowerment in the fictions of writers like Elizabeth Gaskell, George Eliot, and Thomas Hardy.[34] This ambivalence prevails even in working-class periodicals, which seem, as D. G. Paz shows, able to combine No-Popery sentiment with surprisingly positive representations of Catholic priests and nuns and also of the Virgin. Even Murphy, the Irish convert to Protestantism, rabble-rouser, and leader of violent working-class riots against Catholics, was prepared to make an exception for the Virgin, claiming that she "was a Protestant, and no Roman Catholic" and therefore disapproved of nunneries![35] That he felt the need to make such a claim suggests the predilections of his audiences. The figure of the Virgin seems to have had special attractions for same-sex communities, such as the Anglican sisterhoods established under the influence of Edward Pusey, and, as I shall attempt to demonstrate, for homoerotically inclined men and women, both individually and as communities.[36]

Mary as Autonomous Creator

Victor and Edith Turner, tracing the dramatic resurgence of Marian pilgrimages and images in the nineteenth and early twentieth centuries, argue that while Mary as Theotokos (Mother of God) was the most popular iconic representation of the Virgin in the middle ages, "early in the nineteenth century . . . the emphasis began to shift to Mary herself, as an autonomous figure who takes initiatives on behalf of mankind, often intervening in the midst of the economic and political crises characteristic of industrialized mass society."[37]

Confining my argument to England, I suggest that paradoxically, precisely because of the exclusion of the feminine from Protestant orthodox ideas of divinity, the idea of Mary for a Protestant writer constitutes what might be called a site of free signification. A nineteenth-century English Protestant writer could not but be aware of the debates that raged around Mariology within Catholicism. But, unlike a Catholic writer, he or she was free to use the idea of Mary in transgressive ways, since Mary, not being sanctified in Protestant ideology, was not open to blasphemy in the same way, but could nevertheless be a focus for many ideas that had accumulated around her. The most radical of these ideas is that which challenges the model of binary opposition between male creativity excluded from motherhood and female motherhood excluded from creativity ("Men must work and women must weep"), justified in Christianity by the notion of the Fall and secularized via an appeal to biology. This model was especially galling to women like the young Virginia Stephen, who aspired to be writers, and to persons inclined to emotional and sexual attachment for their own sex.

In a 1905 review of *Nancy Stair*, a novel by Elinor McCartney Lane, the twenty-three-year-old Virginia Stephen describes and comments upon the heroine's progress thus:

> She realises "how little value verse-making holds to the real task of living," and understands the real task of living to mean, for a woman at any rate, marriage and motherhood. The genius for poetry seems to be incompatible with the duties of wife and mother, and, as the least important, Nancy has no hesitation in quenching it in order to marry and live happily ever afterwards. This is the eighteenth-century solution of the doubts of the nineteenth century. Such a solution is, of course, the popular one, and it is right, perhaps, that a novelist should take a sentimental point of view and rejoice at the conventional ending. The prosaic mind may be tempted to suggest that the world might, perhaps, be considerably poorer if the great writers had exchanged their books for children of flesh and blood. But Miss Lane does not go very deeply into these problems.[38]

The ungendered use here of the phrase "the great writers" suggests that the young writer perhaps already has in mind the fact on which she was later to comment, that the great nineteenth-century women writers in English had had no children. It also shows her engagement in the debate, begun perhaps by Plato and revived in the nineteenth century by the Romantic poets and by Pater, Symonds, Wilde, Carpenter, Samuel Butler, among others, that posited immortality through biological parenthood against the immortality of art. From Romanticism through Aestheticism to Bloomsbury this debate develops in covert or overt opposition to the nineteenth-century mainstream novel's glorification of marriage and parenthood. The "doubts of the nineteenth century" were many and took many interesting forms. I propose to explore some of the doubts regarding gender and sexuality in relation to ideas of intercourse, conception, and creation—taking these words both in their sexual and in their intellectual connotations.

Conception

The word *conception* has two common meanings—one, the conception of an idea, the other, the conception of a child. Depending on the gender of the noun or pronoun to which the word is attached, its meaning is generally construed to be mental or physical—if a man conceives, he gives birth to an idea, a thought, a text; conversely, if a woman conceives, she gives birth to a child of flesh and blood. The moment of intellectual conception is often pictured in visual art—either as a vision, as when Dante sees Beatrice, or as an act, when a writer is pictured with his hand resting on a book or with a quill in hand. Its ultimate model is perhaps god creating the universe or the human species—Michelangelo's god reaching out to Adam or Blake's god with his pair of compasses. Victorian portraits of individuals often represent the man in his study surrounded by books, the woman surrounded by children. Family portraits bring the man into the feminine space of the drawing room or the garden but rarely allow the intrusion of women and children into the sacred male space of the book-lined study.

As opposed to the conception of an idea, the conception of a child is not susceptible to picturization. When attempts are made, as in paintings of the conception of Helen by Leda, the suggestions of rape, or at least of passivity, and even of pain, rather than joyous activity and conscious intention, are strong. Since a woman can never know, at the moment of conception, that it has actually taken place, since it cannot be undertaken alone (as the conception of an idea can) but only as part of a sexual act with a man, and since it can take place not only in a desired sexual act but equally as a result of rape, it is hard to invest it with the "sublimity" attributed in Christian tradition to the conscious act of making, figured as a divine and male act—the fiat "Let there be light."

This difference between reproduction and creation, heightened into an absolute, lies at the base of arguments justifying separate spheres, gender as biologically given, and the mental and emotional differences between men and women as fixed. Tennyson's famous dictum in *The Princess* may be taken as summing up widely held Victorian beliefs in this matter, which resurface repeatedly in texts by a range of writers who otherwise hold differing worldviews and ideologies:

> Man for the head and woman for the heart
> He for the sword and for the needle she
> Man to command and woman to obey
> All else confusion.

In 1905, the year that the young Virginia Stephen questioned this Victorian wisdom, it was asserted even more vigorously across the Atlantic as essential to nation and civilization. Theodore Roosevelt's 1901 address at the Minnesota State Fair was published under the title "National Duties" in 1905 in a collection, *The Strenuous Life*. Denouncing the "pursuit of mere pleasure as an end in itself," Roosevelt stated, "The wilfully idle man, like the wilfully barren woman, has no place in a sane, healthy, and vigorous community. . . . Exactly as infinitely the happiest woman is she who has borne and brought up many healthy children, so infinitely the happiest man is he who has toiled hard and successfully in his life-work."[39] He went on to say that this manly work might be done with the brain or the hands, in the study or in the field or workshop. The exclusion of pleasure here significantly also excludes ideas of asceticism, celibacy, solitude, associated in many older traditions, in the West and the East, notably the Catholic tradition, with learning and creativity. These excluded ideas cluster around the figures of the Virgin Mary and the saints.

For the one moment in Christian tradition that challenges the creation versus reproduction model is that of the annunciation, one of the most frequently painted moments in Western art. The variety of ways in which this moment is represented testifies to its openness to interpretation. Mary is usually alone, almost always with a book in hand. The appearance of the angel and the dove constructs the moment as a vision, a moment of intense concentration. Mary "conceives"—she has an idea, an inspiration. She is "filled with god." This mystical moment places her, to use the Greek model familiar to nineteenth-century readers of Plato, as the hearer or beloved, and god as lover or inspirer. Unlike the human women in Greek myth who conceived by various gods, Mary does not go through a heterosexual experience at this point. Rather, her intercourse and conception are intellectual because she hears—that her conception took place through the ear (as Eve's fall occurred through her listening to the serpent) was emphasized by the early fathers who posited Mary as the second Eve, a parallel to Christ, the second Adam. Graef notes that "like St. Augustine, Leo, too, holds that she conceived Christ in her mind even before she conceived him in her body."[40] The stillness and light of this moment, when an idea strikes but has not yet been incarnated, is wonderfully suggestive. As Woolf writes, material conditions impede the making of "a work of genius"; if it is made despite those conditions, "it is a miracle, and probably no book is born entire and uncrippled as it was conceived."[41] But before the suffering of making begins, the conception itself is joy—the annunciation represents that conception, and the conceiver, the intellectual par excellence, is a woman, in whose mind the word takes on flesh.

It is important that god almost never appears in person at this moment. Instead, a genderless and often very feminine-looking angel appears.[42] Although the angel is Gabriel, angels were supposed to be, and were represented as, sexless, as was the holy ghost. This stresses the importance of the word. Mary hears and/or reads the word, which is divine, conceives an idea and gives birth to it, for like Christ she too is an "immaculate conception," an idea, the word who was with god. The second important feature of this "conception" is what church fathers termed Mary's fiat—"Let it be unto me." "Fiat Mihi," echoing "Fiat Lux," feminizes the sublime. Mary's active consent was construed by the early fathers as crucial to the incarnation (just as Eve's consent was crucial to the Fall).[43] What could be terrifying—the sudden appearance and announcement by the angel, before which Mary is sometimes represented as shrinking and frightened (Simone Martini, *Annunciation*, 1283–1342)—is contained and controlled in most representations by her speech, which parallels the initial moment of divine creation. In medieval paintings her words often appear on a scroll emerging from her lips. This construction of the annunciation rewrites female conception as conscious and creative. There is a slippage here between the conception of a child and the conception of an idea. Conceiving with full consciousness and intention to do so, Mary achieves conception as thought, as "making." Hearing the word of god and doing it, she becomes a model for independent feminine action and creativity, a model duplicated in innumerable legends of female saints who refuse marriage, see visions, establish communities of women, and proceed to contribute to the community in different ways, often through their writings. As Eve brought about knowledge of one kind, Mary brings about wisdom of another kind. She is identified in Mariology with the figure of Sophia, or Wisdom, who in the Book of Proverbs was present at creation and is the feminized face of divine energy. The second act may even enable celebration of the first, as in that famous medieval lyric that bypasses Christ altogether to celebrate the Fall as productive of Mary's queenhood: "Ne hadde the appil taken ben, / The appil taken ben, / Ne hadde never our lady / A ben hevene quene."[44]

Paintings of the annunciation often emphasize the inwardness of the conception as a mental act. In Robert Campin, the Master of Flemalle's *Annunciation* (1374–1444) Mary is seated alone in a domestic interior, reading. Another book lies open on the table next to her. The angel looks at her, but she does not look at him. Her eyes are lowered, gazing on the book. Hearing the word is thus conflated with reading it. Mary's intercourse is with the book and with herself. Hans Memling's *Annunciation* (1430–1494) shows Mary seated, one hand on the open book, eyes lowered, with an expression of inward concentration. The angel looks at her but she does not look at him; two other angels hover around her and the dove appears in her halo (she is the only one haloed). This kind of representation makes the angel appear an embodiment of her thought at whom she does not need to look. Several other paintings do show her looking at the angel. Frequently, also, as in Jan Van Eyck's *Annunciation Virgin* (1366–1441) and Roger van der Weyden's *The Angelic Salutation* (1399–1464), she looks upward, not at the angel. In the Master of Moulins's *Annunciation* (1480–1500) Mary, seated at her desk, facing the viewer, with the book open before her, looks to her right, into space, hands held apart. The expression on her face strongly suggests that an idea has just occurred to her. In this unusual representation, the angel is behind her, facing her left and the viewer's right, looking upward, not at her. His position makes it impossible that Mary should see him. The dove is directly above her head. This composition suggests very strongly the ideational nature of the experience. The varied relative positions of Mary and angel in various paintings (he kneeling to her, she kneeling to him, both kneeling, she seated while he stands or kneels, both standing, one lower, the other higher, or both at the same level) indicate how varying readings of Mary's role and status were simultaneously possible.

As medieval Marian cults constructed other events in Mary's life (which were officially proclaimed by the pope centuries later—the immaculate conception 1854, the assumption 1950, queen of heaven 1954), these were represented in visual art as iconographic repetitions of the annunciation. Thus St. Anne, conceiving Mary without heterosexual intercourse, in Bellegambe's painting, kneels alone in contemplation before the open book, with the figure of a haloed girl child blazoned on her body.[45] Her body responds ("conceives") to a conception in her mind.[46] Another popular way of envisioning this moment shows Mary as existing, like Sophia, from the beginning. Here, very clearly, Mary is an idea in the mind of god and is independent of her son. The grandeur of the moment makes it an alternative to the biblical story of the creation of Eve from Adam's rib almost as an afterthought. Paintings of the immaculate conception vary in endowing the figure of Mary with different degrees of prettiness or power. Tiepolo's *The Immaculate Conception* (before 1769) shows her as a grave and dignified figure, the center of the universe. Her head is haloed with stars, her feet rest on the earth, and the dove hovers above her head as in the annunciation. Francisco Zurbaran (1598–1662) makes her a more feminized, less powerful figure. Jose Antolinez's 1665 painting encircles her with cherubs, graceful rather than powerful. These representations merge Mary as immaculate conception with Mary as queen of heaven/goddess figure. As bride of Christ, crowned by him queen of heaven, a moment enshrined in numerous Renaissance and Counter-Reformation paintings, Mary is conflated with the bride of the Song of Songs, and the Magnificat with the Canticles. This conflation suggests the eroticization of the figure. Thomas Stehling points out that "the language of religious devotion" was not, as is often assumed to be the case, eroticized only in the case of heterosexual love: "The two lesbian poems that survive from the Middle Ages use language recalling the Song of Songs."[47]

The assumption Virgin is older, more mature, more powerful, and, as in the immaculate conception, without the child. In Velazquez's *Coronation of the Virgin* she forms a quaternity with god, Christ, and the dove. Her eyes are lowered in contemplation, as in so many annunciations. As queen of heaven, Mary takes on various other active roles. She appears alone, holding out her mantle like an umbrella to shield crowds of devotees. Jean Mirailhet's *Our Lady of Mercy* (1394–1497?) shows her in this attitude, treble the size of the men and women she covers with her cloak. Here she has a look of compassion on her face. Piero della Francesca's (1420–1492) *Virgin of the Misericordia*, treating the same theme, shows a less feminine figure, older, grander, much more powerful looking.

Mary as intercessor may kneel at the head of a flock of devotees; she may also actively intervene on her own. In Giovanni da Monte Rubiano's sixteenth-century *Our Lady of Help* she holds a stick up over her head, threatening a terrified devil. With her left hand she protectively holds a child, and a woman kneels appealingly at her feet.

Powerful Marian cults, expressed in sermons, legends, songs, and other texts, ascribed to Mary omnipotence as well as participation in the creation of the universe and in the crucifixion and redemption.[48] Thus Richard of St. Laurent, dean of the Metropolitan Chapter of Rouen, argued in his enormously influential *De Laudibus Sanctae Mariae* (c. 1240) that Mary participates in the passion and crucifixion and that woman, by sharing in the task of redemption just as she shared in the Fall, is made equal with man. This makes it possible for him to modify the Lord's Prayer and other verses, replacing "Our Father" with "Our Mother" and "God so loved the world" with "Mary so loved the world."[49] Bernardine of Siena (d. 1444), an extremely popular Franciscan preacher, even argued that the Virgin was in some respects superior to god, since she accomplished the incarnation, which he on his own could not have accomplished.[50] It was in 1894 that the pope first referred to Mary by the title of "coredemptrix," and it became a common designation of Mary, although even today it lacks the status of dogma.[51] As mediatrix and advocate (titles long-bestowed by devotees upon her although not yet conferred by papal authority), she takes on roles not publicly practiced by women before the twentieth century. Not only does she act as advocate but also as priest. The School of Amiens's fifteenth-century "The Priesthood of the Virgin" shows her in church, dressed as a priest, celebrating a rite at the altar while a monk and other devotees kneel.

I would contest Marina Warner's view that Mary cannot serve as a role model for women because she is by definition inimitable. Like any model, Mary is not duplicable. But, like Christ, she is imitable. As the innumerable legends and life histories of saints show, she acts as a model and justification for unconventional behavior by both women and men, provides a convention for alternative ways of life. I shall explore the radical ideas that are at some level suggested or validated by goddess figures like Mary.

Virginity

The first of these radical ideas is that of virginity. Mary is a woman—like Woolf's Orlando centuries later—who conceives, once, without mating, and reproduces without pain. She is also rewarded and acclaimed for not mating or reproducing thereafter. As the fifteenth-century English carol puts it, she is "a Maiden without make"—where *make* means *equal* but also suggests *mate*. In nineteenth-century England childbirth constituted a very real danger to women's lives. Celibacy in marriage was often the only way a woman could avoid being worn out by a series of childbearings, but this option was of course contingent on her husband's concern for her health and well-being. Before the wide availability of contraception, which constitutes a watershed in the condition of Western women, marriage was not so much the extension of romance (however it may have been represented) as the beginning of compulsory and continual childbearing. If the Victorian novel ends with either marriage or death, for the Victorian woman the two were often simultaneous or linked. Jane Austen's keen awareness of this danger, evidenced in her letters, is not as paranoiac as it sounds when one considers the not untypical life of her contemporary, Mary Wollstonecraft, whose promising literary career was cut short by childbirth-related complications. Woolf had in mind deaths like Wollstonecraft's and Charlotte Brontë's when she remarked that none of the great nineteenth-century women writers had children.

In such a context, to be virgin may be to be despised, but is also to be physically, in at least some respects, safe and free—an idea, as I shall demonstrate later, clearly present in the writings of Austen and of other women both in her time and later. Further, to be virgin was not always to be despised—not even in the nineteenth century. The Ladies of Llangollen were admiringly referred to as "the most celebrated virgins in Europe."[52] From our post-Freudian perspective the idea of virginity may appear to be sexually repressive. This construction, however, is grounded, first, in an assumption that sexuality equals heterosexuality and, second, in an unproven assumption that heterosexual activity is not repressive or oppressive for women. The second assumption is particularly doubtful in a situation where marital rape is not recognized and where contraception is not available. Further, it underestimates the attractions of survival and health. The increased propaganda in the nineteenth century for heterosexual romance leading to marriage may have been in part a reaction to the perception of the power of these attractions for women like Jane Austen and Anna Seward who refused marriage, preferring the company of their own sex. In Victorian texts women may be represented as "sexless," but an unpacking of this word suggests that it equals "uninterested in heterosexual activity"; it by no means equals "uninterested in erotic or romantic emotion." That the Ladies of Llangollen loved one another deeply, for example, was acknowledged by all who wrote about them.

If sex equals heterosexual penetration, a woman who does not engage in heterosexual activity is a virgin. But this says nothing about whether or not she engages in other kinds of sexual activity. Late eighteenth-century and early nineteenth-century England was certainly not devoid of the knowledge of masturbation, private or mutual, or of the existence and importance of the clitoris.[53]

The "sexlessness" of women, then, in the sense defined above, may not be merely a patriarchal stereotype but may have something to do with the material fact that heterosex meant for a woman repeated childbirths and everything that followed—from absence of leisure, increased constraints, confinement and immobilization to the wearing away of youth and health, and shortened longevity.[54] Even if we assume that heterosexual activity is inherently attractive to most women, an assumption by no means proven, it is probable that it would be attended by some degree of fear and anxiety in these conditions. It is significant that in most Victorian fictions the sexual nature of a heterosexual relationship is signaled by a marriage proposal, by hand clasping, or at most a kiss, and then by marriage and childbirth. For instance, sex between David Copperfield and Agnes is evidenced only by their final appearance surrounded by miniature reproductions of themselves. Within this set of signals, where heterosex and childbirth go together as one package, the absence of the latter must signal the absence of the former and the woman be named "virgin," but this has nothing to do, I would argue, with her exclusion from romantic and erotic emotion or even activity. I would also argue, and I hope to demonstrate, that the romantic and passionate but not necessarily sexless friendships between women that, as Lillian Faderman has shown, were acceptable and ubiquitous in nineteenth-century England were also acceptable between men. These romances were displaced, in the Victorian novel (but not in Romantic and Aestheticist poetry), by marriage. Virginity or celibacy, in this economy, draws on long traditions to become the alternative to heterosexuality and a site where same-sex love can be articulated as primary. Importantly, *virgin* in Catholic discourse is not a term restricted to women. Male saints are also described as virgins, and Victorian texts like Newman's novel *Loss and Gain* treat virginity as a condition to which men too aspire and attain.

The utopian desire for such alternatives fuels, I suggest, the persistent popular devotional Marian cults. Her status as Aie Parthenos, ever virgin, can make her (when so constructed, and she often was so constructed) a figure of female autonomy and power.[55] Like so many ideas that precede by centuries their material accomplishment, her giving birth without sexual intercourse (the idea of parthenogenesis) can be seen as anticipating conception by artificial insemination.[56]

Mariology constructed the life of Mary as parallel to that of Christ. The celebration of the birth of a girl is less common in most cultures than that of the birth of a son. Even in religions that have both gods and goddesses, the divine child is usually male. In the Victorian novel the male child is always more desired than a daughter (Tom Tulliver, Paul Dombey, Jane Eyre's son). This preference is, however, constantly contested by the struggling female child who yearns for an education and for appreciation (Jane Eyre, Maggie Tulliver). Looking for a cultural model of an achieving female child, it is significant that George Eliot has to turn to a non-Protestant tradition and presents the child Theresa as well as the Virgin Mary as prototypes for her Dorothea. Mary worship had evolved the stories of Mary's miraculous wisdom as a child, her presentation at, and education in, the Temple (which would have been impossible given Jewish tradition) as models for the desired female child.[57] All of these elaborately worked out stories placed her more and more on a plane of equality with Christ, in whose life these were biblically attested events. For the Protestant nineteenth-century reader, this information would not have been readily accessible. However, some of the most famous paintings by acknowledged masters, paintings hung in the British Museum, the National Gallery, the Louvre, and familiar to educated men and their daughters (to use Woolf's phrase), focused on these models—on Mary reading, being taught by her mother to read, or being presented in the Temple, just as Christ was to be presented later. Pater's way of commenting on and appreciating these paintings in *The Renaissance* constitutes an interesting strategy—he uses the familiar to suggest the strange and unfamiliar.

Equally interesting, the immaculate conception of Mary meant that both she and Christ acquired a matrilineal heritage in opposition to the heavily patrilineal one (a series of names of fathers, where one "begat" the other) with which the Book of Matthew opens.[58] Patriliny is displaced when both Christ and Mary are not children of earthly fathers but of God. This kind of fathering was always capable of a radical antinomian reading. As William Blake put it when asked if he believed that Christ was the son of God, "Yes. And so are you, and so am I." If one kind of "holy family" representation showed Mary and child in the company of a nurturing Joseph or of a hovering father god, another equally popular one showed Mary and child with Anne and/or Elizabeth, and sometimes the infant St. John. This earlier type of holy family or holy kinship is constructed on matrilineal principles, since Elizabeth is Mary's cousin and John her nephew. The community of women is celebrated through such events as the visitation, the Magnificat, and the idea of the three Marys at the cross and at the tomb.[59] As Ashley and Sheingorn demonstrate, an elaborate matrilineal cult developed around the figure of St. Anne, but this powerful and widespread cult was lost to Protestants. Luther vehemently denounced the cult of St. Anne. Following the Reformation she became again the anonymous maternal grandmother of Jesus. Nevertheless, this anonymous female figure replaces the father figure in some of the most famous of Western paintings, a fact Pater exploits to make his points.[60]

Refusing Marriage

The second radical idea connected with Mary is that of the refusal to marry. Most early accounts of her life represent her as refusing all marriage offers until assured that the marriage with Joseph will not be sexual.[61] Her virginity stands as a symbol of this refusal of conjugality. The disavowal of Mary worship at the Reformation had much to do with the Protestant reformers' campaign for married clergy. The Puritan idea of companionate marriage, seen by some feminist historians as liberatory for women, may equally be read as involving the institutionalization of compulsory heterosexuality in a more definite form and the persecution or downgrading of other alternatives, including celibacy, same-sex eroticism, and friendship.

This particular battle was fought out again in a different form at various sites in the nineteenth century, for instance, in Oxford and Cambridge, where unmarried dons like Pater were viewed askance by patriarchs like Leslie Stephen—a battle represented by Woolf in *The Years* and *Jacob's Room*. For women the battle was much more difficult. The refusal to marry when an offer was made was itself viewed as perverse— the archetype for this moment being perhaps Elizabeth Bennett's celebrated refusal of Mr. Collins. To counter the figure of the pitiable old maid or spinster governess figure, "poor, plain and insignificant," in Jane Eyre's words, Protestant literature had little to offer. The celibate figure of Christ, being male, was not an adequate model, and, more important, acceptance of it meant an early death. The heroine who refuses to marry and models herself on the martyred Christ ends up dying young— Richardson's Clarissa is the classic example here. For happy, nonheterosexual, and long-lived creativity, Mary is the dominant model. She is invoked in stories of single mothers such as Mrs. Gaskell's Ruth and Hardy's Tess. For the Victorian young woman inclined to singleness or to the love of a woman, the social statement of intention was not declaration of sexual preference but refusal to marry. Even in the case of the Ladies of Llangollen the refusal to marry was seen as the great defining act of their lives. It is also the central moment in many Victorian fictions. Even if it is later followed (as in *Pride and Prejudice* and *Mansfield Park*) by the acceptance of another man, the refusal nevertheless carries a great deal of emotional and political resonance. To use Roosevelt's phrase, a "wilful choice of barrenness" would be seen as perverse by most parents.

The threatening model available here was that of the female saint. Early stories of the saints (available to such children as Maggie Tulliver in Foxe's *Book of Martyrs*) almost always connect female martyrdom with a refusal to marry. The martyrdom is celebrated and the willful choice to remain barren is represented as the most glorious of choices. Initially, these stories are often about Christian women refusing to marry pagans. However, the theme does not disappear later. In stories of English saints in the second millennium, for example, the women simply refuse to marry. They resist parental attempts to marry them off and flee to convents. Often, they are not martyred but survive to acquire fame, power, and learning as abbesses, and, after a natural death, canonization.[62] Some female saints like St. Catherine of Alexandria, apocryphal queen of Egypt who dreamed of her mystical marriage to Christ, did not enter convents but nevertheless refused to marry any man. In paintings the representation of St. Catherine's mystical marriage underlines its nonreproductive aspect by figuring Christ as a baby. To marry a baby obviously entails refusing to produce babies. In Bernardino Luini's *The Marriage of St. Catherine* the beautiful young Catherine and the equally beautiful young Mary stand side by side while the baby puts the ring on Catherine's finger. Interestingly, Mary, who, in her legends, is very jealous of her own devotees' affections and insists on their remaining celibate, is not jealous of Christ's marrying Catherine and other female saints who, by this marriage, become assimilated to Mary's company of women, similar to the virginal bands of Artemis.[63]

Although she enters into a spiritual nonsexual marriage with Joseph, Mary in her legends is not so burdened by wifehood and motherhood as to be unable to participate in a wider life. As queen of heaven, she is undomesticated and remarkably mobile, constantly appearing unexpectedly to aid and rescue her devotees. She performs numerous miracles that parallel those performed by Christ—curing the sick, raising the dead, calming tempests, and freeing people from hell.[64] The imitable nature of her performances is evident from the legends of male and female saints who also perform such miracles.

That the disobedient daughter who refused to marry constituted a major problem in the Victorian imagination is testified by the recurrence of this figure in fiction, from Clarissa to Fanny Price, Elizabeth Bennett, little Em'ly, and innumerable others in the heyday of the Victorian novel. The nun was represented in paranoid anti-Catholic diatribes, both by educated political leaders like Newdegate and by such popular No-Popery rabble rousers as Murphy, as an unruly, most likely promiscuous, and certainly perverse woman who had chosen the unwomanly path of singleness and barrenness and tempted Protestant daughters and wives to do likewise. How far the temptation factor had a basis in fact and how much was a construction by the threatened and pornographic imagination of the men involved remains uncertain. However, at the level of an idea, the nun as celibate woman was for many reasons a more threatening figure than the mocked or pitied spinster aunt.

Part of the threat may have been her living to grow old and become a figure of authority.[65] Another part was her potential autoeroticism or lesbianism (as in Diderot's *The Nun*). Mary was represented, in several canonical paintings, such as El Greco's *Pentecost*, as the center of the apostolic community on the day of Pentecost and as graciously presiding over the apotheosis of various saints, male and female. In her nineteenth-century incarnation she is the mother superior, the dangerous figure of female rule, who, unlike the reigning Queen Victoria, is not married and fertile, but perversely barren. She may also be the older woman who seduces the younger, whether in fiction and poetry (in Hardy's *Desperate Remedies*) or in life—Katherine Bradley, the aunt and lover of Edith Cooper.

A good example of the way Marian imagery was recuperated by Victorian Protestant feminists to their own ends is the pioneer women's educationist Dorothea Beale's choice of St. Hilda as a model. Herself an ardent Protestant, although accused in her youth of being a Tractarian, Dorothea Beale was also a leading intellectual, principal of the Ladies' College, Cheltenham, for over fifty years, an inspired interpreter of Rossetti and Browning, a friend of many leading feminists, including the pioneer Indian women's educationist Pandita Ramabai, and of such men as Benjamin Jowett, translator of Plato. She remarked, "I grieve over that Protestant spirit which forbids people to read books, to associate with people who do not think precisely in their way."[66] Dorothea Beale was imaginatively inspired by such women as Catherine of Siena, Spenser's androgynous Britomart, and St. Hilda. Of these the most dominant was the seventh-century abbess of Whitby, patron of the first English religious poet Caedmon. St. Hilda's double monastery (for men and women) at Whitby had been sacked by the Danes circa 800 and refounded as an abbey for monks in the eleventh century. In a sense Miss Beale reversed the process when in 1893 she founded St. Hilda's Hall at Oxford. She personally financed it for several years, reclaiming space within the university for women to live the life of the mind. She also founded the first resident training college for teachers, St. Hilda's College at Cheltenham, in 1886. Unveiling the saint's statue on this occasion, Miss Beale spoke of Hilda's work as a teacher. In 1890 she named the teachers' hostel at her college Astell House after Mary Astell, whose plan for a Protestant sisterhood dedicated to higher learning had been turned down by Bishop Burnet on the grounds that it would be too much like a nunnery. Thus she made connections between traditions of women's learning and same-sex community. When Frances Mary Buss, another pioneer women's educationist, died in 1894, her relatives and friends dedicated a window to her memory in the Protestant Church of Holy Trinity of which she was a member. The subject of the window was the sixth-century abbess St. Scholastica, whose features were modeled on those of Miss Buss.[67]

Woolf's imagined Judith Shakespeare, beaten and punished by her father for her refusal to marry, would very likely have run away to a convent, an alternative Woolf does not consider, because, by her time, convents had been identified with repression and frustration rather than female power and learning. Yet, the subtext remains—Woolf talks of female tradition as one of poverty, chastity, and obedience, values that, she suggests, were reinterpreted by Victorian feminists and should be retained in a new form by twentieth-century women. These, of course, are the vows taken by nuns.[68]

Mary and the Book

Western art constructs Mary in symbiotic relationship with the written word. As I have pointed out, St. Anne's conception of Mary is frequently represented in the same way as is Mary's conception of Christ—a woman alone, concentrating on a book. St. Anne teaching Mary is an often represented theme that would seem to validate the education of girls, especially as the representation becomes more realistic and humanized. Georges de La Tour's seventeenth-century *Education of the Virgin* shows the tired-looking mother and the grave little girl reading by the light of a candle in a domestic interior. Murillo's *St. Anne and the Virgin* (after 1674) shows them on a balcony. The little girl, kneeling at her mother's knee, rests her hand on the book while Anne explains something. Delacroix's moving representation shows a peasant mother and daughter out in the open. The mother's arm is round the daughter's shoulders and the daughter's hand is on the book as she reads.

Mary's intercourse with the book continues after the baby appears. It accompanies her into later life, as a symbol of that to which she is wedded. Botticelli paints a less often represented scene in his *Madonna of the Magnificat* (c. 1480). Supporting the baby with her left hand, Mary writes her song in a book with her right hand. Here we have a woman as one of the authors of the Bible, for the Magnificat is inscribed in the Gospel of Luke. Botticelli shows her writing it out rather than dictating to St. Luke. Two angels crown her, and three others, feminized and androgynized, wingless and haloless, form a self-absorbed triangle facing her. As Emmanuel Cooper points out, these creatures, who suggest a third sex, "direct their tender, adoring concern" not at her or the baby but at each other (6). The Madonna's presence seems to legitimate and bless this tender concern, here as in many other paintings.

In Rembrandt's seventeenth-century *Holy Family* she sits at the fire, open book on her knee, checking on the baby who sleeps in a crib beside her while Joseph works at his carpentry in the background. In this composition Mary, the baby, and the book form a triangle of which she is the apex, and the triangle is blessed by hovering cherubs. Henri Rousseau's (1844–1910) *Le Douanier* presents a somewhat comical reading of this configuration. A grim-faced and robust Victorian Mary stares aggressively at Joseph, holding the open book as a barrier between herself and him. Joseph, smoking a long and phallic pipe, looks at her in a mildly puzzled manner. With her other hand she supports the naked baby who drinks at her breast, glaring at Joseph the while!

Mary's relationship with the written word continues into old age. In Mariological tradition Christ appears to Mary after his resurrection and, later, the angel appears again to Mary to inform her of her impending assumption. On both these occasions she is often represented reading. In Frei Carlos's sixteenth-century *The Apparition of Christ to the Virgin* she is reading when Christ appears, and the other Maries look on. In Jean Fouquet's fifteenth-century *The Second Annunciation* she is an old woman in a domestic interior. The kneeling angel faces her and holds out the victor's palm instead of the flowering lily. The open book lies before her on a table.[69]

Iconographic representations of Mary after Christ's departure often

show her dressed as a nun, while the female saints are represented in her company and are modeled on her in appearance. Frequently, all are reading and writing. After her own assumption, Mary presides over a learned community. Gerard David's *Virgo Inter Virgines* (1450–1523) shows her as the center of a company of women. To her right one woman explains something to another who listens, holding an open book. To her left, one woman reads concentratedly while another looks up from her book, as if reflecting on something just read. Two angels in the back row play musical instruments. Other women in the picture tell the rosary or meditate. Some of the women are dressed as nuns.

Mary presides not only over female but also over male learning. In the Master of Flemalle's *Votive Virgin* she is seated above the reading St. Augustine, blessing him, St. Peter, and the kneeling abbott of St. Augustine's order. In Il Moretto's *The Four Latin Fathers* she sits enthroned above the four, two of whom, in the foreground, are reading together. In Fra Filippo Lippi's *The Vision of St. Bernard* she appears to the saint while he is reading. In Sodoma's *Madonna and Child with Saint Lucy and Other Saints* Mary presides over a group, in the foreground of which Lucy is busy writing. Both male and female saints are frequently represented holding the book or reading or writing.

Mary presides over scholasticism, and female saints imitate this action of hers. Paintings of the life of St. Ursula, patron saint of women teachers, show an angel appearing to the learned young woman in a dream, much as Gabriel appeared to Mary, and represent her and her army of eleven thousand virgins ascending the steps to be blessed by the pope much as the child Mary is represented ascending the steps of the Temple to be received by the high priest. In their turn, female saints appear as leaders and teachers. In Francesco Vanni's *St. Catherine of Siena* the saint, a branch of flowering lilies in one hand, holds her other hand to the lips of a woman kneeling before her. The woman kisses two of the saint's fingers. The representation is as erotic in its own way as the more famous Bernini statue of the swooning Theresa being pierced by the arrow of love.

If Mary is often represented worshipping her son, she also appears teaching him and presiding over his relationship with others, especially John the Baptist. In Leonardo's *The Madonna of the Rocks* she and a feminine-looking angel preside over the two boy babies' meeting. Here, as in *The Virgin in the Lap of St. Anne*, two women appear to be blessing two boy children's friendship. In Pietro Lorenzetti's fourteenth-century *Mary Teaching the Child Jesus*, she looks gravely at him and explains something.

In this context it is striking that in the biblical account familiar to most English Protestants the sentiments of the Magnificat prefigure those of the Beatitudes. The main theme of Mary's song is that she is "blessed" because God has raised her from "low estate." God puts down the mighty and exalts "them of low degree," fills "the hungry," and sends "the rich empty away" (Luke 1:46–55). Christ's first and most famous sermon, which centrally defines his teaching, echoes his mother's song, saying that those who are poor and who "hunger now" are "blessed" because they shall be filled, while "the rich" who are "full" now "shall hunger" (Luke 6:20–38). It could be said that women's experience informs Christ's teaching and, thus, that as Plato's Socrates ascribes his teaching on love to Diotima's instruction, Christ's teaching on love is represented as owing its emphases to Mary.

Mary and Sexual Transgression

Victorian Protestants and Catholics alike often terrified children and young people with lurid pictures of hell, especially the tortures awaiting those who sinned sexually. However, unlike Catholicism, Protestantism, having done away with the therapeutic relief of confession, penance, and absolution as well as the saving grace of purgatory, consigned the sinner to a Calvinist legacy of perpetual guilt and doubt regarding his/her salvation. In such a context one reason for the attraction of homoerotically inclined men and women to Catholicism may have been the figure of the Virgin, who was constructed in Catholic belief as all-compassionate.[70] She was believed to be specially compassionate because she shared in Christ's passion—her com-passion. She intervenes to save the innocent, but in many of her legends she also intervenes to save sinners, including thieves and prostitutes, a nun who runs away with a lover and returns to find she has not been missed because Mary has taken her place, an abbess whose illegitimate child Mary delivers and hides, an incestuous empress who drowned her baby, and a man who blasphemes Christ but reveres Mary.[71] She is represented in numerous English churches as intervening when St. Michael weighs the soul against its sins—she tilts the balances to save the soul.

Zimdars-Swartz points out that the image of the Victim Soul pervades modern Catholic piety and especially Marian devotion; it is structured around the idea of the vicarious suffering of Christ and Mary and extends to the suffering and crisis experienced by individual devotees as well as communities of devotees who see themselves as suffering on behalf of the larger community or the world.[72] This self-view fits well with the Romantic view of the artist as martyr and pioneer, suffering the miscomprehension of a philistine society.

In the popular imagination Mary was always on the side of the underdog. All the major nineteenth- and early twentieth-century Marian apparitions (Rue de Bac 1830, La Salette 1846, Lourdes 1854, Fatima 1917) were claimed to have been witnessed by women, girls, and boy children. All the visionaries were poor and uneducated—they included servants, shepherds, a sickly housewife, and a woman accused of being a prostitute. This suggests the structure of Marian cults and their tendency to privilege the underprivileged. Mary's greater popularity as mediator (as compared to Christ) has to do with her being viewed as embodying divine mercy in contrast to divine law represented by God and Christ—hence the many paintings that show her pleading with Christ on behalf of sinners as well as battling the devil to save sinners.[73] In both cases, whether acting as warrior knight or as compassionate mother, she opposes a tyrannical male force, divine or demonic, and is herself on the side of humanity. If the Law is phallic, then Mary, in opposition to it, can be read as standing for nonphallic antinomian Love that, in her mythology, cannot fail to triumph.

More important, her attraction for sexual "sinners" and supposed sympathy for them derives from her own liminal position as one who was viewed as sexually transgressive and was then vindicated. After she agrees to conceive Christ, she is suspected by Joseph of sexual sin. Christ never has to face this particular charge. Mary's experience makes it easy for others who are perceived as sexual transgressors, whether or not they perceive themselves as such, to look to her rather than to Christ alone for inspiration and vindication. Mary's "conceiving," even thinking of having, a child without a man is audacious insofar as it places her outside and above patriarchal family laws, making her unquestionably superior rather than subordinate to her husband. Regardless of the church's insistence on her uniqueness, on her being "alone of all her sex," many nineteenth-century homosexuals identified with her lonely suffering as well as with her nonheterosexual joy. The identification of Mary with Love is also one of her attractions for Victorian homosexuals who, even when they wondered if they were sinning, justified themselves in the name of love, often also evoking the other Mary (Magdalene), forgiven by Christ because "she loved much." The homosexual search for ancestry is simultaneously a search for lovers whose love was defined as sin by their own societies. Mary, exposed to unjust suspicions, fits this pattern.

Furthermore, as nurturer of the divine, mother of her father (god), she represents the paradox of inversion wherein the powerless is the most powerful and the last first, a theme foregrounded both in the Magnificat and in the Beatitudes. This paradox was accepted by some Anglican divines. For example, John Donne, in his sonnet "Annunciation," writes "yea thou art now / Thy maker's maker, and thy father's mother."[74] As Jean Guitton puts it, "She gives to the divinity what is necessary for the earthly life: milk, daily bread, the thoughts, the feelings, the words of a language. . . . Everything is then *inverted* in a manner at once absolute and discrete" (emphasis in the original).[75] In giving both milk and language she undoes the binary opposition of Victorian fatherly and motherly roles, makes the father superfluous, and enacts the possibility of a parenting role beyond biological gender. It is my contention that the various intersecting and often contradictory triangles in which Mary participates—God-Mary-Christ, Anne-Mary-Christ, Anne-Mary-Elizabeth, Anne-Mary-Joseph, Mary-Joseph-God, and so on, as also her shifting and simultaneous status as daughter/mother/bride/teacher/protector/mediator/beloved/friend to both women and men, in different contexts, provide fruitful paradigms for the reading of English literary texts.[76]

The necessarily underground nature of the Marian model in Victorian society is appropriate—it is oppositional both by reason of its Catholic associations and because of its connotations of female power and intellectual and sexual autonomy. It is even possible that it acquires greater radical potential, because of this oppositional quality, within Protestant discourse than in Catholic contexts, where, although popular Mariolatry is in opposition to Church teaching, it is from time to time contained by dogmatic incorporation of popular belief, such as the Vatican's acceptance of the immaculate conception, assumption, and queenhood of Mary, centuries after these were developed and accepted widely by ordinary Catholics.[77]

In the next chapter I shall consider how Marian ideas and images intersected with Sapphic ideas and images in Romantic texts, becoming crucially constitutive of nineteenth-century lyrical elegy and elegiac lyric, forms that, in their turn, influenced lyrical fictional and nonfictional prose.

2

The Sapphic Sublime and Romantic Lyricism

The isles of Greece, the isles of Greece!
Where burning Sappho loved and sung
—Byron

O sweetest lips since those of Mitylene!
—Oscar Wilde, "The Grave of Keats"

I got Sturge Moore's brother to translate me all the
fragments of Sappho. Her touch has left a little trail of
flame in Catullus, Keats, Swinburne.
—Charles Ricketts (1926)

It is generally agreed that Romanticism constitutes a decisive turning point in English literary history.[1] Romantic writers' rebellion against neo-classical order and their shift to valorizing personal emotion is signaled by their experiments with and achievements in the lyric. Numerous sources for the shift have been traced by literary historians. I propose to add a source—the Sapphic ode. I shall argue that the model for the English Romantic ode is less the Pindaric ode or the odes of classical drama and more the Sapphic ode. Drawing on Longinus, the Romantic poets figured Sappho as the sublime lyricist par excellence.

Sappho has often been acclaimed as perhaps the earliest poet to speak in an intensely personal voice, to foreground an emotional subjectivity.[2] This made her an obvious choice for the Romantics in their search for ancestry, since their attempt to redefine value was based on the privileging of emotion over reason. Valuing the ability to love and to suffer over the ability to make a rational or logical argument, the Romantics sought to extend significance and dignity to those commonly categorized as less "rational," for example, children, very old people, non-European races, the poor, and even the insane, criminals, and nonhuman species. The poetics of this attempt was premised on making the poetic persona vulnerable. Instead of constructing a poetic "argument," the Romantic lyrical voice confesses to being overpowered by emotion. Further, the dialogic quality of the Romantic ode is one of the main features that distinguishes it from the neoclassical ode.

The Sapphic ode is a primary chosen ancestor of the Romantic lyric in the following ways:

1. Both adopt a confessional tone: the expression of suffering, pain, and weakness paradoxically constitutes the power of the poem.[3]
2. Both are built around intense love or magnetic attraction for a person, a place, or a humanized, ungendered, or feminized divine/natural force. This love is often nonreciprocal or not fully requited or obstructed by circumstances.
3. Both move between praise/celebration/joy generated by love and pain caused by nonfulfillment of this love.
4. Both construct a confidential dialogue between poetic voice and the object of love and, implicitly or explicitly, between poetic voice and reader.

In Sappho's odes the dialogue and the love is primarily between women.[4] This quality carries over into Romantic poetry. The Romantic poetic voice frequently moves in the direction either of ungendering or self-feminization or both, and the Muse or the beloved object (person/place/natural creature/force) is also moved in similar directions.[5] The paradigm of the Romantic poetic conversation, I will argue, is a conversation between women. This metaphoric conversation occurs in the context of the English Romantics' revulsion from the bloodshed of the Terror in France, which led them to stress, in their writing of radicalism, the ideas of fraternity and liberty over that of equality. For some Romantic writers, notably Shelley, women's freedom was an axiom; for all of them it was, at some level, an idea partially avowed. Thus, in their writings, fraternity often gets displaced by or is modeled on sisterhood. Their revulsion from violence in all its forms, especially martial and "manly" violence but also state and patriarchal violence, and violence toward nature, inclines them to feminize their image of ideal community.[6] The ideal human being is often a woman and always more like a woman than like a man, as those categories were constructed in late eighteenth-century, early nineteenth-century England (consider Coleridge's poet with "flashing eyes" and "floating hair").[7] The girl child (Wordsworth's little Barbara Lewthwaithe or Dorothy who fears to brush the dust off the butterfly's wings) or young woman (the lady in "The Sensitive Plant") or pair of female friends (Shelley's *Rosalind and Helen*) become the models for desirable relationship—between various aspects of the self, between humans, between human and animal, human and plant. These are models for the male poet or narrator and for readers, both male and female, to imitate. Nurturing, tenderness, and mutual parenting, the feelings conventionally associated with mother and child, are imaged as constituting the ideal relation between male friends as well (the relation Coleridge posits himself as seeking from Wordsworth in particular and the world in general).[8] In their search for non-Protestant, nonmale models, the Romantics looked to Greece, to the East, and to the middle ages. Sappho and Mary were, in different ways, very attractive figures to them.

Feminist criticism has by and large assumed that male writers ignore or trivialize women's writing, constituting themselves as sons of literary fathers, while women writers operate within a tradition of their own. An unintended and ironic consequence of this segregative approach is that women writers' influence on male writers goes unacknowledged. In order to challenge this approach I will look briefly at one of its major sources, Virginia Woolf's *A Room of One's Own*.

In this text Woolf constructs what may be termed a Marian tradition. Her narrator tells the reader, "Call me Mary."[9] The narrator is named Mary Beton, for her aunt of the same name who leaves her the legacy that enables her to write. Her friend at Cambridge, a science teacher, is named Mary Seton, and the woman novelist she reads is Mary Carmichael. This naming befits Woolf's claim that "we think back through our mothers if we are women" (79). This important claim, empowering though it has been for feminist criticism, is also at odds with much in Woolf's own text. The list of male writers to whom, Woolf says, it is useless to go for help are all prose writers ("Lamb, Browne, Thackeray, Newman, Sterne, Dickens, De Quincey," 79). This may be appropriate for her consideration of the difference between Austen's and Thackeray's prose, but for the purposes of the general argument, which revolves around the question of the woman poet—the woman Shakespeare—it is less than adequate. Asking why women have more often written poetry than prose, Woolf notes in passing, and without naming her, the presence of Sappho: "The 'supreme head of song' was a poetess" (69). Toward the close she mentions Sappho again, as "an inheritor as well as an originator" (113). Although everywhere allusively woven into her own prose, the Romantic poets and the Aestheticists (to which latter group Vernon Lee and Christina Rossetti, both of whom Woolf mentions, belong) are absent from her argument and so is the lyric. Thus Woolf absents her own immediate ancestors and also the form that most strongly influenced her kind of novel, which has been called the lyric novel. She remarks that the epic and the poetic play are perhaps not suited to women and that "all the older forms of literature were hardened and set" by the time women began to write (80). Yet, Christina Rossetti, the woman poet she quotes as the equal of Tennyson (12–13), wrote lyrics—surely an "older form of literature."[10]

While Woolf's main premise—that the lack of intellectual freedom, based on the lack of five hundred pounds and a room of one's own, inhibited the genius of many women, is crucial to the persuasiveness of her text, her second premise, that women think back through their mothers, is shot through with enfeebling contradictions. It is contradicted by her own writing, even in this text, which is full of enabling allusion to male poets (Shelley, Gray, and even Milton).[11] It is also contradicted by other arguments she makes, for example, that "poetry ought to have a mother as well as a father" (107). This implies that women poets do think through their fathers as well, and, more important, that men poets think through their mothers too. Only once does she mention the influence of a woman writer on a male writer (and this is in passing), to say that we have had enough critical studies of the influence of Joanna Baillie's tragedies on Edgar Allan Poe. It would seem to me that we have had far too few studies of such influence. For Western poetry does have a mother, and not an entirely unacknowledged one, in Sappho. Largely as the result of the red herring Woolf started, the acknowledgment of Sappho's pervasive influence on male writers has been muted, even in feminist criticism, in the later twentieth century.[12] Sappho has been read more as an influence on women writers, specifically lesbian writers.[13] While this influence is undeniable and important, her influence on male writers, indeed on every post-Romantic writer of lyrical poetry and prose, is equally important.

Woolf's famous indecision on the sameness/difference question (are women's minds the same as men's or different and, if they have come to be different, should the difference be preserved?) remains just that: indecision. She remarks that "the nerves that feed the brain would seem to differ in men and women" and suggests that this may require different material conditions of work. However, this alluring idea of difference leads to dangerous ground—her concluding sentence in this section, and her argument on the question, remain incomplete: "If through their incapacity to play football women are not going to be allowed to practise medicine—Happily, my thoughts were now given another turn" (81). Not so happily, however, her speculations bred, or, rather, reinforced, a powerful tendency in feminist and even in mainstream criticism to treat women writers as working within a tradition of their own and men writers as relatively untouched by this women's tradition. Typical is Elaine Showalter's claim that feminist criticism's "primary concern is to develop theories of sexual difference in reading, writing, and literary interpretation."[14]

The contradiction in Woolf's text arises partly from her confusing scholarly academic writing about women, of the kind Woolf's narrator reads in the British Museum, with imaginative writing about women. Woolf's confusion persists in much feminist criticism today. While entirely persuasive in her analysis of the former, she fumbles in her consideration of the latter. Acknowledging the power of representations of women in Greek tragedy, Shakespeare, and Racine (and not mentioning novelists like Richardson or Hardy), she recognizes that Shakespeare's writing, unlike that of the various professors pontificating on women's inferiority, is not driven by anger, that the creative imagination is "incandescent, unimpeded" (59). Such a distinction between the work of imagination and the work of polemics is not fashionable today. Some such distinction would seem to persist in the thought of creative writers, however.

For instance, the novelist Dorothy Allison, who writes as a working-class lesbian feminist, describes, in her essay "Believing in Literature," how, over the years, she has given up the premise of much feminist criticism that mainstream literature is the enemy and has come to make a distinction between the academy and literature:

> The academy may lie, but literature tries to tell the truth. Literature is the lie that tells the truth, that shows us human beings in pain and makes us love them, and does so in a spirit of honest revelation. That's radical enough, and more effective than only publishing unedited oral history.[15]

Sappho in England

Most literary historians assume that Sappho came to be perceived as a lover of women only in late nineteenth-century England and that, before this, the legend relayed by Ovid of her suicide following her unrequited love for the boatman Phaon, was, as Leighton puts it, the "myth which prevailed . . . and which profoundly influenced theories of female art." This view is based on the assumption that of her two longer fragments known in England in the eighteenth century the one about jealous love ("That man seems to me as the gods") was "translated, before 1885" as addressed to a boy.[16] It is also based on reading the writings of sexologists (as opposed to, say, literary commentators) as definitive of how female, and lesbian, sexuality was perceived.[17] I shall demonstrate that Sappho's passion for women was discussed in England in the eighteenth century and was thus available to the English Romantics.

Two of Sappho's odes were known in eighteenth-century England. The "Ode to Aphrodite," in which Sappho prays the goddess to grant her the love of a female beloved, was translated at this time with male pronouns for the beloved. Even in this kind of translation the poem does work as a dialogue between two women—Aphrodite and Sappho, her beloved devotee, yet the human beloved is male. However, the second ode ("That man seems to me") was far more influential because its source was Longinus's *On the Sublime*. I shall demonstrate by an examination of this and other sources that this second ode was translated and presented in eighteenth-century England as addressed by Sappho to a woman beloved.

Longinus's treatise has been described as possibly the most influential text for European literary criticism after Aristotle's *Poetics*.[18] Several translators have remarked that if all Longinus had done was preserve Sappho's ode he would have deserved lasting renown. T. R. Henn and M. H. Abrams, among others, have demonstrated that Longinus's treatise, with its development of an expressive theory of poetry, its emphasis on ecstasy and intensity as the source and the effects of poetry, and its privileging of condensation and brevity, is a major influence on Romantic, Aestheticist, impressionist, and modernist criticism.[19] It follows that the Sapphic ode, cited by Longinus as his only example of a love lyric that is "sublime," must also have been influential, an inference not elaborated by most critics, presumably because of a reluctance to acknowledge a woman writer's influence on male writers. Surprisingly, even feminist critics have not noticed the implications of this. Anne Mellor, for example, ignores Longinus and treats Burke's *Philosophical Inquiry Into the Origin of Our Ideas of the Sublime and the Beautiful* (1757) as "the most famous treatise on the sublime published in the eighteenth century," which leads her to conclude that "the concept of the sublime promoted by eighteenth-century theorists and the male Romantic poets . . . is associated with an experience of masculine empowerment" (85). In privileging Burke over Longinus as influential for Romantic conceptions of the sublime, commentators privilege the later phase of Wordsworth's and Coleridge's lives over their most creative youthful phase and over the lives and writings of Byron, Shelley, and Keats. The "younger" Romantics were vehemently opposed to all that Burke represented and passionately inclined to take classical Greece, including "burning Sappho," as a model of sublimity, creativity, and community.

Longinus's treatise was first translated into Latin in the sixteenth century, and the first modern language edition was Boileau's in French in 1674, which created a literary sensation. The first English translations, made in 1652 (J. Hall), 1680 (Pulteney), 1698 (anon., Oxford), and 1724 (Welsted), relied heavily on Boileau. It was his dissatisfaction with this reliance that inspired William Smith, rector of Trinity in Chester, to work for nine years on his translation, dedicated to the Earl of Macclesfield, which first appeared in 1739, was reprinted in 1751 and 1756, and rapidly superseded all other English versions.[20] The importance of Smith's translation is evident in that his use of the word *Sublime* was picked up by all subsequent English translators. Hall (1652) had entitled his translation "The Height of Eloquence" and Pulteney his in 1680 "The Loftiness or Elegancy of Speech." Leonard Welsted (1724) had first used the phrase *on the Sublime*[21] but Smith in his preface dismisses Welsted's translation as Boileau "misrepresented and mangled" with "every Error" including printer's errors, reproduced (no page number in the original). Smith proclaims on his title page that his translation is "from the Greek."

I am interested in how Smith handles chapter 10, which contains Sappho's poem. In Smith's translation this is the chapter where the word *Imagination*, a key word for the Romantics, is first used, Sappho being cited as an example of "judicious choice" and "skilful connexion" of circumstances that "affect the Imagination" (27). The circumstances are those of "jealous Love" (27). This is the first time love is mentioned in the text. The only subsequent mention of it is in the account of Euripides, who is praised for his rendition of love and madness, but the example cited from his work refers to the second state. Sappho's poem is the only one cited as an example of love.

Smith uses Ambrose Philips's translation of Sappho's poem from the *Spectator*, no. 229. I shall reproduce the translation, as it seems to me open to either heterosexual (if the speaker is assumed to be male) or homosexual interpretation and more inclined to the latter:

> Blest as the immortal Gods is he,
> The Youth who fondly sits by thee,
> And hears, and sees thee all the while
> Softly speak, and sweetly smile.
> 'Twas this depriv'd my Soul of Rest,
> And rais'd such Tumults in my Breast;
> For while I gaz'd, in Transport tost,
> My Breath was gone, my Voice was lost.
> My bosom glow'd; the subtle Flame
> Ran quick thro' all my vital Frame;
> O'er my dim Eyes a Darkness hung;
> My Ears with hollow Murmurs rung.
> In dewy Damps my limbs were chill'd;
> My Blood with gentle Horrors thrill'd;
> My feeble Pulse forgot to play,
> I fainted, sunk, and dy'd away.   (28)

Longinus's commentary praises the delineation of the speaker's simultaneous and contradictory emotions, using the female pronoun throughout. More relevant to my immediate purpose is Smith's commentary in the lengthy "Notes and Observations" appended to his translation. Here Smith imagines the circumstances of the poem as specifically female homoerotic, stresses the violence of the passion, and then, anxiously, proceeds to give examples of heterosexual love from classical and English poetry to counter the effect. Smith writes: "The title of this Ode in Ursinus in the Fragments of Sappho is, To the beloved Fair, and it is the right. For Plutarch (to omit the Testimonies of many others) in his Eroticon, has these Words, The beautiful Sappho says, that at sight of her beloved Fair, her voice was suppressed, &c" (134). Here Smith directly tells the English reader that classical sources confirm the homosexual context of the poem. He then goes on to imagine this context more concretely:

> Besides, Strabo and Athenaeus tell us that the Name of this Fair one was Dorica, and that she was loved by Charaxus, Sappho's Brother. Let us then suppose that this Dorica, Sappho's infamous Paramour, receives the Addresses of Charaxus, and admits him into her Company as her Lover. This very Moment Sappho unexpectedly enters, and struck at what she sees, feels tormenting Emotions. In this Ode therefore she endeavours to express that Wrath, Jealousy and Anguish, which distracted her with such variety of Torture. This in my opinion is the Subject of the Ode. (134)

By using the words "Sappho's infamous Paramour" Smith makes clear the fleshly connotations of the love between the two women. He goes on to insist on the "Rage and Distraction" of Sappho's emotions and criticizes

Boileau for using phrases like "doux transports" and "douces langueurs" and Philips for the similar terms "transport lost" and "gentle Horrors" (135). Softness, Smith insists, is not the characteristic of the poem's sublimity, but rather intense and violent passion.

Sappho's is the only complete poem quoted and analyzed by Longinus. It is also the only lyric. His other examples are drawn from epics, orations, and dramas, and he quotes one line from Anacreon. Given that the development of the lyric is the major achievement of the English Romantics, it is significant that Smith's commentary presents something like this formulation: love between women—intense passion—jealousy aroused by a male lover—infamous—sublime lyric intensity and power.

Smith constructs the dialogue in the sublime lyric as occurring within a triangle consisting of two women and a man, in which one woman speaks to the other. In this, he does not, I think, misrepresent either Longinus or Sappho, but while Longinus does not find it necessary to stress the homosexual nature of Sappho's passion, Smith does. He is shocked by it and proceeds to give examples of heterosexual love poetry. The first example he gives is from *Romeo and Juliet* and he then refers to Otway, Dryden's *All for Love*, and Addison's *Cato*. Finally, he sets up Milton as the best model for the portrayal of love:

> But Adam and Eve in Milton are the finest Picture of conjugal Love that ever was drawn. In them it is true warmth of Affection without the violence or fury of Passion; a sweet and reasonable Tenderness without any cloying or insipid Fondness. In its Serenity and Sun-Shine, it is noble, amiable, endearing and innocent. . . . Eve knows how to submit, and Adam to forgive. (136)

Smith's formulation here posits heterosexual love as conjugal and thus legitimate, and as based on affection, not passion, as reasonable, not excessive, and as based in inequality. He then cites examples of conjugal love from classical authors, Tasso's husband and wife who fight side by side and die together, Homer's Hector and Andromache, Ulysses and Penelope, and concludes: "Milton has followed and improved upon his great Masters with Dignity and Judgment" (137).

In the most influential English translation of Longinus's treatise, then (the translation of chapter 10 and the notes on it quoted above were unaltered in subsequent editions), intense passion was presented as lesbian and illegitimate by Christian standards but as nevertheless giving rise to sublime lyrical poetry and was posited against the Christian ideal of conjugal nonexcessive affection, exemplified in Milton's epic. Smith's Christian and neoclassical didacticism would of course be received differently by different readers. What Blake, Shelley, Byron, and Keats, with their penchant for excess and intensity, found attractive in Milton was his passionate Satan rather than his picture of sweetly reasonable conjugal love. My contention is that the English Romantic poets, in their antinomian tendency to privilege intense and outlawed emotion, and their preference for love and liberty over institutionalized relationships, had as a model Sapphic emotion.

The two central elements of this model of Sapphic emotion were intense passion and intense jealousy arising from the unresponsiveness or inadequate responsiveness of the beloved. These elements were also central to the construction of the Byronic hero. The attraction that the Byronic pose held for a number of women and lesbian writers, such as Emily Brontë, has much to do with the Sapphic inflection of that pose.[22] Sappho is the first Romantic poet-hero—loves deeply and illicitly, is misunderstood and receives no adequate response, expresses her feelings in highly condensed lyrics that become immortal, dies alone for love, and is acclaimed after her death. Chatterton and the younger Romantics enact different dimensions of this scenario set by a Lesbian model. Leighton sees Sappho's leap as connecting "female creativity with death . . . which the Victorian imagination finds endlessly seductively appealing" (35). This formulation seems to me inadequate for failing to recognize that it was not female creativity but creativity itself that the Romantic imagination connected with death, a connection passed on to the Victorians. The model is, I would argue, female, and lesbian, but the imitators are not only women poets. They include several major male poets.

Even the Romantic predilection for the fragment or incomplete poem may have much to do with the Sapphic model, which suggests that the greatest achievement in the lyric form is fragmented. The younger Romantics, Byron, Shelley, and Keats, were particularly beloved by women and lesbian readers throughout the nineteenth and into the earlier twentieth centuries. Frequently accused of effeminacy by male critics, Shelley and Keats had large fan followings among women, which tended to reinforce the charge.[23] If, as Margaret Homans asserts, Keats invokes and writes for "an exclusively male readership" and makes of his poetry "a masculine preserve,"[24] it is strange that women readers have consistently misunderstood his intentions. The lesbian poet Amy Lowell wrote an influential biography of Keats (1925) that is today often dismissed as "excessively fond."[25]

The second major source of Sappho's poetry in eighteenth-century England was the French scholar Madame Anne Dacier's translation of Anacreon's and Sappho's poems into French. Her translation was first published in Paris in 1681, and there were many subsequent editions. Sappho is represented only by two poems and two epigrams. Dacier's biographer, Fern Farnham, argues that Dacier's choosing not to mention Sappho's possible lesbianism was crucially influential for the idealization of Sappho as pure and sexless in England through the nineteenth century, especially as Addison who wrote three essays on Sappho in the *Spectator*, nos. 223, 229, and 233, followed Dacier in remaining "entirely silent" on the subject of lesbianism.[26] Elsewhere, however, Farnham mentions that Dacier reproduced in full in her editions of Anacreon and Sappho her father Tanneguy Le Fevre's notes (35) and that Le Fevre in his notes on Sappho, and even in his life of Sappho written for a twelve-year-old child, had condemned the Greek poet as a lesbian (80). Le Fevre's books and ideas were in circulation, and the French and English literary worlds were not so isolated from one another as to make these ideas inaccessible in England. Even more important, influential English commentaries on Sappho were available in England, as I have demonstrated, and there is no reason to believe that Addison's three essays were more influential than Longinus's treatise, especially since neither Addison nor Dacier states that Sappho was not lesbian; they simply remain silent on the question. Furthermore, many late eighteenth-century and early nineteenth-century writers knew some Latin and a little Greek, and some attempted to read Sappho in the original as well as in translation, as I shall show below.

A third source existed in English for Sappho's poems in the late eighteenth century, and this directly presented her lesbianism through yet another fragment. This book *The Works of Anacreon and Sappho with Pieces from Ancient Authors; and Occasional Essays, Illustrated by Observations on their Lives and Writings, Explanatory Notes from Established Commentators . . .* was printed for J. Ridley in London in 1768. The dedicatory poem, "The Classic," is addressed to a boyhood friend with whom Ridley first discovered the classics. The poem constructs childhood as a time of perfect joy and love: "That age, when *open'd* souls familiar meet / In frolic intercourse, communion sweet" (vi; emphasis in the original), metaphorically contrasting the spontaneity of the ancient childlike past with the modern adult present. Childhood, the time of same-sex friendship and love, is nostalgically contrasted with adult conjugality and, in an interesting double take, the perfect wife and mother of the classics is contrasted with the lesbian modern woman:

> We saw the mother quit, profuse of charms,
> Her *mortal* husband for *immortal* arms;
> Unlike the fair, whom modern whimsy shows
> *Wasting* her toilette-smiles on *sister*-beaus. (v; emphasis in
> the original)

"Sister-beaus" is an interesting phrase, combining as it does the ideas of sisterhood and sexuality, drawn perhaps, as becomes clear in Ridley's commentary on Sappho, from the idea of Sappho's love for her sister-in-law that Smith had imagined as the scenario for the ode of jealous love.

In his "Observations on the Life, and Writings of Sappho," Ridley constructs her as her mother's daughter (rather as Mary of the immaculate conception is Anne's daughter) and as hostile to men. He remarks that seven cities contended for the birth of Homer and eight men contended for the fatherhood of Sappho. But her father remains unknown: "Her mother, Cleis, for the mother is always known, must surely have been injured by the zeal of these wild competitors" (129–30). He says Sappho was married to a wealthy man Cercalas, but the match was "probably not the offspring of love," evidence being her "licentious conduct" as a widow, which shows "she had very little regard for her husband or herself" (130). Sappho is thus constructed as distanced from husband, father, and also brothers, for Ridley proceeds: "Of her three brothers, Larichus, Eurigius, and Caraxus, she acted and wrote against the last with a frenzy of detestation, irritated at his affection for Rhodope, a famous courtezan" (131). Instead of presenting this as competition over a man between his sister and his lover, Ridley constructs the triangle as Smith did: "If this story is built on truth, it may be rather presumed, that disappointment, which the wretched catastrophe of her death proves she could not endure, gave rise to her inveteracy. Why might not Rhodope have been a favorite of a similar cast with Atthis or Andromeda?" (131).

So, by 1768, passion for at least four women has been attributed to Sappho in English translations, and all four are named—Dorica, Atthis, Andromeda, Rhodope. In recounting the story of the passion for Phaon and the suicidal leap from the Leucadian promontory, Ridley emphasizes his "unrival'd beauty" and speculates that "meer vanity" and "the violence of her chagrin" at being rejected may have animated her rather than "affection" (133). He proceeds to praise her as a poet, "inventress of the most harmonious measure in the Grecian, or Roman poetry," the "author of nine books of Lyric performances," notes that "the tenth muse" was her "ancient title," lists her "Eulogists," including Aristotle and Socrates, and mentions that her head was stamped on a coin in Mitylene and her statue erected in Rome (134–35). In this account Sappho's violent passions and lesbian loves, though labeled as "excesses of . . . immorality" and a target for "sarcasms" from "several pens of antiquity" (135, note), are nevertheless presented as not having detracted from her fame as a poet and being possibly constitutive of that fame, insofar as Ridley interprets at least two of her poems as inspired by these lesbian loves.

Ridley, like Smith, is torn between his awareness of the lesbian content of Sappho's poems and his uneasiness with it. He presents his own translation of the ode from Longinus's treatise (which I shall reproduce below, in connection with the "Ode to a Nightingale"), but notes, "I am desirous to understand that the piece owed its origin to the jealousy of Sappho on finding a rival beauty prefered to herself" (145, note). I find these two eighteenth-century scholars more honest and scrupulous in their approach than later bowdlerizers who alter pronouns wholesale without taking the reader into confidence on the nature of their enterprise. Ridley does not alter pronouns or even argue for a heterosexual context; he merely confesses his own predilection for a heterosexual reading, "I am desirous to understand," aware that this reading is different from Smith's, and even contradicts his own translation of the poem, which is addressed to the "thou," the "lovely Fair" who makes "the youth" happy.

Apart from the two odes, Ridley presents three fragments. The third of these is explicitly addressed, in his translation, to a woman:

> Love, thou sweetly-bitter pow'r,
> Ruler of the human hour,
> Why do'st hurl thy wanton dart
> 'Gainst a fond, unguarded heart?
> Gentle pow'r, thy soft control
> Well might melt my yielding soul,
> Did my fav'rite Atthis prove,
> (She to Sappho vow'd her love)
> How I court the charming fair;
> How she loads my breast with care!
> While my rival in her mind
> Rules the place to me assign'd.   (166–67)

The ungendered "rival" here leaves the third point in the erotic triangle uncertain, but two points are clearly female, and Ridley's note, conflating love and friendship as interchangeable terms (his translation uses all the phrases of romantic love), identifies the passion as subsisting between women: "The Teian muse [Anacreon] was divided between Love, and Wine, but the productions of the Lesbian are confined solely to the former. . . . This third Fragment may seem to have been composed upon a favorite companion, who quitted her friendship, and with a very usual frenzy in all ages, and conditions, exchanged the old for new connections!" (167, note). Ridley makes several references to Madame Dacier's edition, which is one of his sources. It is therefore significant that, unlike Dacier, he makes Sappho's lesbianism evident—which goes to refute Farnham's argument that Dacier's silence on the question was crucially influential for the English conception of Sappho as asexual. Ridley takes issue with Madame Dacier on a suggestive point: "Horace gives Sappho the title of *mascula*, which Mad. Dacier has injudicially applied to the extravagant Lover's Leap, which occasioned her death. Porphyrion has more ingeniously attributed it to the manly elegance of her numbers" (136, note).

I hope to have demonstrated that although the legend of Sappho's love and suicide for Phaon may have been better known by the turn of the century than that of her love for women, there was enough speculation, debate, and poetic evidence on the latter issue available in widely influential texts for it to have been known to any interested reader. That her sexual love for women could not be ignored by even the most unwilling editor is clear from the commentary on her in Alexander Chalmers's *The Works of the English Poets* (1810). The encyclopedic nature of this multivolume enterprise probably means that this version of Sappho was the most widely accessible in the first quarter of the nineteenth century. Chalmers's commentary on Fawkes's translation of ode 2 quotes Addison in an uneasy attempt to heterosexualize and masculinize the context, even while acknowledging that it was originally neither, by quoting Addison: "Whatever might have been the occasion for this ode, the English reader will enter into the beauties of it, if he supposes it to have been written in the person of a lover sitting by his mistress."[27] The male English reader's mindset, rather than that of the poet, is Addison's concern here. However, the editor modifies this by also quoting Pearce, who uses the feminine pronoun: "In this ode she endeavours to express that wrath, jealousy and anguish, which distracted her with such variety of torture" (376). The editorial account of "The Life of Sappho," while dwelling in detail on the story of Phaon, does acknowledge that her husband "leaving her a widow very young, she renounced all thoughts of a second marriage, but not the pleasures of love; not enduring to confine that passion to one person, which, as the ancients tell us, was too violent in her to be restrained even to one sex" (371).

It should also be remembered that many Englishmen and a few Englishwomen did read Latin and Greek. John Donne's poem, "Sappho to Philaenis," first published in 1633, and many times thereafter, is a good example of how such reading enabled the image of Sappho as a lesbian to be transmitted into English poetry. This highly accomplished sixty-four-line poem has Sappho clearly say that she has forgotten Phaon because of her "desire," "idolatry," and "love" for Philaenis. The poem follows Sappho's odes in presenting the speaker as desperately longing for a female beloved who has left her. Donne constructs a detailed argument for the superiority of lesbian love as more "mutual" and sweeter than heterosexual love. The poem is sexually explicit, as Donne's poems are wont to be; the speaker's desire is presented unironically, with sympathy.[28]

Thus the Romantics received from many sources the idea of Sappho as a great poet whose lyrics were inspired by love and desire for women. Byron, Keats, and Leigh Hunt referred to Sappho as the greatest woman writer. Keats, while deploring the immodesty of female poetasters who dubbed themselves "Sapphos in poetry," went on to admiringly transcribe for his friend Reynolds one of the best poems of Katherine Philips (who, he notes, was called "the matchless Orinda"). This poem celebrates her undying Sapphic love for a woman friend.[29] In 1812 Shelley ordered Sappho's works both in the original and in translation, "if possible, united."[30] In 1800 Blake was commissioned to do a "head" of Sappho for a series of poets' heads for Hayley's library, but she was later replaced by Milton.[31] Southey wrote a "verse monodrama" called "Sappho" in which the poet declares her unrequited love for Phaon before leaping from the rock. Byron was fascinated by the story of this suicide and, when in love with John Edleston, playfully wrote from Greece that he intended to make the leap and survive. In the legend surviving the leap entailed being "cured" of hopeless love. Writing "Sapphics," poems in the meter Sappho was said to have invented, was a popular pastime, pursued by Charles and Mary Lamb, Southey, and Hunt, among others.

Coleridge, in "Alcaeus to Sappho" (1889), suggests the ambiguity associated with the poet at this time. His poem, loosely based on one of Alcaeus's lyrics, opens by detailing the pleasure experienced when a maiden blushes and "you" know it is because "you" are in her heart. The ungendered "you" in a poem addressed by a male poet to a female suggests that this is an experience they have both known. The male poet goes on to ask if any sight can be fairer than this and replies to his own question in the affirmative. The last stanza is: "Then grant one smile, tho' it should mean / A thing of doubtful birth; / That I may say these eyes have seen / The fairest face on earth!"[32] The phrase "a thing of doubtful birth" indicates that Sappho's smile would be different from the maiden's, would not be a smile of love for a man. The poem also constructs the erotic triangle of two women and one man in which the man is the most excluded angle.

Sappho was associated with women's community and this idea of community was shot through with undercurrents of same-sex love. That Coleridge used a Sapphic model for his dreams of loving community with male friends is pointed out by Koestenbaum: "He had once planned to emigrate with Wordsworth and Southey to the island of St. Nevis, and to make it 'more illustrious than Cos or Lesbos!' " (75). The emulative tone of Coleridge's comment is exactly similar to Byron's on the Ladies of Llangollen:

> I certainly love him [Edleston] more than any human being, & neither time or distance have had the least effect on my (in general) changeable Disposition.—In short, We shall put Lady E. Butler, & Miss Ponsonby to the Blush, Pylades & Orestes out of countenance, & want nothing but a catastrophe like Nisus & Euryalus to give Jonathan & David the "go by."[33]

In this context Byron's identification of Greece with "burning Sappho's" love and song would appear to select her as a model for what Louis Crompton has termed Byron's "Greek love."

Romantic Landscapes: Sapphic + Marian = Edenic

The "language of flowers" that Paula Bennett, among others, has identified as a language of generally female and specifically clitoral eroticism available to both men and women writers in nineteenth-century England can be traced, I would like to argue, to medieval and Renaissance texts that draw on Mariological imagery. Carol Falvo Heffernan has elaborated on the erotic connotations of images such as the garden, the fountain, the sun, and the singing phoenix.[34] While she stresses the fertility ritual element that is transformed in Mariology, the element of autonomous female joy and creativity in these images is equally, if not more, powerful, both in the pagan sources and in the Marian rewritings. In chapter 9 I shall examine the phoenix image as it is rewritten in English homoerotic texts from Shakespeare onward. Images closely associated with garden, fountain, and sun in Mariological texts and paintings are those of flowers like the rose, the violet, the lily, of birds, such as the phoenix, singing to themselves, and of gems, especially the pearl in the oyster. The last is particularly apposite both to the conception of Christ and to that of Mary, since the pearl is produced by the oyster on its own. The pearl suggests both the child in the womb and the clitoris in the vulva.[35] In either case the symbol stresses autonomy, self-generated joy, and creativity. The bird, especially the phoenix, singing to itself as it mounts toward the sun, is often an image of Mary singing the Magnificat as she conceives without pain and of Wisdom singing the canticles.

Famous English "catalogues of flowers," for instance those in Shakespeare, identify them with women's erotic and emotional life. Another source for such identification in late Victorian England is the Homeric "Hymn to Demeter," where Persephone plays with her girl-friends in a meadow full of roses, crocuses, violets, hyacinths, irises. When she plucks the narcissus, the flower symbolic of falling in love with likeness, Hades appears and rapes her—heterosexual violence attempts to foreclose the possibility of love of likeness. Each flower develops over time its own multidimensional significance. I shall examine here the violet, which became, by the early twentieth century, clearly associated with Sapphism (and also with male homosexuality), as did the pansy later.

In the late eighteenth century violets were associated not only with the shy and timid woman but also with Sappho and with women writers' communities. Thus Southey, writing to his friend Bedford in 1793, imagines Nature describing how she framed the hearts of different people, including Rousseau: "Parnassus furnished the clay and the font of Helicon tempered it with a dew from the violet that grew upon the grave of Sappho, but I instilled too much sensibility, the heart was too yielding, it was too much my own, and Rousseau was unhappy."[36] Here, the emotional and sensitive poetic temperament is Sapphic and the sensitive male is modeled on Sappho. Leigh Hunt's "Blue-Stocking Revels or The Feast of the Violets" (1837), a companion piece to his "The Feast of the Poets," lists all the women poets of the time, invited to a party by Apollo. The god summons the spirits of dead women poets at the moment when the living ones are toasting them. Among them is Sappho "as brown as a berry, and little of size; / But lord! with such midnight and love in her eyes!" Apollo presents the living women with violet stockings and hopes that "they may speak / Not with Sappho's eyes only, but even her Greek."[37] One of the most famous Romantic references to the violet, Wordsworth's in one of the Lucy poems, associates the violet with the qualities Paula Bennett identifies with clitoral eroticism—hiddenness, solitary autonomy, and smallness:

A violet by a mossy stone
Half hidden from the eye!
—Fair as a star, when only one
Is shining in the sky.[38]

I suggest, then, two major sources for particular clusters of images and ideas that come together in Romantic poetry—the Sapphic, of the poet who loves, suffers, sings, and dies in solitude, but lives forever in her verse; the Marian, of the creative woman who, phoenixlike, also loves, suffers, and sings, but lives on after death. If Sappho stands for a women's community of learning, so does Mary. Both figures are empowered by tradition, simultaneously available for gendering as ideal women and for ungendering as too unconventional to be "feminine." If Sappho suggests the danger and pain of erotic love in a women's community, Mary suggests its joy, self-sufficiency, and autonomous creativity. The interplay between them aspires toward a new Eden or new Jerusalem—a revolutionary idea of community—in Romantic texts. Different writers make of these possibilities very different things, and the differences indicate the richness of the matrix. I hope to suggest, through exegeses of a few very influential Romantic lyrics, some common strains in the kind of dialogue here begun.

I will begin with the "Ode to a Nightingale," which in the course of the nineteenth century became increasingly valorized as the supreme English achievement in the lyric form. Keats was especially influential for the Aestheticists, but even Rudyard Kipling, a robust anti-Aestheticist, selected three lines from this poem and two from "Kubla Khan" as the five supreme lines of English verse. The "I" and "You" structuring of many Romantic poems, including the ones here examined, allows for an ungendering of the speaking voice. If the gender of the author is not known to the reader (and even when it is), there is a way in which the poem may unstress or even undo the masculinity of the persona (not all poems do this, but some major ones do). If the nightingale is a feminine power (a dryad), the poet at the start is trapped in a male-constructed world ("Here, where men sit and hear each other groan") but behaves in ways normally considered feminine and becomes passive and receptive ("heart aches," "sunk," desires to "fade away" and "dissolve").[39] The poet rejects reason ("the dull brain perplexes and retards") and reaches a world of imaginative and emotional vision presided over by feminine community ("the Queen moon is on her throne / Clustered around by all her starry Fays"). There may be a connection with Sappho in Keats's choice of bird, for Lucian in his *Portraits* had described the infant Sappho as "very ill-favoured, being small and dark, like the nightingale, whose tiny little body is covered with unlovely plumage."[40]

I will reproduce here Ridley's translation of Sappho's ode, which in many of its phrases seems suggestive of Keats's ode, also reproduced below. Ridley's translation encloses the intense and contradictory passions that Longinus praises in a rigid end-stopped rhyme structure. Keats frees the intensity into sentences that overflow rhymed lines, but many of the phrases and images are picked up and rewritten. The speaker is distanced from a beloved addressed as "thee," overpowered by the "music" of the beloved's voice; the speaker is in a "fever," with "senses" and breath oppressed, is drowning, is "pale," overcome with thoughts of death, while one who is with the beloved is in "ecstacy." Where Ridley's speaker is filled with "envy," Keats's speaker repudiates envy. This is possible because the third term—the rival—has disappeared.

I

My heart aches, and a drowsy numbness pains
My sense, as though of hemlock I had drunk,
Or emptied some dull opiate to the drains
One minute past, and Lethe-wards had sunk.
'Tis not through envy of thy happy lot,
But being too happy in thine happiness,—
That thou, light-wingèd Dryad of the trees,
In some melodious plot
Of beechen green, and shadows numberless,
Singest of summer in full-throated ease. . . .

III

Fade far away, dissolve, and quite forget
What thou among the leaves hast never known,
The weariness, the fever, and the fret
Here, where men sit and hear each other groan;
Where palsy shakes a few, sad, last gray hairs,
Where youth grows pale, and specter-thin, and dies;
Where but to think is to be full of sorrow
And leaden-eyed despairs,
Where Beauty cannot keep her lustrous eyes,
Or new Love pine at them beyond to-morrow.

IV

Away! away! for I will fly to thee,
Not charioted by Bacchus and his pards,
But on the viewless wings of Poesy,
Though the dull brain perplexes and retards:
Already with thee! tender is the night,
And haply the Queen-Moon is on her throne,
Clustered around by all her starry Fays;
But here there is no light,
Save what from heaven is with the breezes blown
Through verdurous glooms and winding mossy ways.

All of these elements are also present in Philips's translation, which Keats must certainly have come across.

Ode II

Happy the youth, who free from care
Is feated by the lovely Fair!

Not Gods his ecstacy can reach,
Who hears the music of thy speech;
Who views entranc'd the dimpled grace,
The smiling sweetness of thy face.

Thy smiles, thy voice with subtil art
Have rais'd the fever of my heart;
I saw Thee, and unknown to rest,
At once my senses were oppress'd.
I saw Thee, and with envy toss'd,
My voice, my very breath, was lost.

My veins a throbbing ardor prove
The transport of a jealous Love;
Ev'n in the day's meridian light
A sickly languor clouds my sight;
A hollow murmur wounds my ear,
I nothing but confusion hear.

With current cold the vital streams
Trill, slowly trill along my limbs;
Pale as the flow'rets faded grace
An icy chillness spreads my face;
In life's last agony I lie,
—Doom'd, in a moment doom'd to die.   (144–46)

Keats's inspired rewriting transposes the dialogue into a universe conceived as dualistic. Here, the threat to feminine Eden comes not from an individual male rival but from a world constructed on the masculine principle of divisiveness. The paradisal landscape to which the nightingale belongs is imaged in female erotic terms—unlit, shadowed, hidden by undergrowth.

V

I cannot see what flowers are at my feet,
Nor what soft incense hangs upon the boughs,
But, in embalmèd darkness, guess each sweet
Wherewith the seasonable month endows
The grass, the thicket, and the fruit-tree wild;
White hawthorn, and the pastoral eglantine;
Fast fading violets cover'd up in leaves;
And mid-May's eldest child,
The coming musk-rose, full of dewy wine,
The murmurous haunt of flies on summer eves.

It expands into a celebration of interaction between feminine forces—the seasonable month endows the grass, the thicket, and the fruit tree with flowers. The flowers are hidden, like Shelley's and Wordsworth's, but abundant and self-intoxicating. Maternal and nurturant images are eroticized—mid-May's eldest child, the musk-rose, is full of dewy wine. This imagery of interactive tenderness produces the exclamation—"Darkling! I listen!" The interaction between the flowers (fading violets give way to coming musk roses) structures the poet's direct address to the nightingale as a beloved. The alternative masculine beloved, Death ("called him soft names in many a mused rhyme"), is rejected because he would deprive the poet of the pleasure of listening to and loving the nightingale, even though at a distance. In relation to death, however, the poet's voice is passive and receptive ("to take into the air my quiet breath"). The nightingale's song is not addressed specially to the poet but, like the moonlight in *The Fall of Hyperion*, which falls indifferently on the many "eyes . . . upward cast," is absorbed by many. The divine in both poems is figured as impersonal but compassionate—and feminine.

In stanza 7 the poet imagines that the song he hears was once heard by emperor, clown, and by Ruth; it has often charmed magic casements and made them open onto perilous seas. In the biblical story Ruth left her home for the love of a woman. Keats imagines the song finding a path through her heart; it expresses and soothes women's love, longing, and sadness; it opens the windows of imagination to dangerous depths, "perilous seas," in magical female places—"faery lands forlorn." The open window in nineteenth-century writing is a recurrent motif for a woman's yearning. The mind opened by the song is figured as feminine here. Both the individual self and the universal self with which it seeks to fuse are figured as feminine.

VII

Thou wast not born for death, immortal Bird!
No hungry generations tread thee down;
The voice I hear this passing night was heard
In ancient days by emperor and clown:
Perhaps the self-same song that found a path
Through the sad heart of Ruth, when, sick for home,
She stood in tears amid the alien corn;
The same that oft-times hath
Charm'd magic casements, opening on the foam
Of perilous seas, in faery lands forlorn.

The interaction/conversation is paradigmatically set up as between women and thus can include the poet only temporarily. Exclusion has something to do with the imagination being a "she"—a female elf, a denizen of the "faery lands" where windows are opened by the song that now retreats from the poet. At the close the nightingale undertakes the actions the poet desired to undertake ("fades" and "fled" recall "fade away" and "I will fly") and moves not toward the poet but into a female place—it is "buried deep in the next valley glades."

In *The Fall of Hyperion* the poet attains vision only after undergoing death and rebirth. Unlike the poet-lover of "La Belle Dame Sans Merci," who tries to contain and possess his vision of feminine presence (encircling her head, waist, and arms with garlands, putting her on his horse, fixing her with his gaze and shutting her eyes) and who is unable to understand her language, the poet in *The Fall of Hyperion* is overpowered by this presence. The knight of "La Belle" is a dreamer—his dream shows him the ancestry of failed male poets to which he belongs. His kind of love is unamenable to creativity. It belongs in the "here" where "men sit and hear each other groan" and where "beauty cannot keep her lustrous eyes." In *The Fall of Hyperion* the poet envisions a kind of love that is not premised on possession but on "holy dread." The poet does not make the bridegroom's gesture of unveiling Moneta's face; she unveils it and reveals to him an ancestry conceived as female. Moneta recalls many powerful figures—Diotima, Mary, Demeter. She shows him a trinity ("three fixed shapes") that consists of two women and a man (Thea, Moneta, Saturn) and is (like the unravished and inviolate Grecian urn) herself the only survivor, the historian of the lost past. The pre-Christian world, here Greek, as it was Eastern in "Kubla Khan," is conceived as a lost matrilineal world.

The poet approaches Moneta's shrine through yet another female landscape—the images of enclosure, flowers, and fountain appear (arbor, vines, bells, blooms) and on a mound of moss are spread fruits that "seem'd refuse of a meal / By angel tasted or our Mother Eve." Images of drinking and intoxication lead in both poems to a transportation of the poet into feminine presence.[41] This is an Eden without Adam—only Eve and a genderless angel inhabit it; it also evokes Persephone not as raped by Pluto but as returning to her mother's home and bringing springtime: "For Proserpine return'd to her own fields / Where the white heifers low." This feminine paradisal past, though lost, is also timeless in memory— biblical language suggests this: "In that place the moth could not corrupt." The revived poet is twice compared to winged and ungendered angels.

The famous description of Moneta's face, like Shakespeare's image of Hermione turned to stone, evokes the survival of women despite their suffering, the survival of memory despite death and destruction. Here, as in the "Ode to a Grecian Urn," the Christian who would turn pagan looks with awed guilt at the relics of a religion violently destroyed by Christianity and yet somehow surviving. The metaphor used in both cases is that of the man who wishes to take woman for a model, looking with guilt at the historical violence inflicted by men on women. The ritual of drinking before he approaches Moneta's shrine is like the black mass often performed by medieval heretics attempting to invoke pagan deities. The description looks forward to Pater's description of La Gioconda. Moneta, like the Grecian urn, is both historian and tragedian. She is the repository of wisdom only partially granted to men—Apollo is only her "foster-child." The poem remains incomplete, perhaps because the poetic demand of its opening would be a narrative more focused on women than that of the fall of Saturn. The way *Hyperion* ends is suggestive. Apollo's orgasmic ecstasy, inspired by a goddess, seems to be leading up to his transformation into a woman. The "Knowledge enormous" that pours into the feminized "wide hollows" of his brain seems similar to Teiresias's great knowledge, which arises from his having been both a man and a woman. The unfinished last sentence strongly suggests metamorphosis. The feminine images surrounding it ("a ravish'd Nymph") suggest that Apollo is ravished by the presiding Mnemosyne, through death as a man into life as a woman. The frightening implications of this feminization of his god/muse may have led Keats to leave the poem unfinished. Apollo is surrounded even in infancy with female erotic imagery—the glowing rose, red wine in a goblet, a bubbling well, labyrinthine vermilion shells, and murmurous echoing caves.

Keats's erotic landscapes and images generally suggest female autoeroticism or oral eroticism.[42] In *Endymion* the nymph Echo lives in a cell or grotto where fountains rise from the abyss toward bowers and chambers decorated with pearls and crimson-mouthed curly shells.[43] In "The Eve of St. Agnes" the heterosexual encounter is imaged in completely oral, nonpenetrative terms. Suggested by the fruits and other Edenic foods that Porphyro prepares (but does not consume), this eroticism culminates in the nonphallic feminine images of the star and of the mingling of fragrances: "Into her dream he melted, as the rose / Blendeth its odour with the violet,— / Solution sweet." Recent commentators, such as Stillinger, read these as images for heterosexual intercourse, which seems to me highly unlikely, given that Madeline continues to think she is dreaming while it proceeds, until enlightened by Porphyro.[44] Such a reading proceeds more from a refusal to see anything but penetrative intercourse as "real" sex than from attention to the poem's figurings. Madeline is figured in a series of nonheterosexual images as a mermaid, a madonnalike saint, and a dove. The images of rose and violet, both feminine, coming together, suggest kissing more than anything else. Words like "melt" suggest the sensation of female orgasm as well as of what Mellor terms Keats's "unbounded, fluid, decentered" poetic self, which is "conventionally associated with the female."[45]

Keats's eroticism is in general much more oral than penetrative, given to such activities as kissing and sucking, and expressed in his well-known ability to evoke the sensations of taste and smell.[46] There seems to me no compulsion to read Freud backward into this and insist, as Hoeveler does, that it is "blatantly oral and regressive imagery," as if the oral is necessarily regressive.[47] One might cite, in rebuttal, Socrates in Xenophon's *Symposium*:

> Nothing gives more fuel to the fire of love than kisses. For this pleasure is not like others, which either lessen or vanish in the enjoyment; on the contrary, it gathers strength the more it is repeated; . . . . Thence it may be that to love and to kiss are frequently expressed by the same word in the Greek.

Terry Castle has offered strong evidence that Keats's contemporary, Anne Lister, used the word *kiss* as a code word for a female orgasm experienced in a sexual relationship between two women.[48] It is possible that the code was not an entirely private one.

Another poem that addresses an ungendered object figured in images of power and tenderness that are associated with women is Shelley's "To a Skylark."[49] The skylark is associated with the moon/Venus ("that silver sphere") and then evoked in a series of erotic images whose eroticism consists in their simultaneous hidden and diffusive quality—the singing maiden, a rose embowered in green leaves, a golden glow worm in a dewy dell. The ungendered "poet hidden in the light of thought" is assimilated to this series of feminine images. These qualities of hiddenness are self-contained and joyous; the song they figure is different from songs of married love and war ("Chorus hymeneal or triumphal chaunt"), which claim completion but are actually characterized by "some hidden want." Thus songs of marriage and of war (the tragic/epic and the comic themes) are premised on lack, while the lyric theme, conceived as feminine in relation to itself, is potentially inexhaustible—it arises from a non-goal-oriented love and is therefore never satiated. The love of likeness ("love of thine own kind") is represented as perfect, inviolate, and whole. Implicit in this perfection is a notion of eroticism that is emotional rather than specifically sexual, sexual being equated with heterosexual. This is the kind of "perfect" love attributed, as I shall later demonstrate, to the Ladies of Llangollen and aspired to by Byron with Edleston. It also has another ancestor in Shakespeare's Phoenix and Turtle, who are simultaneously two and one, who live in "married chastity" and generate beauty, truth, and rarity, but not offspring.

"The Sensitive Plant" presents the eponymous protagonist, the plant, as ungendered ("it") and as fed, nourished, and "kissed" by natural forces. It is not beautiful in appearance but "it desires what it has not / the beautiful." It is thus the emblem of love as defined by Socrates in *The Symposium*—not beautiful itself but desiring the beautiful. Shelley's explicit reference to Plato's text strengthens the homoerotic quality of his poem. Sensitivity and emotion are premised by the poem as the most valuable qualities, which make a plant capable of being a protagonist. Its erotic quality is evoked through feminine images ("trembled and panted with bliss . . . like a doe") and placed in the midst of a series of homoeroticized, feminized plants and flowers (narcissi dying of their own loveliness, the "Naiad-like lily," the hyacinth, the "rose like a nymph," the lily like a "Maenad"). These flowers are all "tremulous" with erotic emotion and are in interaction with the elements ("the fainting air," "the tender sky," "the soft stream"). This interaction is not penetrative but works in feminine orgasmic terms—"trembled," "panted," "fainted"; it occurs between likenesses—the water lilies "lay tremulously" on the "bosom" of the stream that glides and dances around them. Penetration is assimilated to this diffusive eroticism—"For each one was interpenetrated / With the light and the odour its neighbour shed"—an eroticism that is clitoral ("a hidden gem") and also maternal (the flowers look to the sky as an infant looks to its mother and the sensitive plant is a "sweet child," the feeblest and favorite child embraced by night). The lady in part 2 is an Eve without Adam—"an Eve in this Eden" and is to the flowers "as God is to the starry scheme."

The garden is destroyed by forces constructed as masculine: phallic "roots knotted like water snakes," mandrakes, toadstools and nameless "prickly and pulpous" plants overrun it, and finally Winter, personified as a man with a whip, appears. The male pronoun is repeatedly used for this force who chains and imprisons—"The wind was his whip / One choppy finger was on his lip / He had torn the cataracts from the hills / And they clanked at his girdle like manacles; / His breath was a chain which without a sound / The earth, and the air, and the water bound; / He came, fiercely driven." The northern whirlwind is similarly compared to a male wolf devouring a dead child.

The poem is a parable of the destruction of a female homoerotic Eden by a devastating male heterosexual power, but its conclusion asserts the survival of that Eden as a paradigm:

> That garden sweet, that lady fair,
> And all sweet shapes and shadows there,
> In truth have never passed away:
> 'Tis we, 'tis ours, are changed, not they.
>
> For love, and beauty, and delight,
> There is no death nor change: their might
> Exceeds our organs, which endure
> No light, being themselves obscure.

One may compare with this formulation Wordsworth's celebration of the Ladies of Llangollen as having attained a love that is "above the reach of time."

A similar paradigm structures the poet's yearning in Coleridge's "Kubla Khan." In different ways these poems set up the Muse/beloved as a powerful female force, self-sufficient in its abundant and orgasmic eroticism. The poet assumes or desires to assume a feminine persona, to become like a woman, in order to attain such self-sufficiency, but this attempt is only partially successful. I would call this structure Sapphic because the poetic voice pursues an indifferent (not cruel, as in the Petrarchan lyric) but lovable, even somehow tender and compassionate, object, yet (this is the crucial difference from the Petrarchan heterosexual pattern) is not disillusioned in this search and does not seek to transcend it. There is no "Leave me O love that reachest but to dust / And O my soul aspire to higher things" kind of move. Rather, the poetic voice laments being left and seeks reunion.

"Kubla Khan" begins with the attempt by a powerful masculine force to contain the natural/feminine—to ring round the "fertile ground," imprison it in fortresses and top it with a phallic dome. The futility of the attempt is evident from the start because of the subterranean power of the river Alph running through female "caverns measureless to man." The feminine landscape is elaborated in the second movement—a landscape that influences many such symbolic places in Victorian writing, for instance, George Eliot's Red Deeps and Michael Field's slopes, woods, valleys, and dells. It is inhabited by a woman wailing for an ungendered "demon-lover." Most commentators assume that the lover is a male, but this is not at all evident in the poem—homosexuality was frequently attributed to witches and demons. Coleridge's representation of the landscape, unlike Shelley's, is vulval rather than clitoral. The "deep romantic chasm which slanted / Down the green hill athwart a cedarn cover" leads into the powerful evocation of an orgasmic fountain flowing from the chasm. Heffernan demonstrates, in another context, that the spring, well, fountain, are Marian images and suggests that they are menstrual. The fountain becomes, in later texts, such as Michael Field's and Woolf's, a major image of love between women.

While this uncontrollable activity terrifies Kubla Khan, the archetypal warrior male, it delights the poet who, like Socrates taught by Diotima, wishes to revive within himself the "symphony and song" of the Abyssinian maid whom he once saw in a vision. His music would evoke phallic symbols—the dome and the ice Shivalinga from Kashmir that Coleridge had read about in Maurice's *History of Hindostan* (1795). It is significant that the dome and the caves of ice are not in direct contact with the caverns measureless to man and the fountain. The shadow of the former plays on the waves where the sound of the fountain and the echo of the river running through the caves are "heard." The feminine images of river, caves, and fountain are "heard" (an old image of inspiration) by the poet, as is the song of the damsel with the dulcimer. Inspired by them, the poet would like to make music celebrating the male images of the dome and the caves of ice. In my reading, then, "Kubla Khan" suggests, among other things, what Koestenbaum calls Coleridge's "wish for [a] Lesbian utopia" (75). It envisions a self-sufficient female erotic power (what would today be called lesbian) that inspires a similar vision of a self-sufficient male erotic power (homoerotic male). The former is envisioned as timeless, uncontrollable by man, and connected with lost Eastern wisdom (Xanadu, Abyssinia). The latter also has Eastern sources (Kashmir) but is not fully envisioned and evoked because the poet, unlike the damsel, is not able to play and sing as powerfully as he aspires to.

The poem concludes not with achievement but with aspiration. It is premised on the "could" of "Could I revive within me / Her symphony and song." If this revival of the vision of a woman playing to herself could occur, the poet would be nourished by it, would partake of the Edenic "honeydew" and "milk of paradise," and would be transformed into a feminized figure with "flashing eyes" and "floating hair." He would be filled with "deep delight" and would play to himself. His music and vision would, in turn, provoke a mixed readerly response—Kubla Khan-like fear ("Beware, beware") and desire to contain ("weave a circle round him thrice"), but also receptiveness ("Shut your eyes with holy dread"). The opposition between the achievement of the feminine creator figure (the damsel) and the humility of the male creator desiring to attain even a partial approximation is evident in the conclusions of both the "Ode to a Skylark" and "Kubla Khan." In the latter Coleridge's perception of the poem as a fragment enacts the sense of incompletion stated in conclusion.

For later nineteenth-century writers such as Pater, Simeon Solomon, Wilde, Michael Field, Vernon Lee, Edward Carpenter who were engaged in the exploration and/or celebration of a homosexual identity, and also in the espousal of an anarchist worldview in opposition to dominant Victorian imperialist and patriarchal ideologies, the writing of fictionalized biographies of Romantic, Renaissance, and Greek writers and artists was one part of the project of constructing an ancestry at once literary and homosexual. Another part of this project was a continuation of Romantic privileging of "feminine" modes of relating. These Victorian writers were, in one way or another, connected with various nineteenth-century women's movements for education, for political rights, for visibility in many spheres, including the religious and the literary. The idea that both the male artist and the homoerotically inclined man are more feminine and more creative than other men is espoused and foregrounded in texts by both men and women at this time. This can be read as being in accordance with the demands of contemporary women's movements, such as the temperance and chastity-for-men movements, which suggested that society would be better off if men imitated women rather than if women imitated men. In response to repeated charges of effeminacy and unmanliness (charges brought against Shelley, Keats, Pater, Wilde, among others) the strategy adopted was Wilde's one of "picking up a brickbat and wearing it like a bouquet." This strategy had the advantage of appealing to the conventional Victorian idea of woman as angelic, and therefore an appropriate model for men, while simultaneously subverting conventionality by linking womanly virtue with pagan images of woman as goddess. Virtue thus combined with power and autonomy in an unsettling way.

These writers drew on and rewrote Marian and Sapphic triangulations, tropes, and ancestries, setting up a dialogue with their forebears and their contemporaries through these shared metaphoric languages.

3

Ecstasy in Victorian Aestheticism

To burn always with this hard, gem-like flame, to
maintain this ecstasy, is success in life.
                                        —Walter Pater

In this chapter I will argue that Walter Pater drew on medieval, Renaissance, and Romantic models of love between women to develop his new
hedonism. His aesthetic of intensity was built around images of clitoral
ecstasy. Pater's disciples, most notably Simeon Solomon and Oscar
Wilde, envisioned women's freedom as crucial to the development of a
free society and love between women as a model for love in general, especially for love between men. Their anarchist worldview was contested by
thinkers like Ruskin and J. A. Symonds, who legitimized male comradeship as the basis of a Christian nation. In the ideal imperialist phallocentric society that they imagined, women were to be good wives and mothers. I shall examine the contest between these two highly influential sets
of thinkers.

Studies of male and female homoeroticism in the nineteenth century
have tended to examine them as mutually exclusive, if not antipathetic, to
one another.[1] Thus, Linda Dowling shows how Symonds's conception of
male homoeroticism is closely tied in with ideals of manliness, militarism,
and imperialist nation building and argues that this discourse is equally
present in Pater, Wilde, and Carpenter. She demonstrates that Oxford
Hellenism developed a language to express a particular kind of male
homoeroticism.[2] I dispute Dowling's argument by highlighting the
Romantic component of this language, which she disregards.[3] The Oxford
Hellenists saw themselves as heirs not only to Romantic Hellenism but

also to Romantic medievalism. Their language legitimizes homoeroticism by a simultaneous appeal to various different pasts—to classical Athens, to Sapphic Mytilene, to the medieval saint and the Renaissance artist, and to many Romanticisms. In making this appeal, they wrote from a homoeroticism that is not definitively and constitutively male, as it might be if it appealed only to classical Athens.

Consider, for example, the story of St. Frideswide, the patron saint of Oxford. In the most popular form of her legend, this young lady was a late seventh-century Saxon princess who was betrothed by her father to a wealthy nobleman named Algar (or Aethelbald). When Algar came to claim her, Frideswide, who had already decided to devote her life to God, made off with her maidens and crossed the Thames in a boat miraculously provided for them. They were pursued by Algar, but, just as he was about to seize Frideswide, she called on SS. Cecilia and Catherine, who immediately struck Algar blind. In the words of the Victorian woman reteller of this legend,

> Algar was led away by his attendants, but whether his sight was ever restored to him the legend does not say. Having got rid of her lover in this very dramatic manner, St. Frideswide settled down happily in the forest, where she was joined by other maidens, and after a few years of retirement she removed to Oxford, where she founded an important monastery, supposed by many to have occupied the site of the present Cathedral of Christ Church.[4]

Miracles of healing lepers and the blind are attributed to her, and her emblem is an ox (from her association with Oxford where she died).[5] It is noteworthy that her two patron saints, Cecilia and Catherine, are connected with music and scholarship respectively. The university thus acquires a female ancestry for its dedication to learning.

The presence of this saint, who refused marriage and chose life in a same-sex community, is inscribed in the university she is supposed to have founded and which constituted in the nineteenth century a space for the repetition of her life choices by many men. Her statue stands in one of the transept turrets of Christ Church cathedral; her figure is among the ancient sculptures above the altar in the choir; she appears on the modern lectern with Cardinal Wolsey and Bishop King; and her legend is told in a window in the Latin chapel, designed by Sir Edward Burne-Jones. Such female ancestors are central in Pater's writings, which became the bible of Aestheticism.

Many recent commentators have demonstrated that Pater's *The Renaissance* is crucially concerned with employing suggestive strategies to celebrate the homoeroticism of the lives and work of such figures as Michelangelo, Leonardo da Vinci, and Winckelmann.[6] However, only Richard Dellamora has recognized that this text is also suggestive of female homoeroticism. He argues that Pater is a major figure in a tradition of philosophical radicalism that brought homoeroticism and feminism into close conjunction.[7] My approach is close to his, with the difference that I focus much more intensively on lesbian images and also look at alliances between male homosexual radicals and lesbians/feminists.

In the diffused atmosphere of "strange" desire that Pater creates in *The Renaissance*, opposed to what he posits as the "stereotyped" and "habitual" way of life of conventional society, images of love between women play a crucial part and occur at important moments. I will examine some of these moments and suggest how they build toward a climax in the conclusion, a climax figured in terms that may be read as clitoral rather than phallic, concentratedly and continuingly intense rather than goal oriented.

In choosing to write about the Italian rather than the English Renaissance, Pater largely avoids the Reformation and focuses on images that he stresses were close to the pagan. In his second essay, "Pico della Mirandola," he provides a self-reflexive clue to his project when he says that in the fifteenth century the "only possible reconciliation" between Christian and pagan imagery, "the sacred with the profane," was "an imaginative one," while a later age would effect a "scientific" reconciliation (30). His own attempts to reconcile homoerotic with religious imagery, also a reconciliation of the sacred with the profane, seem similar. For this project the Madonna becomes one of his primary tropes. He points out, first, that Michelangelo's Doni Madonna has the "uncouth energy" (31) of the primitive mother goddesses. In the next essay he makes the controversial point that Botticelli's Madonnas are peevish-looking, wan, and cheerless, and seem to shrink from the pressure of the divine child and from the "intolerable honour"(37) thrust upon them. He goes on to say that Botticelli's famous Venus (in *The Birth of Venus*) looks sad and that "you might think that the sorrow in her face was at the thought of the whole long day of love yet to come" (38)! This idea, that Botticelli's women are saddened by heterosexual love and by motherhood, would occur to a rather unusual "you." Pater, however, claims that "what is unmistakable is the sadness with which he has conceived the goddess of (486) pleasure" (39). Pater's readings invest the obviously heterosexual with sadness and write the suggestive as homoerotic.[8]

In the next essay, on Michelangelo, Pater refers to the artist's non-platonic loves for young men, connecting these to "some secret spring of indignation or sorrow" in the "depths of his nature" (52). In imagining the old age of Michelangelo, Pater hints at the reasons for the heterodox attraction of Catholicism to men like himself in Victorian England. He points out that the Catholic church during the Counter-Reformation, by fixing itself in a "frozen orthodoxy" (57) and opposition to art, had alienated itself from Michelangelo. He then suggests that ideas generated by religion may be in excess of their institutionalization:

> For himself, he had long since fallen back on that divine ideal, which above the wear and tear of creeds has been forming itself for ages as the possession of nobler souls. And now he began to feel the soothing influence which since that

time the Roman Church has often exerted over spirits too independent to be its subjects, yet brought within the neighbourhood of its action"(57).

In a famous passage in his essay "Leonardo da Vinci" Pater comments on the "strange likeness" of Leonardo's St. John the Baptist to his Bacchus, and notes that the saint's "treacherous smile would have us understand something far beyond the outward gesture or circumstance."[9] That this "something" is homoerotic is suggested by Pater's description of the St. John as "one of the few naked figures Leonardo painted—whose delicate brown flesh and woman's hair no one would go out into the wilderness to seek" (75). He goes on:

> We recognise one of those symbolical inventions in which the ostensible subject is used, not as a matter for definite pictorial realisation, but as the starting-point of a train of sentiment subtle and vague as a piece of music. . . . And so it comes to pass that though he handles sacred subjects continually, he is the most profane of painters; the given person or subject, Saint John in the Desert, or the Virgin on the knees of Saint Anne, is often merely the pretext for a kind of work which carried one altogether beyond the range of its conventional associations (76).

In what way may Leonardo's painting of the Virgin on the knees of St. Anne carry one altogether beyond the range of conventional associations? In this humanized version of a conventional medieval theme, Leonardo represents an adult Mary sitting on a youthful St. Anne's lap and leaning languorously toward the Christ child, who has slid off her lap and is playing at her feet with a lamb. He has one foot over the lamb's neck and is looking mischievously up at Mary over his shoulder. Anne smiles proudly down at Mary, the expanse of whose bare neck lies directly beneath her gaze. There are no halos, and no angels or other personages around, so that we see two women in a very intimate relationship, presiding over the growth of a child. While Leonardo's audience would have been familiar with this matrilineal version of the holy family, following the post-twelfth-century evolution of what was known as the holy kinship—the cult of St. Anne, her daughters, sisters, nieces, nephews, and grandchildren—most of Pater's readers would not.

Pater suggests that Leonardo's version of this scene is different from other, more conventional, versions. Before I had read Pater's commentary and before I knew anything about St. Anne, this painting was for me a compelling lesbian image.[10] Comparing it with many conventional medieval representations confirms this feeling. When medieval artists show Mary sitting on St. Anne's lap, Mary is an infant and St. Anne a young woman, or Mary a young adult and St. Anne a wrinkled old woman. When the point of the icon is to stress the matrilineal descent of Christ, both women may be adults, but the positioning is rarely suggestive of intimacy. It tends to be stiffly vertical, each child on the lap of its mother. Anne is almost always represented as a grandmotherly figure, and her attention, like Mary's, is focused on the Christ child. Frequently, angels, donors, saints, or other members of the holy kinship crowd the picture. Leonardo's version is different in the youthfulness of Anne, the focusing of her attention on Mary, the sense of privacy and intimacy, and the child's—very unusually—not being on the lap of either woman. The composition concentrates the fusion of the two women.

Two pages later Pater refers to the excited response of the people of Florence to Leonardo's cartoon on the same subject.[11] Pater's explanation of Leonardo's triumph is that "his work was less with the saints than with the living women of Florence" (78). Pater's account of what he imagines was Leonardo's artistic response to "these languid women" of Florence and to the "polished society" (78) in which they moved, leads directly into his celebrated meditation on La Gioconda. Here occurs Pater's third reference to St. Anne. After accumulating in the space of one paragraph all the words he has associated with the homoerotic—"subtle," "strangely," "strange," "exquisite passions," "maladies,"—he continues: "She is older than the rocks among which she sits; like the vampire, she has been dead many times, and learned the secrets of the grave; and has been a diver in deep seas, and keeps their fallen day about her; and trafficked for strange webs with Eastern merchants; and as Leda, was the mother of Helen of Troy, and, as Saint Anne, the mother of Mary." (80).

St. Anne is certainly in "strange" company here. In what way is she similar to Leda or, indeed, to Mona Lisa? Through the accumulation of apparently disparate images, Pater constructs homoeroticism as ancient and indestructible: "older than the rocks" and alive although "dead many times." His first image for this living of many lives and dying of many deaths is that of the vampire. Sheridan Le Fanu's story *Carmilla* (1872) had appeared just one year before *The Renaissance* was published. In this story the narrator, a young English girl living in Austria, by accident receives into her home a girl, Carmilla, whose face she had dreamed of in childhood. Carmilla calls her "darling" and declares herself in love with her. She visits her at night and sucks her blood, leaving two marks on her throat, an obvious image for a love bite.[12] The female vampire, as Lillian Faderman has demonstrated, was, from the time of Coleridge's "Christabel" (in which the older woman, Geraldine, becomes lover and mother surrogate to the younger Christabel), connected with lesbianism. Pater, writing at the same time as Le Fanu, gives the reader an obvious clue to the "chain of secret influences" that, he argues, Leonardo's "type of womanly beauty" passes "on to us" (74). The next image, that of "a diver in deep seas," is again a homoerotic image, witness the drowned Narcissus and Charmides who were to figure so prominently in Wilde's poems and the marine imagery of such lesbian poems as Renee Viven's "Undine."[13] The word "traffic," with its sexual suggestiveness, is combined with the East, the "return of the Pagan world" (80). The odd juxtaposition of Leda with St. Anne now becomes more explicable—both produce divine daughters who focus cultural ideas of female beauty, power, and danger.

In the last essay, on Winckelmann, Pater's homoerotic imagery intensifies—words like "penetrated," "possessed," "temperament" and references to intimacy, friendship, love of beauty and of young men proliferate and are associated with "the absence of any sense of want, or corruption or shame" (142). In this essay Pater moves backward in time, suggesting that Winckelmann used Catholicism merely as a medium to approach the Hellenic. He inaccurately remarks that "there is no Greek Madonna, the goddesses are always childless" (139), but corrects this toward the close, where he cites three figures, connecting well-known stories of male homoerotic love and loss with a story of passionate love between mother and daughter, thus suggestively linking Demeter-Persephone with Anne-Mary: "for Greek religion has not merely its mournful mysteries of Adonis, of Hyacinthus, of Demeter." (144).

"The Myth of Demeter and Persephone" (1894) is Pater's most extended meditation on love between women.[14] He defines the myth as the earliest and the central subject of Greek worship. Examining and citing at length four major accounts of the myth, Pater makes of it an archetypal pattern followed by other myths. Thus Demeter is "the type of divine grief" (92–93) and Dionysus, dual god of summer and winter, is "almost identical" with her and with Persephone.[15] Pater describes Orphic mysteries as developing from the worship of Demeter and Dionysus. In his schema, then, cults of male love (Orpheus was a lover of boys after his return from Hades) are modeled on cults of love between women. Persephone's story is, for Pater "the story, in an intenser form, of Adonis, of Hyacinth, of Adrastus" (110). These analogies make of it not just a mother-daughter but also a, indeed *the*, lover-beloved story. As Dellamora points out, "what captures Pater's imagination is the story of love between two women."[16]

Pater insists that the Greek religion is not a religion of "mere cheerfulness" (111) but is imbued with the romantic spirit that extracts beauty from sorrow. In Pater's view the Greeks represented primal sorrow as a separation between two women. Pater describes Demeter as "our Lady of Sorrows, the *mater dolorosa* of the ancient world" (116), but also, repeatedly, as a "strange, dual being" (95), the double of Persephone, "almost interchangeable" (109) with her. He remarks that in their images on coins it is "hard to distinguish" (141) one from the other since Persephone looks only slightly younger than Demeter. As with his description of Leonardo's St. Anne and the Virgin, Pater strongly suggests the loverlike quality of the two women's intimacy. Remarking on the mingling of the cosmic with the "personal interests" of the story, he says that "the strange Titaness," Hecate, "is first a nymph only; afterwards, as if changed incurably by the passionate cry of Persephone, she becomes her constant attendant" (118). Since he has earlier noted that offerings for Demeter were left at the crossroads (where Hecate/Diana was also worshipped), the connection between Demeter and Hecate suggests that although separated from Persephone for three months of the year Demeter in shadow form remains always with her. The translation of the Homeric hymn that Pater quotes makes clear that the yearning and grief are not Demeter's alone. Sitting with her husband in Hades, "the shrinking Persephone [is] consumed within herself by desire for her mother" (89). Toward the close of the essay, Pater quotes Wordsworth and Keats to indicate the powerful influence of this myth on Western conceptions of love and death. He reads the myth as illustrating the power "of pure ideas—of conceptions" in Greek religion, of "symbols" as distinct from "historical fact" (155).

In Pater's mythmaking the mother-daughter relation is the type of love and desire between women, as the Socratic-Platonic teacher-student relation is the type of love and desire between men. How close he was to the pulse of feeling between some women is suggested by Mary Campbell's letters to her lover, Vita Sackville-West: "She called Vita her St Anne, her Demeter, lover, mother, 'everything in women that I most need and love.' . . . 'It is a lovely moment when the mother's voice and hands turn into the lover's.' "[17] E. M. Forster was to pick up the image of Demeter as a symbol of perfect love in *The Longest Journey*. Both Judy Grahn and Christine Downing have recently gone over the same ground as Pater in reading the Demeter-Persephone-Hecate story as a lesbian myth.[18]

Throughout *The Renaissance* Pater suggests that the homoerotic narratives he is dealing with are narratives of creativity and of sadness. This is the keynote of each story as he tells it—Michelangelo has a secret sorrow, Leonardo's life is solitary and mysterious, Winckelmann is born too late and is killed by a young man in whom he takes an interest just at the point when he is about to meet Goethe. The Demeter and Sappho myths of love between women rather than the Platonic myth of love between men are models for Pater's homoerotic narratives insofar as separation is integral to the former. In opposition to the facile lived-happily-ever-after Victorian heterosexual narrative, Pater constructs homoerotic narratives as compensating for loss with freedom. "And what does the spirit need in the face of modern life?" he asks, when moving toward his vision of a new Renaissance, and answers, "The sense of freedom."[19]

The end of the Winckelmann essay builds a continuous argument with the famous, or notorious, conclusion to *The Renaissance*. It calls for action, persuading readers to transform their way of life, on the model of the Renaissance artists Pater has imagined. He argues that "we," modern people, require freedom and recognize necessity only as the intricate laws of one's own nature that bear the "central forces of the world" (148). Pater suggests that unfrightened self-acceptance rather than battling with antagonistic social forces is the way to freedom.

Significantly, the "you" addressed by Pater at this point, and the "we" and "us" he constructs, are both male and female. The peroration

carefully includes both men and women as being caught up in these per-
plexities and as looking for freedom for themselves:

> For us, necessity is not, as of old, a sort of mythological personage without us,
> with whom we can do warfare. It is rather a magic web woven through and
> through us, like that magnetic system of which modern science speaks, pene-
> trating us with a network, subtler than our subtlest nerves, yet bearing in it the
> central forces of the world. Can art represent men and women in these bewil-
> dering toils so as to give the spirit at least an equivalent for the sense of free-
> dom? (148–49)

He goes on to say that modern art, in trying to accomplish this, must
accept "natural law," however much this natural law may "embarrass us."
The tragic situations in which this law may place us become the occasion
for "certain groups of noble men and women" to work out for themselves
"a supreme denouement" (149). Pater suggests that the figures whose stories he has told are models for a new Renaissance. He proposes that his
readers undertake a quest for freedom. Though reviewers criticized the
conclusion for its possible encouragement of immorality in "young men,"
it is remarkable that all the pronouns Pater uses are ungendered. By use of
the infinitive ("To regard all things," "To burn always with this hard gem-
like flame") and of the ungendered pronoun—the repeated "we," "us," and
"our" giving way at the close to "you"—Pater includes readers of both
sexes. He presents a manifesto for an entire society or an unconventional
minority, depending on how the reader chooses to read the collective
first-person pronoun and the singular/plural "you."

In the conclusion's most famous sentence, Pater introduces two
images that together constitute an immensely influential trope for homoerotic and, specifically, lesbian love, as I shall attempt to demonstrate in
readings of various texts, including Woolf's fictions. These are the gem
and the flame. The flame is an image from conventional love poetry and
also from mystical poetry. The gem is a clitoral image—in contrast, for
example, to the phallic arrow that appears in conjunction with the flame
of love in the visions of St. Theresa. "To burn always with this hard, gem-
like flame, to maintain this ecstasy, is success in life"—Pater's formulation
here is oxymoronic and paradoxical ("hard" with "flame") and suggestive
of clitoral sexuality that is not linear but continuous ("to burn always").[20]
There may also be a defiant allusion to St. Paul's dictum, frequently cited
by Protestants arguing in favor of a married clergy: "It is better to marry
than to burn." Pater reverses this to claim that burning, the condition of
desire itself, is a creative condition. He even terms it "success," a remarkable reversal of normative Victorian goal-orientedness. Since the clitoris
is the only organ in the human body whose sole function is to give pleasure, it is particularly apt as a symbol for Pater's antididactic hedonism.

The link here established between flame, gem, burning, and ecstasy
occurs too in Woolf's *Mrs. Dalloway*, when Clarissa remembers her youth-

ful love for Sally Seton as a burning diamond. She attributes her loss of that love to her desire for "success": "She had schemed; she had pilfered. . . . She had wanted success."[21] Toward the close of *Orlando* the protagonist, trying to decide what is important in life, concludes that money-making or even writing, the common indicators of "success," are not important, but "ecstasy" is: " 'Ecstasy!', she cried. 'Ecstasy!' ."[22]

Pater's reading of Renaissance art could not but have been received as a refutation of what was earlier the most famous Victorian reading of that art—Ruskin's, in *The Stones of Venice* (1853).[23] Ruskin's blatant Christian and Northern European chauvinism drew its force from an imperialist conception of Northern Europe as manly and the rest of the world as less than manly. Thus Ruskin's advice to the reader on how to identify Gothic features is "First, see if it looks as if it had been built by strong men" (189). He posits the "veracity" (170) of the Northern Gothic medieval workman against the "corrupt" (235) and "pagan" (read, Catholic) spirit of the Italian Renaissance artist. He characterizes Renaissance lintel architecture as "effeminate" (182) and denounces it as infidel for its "unscrupulous pursuit of pleasure" (236) as well as for its sinful pride, its exaltation of the human over the divine.

That Ruskin's analysis is as much about Victorian Britain as about the periods it purports to examine becomes clear from the hysteria with which he ascribes all qualities he considers positive, including democracy, to the medieval Christian workman and the way in which his diatribe against Renaissance art inevitably leads from its womanly to its decadent qualities. Grotesque Renaissance statuary, according to Ruskin, is evidence "of a delight in the contemplation of bestial vice" (238). He marshals several words and images that suggest the nature of this vice, culminating in an explicit reference to Sodom and Gomorrah:

> Year after year, the nation drank with deeper thirst from the fountains of forbidden pleasure, and dug for springs, hitherto unknown, in the dark places of the earth. . . . That ancient curse was upon her, the curse of the Cities of the Plain. . . . By the inner burning of her own passions, as fatal as the fiery rain of Gomorrah, she was consumed from her place among the nations" (243).

Ruskin concludes by putting forward an agenda for his own times. He denounces "the Byronic ideal of Venice" (126), with its sympathy for prisoners and other oppressed people. In contrast to this Romantic humanism, he glorifies "the dominion of Venice," the Christian spirit in which "she went forth conquering and to conquer" (139). England should, in Ruskin's view, take her own medieval past and medieval Venice as models, should cast out the feminine, sodomitical, and pagan humanist principle of pleasure and should revive the Gothic style "worked in a broad and masculine manner" (246), "symbolical of the faith of Christianity" (245). He recommends "the revival of a healthy school of architecture in England. . . . First, let us cast out utterly whatever is connected with the

Greek, Roman, or Renaissance architecture. . . . It is base, unnatural, unfruitful, unenjoyable, and impious. Pagan in its origin" (244).

It is clear how Pater's text answers Ruskin's at every point, putting forward exactly the opposite agenda—for the revival of a new hedonist humanism. J. A. Symonds's response to Ruskin's enormously influential and controversial opinions is more anxiety-ridden. Symonds disputes the identification of the sodomite with effeminacy and hedonism. Displacing these qualities on to Sapphism, he seeks to recuperate male homoeroticism for the manly imperialist ideal. Symonds's argument is important because he was a prominent member of the literary establishment and an early apologist for homosexuality. He collaborated with Havelock Ellis in working out the concept of sexual inversion. Symonds tends to endorse marriage and legitimate reproduction as one aspect of men's life (by implication, the primary or only aspect of women's life) and homosexual friendship/love as the other. His uneasiness with fully physical homosexuality and his desire to transcend it inflect this conception. Pater's writing of Sapphism influences not only writers like Wilde and Solomon but also lesbian writers like Michael Field and Vernon Lee and, later, Woolf, Forster, and Lytton Strachey. Symonds's use of Sapphism as a scapegoat for the displacement of homophobia influences writers like D. H. Lawrence, whose heroes undertake unequal marriages with women and search for mystical blood brotherhood with men while expressing revulsion toward lesbianism.

In his *Studies of the Greek Poets*, published in two volumes in 1877 and 1879, Symonds, having identified male love with the Dorian lyrists of chivalry "who culminate in Pindar," places Sappho "at the head" of Aeolian lyrists.[24] Describing Aeolian culture, he begins by listing everything Aeolians did not do: "They produced no lawgivers like Lycurgus and Solon; they had no metropolis like Sparta and Athens; they played no prominent part in the struggle with Persia, or in the Peloponnesian war" (136). Lest we should think this detachment from militarism worthwhile, he goes on to identify it with a series of increasingly derogatory adjectives and nouns:

> Lesbos, the centre of Aeolian culture, was the island of overmastering passions:the personality of the Greek race burned there with a fierce and steady flame of concentrated feeling. . . . At first this passion blossomed into the most exquisite lyrical poetry that the world has known: this was the flower-time of the Aeolians, their brief and brilliant spring. But the fruit it bore was bitter and rotten. Lesbos became a byword for corruption. The passions which for a moment had flamed into the gorgeousness of Art . . . remained a mere furnace of sensuality, from which no expression of the divine in human life could be expected. . . . As soon as its freshness was exhausted there was nothing left for Art to live on, and mere decadence to sensuality ensued. (136–37)

The series of images is telling. Symonds becomes complicit with Ruskinian ideology in condemning passion that is barren. He identifies the pleasure Ruskin had termed "corrupt," "unfruitful," and "unnatural" with Sappho of Lesbos. Symonds picks up Pater's image of the flame and identifies it with "concentrated feeling," only to condemn it because it does not transcend the human and become the "divine."

"Decadence" and "sensuality" are, of course, the terms used to condemn Pater and Wilde, not only by their contemporaries but by later establishment critics who labeled aestheticism "decadent." Immediately after this Symonds goes on to describe the freedom of Aeolian women, their education and self-expression in literature. Framed as his description is by the passage cited above, his praise of their literary "success" sounds very different from Pater's celebration of maintaining a flamelike ecstasy as "success in life." Symonds further colors the description by using words that point to a lack of control: "The Lesbian ladies applied themselves successfully to literature. . . . Unrestrained by public opinion, and passionate for the beautiful, they cultivated their senses and emotions, and indulged their wildest passions" (137).

In this promising context 3 pages (in a volume of 438) are devoted to Sappho. Her verse is not quoted, even though Plato's, Aristotle's, Longinus's and others' praises of her work are cited. In contrast, most male poets are quoted at length, with Symonds often picking out their poems in praise of boys; for instance, a fragment of Pindar's about his love for boys is translated. In an appendix Symonds translates Sappho's "Ode to Aphrodite," presenting the beloved as a "he," not a "she"! Although he mentions Sappho's love for women, Symonds does not demonstrate it in her verse—while a major part of the *Studies* as a whole is devoted to analyzing and demonstrating men's love for men. More damagingly, he places it in the context of women's freedom and education only after he has first identified these with corruption, decadence, and sensuality. Men's love for men is identified with democratic battles against tyranny, love of country, martial courage, philosophy, transcendence, and civilization itself.

Similarly, in his essay "A Problem in Greek Ethics," appended to Havelock Ellis's 1897 edition of *Sexual Inversion*, Symonds devotes two and a half out of eighty-six pages to lesbianism. He acknowledges that Aristophanes' myth in Plato's *Symposium* places lesbianism on the same plane as male homosexuality and heterosexuality and mentions Sappho but does not quote a single line by her. He then goes on explicitly to state that the Greeks did not build any civilizational, military, or educational ideal on the basis of women's love for women and that later they viewed it as an "eccentricity" or a "vice" (249).[25]

In his 1893 collection of essays *In the Key of Blue*, Symonds develops a cultural ideal of manliness.[26] Here he shifts uneasily between the impressionistic and subjective Paterian style in such essays as "In the Key of Blue," "Among the Euganean Hills," and "Clifton and a Lad's Love" and the Arnoldian style of statement and dictum in essays like "The

Dantesque and Platonic Ideals of Love" and "Culture." The essay "Edward Cracroft Leroy" purports to be a sympathetic appreciation of a homo-erotically inclined man who, as Symonds notes, belonged to a camp ideologically opposed to Symonds's own. Leroy was a writer of sonnets appreciative of youthful male beauty but was also an adherent of Kingsley's Muscular Christianity, which was aggressively opposed to Paterian Hellenism. Although Symonds mildly criticises Leroy for believing that Christianity is a divinely appointed way to transcend nature, he praises him for having by "instinct" hit upon "the right solution" of problems that "less well-balanced natures seek after in vain, because they are too coarsely fibred, too revolutionary, or peradventure too intemperate."[27] This set of epithets once more connects sensuality with subversion and condemns both.

Symonds seems to place himself halfway between Leroy and Pater/Wilde, a position very clear in the essay "Culture." Here, he defines culture in terms similar to Tennysonian or Rooseveltian manly work: "Culture is self-tillage, the ploughing and the harrowing of self. . . . The method of self-exercise which enables a man, by entering into communion with the greatest intellects of past and present generations . . . to make himself . . . an efficient worker, if not a creator" (200–1). The recurrent references throughout this essay to "men of culture," the "man of educated faculties," and to the human being as "him" are not fortuitous. Where Pater, outlining an ideal culture in the conclusion, carefully avoids the male noun or pronoun: "Art comes to *you*, proposing frankly to give nothing but the highest quality to *your* moments" (emphasis mine), Symonds's culture "makes a man to be something; . . . prepares him to exert his innate faculties . . . with a certain spirit of freedom" (204). Freedom thus becomes an ideal for men but not for women. For women it is associated with decadence; for men, with culture. This is a very different definition of freedom from Pater's—as I showed above, he explicitly defines freedom as sought by modern "men and women."

In this essay Symonds also makes a distinction between men of genius and men of talent. The former, "peculiarly constituted natures," like Dante and Plato, in "The Dantesque and Platonic Ideals of Love," may produce "fires of the imaginative reason" and become "fruitful" (86) when engaged in passionate mystical love, but other less special people will find such loves "for all practical purposes . . . sterile and ineffectual" (85). Symonds even argues that "social evils of the gravest kind" arose from Dantesque and Platonic love "because each had striven to transcend the sphere of natural duties and of normal instincts" (78). This endorsing of the natural and normal is necessary if Symonds is to plead the special case of peculiar natures, men of genius, rather than treating them as inspiring models for everyone, as Pater does. Pater assumes that the desires of all human beings are capable of transgressive direction. For Symonds male homoeroticism is a peculiar aberration connected with genius, and, if allowed to flourish, it can be assimilated to and even basic to the overall manly, martial, and Christian aims of national culture. Men can be fathers as well as lovers of men, as many Greeks were; women must be either decadent unfruitful Sapphists or wives and mothers. In "Culture" he lauds the "national spirit" of the Germans (212). The essay concludes by insisting on the necessity of strife and contention (as opposed to the Paterian ideal of peace) and with a sudden but unsurprising reversion to the "Onward Christian Soldiers" or "Charge of the Light Brigade" kind of image: "All the soldiers in all the armies, if they act with energy, sincerity, disinterested loyalty, serve one Lord and Master" (216)

Interestingly, the only moment in this set of essays when Symonds moves toward a nonstereotypical image of femininity is in the essay "In the Key of Blue" when he is constructing a series of poem-paintings of his Italian beloved, Augusto. In one of these poems he describes Augusto holding on his lap their host's little girl. The poem constructs Augusto as a kind of male Madonna/Anne, with the child as an infant Jesus or Mary:

> Your strong man's stature in those three
> Blent azures clothed, so loved by me;
> Your grave face framed in felt thrown back;
> Your sad sweet lips, eyes glossy black,
> Now laughing, while your wan cheeks flush
> Like warm white roses with a blush.
> Clasped to your breast, held by your hands,
> Smothered in blues, the baby stands:
> Her frock, like some carnation gleams;
> Her hair, a golden torrent, streams . . .
> Your beautiful pale face of pain
> Leaned to the child's cheeks breathing health . . .
> Such was the group I saw one night
> Illumined by a flaring light.   (9–10)

The combination of strength and sweetness ascribed to Augusto here is reminiscent of Pater's recurrent characterization of Michelangelo by the use of those two epithets together. Associating the blue of maleness with the traditional blue of the Madonna's mantle, Symonds paints an Italian portrait of his lover as our lady of sorrows who paradoxically combines warmth and paleness, whiteness and a blush, pain and beauty.[28]

It is through the proliferation of such images that Pater's disciples, Simeon Solomon and Wilde, developed a homoerotics that foregrounded love between women. Solomon, an enormously influential and fashionable painter before his arrest for a homosexual "offence" in 1873 put him outside the pale of "respectable" society, was a pioneer in this regard. Although he lived on to 1905, beyond Oscar Wilde, and his paintings are preserved in major museums, the significance of his contribution has not been adequately acknowledged, nor has he become an icon for the modern gay community as Wilde has. His being a Jew, doubly outcasted by his own community and by the English artistic community he had joined but that cruelly repudiated him after his fall, may have something to do with this. Born in 1840, Solomon was heavily influenced as a young man by Pater; other influences were the Pre-Raphaelites and his favorite poets, Keats and Shelley.

Solomon's paintings explore images of homoeroticism, both male and female, in Hebraic, Hellenic, and Catholic settings.[29] One of these images is that of the same-sex couple; another is that of the triangle, consisting of two men and a woman or two women and a man. An 1865 drawing, "The Bride, Bridegroom and Sad Love," features a man in the center embracing a woman with one arm. His face turns toward her but, behind his back, his other hand clasps that of a sorrowful young man, also touching his genitals. All three are nude. A drawing of 1868, developed into a much-admired watercolor of 1870, entitled "The Sleepers and the One That Watcheth," repeats the theme, reversing the genders. Here, a woman is in the center, with a man embracing one of her shoulders and a woman the other. While the man and the woman in the center have their eyes closed and an expression of satisfaction on their faces, the woman to the left looks down, away from them, with open, pensive eyes. What is interesting is that both kinds of triangles are similarly conceived. In each, a same-sex lover is marginalized by a heterosexual couple, but represents a hidden life unperceived by the other-sex lover.

Other pictures show suggestive mythological or religious figures, such as Bacchus (1867, an oil painting much-admired by Pater), Sappho (an 1862 drawing, showing her crowned with laurel, eyes shut as if meditating), and "A Saint of the Eastern Church" (an 1867 watercolor of a beautiful young man holding a flowering branch). Several pictures represent same-sex couples. "Two Acolytes," an 1863 watercolor, shows two beautiful, robed young men in church, with censers and flowering lilies in their hands. "Socrates and His Daemon" shows an old bald Socrates with a beautiful nude youth. "Righteousness and Peace Have Kissed Each Other," an 1865 wood engraving, shows two female figures embracing, lips meeting. They are in a forest, surrounded by doves and flowering lilies. This painting is probably based on medieval mystery plays that dramatized mercy and judgment, peace and righteousness, the new law and the old, as female figures kissing one another.

The most explicit pictures of same-sex couples are perhaps those of David and Saul and Sappho and Erinna. The 1859 pen and ink drawing, "David Playing to King Saul," shows the older man, bearded, clothed, holding a harp, and leaning back, eyes closed, against the nude body of the beardless young boy who is playing the instrument. A much later (1896) drawing on the same theme shows the older and the younger man gazing at one another with expressions of mingled desire and fear. Both hold phallic weapons, and the harp is barely visible in the background.

An equally erotic 1864 watercolor, "Sappho and Erinna in the Garden Mateiene," shows the two women on a garden bench, Sappho (her face is the same as in the study of her head) embracing Erinna, lips to cheek. Erinna's dress is drawn down to expose half her bosom. "Ruth, Naomi and the Child Obed" is an interesting Jewish version of the Anne-Mary-Christ theme. Here, the older woman, standing, holds the baby (whose face is not visible) in one arm and with the other embraces the seated younger woman. A flowering branch encloses them from above in a semicircle. "The Mother of Moses," an 1860 oil, is again a group of two females and a male—the older woman holds the baby, whose face is not visible, and the younger woman (Miriam), holding her arm, leans up to look at the baby. "The Finding of Moses" shows the two women returning joyfully with the baby. The absence of father figures from these groups is noteworthy. When older male figures appear, it is in company with younger males.

Solomon picks up well-known religious, mythological, and emblematic themes, to rewrite cultural history as infused with homoeroticism. In his more "realistic" paintings of drawing room or garden scenes in what looks like contemporary England, heterosexual couples are seen embracing, in the company of pairs of women, who are also embracing. These are conventional Pre-Raphaelite paintings. In this context I find most interesting his 1870 oil "A Youth Relating Tales to Ladies," where a young man sits facing five women, telling them a story. The women, all with dreamy looks on their faces, seem sunk as much in their own emotions as in the story. One sits on the lap of another, embracing her with one arm and holding her hand with the other. This group almost constitutes a Victorian redoing of the Leonardo painting of the Virgin and St. Anne. A third woman leans on the back of their chair. Another couple stands against the mantelpiece, facing the viewer. The younger woman in this pair leans her head against the older woman's neck and has her eyes closed. A story that induces this kind of emotion and action must be of a very special kind, in fact, precisely the story that Solomon and Pater were telling!

Solomon's fall in 1873 was attributed by some of Pater's enemies to his corrupting influence. It may have been in response to this charge that Pater excluded the conclusion (first published in 1868) from the 1877 second edition of *The Renaissance*.[30] Solomon's paintings were criticized by Sidney Colvin for "insufficient manliness" (27) and by Robert Browning for being "affected and effeminate" (28). Browning had added that an exhibition of the old masters should act as a tonic on "these girlish boys and boyish girls" (28). Solomon's celebration in his paintings of Sappho on the same plane as Socrates, and his fuller development of the idea of love between older and younger women and older and younger men as also of the maternal in both men and women, ideas at which Pater had hinted, seem to have contributed to his work being seen as shocking and effeminate.[31]

In his prose poem entitled "A Vision of Love Revealed in Sleep" Solomon undertakes an interesting exercise, the writing of a homoerotic narrative into a Judaic framework. Using elements of the Hellenic, and also of the Christian (notably, of the Eastern or Greek Orthodox Church), Solomon frames his text with Hebraic imagery. The vision begins with "three sayings of the wise King" (43), that is, three phrases from the Song of Solomon, which "came" to the narrator. The sayings of the author's namesake inspire his meditation on love, conceived very differently from the Christian reading of this text (as involving the mystical marriage of Christ and the Church). The narrator asks his spirit "to show me, as in a glass, what I sought" (43). The text written by his namesake thus becomes the starting point for an inner journey, into the self and into his culture and religion, to find what will empower him. He figures himself as a pilgrim, carrying a staff and wearing a colorless garment. He is accompanied on this journey by his Soul. Here Solomon anticipates many of Wilde's stories in which the embodied soul or self often plays an important part.

The journey carries the narrator "back in the spirit to the time past" (45) and his gaze is "drawn inward" (45) where he sees innocent creatures frolicking with the female figure of Pleasure who does not know "the sickness of the soul" (46). This early phase past, he encounters the wounded male figure of Love who is like a winged dove that has been battered and shamed so that he can no longer fly. The narrator realizes that he too has been one who has held "Love in contumely" (48) by planting rue or bitter things and hoping for myrtles or sweet things. Love is seen bound to a tree, wounded and bleeding, and tells the narrator: "Thou hast wounded my heart" (49). The narrator's soul tells him to purify his spirit so that Love can enter into that temple. This episode looks forward to such stories as "The Star Child" and The Picture of Dorian Gray, where the physical desire for male beauty unsuccessfully attempts to displace the desire for love between men, love that will be both physical and emotional. He next encounters the female figure of Passion whose unsatisfied cravings have nearly killed Love with their fiery breath. The narrator realizes that she is in fact himself. As a warning, the Soul then shows him "a vision of that which may yet be averted" (51). This proves to be a vision of Love lying dead. After this, they meet the figures of Death, Eternal Silence, and Sleep, all male. Next they see the wounded Love lying in the arms of Time, a maternal male figure: "His mien had in it the great tenderness of one unconquerable; as a mother encircles with her arms a beloved and sorrowing child . . . so he pressed his bruised and smitten charge to his breast, comforting him" (59).

The narrator realizes that by his neglect and maltreatment of Love he has helped "consign Love to the arms of Time" (59). This is an interesting rewriting of the figure of Time, who, since Shakespeare's Sonnets, had been conceived of primarily as destructive of and opposed to Love.

Solomon's image suggests that Time preserves despised love, keeping it asleep but not dead, waiting for a period when it will be less despised. This is an idea that recurs in Wilde's statement "Dorian [is] what I would like to be—in other ages, perhaps,"[32] and also in C. P. Cavafy's poem expressing the hope that someone in some more congenial future will live out all the unlived desires of the poet. The figure of Time is followed by the maternal figure of Night, a healing female who carries the weary male Day, in a pieta posture. The Soul then tells the narrator that he will see "the history of [the] shame" (61) of love, how men have buried him in darkness. They see the sleeping figure of love in a gloomy and ruined temple, on which the legend of "the joyful creatures who sported" in earlier times is "in decay, time-discoloured and riven" (62). Solomon now alludes to Sappho's lyric about night who brings the lamb to the fold and the child to its mother's breast. This idea is used to suggest that love lies sleeping in a night that preserves it until human beings are awakened to its significance. Night here is not a destructive but a healing and rejuvenating figure:

> Upon her all-supporting arms, and hidden in her raiment, she bore those who slept and dreamed, and those who watched; . . . she put away from them the sword, and healed the wounds that gape and bleed when she is not by to close them, . . . and in her arms the long-separated were brought together; beneath her shadow the lost little one yet again nestled upon her mother's breast; she hid the stricken in her heart, by her the forsaken were taken back to the hearts of the forsakers; she brooded over the uncared-for with the soft care of her wings, and by her the forgotten were brought to remembrance. (63–64)

Though this passage begins with the idea of mother and son, it ends with the idea of mother and daughter (the "lost little one" is "her"), connecting with it the idea of the outcast.[33]

He then has a vision of Love turning his head to the East, and sees many whom he knows "by name" in a group "clad in garments of beauty," with his beloved among them (68). When he sees his beloved's face, he feels as if his sorrows are almost over. Finally he sees the figure of Love rising up from the waters, naked and glowing, healed of his wound, and a flame burning on his heart. The flame comes and touches the narrator's heart and engraves on it the words "Many waters cannot quench Love, neither can the floods drown it" (70). This is followed by a vision of a double soul, reminiscent of Aristophanes' image in Plato's *Symposium* and of the winged beasts in the Book of Revelations: "I saw a happy light . . . and . . . within the light an inner living glow, and the glow divided itself in twain, and became two Holy Ones, each having six wings" (71). This image of doubleness is homosexual:

> As one sees in a soft air two flower-laden branches bend one towards the other, and, mingling, send forth a two-fold fragrance, so I saw one of these impelled towards his fellow and lightly touch him, and a living pulse seemed to beat in the flame that went forth from them, and a form was given to it, and

a heart informed it, all the fire-coloured air about it breathed hymns at this marvellous birth. (71)

The double soul composed of two similars thus creates a third being. This Platonic vision springing from a Judaic source lights in the narrator's heart an "inmost, secret flame" (79). The *Vision* ends with a prediction of the dawn to come, as the narrator remembers "the words of the wise king, Until the day break, and the shadows flee away. And a strong yearning was begotten within me, and a sob burst forth from my mouth up out of my heart, and my lips said inaudibly, Ah, that the day would break, and the shadows verily and indeed flee away" (65).

This text appears to critique, sympathetically and from within, that kind of male homosexual desire that restricts itself to furtive physical encounters and does not dare claim the fullness of love for a relationship between men. Such practice is represented as wounding, shaming, and killing love. The narrator, in his spiritual journey, has to pass through and survive this "night" of pain in order to emerge into the dawn of an open and creative love. His journey is mediated by female figures whose love is extended both to females and to males. Metaphorically, the text sets up women's way of loving, completely outside of a heterosexual complementarity model, as a paradigm for men to learn to love one another.

Wilde's lyrics, too, develop Marian images as an ideal toward which the homosexual male speaker looks for inspiration from his night of pain and despair. Wilde's lyrics have received much less attention than his plays, fiction, and essays, even in the recent revival.[34] The lyric was, in Victorian England, cast as a women's form (as opposed to the manly epic), and Wilde's lyrics self-consciously follow Shelley and Keats in ungendering and/or feminizing both speaker and addressee. A transgressive Mary and a feminized Christ play important parts in this project.

In the sonnet "Ave Maria Gratia Plena," written in Florence, Wilde contrasts the annunciation with Greek myths of the union of Zeus with mortal women like Semele and Danae. Describing himself as having expected "such glad dreams" of a heterosexual encounter, the poet stands before "this supreme mystery of Love." The destructiveness of Zeus's appearances, which "slew" Semele and "broke open bars and fell on Danae," is described in the octet. In the sestet these are replaced by stillness and the dove.[35] The violence of heterosexuality as it is experienced by many women is contrasted with the emphasis on emotional rather than merely physical experience in the Marian syndrome.

Another sonnet, "On Hearing the Dies Irae Sung in the Sistine Chapel," pursues this contrast between violence—here, of God's wrath—and the peace of the annunciation.[36] Christ is asked not to come in "terrors of red flame and thundering" but with "white lilies in the spring / Sad olive-groves, or silver-breasted dove," which teach "more clearly of thy life and love" (730). "Easter Day" contrasts the pomp and splendor of the papal appearance, which strikes the kneeling people with awe, to the weary and lonely Christ who had nowhere to lay his head. Christ becomes approachable by the outcast (in this case, the homosexual out-casted by society) when himself imagined as an outcast. Thus "E Tenebris" (Out of darkness) asks Christ for help because the poet is drowning in a stormy sea and his "wine of life is spilt upon the sand" (731). This is exactly the phrase Wilde used when writing to Robby Ross about the marquess of Queensberry having accused him of "posing as a somdomite": "The tower of ivory is assailed by the foul thing. On the sand is my life spilt."[37] Representing himself in this poem as convinced that he would go to hell if he had to stand that night "before God's throne," the poet finds peace in the thought that "before the night" he will behold the outcasted Christ: "The wounded hands, the weary human face" (731).

Interestingly, Mary proves equally compassionate and approach-able, because of her experience of pain. The subtext here, I suggest, is that Mary too knew the pain of persecution for supposed sexual transgression. The poet in "San Miniato" addresses her as crowned queen of heaven, who is at once "virginal," "mother of Christ," and "mystic wife," and ends with the telling lines: "O listen ere the searching sun / Show to the world my sin and shame" (725). "Shame," as is well known, was a code word for homosexuality at this time, most famously used at the end of Alfred Douglas's poem "Two Loves" when the figure representing heterosexual love accuses the figure representing homosexual love of not being love at all: "He lieth, for his name is Shame" to which the latter responds : "Have thy will, / I am the Love that dare not speak its name."[38] The appeal in "San Miniato" from the "searching sun," the judgmental male principle, to the feminine principle, Mary "throned upon the crescent moon," is also an appeal against Victorian Protestantism to outcasted Catholicism, with its pagan suggestions. The crescent moon connects to Islam as well as to moon goddesses like Isis and Diana.

In "The New Helen" (733–35) Wilde identifies Helen with pagan love that vanished with the ancient world but has reappeared in the poet's own time. In the fifth stanza she is explicitly contrasted with Mary and is said to have hidden away so that she might never have to see this Christian goddess who got from love "no joyous gladdening / But only Love's intolerable pain." However, in the sixth stanza the poet begs Helen to admit him into her temple and characterizes himself in Shelleyan terms as "bowed and broken on Love's terrible wheel." He fears that Helen will refuse and will return to Greece, leaving him imprisoned in "this poiso-nous garden," crowning his brows "with the thorn-crown of pain." The poet here becomes a Christlike figure, paradoxically imprisoned by Christianity but wishing to be liberated by Helen. Repeating his appeal, he suddenly declares his two deities to be Helen and the god "before whose feet / In nets of gold the tired planets move, / The incarnate spirit of spiritual love / Who in thy body holds his joyous seat." Since the next stanza seems to identify Helen with Aphrodite born of the sea, this god might be Eros or Christ "the incarnate." Helen and Aphrodite are thus surprisingly assimilated to Mary, who too was constantly identified by her worshippers with the sea, in consequence of her title "Stella Maris" (Star of the Sea), and was supposed to be the patroness of sailors. The reference to her uncommon birth could thus refer to the immaculate conception, which had just been declared a dogma by the pope (in 1854):

> Thou wert not born as common women are!
> But girt with silver splendour of the foam,
> Didst from the depths of sapphire seas arise!
> And at thy coming some immortal star,
> Bearded with flame, blazed in the Eastern skies,
> And waked the shepherds on thine island-home, . . .
> Lily of love, pure and inviolate!
> Tower of ivory! red rose of fire!
> Thou hast come down our darkness to illume:
> For we, close-caught in the wide nets of Fate,
> Wearied with waiting for the World's Desire,
> Aimlessly wandered in the house of gloom,
> Aimlessly sought some slumberous anodyne,
> For wasted lives, for lingering wretchedness,
> Till we beheld thy re-arisen shrine,
> And the white glory of thy loveliness.

Through its many twists and turns this poem finally suggests that the worship of Mary is a rebirth of the worship of Aphrodite ("re-arisen shrine") and the worship of Christ a rebirth of the worship of Eros. This Mary of the poet's imagination is explicitly distinguished from the Mary of Catholic countries, who embodies pain, not love: "before whose mouldering shrine / To-day at Rome the silent nations kneel." Mary as an oppositional figure is evoked in images from Greek poetry and from medieval sermon and litany (rose, lily, star of the sea, inviolate, tower) and contrasted to the biblical Mary whose pain is emphasized by the Church: "Only a sword to pierce her heart in twain / Only the bitterness of childbearing." In both Christ and Mary love is figured as triumphing over pain, but this is clearer in Mary's case, because she is not identified with a wrathful and judgmental god, as Christ may be. The poem suggests the complexity of the figure of Mary and wrestles with its various significations—sexlessness and pain, but also autonomous eroticism, love, and joy.

In the next chapters I will examine the Romantic roots of Aestheticist images of feminized homoeroticism by looking at the mother-daughter-female lover syndrome as it appears in Shelley's *The Cenci*, in Jane Austen's *Emma*, and in the writings of the Ladies of Llangollen, concluding with the way this inheritance was received by lesbian Aestheticists. Austen's writings have conventionally been treated not as Romantic texts but as continuations of the eighteenth-century novel and as examples of women's writing. Recently this model has been challenged, insofar as Susan Morgan and others have convincingly demonstrated her Romantic and feminist affiliations.[39] I wish to explore the ways in which Austen is concerned with issues of nonmarital and nonfamilial love, nurturing, tenderness, friendship, and community, which were also issues that preoccupied the Romantic poets. I see this preoccupation as having been inherited by homoerotically inclined writers, male and female, in the later nineteenth century, whose writings in this respect were different in emphasis (although not entirely in concerns, as I have argued earlier) from the mainstream Victorian novel.

4

Anarchist Feminism and the Homoerotic
Wilde, Carpenter, Shelley

It is indeed a burning shame that there should be one
law for men and another law for women—I think that
there should be no law for anybody.

—Oscar Wilde

From 1887 to 1889 Oscar Wilde was editor of the *Woman's World*, a journal to which he gave a decidedly feminist tone. The feminism Wilde
endorsed was significantly different from the kind of Victorian feminism
that argued that women should be educated to be better mothers and
equal partners within marriage. In the issues Wilde raised he often anticipated Woolf's arguments. His anarchist tendency is visible in his greater
stress on freedom rather than equality.[1] This stress is inherited from
Romantic thinkers like Shelley and integrated with the Paterian homoerotic discourse of which Wilde was an exponent.

Linda Dowling has demonstrated that the New Woman and the
Decadent shared antinomian energies and an unconventional vision of
sexual identity and were perceived by conservative Victorians as constituting a combined threat to establishment culture, but her insights have
not been incorporated into the general view of the period.[2] For instance,
Teresa de Lauretis remarks, "The fact is, 'the patriarchy' does not like lesbians any better than gay men, but some women, straight or lesbians,
have produced a feminism (some say several feminisms) while men,
straight or gay, have not produced one."[3] I would argue that some men,
straight and gay, participated crucially in the production or reproduction
of "several feminisms" in nineteenth-century England.[4] Some homoerotically inclined men's participation in the kind of feminism in which I am
interested, one that privileges women's freedom and creativity over their

'equality' within marriage and their rights as mothers, constitutes an important part of the history of that kind of feminism.[5] Its two signal features are an emphasis on women's autonomy and agency rather than their victimhood and a trenchant critique of marriage and the family. I shall examine one strand in the heritage of this feminism by tracing it backward from Wilde and Carpenter to Shelley's *The Cenci.*

Wilde changed the name of the journal *Lady's World* to *Woman's World* and set out to "deal not merely with what women wear, but with what they think, and what they feel."[6] The main focus of his writings in this journal, and in other essays and reviews at this time, is on women as artists. One strand of his argument is that various kinds of art by women have not been recognized as art, for example, embroidery, tapestry, and lace making, as also letter writing.[7] He also argues at length for women's education, connecting it with the development of their creative abilities.[8] Reviewing the poems of Miss E. R. Chapman, Wilde points out that the paucity of women poets in the past is attributable not to biology but to material circumstances.[9] In a review of an anthology of women poets, entitled *Women's Voices,* edited by Mrs. William Sharp, Wilde reveals an astonishingly wide acquaintance with the writings of women. After enumerating the poets anthologized, an enumeration that occupies two pages, he notes:

> It is not, however, by any means a complete anthology. . . . Where is Anne Askew, who wrote a ballad in Newgate; and where is Queen Elizabeth, whose "most sweet and sententious ditty" on Mary Stuart is so highly praised by Puttenham as an example of "Exargasia." . . . Why is the Countess of Pembroke excluded? Sidney's sister should surely have a place in any anthology of English verse. Where is Sidney's niece, Lady Mary Wroth, to whom Ben Jonson dedicated the "Alchemist"? Where is "the noble ladie Diana Primrose," who wrote "A Chain of Pearl, or a memorial of the peerless grace and heroic virtues of Queen Elizabeth, of glorious memory"? Where is Mary Morpeth, the friend and admirer of Drummond of Hawthornden? Where is the Princess Elizabeth, daughter of James I; where is Anne Killigrew, maid of honour to the Duchess of York? The Marchioness of Wharton, whose poems were praised by Waller; Lady Chudleigh, whose lines beginning—
>
> "Wife and servant are the same,
> But only differ in the name,"
>
> are very curious and interesting; Rachael Lady Russell, Constantia Grierson, Mary Barber, Laetitia Pilkington; Eliza Haywood, whom Pope honoured by a place in the "Dunciad"; Lady Luxborough, Lord Bolingbroke's half-sister; Lady Mary Wortley Montagu; Lady Temple, whose poems were printed by Horace Walpole; Perdita, whose lines on the snowdrop are very pathetic; the beautiful Duchess of Devonshire, of whom Gibbon said that "she was made for something better than a Duchess"; Mrs Ratcliffe, Mrs Chapone, and Amelia Opie, all deserve a place on historical, if not on artistic grounds. (194–96)

I have quoted this passage to demonstrate that Wilde could make catalogues of other things besides jewels and perfumes and that in this catalogue of women poets he proves himself an ancestor of Woolf and later feminist critics.[10] Wilde himself had a Romantic ancestor in this project. Leigh Hunt had written a three-part essay, "Specimens of British Poetesses," in which he listed many, although not all, of the same poets. His tone, however, is different—condescending, flirtatious, and insensitive to difference. For instance, he imagines that Katherine Philips, "the matchless Orinda," writing a love poem to Lady Elizabeth Boyle, must have "written in order to assist the addresses of some young courtier," even though the occasion of the poem (Lady Boyle singing a song composed by Orinda) makes the direct nature of the address evident.[11]

Nowhere does Wilde's argument for women's education, unlike other such arguments of the time, make a plea that women be educated in order to educate the future leaders of the race. On the contrary, women's education, in Wilde's argument, is linked to creativity. Motherhood scarcely makes an appearance in his writings in this journal. He links women's education directly to politics and to earning a living, as Woolf was to do in A Room of One's Own.[12] In a survey of "The Englishwoman's Yearbook," which is worthy of comparison to one of Woolf's famous footnotes in Three Guineas, Wilde notes that in the 1831 census, six years before the queen ascended the throne, no occupation was specified for women except domestic service, but more than 330 are specified in the 1881 census. He enumerates some of the more innovative of these, such as stockbroking, but points out that the historical account in the yearbook of literary work done by Englishwomen is "inadequate, and the list of women's magazines is not complete" (294–95). Wilde congratulates Miss Ramsay on her "brilliant success at Cambridge . . . in intellectual competitions with men" (230), and also reports with approval the participation of women in public life. In the context of a raging debate on women's suffrage at this time, he ranges himself uncompromisingly on women's side and remarks: "Nothing in the United States struck me more than the fact that the remarkable intellectual progress of that country is very largely due to the efforts of American women" (198–99).

Recalling the misogynist remark of a Bostonian that "in the twentieth century the whole culture of his country would be in petticoats," Wilde neatly turns it on its head: "By that time, however, it is probable that the dress of the two sexes will be assimilated, as similarity of costume always follows similarity of pursuits" (199). He immediately follows up this prophetic line of thought by quoting a recent article that had argued that in another hundred years the sexes would equally share the task of breadwinning and that women's dress would then have to change so that "they can compete with men upon their own ground" (200). The male author of this article added that he was glad he would not see the end of this revolution, but Wilde, in contrast, proceeds to attack Victorian fashionable women's dress on the grounds that "it not infrequently violates every law of health, every principle of hygiene" (200–1). He quotes a speaker at a medical congress in Washington to the effect that the contortion of Chinese women's feet is not more barbarous or unnatural than this dress. Wilde adds that the dress of the milkwoman, the fishwife, or the factory girl is much more sensible:

> It is really only the idle classes who dress badly. Wherever physical labour of any kind is required, the costume used, is, as a rule, absolutely right, for labour necessitates freedom, and without freedom there is no such thing as beauty in dress at all. In fact, the beauty of dress depends on the beauty of the human figure, and whatever limits, constrains, and mutilates is essentially ugly, though the eyes of many are so blinded by custom that they do not notice the ugliness till it has become unfashionable. (201–2)

Wilde associates the key word *freedom* with beauty, as did Pater, but also with labor and with the human figure. He notes that it is difficult to say what the dress of the future will be and that men's dress is not by any means an example of a rational dress.

In another passage he quotes from various contemporary and historical sources, including Montaigne, to protest against the "mutilation and misery" (224) women have to suffer : "From the sixteenth century to our own day there is hardly any form of torture that has not been inflicted on girls, and endured by women, in obedience to the dictates of an unreasonable and monstrous Fashion" (223). He protests also against the romanticization of slimness:

> To begin with, the waist is not a circle at all, but an oval; nor can there be any greater error than to imagine that an unnaturally small waist gives an air of grace, or even of slightness, to the whole figure. Its effect, as a rule, is to simply exaggerate the width of the shoulders and the hips; and those whose figures possess that stateliness which is called stoutness by the vulgar, convert what is a quality into a defect by yielding to the silly edicts of Fashion on the subject of tight-lacing. (224–25)

Here, Wilde was in tune with the efforts of feminists of his time. Frances Mary Buss, principal of the North London Collegiate School, and Dorothea Beale, principal of Cheltenham College, both "waged continuous warfare" against tight lacing, stiff stays, and unhealthy fashionable clothing.[13] Their students were often inclined to go the way of fashion; Wilde being an arbiter of fashion, his opinion was likely to carry weight of a special kind with young women.

One of the most striking features of Wilde's writings in the *Woman's World* is his sensitivity to the expressed needs of women themselves and his appreciation of all kinds of public activity by women, even kinds with which he is not entirely in sympathy. For instance, in a very long review of the memoirs of the princess of Oman and Zanzibar, who had worked to introduce women doctors into her country, he quotes her at length but refrains from passing derogatory judgments on her society. In this he is radically unlike most Britishers, even feminists, of his time, who generally tended to characterize Asian societies as backward and to link this with their being non-Christian. He notes that throughout her book "the Princess protests against the idea that Oriental women are degraded or oppressed, and in the following passage she points out how difficult it is for foreigners to get any real information on the subject" (287). This is followed by a lengthy extract in which the writer comments amusingly on the visit of a European lady to a harem, where "the enormous circumference of her hoop" strikes Arabian women with wonder, and "the meager conversation" that ensues, the lady retiring "as wise as she was when she came," having seen the "much pitied Oriental ladies" but not really communicated with them at all (289).

Similarly, when reviewing *The High Caste Hindu Woman* by Pandita Ramabai, the well-known Indian educator, Wilde reproduces her account of her life, her "very eloquent" proposals for reform, and her critique of the British educationist Miss Mary Carpenter's reforms, which the government had implemented with little success (156–59). He defends the French bluestockings, the Precieuses, against the French minister of education's attack on them (228–30) and writes sympathetic accounts both of activities of which he strongly approves, like holding life classes for women artists to paint nude models, and also of philanthropic activities even when he differs with their approach to social questions. Pointing out that "the poor are not to be fed upon facts" and that even "Shakespeare and the Pyramids" (218) are useless to people unless they have the material conditions wherein culture can be realized, he nevertheless praises Mary Carpenter's efforts to educate street boys, commenting on her and Bacon's opinion that unmarried people do the best public work and noting that she gave "the children of the poor not merely her learning but her love" (219).

Contrary to Symonds's strategies of quotation, Wilde quotes at length from the women writers he reviews, selecting poems about freedom and about love between women. For instance, reviewing Miss Nesbit's *Leaves of Life,* he presents two poems apparently addressed to a female beloved. In one of these the poet, alone in the forest, dreams of her explicitly gendered beloved. She describes her as "my heart's delight" and "the sweetest woodland thing of all" but never meets her again and hopes one day to do so: "And then—I will not let her pass" (103–04). In the other poem the "Dedication" to the book, the ungendered beloved is addressed as "you," but the floral imagery, nostalgically recalling "the sweetness of my long ago," creates a Sapphic atmosphere (105–6).[14] Wilde comments, in an encoded Paterian phrase, on the "subtle sweetness" (106) of the verse.

Reviewing Miss E. R. Chapman's *The New Purgatory and Other Poems,* he quotes her elegy "A Strong-Minded Woman." This poem addresses the dead woman as "my dear, my lost delight" and makes an elaborate argument to the effect that just as the rich cannot enter the kingdom of heaven, so, too, those most richly endowed with love do not enter the realm of human happiness on earth, "love's fruition"—apparently a reference to marriage and parenthood—being reserved for those who suffer from "a certain lack—a certain dearth" (241–43)!

Wilde's emphasis on freedom over equality arises from his desire to free erotic love from law. This is partly an inheritance from Romantic thinking, for instance, from the Blakean definition of love: "Love to faults is always blind / Always is to joy inclin'd / Lawless, wing'd and unconfin'd / And breaks all chains from every mind." Late Victorian homosexual writers' choice of the Romantics as ancestors is crucially connected to the Romantics' antinomianism, especially in relation to lawless love.

Shelley, as the prophet of free love, seems to have exercised a very special fascination for these writers. He was the favorite poet of numerous suffragists, antivivisectionists, vegetarians, socialists, and anarchists. Edward Carpenter describes an occasion when Shelley was used in the campaign for women's suffrage. In October 1912 Carpenter chaired a meeting of the Sheffield Women's Freedom League. Mrs. Despard, a feminist and "ardent vegetarian" (264),[15] lectured at this women's freedom meeting on Shelley's *Prometheus Unbound*! Carpenter reports that she held her audience's rapt attention for two hours as she quoted the poem at length and expounded it.[16]

In the late nineteenth century Shelley was made a site for debating the nature of gender in its relationship to art as well as for the alliance of feminists and male homosexuals against the establishment. Shelley's life and verse caused acute discomfort to Victorian critics like Leslie Stephen and Edward Dowden, who, while they could not deny his poetic genius, were uncomfortable with his unmanly effusions of self-pity and feminized self-construction in such poems as *Adonais* and "Ode to the West Wind." Stephen censures Shelley's Godwinian inclinations to anarchism, pantheism, and free love: "In Shelley's theory, duty seems to vanish, and the one ultimate reality to be rather love or the beautiful."[17] Shelley's undutiful behavior as a husband and father provoked Stephen's ire, and he remarked caustically on the poet's disregard of the categorical imperative: "Shelley . . . had learnt what system he had rather from Plato than Kant" (94).

Shelley's Platonism constituted part of his attraction for men like Symonds, Pater, and Wilde who were engaged in rewriting Platonic homoeroticism.[18] The work of all three writers is full of allusions to Shelley. In the extracts from his diary reproduced in the essay "Among the Euganean Hills," for instance, Symonds represents himself as following the track of Shelley on his Italian journeyings. Despite his very sympathetic readings of the poet, Symonds's characterization is ultimately not so different from Arnold's famous "ineffectual angel." In his 1879 biography of Shelley, while praising the poet's "profound sentiment of friendship,"[19] he sees his "virtues marred by his eccentricity, by something at times approaching madness" (33). Symonds sees Shelley as "too tolerant, too fond of liberty" (33). He is uncomfortable with Shelley's political idealism, especially his ideological opposition to the institution of marriage: "He had kicked against the altar of justice as established in the daily sanctities of human life; and now he had to bear the penalty" (94).

In Symonds's reading of Plato the love of "some mere mortal object" (142) is only intended to lead to transcendence. Ignoring Plato's second step, "the love of many beautiful forms," Symonds sees "Shelley's identification of Intellectual Beauty with so many daughters of earth" as "spurious Platonism" (142). Summing up in the epilogue, Symonds ranges himself on the side of Victorian convention:

> The right he followed was too often the antithesis of ordinary morality: in his desire to cast away the false and grasp the true, he overshot the mark of prudence. The blending in him of a pure and earnest purpose with moral and social theories that could not but have proved pernicious to mankind at large, produced at times an almost grotesque mixture in his actions no less than in his verse. (184)

Symonds continues: "We cannot, therefore, wonder that society, while he lived, felt the necessity of asserting itself against him. But now that he has passed into the company of the great dead, and time has softened down the asperities of popular judgment, we are able to learn the real lesson of his life and writings" (184). This curious argument almost amounts to endorsing persecution in order simultaneously to uphold convention and to remove those who challenge it into the arena of martyrdom. This approach was to be reenacted once more in the reactions of many like Symonds to the trials of Wilde and their aftermath.

Edward Carpenter, with Pater, Wilde, and Symonds, is perhaps the fourth most influential writer of the late Victorian period who was engaged in the construction of the modern gay identity. His strategies derive in some ways from Pater's and anticipate in others (the tying-in of the question with feminism, antiimperialism, and socialism) some influential modern gay studies approaches. For instance, in 1902 he published *Iolaus: An Anthology of Friendship* (by George, Allen and Unwin, in London). This collection of extracts is divided into five parts: "Friendship-Customs in the Pagan and Early World," "The Place of Friendship in Greek Life and Thought," "The Poetry of Friendship Among the Greeks and Romans," "Friendship in Early Christian and Mediaeval Times," and "The Renaisssance and Modern Times." Although his subtitle does not make it clear, Carpenter deals only with same-sex friendship and love or what he calls "comrade-attachment" (3). This slant is indicated in the title, since Iolaus was the name of Hercules' beloved, at whose tomb male lovers were said to have plighted their faith. Carpenter's anthology compares favorably with similar anthologies compiled in the 1980s and 1990s. In addition to the usual extracts from *Phaedrus*, *The Symposium*, the Greek lyric poets, and accounts of homoerotic myths in Plutarch and others, he also includes information on African tribes, on Polynesians, Tahitians, and Indians. These are interspersed with extracts from the Bible (Saul, David, and Jonathan). Extracts from the writings of St. Augustine, Anselm, and other monks, and the story of Amis and Amile (with due acknowledgments to Pater) figure in the medieval section, Rumi, Hafiz, and other Sufi poets in the Eastern section.

In his introductory remarks to the medieval section, Carpenter notes the survival of same-sex love in monastic life but adds that it was looked upon with disfavor following the exaltation of the holy family and that lapses from chastity were "violently reprobated" (98). In contrast, he sees in the Sufi poets a freedom from matter and spirit dualism: "To these poets of the mid-region of the earth, the bitter antagonism beteen matter and spirit, which like an evil dream has haunted so long both the extreme Western and the extreme Eastern mind, scarcely exists; and even the body 'which is a portion of the dust-pit' has become perfect and divine" (110).

Carpenter's selections map out the territory that would be explored more than half a century later. In the Renaissance and modern section, he includes Sidney and Languet, Browne, Montaigne, Michelangelo's sonnets (translated by Symonds), Richard Barnefield, and Shakespeare. Most interesting, he includes not only Shakespeare's sonnets but an extract from *The Merchant of Venice*, commenting that "the figure of Antonio over whom from the first line of the play ('In sooth I know not why I am so sad') there hangs a shadow of destiny" demonstrates "the devotion which one man may feel for another, as well as the tragedy which such devotion may entail" (141–42). This is followed by the death scene of Suffolk and York from Henry V, which Bruce Smith has recently commented on in his study of homosexual desire in England. The range is more exhaustive for the eighteenth and nineteenth centuries, including Goethe, Schiller, Frederick the Great, Winckelmann, Byron, Shelley, Tennyson, Thoreau, and Fitzgerald. Carpenter's courage does not extend to include Wilde, and the only women included are Sappho, Princess Anne and Lady Churchill, and the Ladies of Llangollen.

Clearly, his knowledge and interest in this latter area is limited, since he even misses out Katherine Philips. However, he quotes the 1807 letter from Byron to Miss Pigot that shows Byron engaged in the same project as himself, claiming an ancestry and including women in it. Perhaps the most interesting text to emerge from this claiming is an unfortunately little-known book, *The Psychology of the Poet Shelley* (1925; published in London by George Allen and Unwin) by Edward Carpenter and George Barnefield. Carpenter's fifty-one-page introduction presents the book as written by Barnefield, but it was presented on the title page as coauthored. Carpenter begins with a disclaimer, "I do not pretend to certify to the absolute truth of the theories put forward by Mr Barnefield" (7), but goes on to suggest the viability of these theories. He remarks in a footnote that Shelley was a contemporary of his (Carpenter's) father, who strongly disapproved of Shelley's ideas, especially on the subject of marriage, and that this enabled Carpenter himself to "appreciate all the more the mental clarity and boldness of the growing boy . . . who so decisively cast aside the conventions that surrounded him" (8–9, note).

He then begins his exegesis by pointing out that Shelley's poetry is saturated with the idea of love and faces sexual questions boldly yet exudes a childlike innocence with regard to physical acts. Carpenter places this simultaneity of intense passion with the absence of heterosexual eroticism in the frame of Freudian theories of repression. Carpenter sees Shelley's tendency to idealize the love object, whether a woman as in *Epipsychidion* or a man as in *Adonais*, as prophetic because it holds a promise of deliverance from sex harnessed to the aims of profiteering and violence. He goes on to quote Shelley's many references to hermaphrodites, especially the "sexless" being created by the Witch of Atlas. Carpenter suggests that Shelley is here envisioning an androgynous being of the future who will be less "sexually excitable" (32) than ordinary men. When Carpenter refers to "sex," he clearly means the heterosexual variety: "Sex in its ordinary procedure seems to belong to a somewhat ancient and prehuman order of things, clumsy and elephantine and, like many ancient institutions, oppressive in the last degree to *women*" (32; emphasis in the original) He then describes "intermediate types" who combine the functions of male and female in some American Indian societies and suggests that they represent the new type of human being who may emerge in a less oppressive future.

Carpenter explicitly states that such types emerge in societies free from the idealized and rigidly gender divided roles that characterize Victorian society. He cites the androgyny of Dionysus as well as Lao-tze's idea of the being who is both masculine and feminine and who "will return again to the state of an infant" (39). Repeatedly warning that such ideas will be "scoffed at" as foolish and impractical, Carpenter defends Shelley against critics like Symonds and rereads Shelley's yearning for ecstatic oneness with the universe and with nature in the context of Eastern pantheistic religions. Finally, Carpenter, following Freud, identifies the "bi-sexual" temperament with the child and with the leaders of humanity such as Shelley, Byron, St. Francis, Jesus, Buddha, Dionysus, Osiris, claiming that Shelley had "reached a *higher* level of evolution than usual" (46; emphasis in the original). Carpenter links homosexuality with "the great cause of human emancipation" and sees Shelley as forwarding this not only through his opinions but through "his love-nature" (51).

This preface is followed by Barnefield's closely argued and very persuasive study, based on close readings of Shelley's works and of comments on his personality by his contemporaries.[20] He begins this exegesis with the idea that "Shelley was pre-eminently the poet of unsatisfied love, through whose every poem there sounds the note of vague, often formless, erotic longing" (56). Recording the femininity of Shelley's appearance and voice attested by many contemporary accounts, Barnefield enrolls him in artists of the "intermediate type," including also Wilde, the latest addition to the roll of honor already written by Pater and Wilde: "Shelley, in fact, belonged to the class of double-natured, or intermediate, types . . . for example, Leonardo, Michelangelo, Wilde, and Tchaikowsky" (58). The inclusion of Wilde leaves the reader in no doubt as to what is under discussion here. On the next page Barnefield names it: "the repressed homosexual component of his nature" (59). Shelley's hopeless yearning for fulfillment in love is put down to "the tragedy of his life that he lived in a society, whose whole influence, acting on him by suggestion from his earliest infancy, forced his conscious mind to seek love in the form of an idealised woman" (61). Barnefield argues that Shelley's marriages prove nothing because "many quite inverted men have married" (64), either through not understanding their own natures or through deference to social convention. He attributes Shelley's marriages to the first cause. He quotes Shelley's letter to Hogg on the eve of his first marriage: "Your noble and exalted friendship, the prosecution of your happiness, can alone engage my impassioned interest. This [i.e., his approaching marriage] more resembles exerted action than inspired passion" (65). While acknowledging that the marriage to Mary was relatively more romantic and happier, Barnefield notes that Shelley's search for an ideal love and his melancholy persisted to the end of his life.

Barnefield argues that Shelley, unlike Blake (with his decidedly masculine and feminine figures), is "continually striving to create an ideal *bisexual* character" (69; emphasis in the original), like the sensitive graceful Athanase or Laon or the Amazonian rebel Cythna. In the next chapter Barnefield analyzes Shelley's romantic friendships with men, starting with his devotion to his schoolteacher Dr. Lind and the passionate attachment to a classmate that Shelley describes in his fragmentary essay on friendship: "I recollect thinking my friend exquisitely beautiful. Every night, when we parted to go to bed, we kissed each other like children— as we still were!" (75–76). Barnefield points out that many boys experience this kind of friendship, but what is noteworthy is that Shelley in his last years vividly remembered the intensity.

Barnefield quotes extensively from Shelley's letters to his male friends to testify to the extraordinary quality of his devotion and of his generosity, monetary and otherwise, to them. In the fourth chapter Barnefield quotes Shelley's comments on Greek sculpture in Italy and the way he dwells on the beauty of male figures like Ganymede and Apollo and on the embraces between male figures like Bacchus and Ampelus, even telling Peacock in an 1818 letter about an explicitly homosexual statue: "A Satyr, making love to a youth: in which the expressed life of the Sculpture and the inconceivable beauty of the form of the youth, overcome one's repugnance to the subject" (90). From this Barnefield proceeds to what has today become a commonplace of Shelley criticism, namely, that Shelley's conception of love is based on likeness, not difference. He makes the very important point that Shelley's interest in incest is related to his notion of fusion between two natures, a notion also found in the hermaphrodite created by the Witch of Atlas. He continues:

> It is important to remember that love, in Shelley's mind, depended upon the perception of the similarity of two lovers; not upon any polar, or complementary attraction. Thus Alastor's mind "thirsts for intercourse with an intelligence similar to itself"; while Laon refers to "That *likeness* of the features which endears the thoughts expressed by them." . . . In real life, too, Shelley always sought a similar soul to mate with. Thus, he calls Hogg: "The Brother of my soul"; and Miss Hitchener, before he knew her intimately, was his "spiritual sister." And in the same key he cries to Emilia: "Would we two had been twins of the same mother!" (92–93)

Barnefield concludes that brother-sister incest in Shelley's work is a disguise for bisexuality. Noting Shelley's fascination with Plato's *Symposium*, he reads Shelley's omission, in his translation of it, of all the definitely homosexual passages as attributable not to prudism (given Shelley's daring in such matters) but to his inability to face up to a subject that came too close for comfort. To this too he attributes Shelley's breaking off his essay on Greek love before he had addressed the question of pederasty. Barnefield suggests that Shelley's choosing to begin this essay and also choosing to translate the *Symposium* indicates a fascination with the subject. Barnefield quotes what he reads as Shelley's "self-analysis" in *Prince Athanase*:

> For all who knew and loved him then perceived
> That there was drawn an adamantine veil
> Between his heart and mind—both unrelieved
> Wrought in his brain and bosom separate strife.

Barnefield points out that Shelley has no Blakean "excessively and entirely masculine picture of unrestricted indulgence" (63) in heterosexual pleasures; rather, his view of free love, like a woman's, "meant sympathy and the passive experience of emotions and sensations" (63). Barnefield's association of heterosexuality with masculinity indicates that women's way of loving, which is empathetic and not exclusively masculine or feminine, was also Shelley's way—and, by implication, homosexual men's way. Barnefield ascribes Shelley's passionate espousal of women's rights and equality partly to this empathy with them, that is, to the empathy of a gay man with women.

Did Carpenter and Barnefield read the feminism of their own times into Shelley or do Shelley's writings actually present a feminist and homoerotic critique of marriage, the family, and heterosexual relations? I shall argue that the Romantic search for love, friendship, and community emerges from a critique of the kind of love that is based in the inequality of heterosexual and family relations. Perhaps the most trenchant critique of this kind is to be found in *The Cenci*. This play brings into the open the question of sexual abuse by a father, at least a hundred years before any other writer did so. Departing from the presentation in Jacobean drama of women as willing participants in such situations—a presentation Freud was to endorse by rewriting molestation as the daughter's fantasy—Shelley straightforwardly presents it as violence by the father. The play could not be staged in Shelley's lifetime because the presentation was too radical; although based on a historical event, it came in some ways very close to family life in contemporary England.

The theme of so-called father-daughter incest in this play (it is actually not incest but rape as Shelley presents it—that is, the horror lies in the absence of consent, not in the breaking of a taboo) often obscures the fact that Count Cenci is only an exaggerated version of what was fairly normal fatherhood in nineteenth-century England. If such Victorian fathers as Mr. Murdstone, Mr. Dombey, and Mr. Pontifex exemplify what Virginia Woolf was to call "the tyrannies and servilities of family life," so too does Count Cenci, with the difference that Shelley dares to read the situation from the female child's perspective. More important, the play, after placing the women in the most extreme situation of victimization possible in a family—prisoners of a murderer and a rapist—proceeds to embody the principle of human agency in them. It achieves this transition, transforming victims into agents, via nurturing love between women represented in a Marian triangle of two women and a boy.

Count Cenci punishes his children in ways that many parents of Shelley's time did—beating them, locking them up in the dark, forcing them to eat nauseating food. Although the details are exaggerated, they are still recognizable. Beatrice generalizes her experience when she says, "Who tortured me from my forgotten years / As parents only dare" (3.i.72–3).[21] Against the myth that "blood is thicker than water," Shelley sets the experience of many ordinary people when he makes Giacomo say of his tension-ridden marital household, "I looked, and saw that home was hell" (3.i.330). That this was part of Shelley's intention in writing the play is indicated by the terms of the dedication to Leigh Hunt in which he praises him for his "patient and irreconcilable enmity with domestic and political tyranny and imposture" (209).

The Cenci exposes the ideal of domesticity within the nuclear family, which was on the ascendant in the early nineteenth century. The ideological basis of the family as an institution is the supposition that biological ties automatically breed love and altruism. The play challenges this basis by showing that the family is as often bound together by hate as by love, the terror of the victim inspiring further unrestrained cruelty in the oppressor: "Thy milky, meek face makes me sick with hate!" (2.i.122), the count tells his son. This critique centers, as in so many of Blake's poems, on the oppression of the child. Beatrice's status, as an unmarried daughter, is that of a child, which is why her father is supported by state and church authorities in characterizing her revolt as impious: "A rebel to her father and her God" (4.i.90). Breaking the child's will was an accepted part of Christian upbringing and educational policy, and the rape of Beatrice is used by her father as a way of forcing her into submission. It is another kind of corporal punishment. The language used by the count stresses his intention of silencing her. After she shames him at the feast with her forthright speech, he decides to make her "meek and tame" (1.iii.167). The first attempt to murder is the count's—he wants to kill her spirit. This drama is enacted in many Victorian novels, only it is often disguised by transferring the murderous impulse to parent substitutes—a stepfather (Murdstone), an aunt or guardian (Jane's Aunt Reed and Mr. Brocklehurst), a sibling (Pip's sister). Emily Brontë and Samuel Butler are perhaps the only two major nineteenth-century writers after Shelley to present parental violence without such disguise.

What is missed by most commentators, however, is that this is also a play about nurturing love. Count Cenci gave Beatrice biological life but wants to kill her spirit, strike her dumb. Lucretia is the life-giving force in the play who has kept the children alive in spirit. The ability of the children to love and care, even though they have grown up in such a love-denying atmosphere, is made psychologically viable by the presence of Lucretia, who has created an inner circle of love within the outer circle of Count Cenci's hate. Shelley daringly reverses the wicked stepmother stereotype, to set the chosen family against the biological family. Both Beatrice and Bernardo refuse to escape, if this involves leaving Lucretia behind. Beatrice's declaration is reminiscent of Ruth's declaration to Naomi and fraught, as that is, with emotion that is not based in biological ties:

> Talk not to me, dear Lady, of a husband.
> Did you not nurse me when my mother died?
> Did you not shield me and that dearest boy?
> And had we any other friend but you
> In infancy, with gentle words and looks,
> To win our father not to murder us?
> And shall I now desert you? May the ghost
> Of my dead mother plead against my soul,
> If I abandon her who filled the place
> She left, with more, even, than a mother's love!   (2.i.88–97)

In a complete reversal of the normal pattern, found in fairytales and in Coleridge's "Christabel," where the biological mother's ghost appears to warn or protect the daughter from the stepmother, here the three women appear in a bonded triangle. Refusing to set up a family of her own, Beatrice constructs instead a new kinship consisting of two women, one older, one younger, and a young boy. This kinship has a life of its own within the patriarchal nuclear family and is in rebellion against that family. Lucretia is both a "friend" and more than a mother. She demonstrates her role as mediatress when Count Cenci enters immediately after these declarations of love. She tries to remonstrate with him on Beatrice's behalf. The ironies of her role are apparent—like the Christian madonna in relation to her worshippers, she is the spiritual, not the physical, mother of the children, yet her mediation is ineffective. But Lucretia's effectiveness operates at another level.

Beatrice is enabled to speak what for most women in most societies remains unspeakable, even to their mothers. That she can do so is entirely due to Lucretia. When the count first makes his intentions clear, Beatrice becomes hysterical. Lucretia asks, "Oh, dearest child! / Are you gone mad? If not, pray speak to me" (2.i.32–33). Beatrice manages to respond, "You see I am not mad; I speak to you" (34). Lucretia questions her, but Beatrice is unresponsive and considers suicide. Lucretia again insists, "Speak to me." (61). Bernardo follows her lead: "Oh, sister, sister, prithee, speak to us" (62), and Beatrice then describes the count's behavior. The dynamic of this scene is repeated again after the rape, when Beatrice tries to speak but cannot: "Mother, come near me; from this point of time, / I am—(her voice dies away faintly)" (3.i.67–8). Her inability to name herself also signals the victim's response of blaming herself—"I am" rather than "he is." Lucretia immediately reverses this trend of thought by focusing on the count as agent and Beatrice as victim of his violence: "Alas! what has befallen thee, child? / What has thy father done?" (68–69). Beatrice responds by accepting this view of things: "What have I done? / Am I not innocent?" (69–70). Lucretia insists that Beatrice name the crime and repeats the invocation that is to undo the count's attempted silencing of Beatrice: "Speak to me" (82). Beatrice is not able to shake off unnecessary guilt and says she is unable to find words for what has occurred:

> . . . of all words
> That minister to mortal intercourse,
> Which wouldst thou hear? for there is none to tell
> My misery; if another ever knew
> Aught like to it, she died as I will die,
> And left it, as I must, without a name.
> Death, death! our law and our religion call thee
> A punishment and a reward; oh which
> Have I deserved?   (3.i.111–19)

Following the classic pattern of the rape story, Beatrice sees herself as at best a Lucrece and at worst a Myrrha, in either case doomed to die. In a powerful rejoinder Lucretia insists on Beatrice's innocence and introduces the idea that precipitates the rest of the play's action—the idea that it is the criminal who deserves to die, not the victim, and that the death of one who punishes a criminal is a righteous death, the death of a martyr:

> The peace of innocence,
> Till in your season you be called to heaven.
> Whate'er you may have suffered, you have done
> No evil. Death must be the punishment
> Of crime, or the reward of trampling down
> The thorns which God has strewed upon the path
> Which leads to immortality.   (119–25)[22]

This idea is received by Beatrice as a new one, "Ay, death— / The punishment of crime" (25–26), and she goes on to meditate on this idea, until, when Orsino enters, she is able to approach him with a new reading of the situation, a reading introduced by Lucretia: " I have endured a wrong so great" (139). In the ensuing conversation the two women argue with Orsino, who advises them to go to law against the count. The women are convinced that the count has too much power and influence for them to succeed against him and that such a course will only result in more suffering for Beatrice. Lucretia insists on the idea of revenge and that they should consider "if there were any way to make all sure, / I know not— but I think it might be good / To—" (196–98). Orsino interrupts her to concur, and Beatrice then states the idea that Lucretia has already introduced and everyone has by this time understood. The rape is not named but is communicated effectively through mutual understanding; so too the idea of murder. One unspeakable event, rape by the father, is countered by another unspeakable event, the parricide.

It is significant that the first to actually name the plan is again Lucretia. Beatrice asks Orsino to swear his friendship before she reveals her plan. After he has sworn, before Beatrice can speak, Lucretia says, "You think we should devise / His death?" (226–27). Beatrice completes the sentence, "And execute what is devised, / And suddenly" (227–28). By stepping in at this crucial juncture, Lucretia shares Beatrice's burden, makes the unspeakable speakable. It is only through Lucretia's intervention that Beatrice is enabled to revert from her "wild and whirling words" to measured speech. The sympathy between the two women is conveyed by their ability to complete one another's sentences. This intermeshed converse stands in stark opposition to the violent debates between the count, his allies, and Beatrice. Through language the dramatist enacts the bonding between the two women, which replaces the master-slave bonding premised on the slave's silent submission that the count seeks to impose on Beatrice. If hatred can only culminate in silence, love expresses itself in speech. It is interesting that Lucretia has the name of one of the most famous rape victims in Western mythology, Lucrece, who earns her fame by killing herself after she is raped. Lucrece proves her fidelity to her husband by her suicide. Shelley's Lucretia is also implicitly a victim of that far more common form of rape, marital rape, and she reverses conventional wisdom when she asserts her fidelity to another rape victim rather than to her husband.

Almost all commentators have seen Lucretia as a weak and passive figure, but I hope to have demonstrated that she in fact plays a crucial role as an empowering figure, who, through her spoken love, counters the count's hatred and cruelty.[23] Through her Shelley dramatizes a favorite Romantic thesis—that the apparently helpless are not helpless; they help one another even when they cannot help themselves. The idea of a community of suffering draws on the interaction between the three Maries, Christ, St. John, and the thief at Calvary.

In the figure of Lucretia Shelley also embodies the ideal of parenting that is explored by many Romantic writers. This is an ideal of nurturance based only in love, without any admixture of fear. It is thus in excess of the Christian ideal of familial parenting dominant in eighteenth- and nineteenth-century England. This excess is stressed in the children's praise of Lucretia's love for them, Beatrice's "more, even than a mother's love," and Bernardo's "Oh, more, more / Than ever mother was to any child, / That have you been to me!" (2.i.7–9). The phrasing resonates with the idea of divine mothering. As the eighteenth-century hymn puts it: "Can a mother's tender care / Cease towards the child she bare? / Yes, she may forgetful prove / He will never cease to love." By embodying this idea in a woman who is not a biological mother, Shelley rewrites divine love as the "fraternity" of the revolutionary slogan that the English Romantics found unfulfilled in the Terror and sought to fulfill in other ways in their own imagined communes and extended households. Friends or lover and beloved who mutually parent one another (through such episodes as nursing in sickness, watching over sleep, feeding) are a common motif in English Romantic narratives. This ideal flowers in the second half of the play, when Lucretia mothers Beatrice and Bernardo, and Beatrice, too, mothers Lucretia and Bernardo. The cluster of Anne-Mary-Christ child is thus rewritten, with the focus shifted from the child to the two women. Mary, the daughter of god and of St. Anne, is also mother and mystic beloved, all of these roles fusing in ambivalence. Shelley's rewriting shifts the gender focus altogether toward closure when the two women are crucified and the boy child left to live on in agony.

The play's imitations of Elizabethan and Jacobean tragedies has often been noticed, but its ending is altogether different from any of those models. It closes not with the spectacle of corpses littering the stage but with that of two women doing up one another's hair, an image of ordering, of peace, of mutuality and intimacy, almost, of play. The women triumph by belying the count's curses and prophecies. He had predicted that Beatrice would become fascinated by him ("for what she most abhors / Shall have a fascination to entrap / Her loathing will" 4.i.85–7) and would be "shelterless," self-hating and unloved, and die abandoned. He made this prediction to Lucretia, who listened in silence. Lucretia's response, as enacted in the play, renders his prediction void. The Jacobean horrific ending, premised on the fascination and destructive power of male-dominated heterosexuality, is replaced with a new, feminized, Sapphic-Romantic closure.

This closure presents the family remade on different terms, but not destroyed—Bernardo remains, the spiritual son of two mothers. He now is "The Cenci," and embodies the opposite of everything his father stood for. Bernardo is the physical son of his father but the spiritual son of his stepmother and his sister. The women's creation and intentions have, in this very tangible sense, triumphed. Uniquely, the play ends with a woman's words (Renaissance tragedies almost always end with a man's words, silencing women). Bernardo repeats Lucretia's earlier invocations when he asks Beatrice to speak: "Oh, let me hear / You speak!" (5.iv.139–40). While the men are silenced and stammering, Beatrice speaks with composure, and the series of words she uses stress the importance of faith, hope, and love, not in god but in human beings: "mild, pitying thoughts . . . the love / Thou bearest us . . . the faith that I . . . Lived ever holy . . . never think a thought unkind." This feminine ending is anticipated in Beatrice's speech, just before Bernardo's entrance, when she contrasts man's mercilessness with a dignified and chosen death conceived of as maternal:

> . . . plead . . . not with man—
> Cruel, cold, formal man; righteous in words,
> In deeds a Cain. No, mother, we must die . . .
> Come, obscure Death,
> And wind me in thine all-embracing arms!
> Like a fond mother hide me in thy bosom. (5.iv.105–17)

By shifting the dramatic action from the world of men's power to the world of women's interaction, Shelley moves the tragedy to the kind of visionary matrilineal ending found in Shakespeare's last plays, where a possible future world is imagined. As Paulina says, when calling Hermione to life, "It is requir'd / You do awake your faith" (*The Winter's Tale*, 5.iii.94–95).

Love based on likeness between women becomes the fulcrum for a shift in the play from Count Cenci's power over words to the women's seizing that power and silencing him. In the next chapter I shall examine the trope of likeness as it was inherited and rewritten by women in the course of the nineteenth century.

5

The Search for a "Likeness"
Shakespeare to Michael Field

My two lips, eyes, thighs, differ from thy two,
But so, as thine from one another do;
And, oh, no more; the likeness being such,
Why should they not alike in all parts touch?
Hand to strange hand, lip to lip none denies;
Why should they breast to breast, or thighs to thighs?
Likeness begets such strange self flattery,
That touching myself, all seems done to thee.
. . . Me, in my glass, I call thee; but alas,
When I would kiss, tears dim mine eyes, and glass.
O cure this loving madness, and restore
Me to me; thee, my half, my all, my more."
                —John Donne, "Sappho to Philaenis"

It was deep April, and the morn
Shakespere was born.
The world was on us, pressing sore;
My Love and I took hands and swore,
Against the world, to be
Poets and lovers evermore . . .

                        —Michael Field

This chapter will examine some nineteenth-century women writers' reception and writing of the trope of "likeness." This trope had multifarious significances, derived from many sources. It could indicate a relationship with a beloved, friend, or sibling as similar/double/other self and also the picture/reflection/work of art engendered by and in such relationships. It could be reassuring or threatening, point to perfection or to destruction of identity. Some of the most famous nineteenth-century texts built around this trope explore male-male relations, for example, Frankenstein and his monster, Dorian Gray and his portrait, Dr. Jekyll and Mr. Hyde. I shall consider its development by women writers—Jane Austen, the Ladies of Llangollen and their circle and the two women who wrote under the pen name Michael Field—to forge mythologies of love between women. These mythologies were not purely personal or private. They derived from women's readings of a general literary ancestry and became mainstream cultural myths. They offered images of same-sex love as a space for resistance to marriage and parenthood and for experimentation, education and self-realization.

Austen and the Ladies of Llangollen wrote in the Romantic period, and the texts they produced contributed to the making of Romanticism. Michael Field were Aestheticists and thus among those Yeats defined as "the last Romantics." The Romantics received two major paradigms of love as likeness. One was the biblical story of creation, where god makes human beings "in our image, after our likeness" (Genesis 1:26). The other was Plato's story of the beloved appearing to the lover as the earthly "likeness of the world above" the "image" and "reflection" of true, heavenly beauty.[1] I will consider the first as channelled through Milton's reading of the biblical account and the second through Shakespeare's reading of Neoplatonic traditions. Milton and Shakespeare were the two English ancestors most ardently claimed by the Romantics. They admired Milton as a republican opposed to monarchy and a lover of liberty who suffered for his unconventional views on freedom of speech and freedom to divorce. But this admiration was tempered, for Shelley, as for Blake, by the contradiction in *Paradise Lost*—the narratorial support for a tyrannical god against rebellious Satan. In the context of the Romantics' concern with the position of women, it is noteworthy that the other rebellious figure in the epic is Eve. She consciously disobeys god's command while Adam disobeys unwillingly, from love of her, not because he is attracted to knowledge. The paradox that Blake and Shelley noticed in Milton's simultaneous attraction to and denunciation of the energies of Satan is evident also in his schizophrenic portrayal of Eve. Despite his obsessive insistence on her inferiority, he gives her some attractive philosophical arguments against inferiority; while debating whether or not to share her newfound wisdom with Adam, she remarks to herself, "inferior, who is free?" (9:825).[2] Her experience of imposed inferiority as a woman leads her to challenge the idea of human inferiority to god.

The Miltonic economy of likeness requires that Eve be the inferior "likeness" (8:450) of Adam as Adam is of god, and that this hierarchy be reproduced thereafter, children being the likenesses of their parents, subordinate to them: "like of his like, his Image multiplied" (8:424). The principle of inferior and complementary likeness structures Miltonic heterosexuality, which is the ordering principle of his ideal universe—witness his invocation to "wedded love" as "perpetual fountain of domestic sweets" (4:750, 760). accompanied by his denunciation of celibacy, and of Catholics who glorify it, as Satanic. However, his picture of marital bliss is full of erotic undercurrents that never get resolved. One of these is that Eve's first experience of erotic attraction is not to Adam at all but to herself. She sees herself in the water and feels that her image returns her admiration with "looks / Of sympathy and love" (4:464–65). When she sees Adam, she thinks him "less fair / Less winning soft, less amiably mild" than the "image" (4:480) she had earlier seen, which she does not know was a reflection of herself. Adam chooses to misread her turning away from him as feminine modesty, even after she has told him about her amour with her reflection. This episode, susceptible to the Freudian reading of feminine narcissism, can also be read as indicating Eve's desire for a "likeness" more like herself, an equal, not a complementary but a similar partner. It resonates too with the legend of Lilith and that of the serpent as a female sexual tempter of Eve. Milton's phrasing here is not far from that of his contemporary Donne in "Sappho to Philaenis": "Plays some soft boy with thee, oh there wants yet / A mutual feeling which should sweeten it. . . . / Thy body is a natural paradise, / In whose self, unmanured, all pleasure lies, / Nor needs perfection; why shouldst thou then / Admit the tillage of a harsh, rough man?" I shall return later to Milton's conception of heavenly homoerotic love between angels, which is depicted as surpassing earthly heterosexual love.

All six major Romantics tried to emulate Milton by writing epics of a sort, but they also all wrote sonnets, influenced both by Milton and by Shakespeare.[3] Shakespeare was attractive to the Romantics as the poet of nature and human nature, sensitive to emotional reality. Shakespeare's *Sonnets* are structured around the move away from heterosexual reproduction to love for a same-sex similar. The first seventeen sonnets urge the male beloved to produce a child, who will be his "image" or likeness, "another self," just as he is his mother's image. Sonnet 18 accomplishes a shift to the idea of the beloved as the likeness of the poet/lover. This becomes one of the most powerful tropes in the whole sequence. The idea of the "likeness" as picture is played with, when the poet/lover's heart is compared to a shop window where the "true image" of the beloved is framed (24).[4] The beloved is made anew by the poet/lover, in the "images" of all his past loves (31) as well as in the image of literary and mythological ancestors like Adonis and Helen (53) whom he is declared to have surpassed. Seeing him everywhere, the poet/lover beholds him in natural objects such as flowers but also in what he reads: "Show me your image in some antique book" (59). The words "image" and "like" are among the most frequently recurrent words in the *Sonnets*, as in *Paradise Lost*. The "image" of the beloved constitutes the poet/lover's waking fantasies and sleep dreams (43, 45, 46, 61) and is transmuted into the poems themselves, which in turn pass that image on to future descendants: "You live in this, and dwell in lovers' eyes" (55).

The Shakespearean economy of likeness, then, is homoerotic and is developed in opposition to heterosexuality.[5] The dark lady is never a "likeness"; her attraction lies in her difference. If her "eyes are nothing *like* the sun" (130, emphasis mine), where the sun has already been described as falling short in comparison to the fair youth ("Shall I compare thee to a summer's day?"), her unlikeness makes her as good as other women ("as rare / As any she") but less than the perfect mirror likeness of beauty that the fair youth is.[6] The speaker's love for the fair youth as his likeness produces dreams, images, and works of art that are likenesses of another kind. These displace the production of children. Poet/lover, the beloved/likeness/other self and the ungendered readers/lovers, who will receive their "likeness" or portrait through the poems, constitute a homoerotic triangulation. The woman rival enters the sequence as late as sonnet 40, disappears after 42, and the final sonnets to the dark lady are only 28 in number (in several of which the youth also appears) as compared to 123 to the fair youth (omitting the three that deal with both). These 123 sonnets include some of the most famous, influential and frequently anthologized such as 18, 29, 30, 55, 60, 65, 99, 106, 110, 116, most of which are eulogies to ungendered love of likeness and make no mention of a rival.[7]

Addressed by an ungendered "I" to an ungendered "you," these sonnets came to acquire meaning as statements of homoerotic love outside of their sequential context. They were open to use by homoerotically inclined women and were frequently so used. The comparably famous sonnets to the dark lady alone are 127, 128, 129, 130, none of which are eulogies to love. For the Romantics, with their philosophical interest in love as an organizing principle, these clever exercises in quibbling with words ("will" and "lie") and reversing literary convention were less interesting and attractive than the exploration of the concept of "likeness" and its implications for human relationships. The explorations of likeness constitute the "difference" of Shakespeare's *Sonnets*—they are, apart from Richard Barnefield's, the only such extended sonnet sequence to a man in their time and for a very long time afterward. The sonnets to the dark lady, both in their eroticism and in their misogyny, are paralleled and outdone by any number of other sonnet sequences and poems such as Donne's, and as such do not constitute a significant ancestry. Further, the Romantics' interest in love as likeness rather than love as difference is consonant with their attraction to antinomian traditions and to pagan, Greek, and Eastern models of love such as Plato's rather than to dominant Protestant models of love such as Milton's.

I shall consider some Romantic women writers' development of tropes of same-sex love as Edenic, heavenly, "perfect" likeness, as likeness between older parent/lover and younger child/beloved, and as picture or mirror image, in the context of their reception of these tropes from literary ancestors.

Emma was published in 1816, the same year as *Childe Harold*, part 3. Like the male protagonists of this and other Romantic long poems, Emma is in search of her "likeness." She takes on the active role in this search. In this, she is different from most women in poems and novels of the time, who exist in a condition of perpetual waiting.

By creating a heroine without brothers and endowing her with wealth, social status, beauty, Austen provides the woman reader with a fantasy and asks the implicit question "What would a woman do and want if she had all that most women are deprived of by virtue of being women?" Emma starts off with the advantages of the average Romantic hero like Don Juan or Childe Harold, and therefore her quest goes beyond the quest for a husband. Byron in *Childe Harold* describes this quest:

> 'Tis to create, and in creating live
> A being more intense, that we endow
> With form our fancy, gaining as we give
> The life we image, ev'n as I do now.[8]

For Austen her novel represented this kind of creative enterprise. She wrote to her sister Cassandra about *Emma*, "I want to tell you that I have got my own darling child from London."[9] Like Austen, Emma attempts to write a novel or paint a picture of which Harriet shall be the ingenue heroine. In the act of writing about a heroine who marries and will have children, Austen frees herself from the need to follow that path—the novel becomes her child, a child that is life-giving rather than death-giving.[10]

The novel begins with the tragedy of loss. What is lost is intimacy between women.[11] Reversing the trajectory of the romantic novel, which concludes with the celebration of a wedding, *Emma* opens with the mourning that accompanies matrimony. Although this mourning becomes comic in Mr. Woodhouse, Emma does share it and it is justified—marriage is in fact a kind of death. "Miss Taylor" is gone for ever and "Mrs Weston" is an inadequate replacement.[12] Miss Taylor is introduced in the novel's second sentence and the various terms used to describe her relationship to Emma—"governess," "little short of a mother in affection," "less as a governess than a friend," "the intimacy of sisters," "friend and friend very mutually attached," "beloved friend"—all suggest the impossibility of adequately categorizing the relationship.[13] What Emma is in need of is not marriage but intimacy; robbed of this by one marriage, she is ultimately compelled to seek it in another, her own, but before that denouement, she makes attempts to seek it elsewhere, outside of marriage.[14] The word *friend* occurs seven times in the first two pages of the novel, signaling the nature of Emma's search. She realizes that while she has many acquaintances in Highbury she has no friends there; significantly, the idea of Mr. Knightley does not occur to her until he appears. At this point in the novel he does not exist for the reader either, and the ideal friend is conceived only as a woman.

Sighing over Miss Taylor's marriage, Emma, we are told, cannot but "wish for impossible things" (39). The phrase is a telling one, suggestive of futuristic Romantic projects. The word *impossible* was to become, in the writings of Pater, Wilde and others, a euphemism for the socially "impossible" homosexual relationship. What these impossible things are, we are not told, but clearly they relate to the desire for a female friend who will remain single and in whose affections Emma will remain primary.

Emma's attachment to Miss Taylor does not cease with the latter's marriage. It continues as a powerful undercurrent. For instance, when

Mrs. Weston is nervous about her first meeting with her stepson she tells Emma to think of her at the hour of his arrival. Emma faithfully thinks of her not only at that hour but at every succeeding hour, and in a "mental soliloquy" imagines her, in her "little fidgets" (202), going repeatedly into Frank's room to check that everything is prepared for him. Her closeness to her friend is evident in the concreteness with which she is able to imagine her nervous activity. Shortly after, when Frank visits Emma, the romantic element of Emma's attachment is suggested. Frank praises Mrs. Weston's youthful beauty and Emma responds: " 'You cannot see too much perfection in Mrs Weston for my feelings. . . . Were you to guess her to be eighteen, I should listen with pleasure' " (204). Even when deprived of the "pleasure" of "uninterrupted communication" with her, "the very sight of Mrs Weston, her smile, her touch, her voice was grateful to Emma" (138). *Emma* provides an early example of a romantic attachment between woman teacher and woman pupil, an attachment central to many twentieth-century English novels.

It is possible to read the whole novel as the story of Emma's search for a substitute for Miss Taylor. Harriet is the first substitute she finds, Mr. Knightley (and perhaps also Mrs. Weston's daughter) the last. Along the way, she considers Jane Fairfax as a possibility. Jane, however, appears in the novel as a "man's woman," not capable of openness with a woman. Mr. Knightley agrees with Emma that Jane's extreme reserve is a flaw that inhibits intimacy.

Mrs. Weston understands Emma's desire for a female friend but Mr. Knightley cannot. When they discuss the Emma-Harriet intimacy, of which Mr. Knightley disapproves, Mrs. Weston says: "I have been seeing their intimacy with the greatest pleasure. How very differently we feel!" (65) The signal word is *feel*—not *think*, but *feel*. Miss Taylor follows up her exclamation with analysis:

> Mr Knightley, I shall not allow you to be a fair judge in this case. You are so much used to live alone, that you do not know the value of a companion; and perhaps no man can be a good judge of the comfort a woman feels in the society of one of her own sex, after being used to it all her life. (65)

Austen knew from experience what she was talking about here. It was a commonplace in the Austen family that Jane and Cassandra were wedded to one another, their mother even going so far as to say that "if Cassandra were going to have her head cut off, Jane would insist on sharing her fate."[15] In a more sober vein their niece Anna Lefroy wrote: "They were everything to each other. They seemed to lead a life to themselves within the general family shared only by each other. I will not say their true, but their *full* feelings were known only to themselves. They alone fully understood what each had suffered and felt and thought."[16] These descriptions are borne out by Austen's own letters, where she tells Cassandra that she fell ill as a result of Cassandra's departure on a short trip and refers to the pleasures of dressing together, discussing everything as they dress.[17] "The Beautifull Cassandra," the humorous "novel" Austen wrote as an adolescent and dedicated to her sister, sets up Cassandra, described as "singular" and imaged as a "phoenix," as a self-sufficient independent young woman whose equanimity is upset only by another woman. Cassandra merely curtsies and walks on when she encounters a highly eligible young bachelor, and she deals summarily with an importunate coachman, but when she meets the mysterious "Maria" in Bloomsbury Square, "Cassandra started and Maria seemed surprised; they trembled, blushed, turned pale and passed each other in a mutual silence."[18] This is the only occasion when Cassandra betrays signs of emotion, and the emotion is definitely signaled as romantic in the recognizable terms of the romantic novel and poem of Austen's time.

Why is Emma attracted to Harriet?[19] Critics tend to assume that Emma is attracted to Harriet's malleability. While this is an element in the attraction, the more important element is Harriet's beauty. The first sentence that introduces Harriet into the novel clearly states that Emma had "long felt an interest in [her], on account of her beauty" (53). Emma's wish to influence Harriet, to draw on this virginal surface, has much to do with Harriet's beauty, which "happened to be of a sort which Emma particularly admired" (53). The phrasing here is a near equivalent of Harriet being Emma's "type." Emma is hardly conscious of her own looks. As Mrs. Weston remarks, she is free from personal vanity, her vanity centering on the quality of her intellect. But Emma is highly susceptible to other women's beauty. Although she dislikes Jane, when she sees her after an interval of two years, she notes all the details of her person, "her face—her features" and "her figure," "could not but feel" their "very pleasing beauty," and sits through the first visit, admiring her with "the sense of pleasure and the sense of rendering justice" (180–81).

When Mr. Elton remarks that Emma, by adding to what nature had done, has made Harriet what she is, Emma conceives the idea of taking Harriet's "likeness." Harriet says she has never sat for her picture. Beginning as an admirer, Emma soon wishes to capture and possess her own vision of feminine beauty. As she puts it, "What an exquisite possession a good picture of her would be!" (71). Austen plays on the word *likeness* in this context. Emma "takes" Harriet's "likeness" both in the sense of drawing her picture and in the sense of possessing her as her mirror image. Although Emma has scarcely ever finished a picture before, she does finish this one, which suggests its importance to her. Emma gave up drawing in disgust when her sister Isabella, blinded by admiration of her husband's looks, declared that Emma's drawing of him did not do him justice. Emma returns to drawing because her relationship to Harriet is not mediated by any man: "for Harriet's sake, or rather for my own, and as there are no husbands and wives in the case at present, I will break my resolution now" (73).

Emma deliberately "improves" Harriet's figure while drawing it, an exercise endemic to the praise-of-the-beloved genre in which her text participates. The terms in which she envisages her enterprise are close to the standard notion of the text as monument to love, found, for example, in Shakespeare's *Sonnets*. Emma declares that the picture will be "a standing memorial of the beauty of one, the skill of the other, and the friendship of both" (74). In the next chapter Emma determinedly retains the friendship by ousting Robert Martin from Harriet's affections. When Harriet finally decides against him, Emma exclaims, "Thank you, thank you, my own sweet little friend. We will not be parted" (81), and also, "I am secure of you for ever" (80). "For ever" is a long time, and Emma's apparently successful attempt to frame Harriet must fail, since no person can be so framed. The attempt is, however, inevitable—and this is often understressed by commentators. Emma is not the only one to engage in such activity—everyone in the novel, including Mr. Knightley, engages in it.[20]

Emma's declaration of her preference for the single life is often dismissed as a consequence of not knowing herself. However, it is perfectly possible to read it as a real preference that she retains as long as she hopes she will have a community of unmarried friends. It is only when, at the end of the novel, she is threatened with a repeat performance of the beginning—the loss of Mr. Knightley through marriage repeating the loss of Miss Taylor—that she realizes "Mr Knightley must marry no one but herself" (398). The negative phrasing of this famous insight is significant—not "she must marry Mr. Knightley" but, rather, Mr. Knightley must not marry anyone else. The difference is of crucial importance. Emma's ideal still remains a mutual singleness and a perpetual intimacy of friendship and flirtation. So long as she can remain first in his affections, she tells herself she will be perfectly satisfied. While this may be partly self-deception, it is also partly a desire not to lose the specialness of wooing for the routine of marriage, a desire voiced by many heroines, from Shakespeare's Rosalind to Hardy's Tess. This is one of the "impossible things" a woman may wish for but in which a man rarely concurs.

Mr. Knightley himself is just such an impossible thing, as Austen indicated, when she said that he was "far from being what I know English gentlemen often are."[21] She indicated the improbability more clearly in a letter to her niece Fanny Knight, who was uncertain whether or not she loved a young man who was wooing her. Coolly reversing the idiom in which men describe women, Austen writes, "There *are* such beings in the World perhaps, one in a Thousand, as the Creature you and I should think perfection, Where grace & Spirit are united to Worth, where the Manners are equal to the Heart & Understanding, but such a person may not come in your way."[22] Mr. Knightley, like Blake's new Jerusalem, Wordsworth's "milder day," or Shelley's imagined world in the last act of *Prometheus Unbound*, is a fantasy, not a type. He is conceived less as a mate and more as an ideal friend. The word *friend* recurs repeatedly toward the close, both in Emma's fear of being left friendless and lonely if he marries Harriet and, crucially, at the moment of the proposal, when she explicitly asks him to speak openly to her "as a friend" and he responds: "Emma, I accept your offer—Extraordinary as it may seem, I accept it, and refer myself to you as a friend" (417). Emma's offer of friendship thus linguistically displaces the expected proposal of marriage; and the wedding finally takes place among a "small band of true friends" (465). It is possible to see Mr. Knightley, at the end of the novel, as a substitute for the friend Emma lost at its start. In other words, Emma makes the kind of marriage Virginia Woolf made.

The brotherliness of the husband emphasizes that trust in the known rather than attraction to the unknown is more empowering for a woman in a heterosexual situation. It simultaneously divests the heterosexual narrative of romance in the usual sense. Many critics have noticed the sense of circumscription that the closure of *Emma* entails. I would suggest that this is related to the text's reconciling itself to the "impossible" nature of her quest for a "likeness" and the sadness consequent on this reconciliation.

Emma's mistake in valuing physical beauty over inner beauty is a mistake of potentially tragic dimensions, as in much Romantic poetry and in later developments of the theme such as *The Picture of Dorian Gray.* It is interesting that the self-reflexive critique of same-sex love undertaken by Wilde and Solomon should have been explored before them by a woman writing about a woman-woman relationship. Emma's admiration of women's beauty casts her as the romantic searcher. As "imaginist," she takes the risks that the creator takes, the risk of her vision and her creation being shattered. As Mr. Knightley remarks, Harriet "is a girl who will marry somebody or other" (90–91), so the risk taken by her only involves the relative socioeconomic advantages of the match she will finally make. Frankenstein's creature kills him, Dorian kills Basil, and Harriet has the potential to destroy Emma's life. The conflict of creator-creature, parent-child, mentor-follower, lover-beloved, contains a tragic force that comes to the surface in Emma's cry: "Oh God! that I had never seen her!" (401).

If we read *Emma* as an exercise in the making of a "likeness," a portrait by a woman of a woman's "mind delighted with its own ideas," an element in the closure acquires some importance. Unlike many Victorian novels, which end with the birth of a child to the protagonist (*Jane Eyre*), this novel ends with the birth of a child to her friend. Mrs. Weston has a daughter, which delights Emma: "If the satisfaction of her well-doing could be increased to Emma, it was by knowing her to be the mother of a little girl. She had been decided in wishing for a Miss Weston" (444). Anna Weston, named perhaps in compliment to Austen's beloved niece, provides an occasion for Emma's renewed self-assertion—to wish for a daughter is to

wish for a furtherance of the self; to wish for a friend's daughter as a furtherance of oneself suggests how closely one is bound up with that
friend.[23] The joking interpellation regarding Emma's plans for Anna's marriage with one of Isabella's sons signals Emma's untamed state and also her
wish to unite the next generation through marriage, since the older generation (Emma-Miss Taylor) were separated through marriage. The baby
is explicitly conceived as another Emma—she and Mr. Knightley discuss
how it is likely to be spoiled, since it will be brought up by the same
mother figure. Mr. Knightley, in a significant shift, now thinks that
indulging a girl child is "nothing very bad" (444) and that all his castiga-
tion of Emma did him more good (by making him love her) than it did her.

Emma's conception of a daughter as "a child never banished from
home" (444) is at odds with the social conception wherein a daughter
must marry and leave the parental home, which is inherited by the son.
This fantasy of the daughter as heir, enacted in so many of Austen's novels, is one of the "impossible things" she imagines, which Woolf, in the
next century, was to imagine in *Orlando* to compensate Vita Sackville-
West for the social reality of disinheritance.[24] The appearance of Anna
Weston, not at all required by the novel's action, serves to create a subdued but nonetheless real triangle based on female spiritual kinship—
Miss Taylor-Emma-Anna, which, to an (admittedly limited) extent, com-
pensates for the marriages that separate women friends.[25]

Emma's portrait of Harriet, which glorifies her physical beauty, is
framed by Austen's portrait of Emma herself, a portrait that valorizes the
mind and imagination. Emma is constantly described in terms of her
mind. As Michael Williams says of this novel, "Its subject is the imagination,"[26] and in figuring this imagination as female Austen writes
Romanticism differently.[27]

Austen's pen and ink portraits of her women friends also celebrate
the inner life. In a well-known letter to Fanny Knight, for instance, she
stresses the inner life as material for a portrait and as attracting love and
creating pleasure: "You can hardly think what a pleasure it is to me, to
have such thorough pictures of your Heart.—Oh! what a loss it will be
when you are married. . . . I shall hate you when your delicious play of
Mind is all settled down into conjugal & maternal affections."[28] The delicious play of mind is the subject of Austen's superb poem on Anna Lefroy,
which deftly inverts, in Donne's own idiom and rhythms, his portrait of a
woman as a land to be conquered and "by one man manned":

> In measured verse I'll now rehearse
> The charms of lovely Anna
> And first her mind is unconfined
> Like any vast savannah.
>
> Ontario's lake may fitly speak
> Her fancy's ample bound:

Its circuit may, on strict survey
Five hundred miles be found.

Her wit descends on foes and friends
Like famed Niagara's Fall,
And travellers gaze in wild amaze,
And listen, one and all.

Her judgment sound, thick, black, profound,
Like transatlantic groves,
Dispenses aid, and friendly shade
To all that in it roves.

If thus her mind to be defined
America exhausts,
And all that's grand in that great land
In similes it costs—

Oh how can I her person try
To image and portray?
How paint the face, the form how trace
In which those virtues lay?

Another world must be unfurled,
Another language known,
Ere tongue or sound can publish round
Her charms of flesh and bone.[29]

In contrast to the conventions of heterosexual poetry, where a woman is generally praised through comparisons to tender and delicate natural objects, this poem empowers its subject by drawing on huge, powerful, and active natural forces that strike observers with awe. Whereas for Donne's lover-speaker America and the woman are equally passive objects, Austen's observers passively gaze and listen, while the beloved is in movement through active verbs ("descends," "dispenses"). The poet-lover-speaker participates in the awe of the other observers insofar as she acknowledges her inability to "portray" the beloved in language. This awe does not result in the pain and humiliation endemic to the Petrarchan tradition. The poem's playfulness and bounding rhythm suggest the speaker's rejoicing in the power of the beloved. The rhyming of "mind" with "unconfined" creates a liberatory effect similar to that in Blake's encomium of love as a force that is "Lawless, wing'd, & unconfin'd, / And breaks all chains from every mind" (175).

The word "charms" in the first line is wittily reconstructed through its unusual application to mental abilities. The poem projects its subject's attractiveness as consisting of her intelligence; this redefinition is also one of Austen's most important contributions to the English novel. However, the poem also eulogizes its subject's physical attractions via rhetorical questions, a mode employed by Katharine Bradley's love poems to Edith Cooper, which I shall examine later in this chapter. The strategy of simultaneous playful wit and serious intention employed throughout the poem is perhaps at its most effective in the last stanza. The desire for "another world" and "another language" gestures towards Austen's experimental and innovative "picture-making" as an exercise between women; the phrase "flesh and bone" toughens the idea of the subject's beauty by complementing its fleshliness with its structural solidity (contrast Donne's woman who is all fleshy curves) and also, by its awareness of the skull beneath the skin, subordinates physical to intellectual charms.

A poem in a very different tone, "To the Memory of Mrs Lefroy, who died December 16, my Birthday, written 1808" (when Austen was twenty-eight years old), is similar in its project. It figures its subject as "past my power to praise" and, via an interesting move, empowers this unknown young woman by placing her with two powerful men, whose power was enhanced after their death—Dr. Johnson, and, through the Shakespearean allusion in the line "We ne'er may look upon thy like again," Hamlet's father. The speaker calls upon fancy to recreate the dead woman: "Let me behold her as she used to be." After a series of encomiums on her "looks of eager Love, her accents sweet," her voice and face "almost divine," her heart, mind, eloquence, and spiritual energy, the speaker asserts that the crowning touch in all this perfection was Anne Lefroy's particular love for her: "Her partial favour from my earliest years / Consummates all.—Ah! Give me yet to see / Her smile of Love.—the Vision disappears" The image of the dream that vanishes recalls Milton's famous sonnet to his dead wife, and the word "consummates" is picked up in the word "union" in the last stanza, when the poet expresses her desire to read the accident of Anne's death on her birthday as expressive of a special connection between them. The imperatives in the last line ("Indulge" and "spare"), with the stark separateness of the last two words and the concluding dash, return the poem to the first line's tone of pain barely held in control, a tone that surfaces occasionally and therefore more powerfully in a poem otherwise cast in conventional neoclassical elegiac rhetoric:

> Fain would I feel an union in thy fate,
> Fain would I seek to draw an Omen fair
> From this connection in our Earthly date.
> Indulge the harmless weakness—Reason, spare.—[30]

In Austen's texts relationships of likeness are less than perfect because separation, through marriage or death, inhibits them. But Austen's contemporaries, the Ladies of Llangollen, succeeded in constructing a public myth of themselves as perfect likenesses of one another and their togetherness as a perfect likeness of various literary ancestors. They were assisted in this enterprise by their friends, especially their women friends. "Perfection" was often attributed to the Ladies' way of life by their contemporaries, and so long-lasting was this view of them that, a century later, when Virginia Woolf considered writing a novel about them, she read their journal and then wrote to Ethel Smyth: "No, I can't 'do' the Ladies. They've done themselves too perfectly for anything to be written."[31]

The story of the Ladies' fifty years lived together at Llangollen, Wales, has been told not only in their journal but many times thereafter. But the story of the battle they waged to achieve that life does not constitute part of the journal. When they eloped together in 1778, Eleanor Butler was about thirty-nine and Sarah Ponsonby about twenty-three. These two Irishwomen, one Catholic, the other Protestant, belonged to aristocratic families who virtually disowned them for their scandalous behavior. Their first attempt to elope was thwarted and rumours were rife that a man or men were involved. The widespread credence that the Ladies' story later achieved was the result of their determined enactment and narration of it, in which they were assisted by several women.

Primary among these women was Mary Carryl, a servant who aided and abetted the romance and the elopement. As soon as they were settled at Llangollen, the Ladies sent for her and she lived with them until her death in 1809. She was buried in the tomb where the Ladies themselves were buried later. The poem inscribed for her on this tomb ends with the lines:

> Attachment (sacred bond of grateful breasts)
> Extinguished but with life, this Tomb attests,
> Reared by two friends who will her loss bemoan,
> Till with her ashes here shall rest their own.[32]

Normally, members of a biological family lay buried together in a common tomb. By appropriating this custom, these Irishwomen indicated that they constituted an alternative kind of family. The dream of such alternatives haunted many people of their generation, including Coleridge and Southey with their scheme of Pantisocracy. This was one reason why the Ladies' way of life was so widely admired. It recalled to many apparently conventional members of society the long-abandoned dreams of their youth. The Ladies paid a price to accomplish this dream. They never returned to Ireland. Eleanor Butler had next to no contact with her family and suffered substantial financial loss by this break. In 1784, recording in her journal how she was cheated by her brother's heirs, she counters this disinheritance with her own intention to endow Sarah and protect her against the possibility of future impoverishment:

> Informed the Talbots of the measures I mean to pursue. . . . They agree in thinking I have been barbarously Cheated. I also acquainted them with my having

sign'd sealed and delivered My Last Will and Testament That I might Secure all
I am possess'd or Entitled to to the Beloved of My heart—They will See Justice
done her when I am no more.[33]

As the language here indicates, the Ladies constructed themselves
as married. In their society, and in the texts of the times, marriage signified the closest bond possible. In novels of the time, once a couple marries their sex life is not discussed. Its only signifier is the shared bedroom
and the appearance of children. The Ladies prided themselves on never
spending a night away from their cottage, and they always shared a bed.
They also presented their home as a household, their pets as near children, and their intellectual pursuits as a choice deliberately exercised, not
a pastime. In this construction they drew on literary and religious models
and tropes to set up an ancestry for themselves.

One trope they used, and which many who knew them also began
to use, was that of Eden.[34] It appears in the title page inscription of the
journal that Eleanor Butler began in January 1788:

JOURNAL
of E.B. and S.P.
Inhabitants of a cottage in the
Vale of Llangollen, N. Wales.
Written by
E.B.

Society is all but rude
To this delicious solitude
Where all the flowers and trees do close
To weave the Garland of repose.

M.DCC.LXXXVIII.[35]

Marvell's poem is quoted here with a significant shift. Marvell's nostalgic
yearning for the garden of Eden may be read as an antiheterosexual move;
however, this move wishes the woman away: "Where first man walked
without a mate." The solitude it imagines is unitary. Eleanor Butler quotes
four lines in a context that wishes the man away and creates a female dual
solitude, an Eve and Lilith situation. She thus rewrites the most famous
English representation of Eden—Milton's unequal conjugality. The image
is picked up by their friend, the poet Anna Seward, herself disappointed
in an intense love relationship with a woman.[36] She refers to their home
at Plas Newydd as "little Eden" and "little Elysium" and repeatedly also to
the Ladies as Rosalind and Celia, thus conferring on them a second,
Shakespearean, ancestry.[37]

As You Like It, a play much studied by recent gay studies theorists,
has an interesting history in the nineteenth century. A performance of
the play is crucial to the unraveling of bisexual relationships in Gautier's

Mademoiselle de Maupin and also in *The Picture of Dorian Gray*. In these performances, as in most recent studies of the play, the interest arises from
the piquant androgyny of the girl dressed as a boy. Anna Seward, on the
other hand, is not interested in Rosalind's Ganymede persona but in the
Rosalind-Celia relationship, which is not based on disguise. While disguise occasions such mistaken loves as Olivia's for Viola and Phebe's for
Rosalind, Rosalind and Celia love one another as women. They assume
disguise and elope in order to preserve this love. Celia gives up her allegiance to her father and her prospects of marriage and inheritance, solely
for love of Rosalind. They buy a house together in the Forest of Arden.
Their life together there is not presented onstage but is figured in terms
of idyllic privacy.[38] For these reasons Anna Seward sees them as prefig-
uring the Ladies. In her reconstruction, Llangollen Valley is "the
Cambrian Arden," Mary Carryl is "Orlando's Adam," and the Ladies
themselves the "Rosalind and Celia of this lovelier Arden."[39] The
Miltonic Eden of unequal likeness is replaced by a Shakespearean ardent
Eden that is rewritten as "lovelier" because it is not destroyed by heterosexual closure.

A third kind of ancestry is that of the convent. Although Eleanor
Butler had explicitly refused to enter a convent and had fled from that
pressure, she retained connections with her Catholicism. One of her
cousins was a Carmelite nun at St. Denys. The mother superior was a sister of Louis XV. Sarah sent her some embellished mottoes and received an
invitation to the convent, with permission to see and converse with the
nuns. Sarah noted that this was "a favour seldom granted to any Protestant
(My Beloved would be admitted of Course) as strangers are never allowed
to see them but through the Grate."[40] In their walks in the Llangollen valley they discovered traces of Protestant iconoclasm in the ruined abbey
of Vale Crucis: "In the Church Yard—had the Rubbish removed and there
discovered the Mutilated Statue of Saint Cuthlin of which we had already
some fragments."[41] The Ladies linked themselves with this past by making a drinking fountain here from an old font and other stones they had
found. It was inscribed with a poem that addressed the reader as a "gentle
pilgrim," described the "holy font" blessed by "holy men" and "o'erthrown"
in "Vale Crucis' shadows," and concluded, "Pray for the souls of those who
gave / This font that holds the limpid wave E.B. S.P. 1782."[42]

Tombstones and inscriptions on such objects as fountains, arches,
benches were ways in which families and poets inscribed themselves on
the landscape, thereby writing its history and attempting to speak to
posterity. Such inscriptions form a considerable part of the output of
most poets of the time, for instance, Wordsworth, Coleridge, and
Southey wrote many place poems, connected with specific bowers,
walks, trees. By undertaking this poetic enterprise together, the Ladies
participated in making an enduring monument to their love and their
unusual life together.

Their journal, modeled, like so many women's journals of this time, on the literary example of the journal of Richardson's Clarissa, is remarkable for its persistent use of the trope of married love. They habitually refer to each other as "My Beloved" (or, more succinctly, "my B."), "the darling of my heart," "my Love," "the delight of my heart," "the joy of my life."[43] Their women friends concurred in this construction of their love as marriage. For instance, Sarah Tighe concludes a letter to Sarah Ponsonby on October 9, 1798: "Give my love to your better half and believe me ever your affectionate S.T."[44] Sarah Ponsonby herself used the same phrase to refer to Eleanor: "My Better Half contented herself with opening the Box."[45] In a very telling Shakespearean allusion, in a letter to Mrs. Tighe, Sarah reports that Mrs. Goddard had heard and believed a rumor that Sarah was going to marry a man. Sarah writes: "But I am more tormented by Mrs G's having a momentary doubt of its truth than at the report. I have reproached her for her folly and told her in the words of Mrs Ford in the Merry Wives of Windsor—'what—have I 'scaped such reports in the holy day time of my beauty and am *now* fit subject for them!'- If you hear it—I need not bid You do me justice."[46] In the speech that Sarah quotes, Mrs. Ford is protesting against a report that she is having an extramarital affair. Sarah feels equally outraged at the idea that she could abandon Eleanor to marry a man and speaks with the indignation of a respectably married woman!

The Ladies were enraged when a newspaper published an article constructing Eleanor as the masculine and Sarah as the feminine partner in the marriage and they appealed to Edmund Burke, who had earlier visited their home, to arrange legal action against the publisher. He responded sympathetically, saying that although legal action might be difficult they ought to "despise . . . the violence of calumny" and to remember that they suffered it "along with everything that is excellent in the world."[47] Yet, in their correspondence with their friend, Harriet Bowdler, they seem to have enjoyed playing with the idea of Eleanor's masculine persona. Harriet carried on an elaborate flirtation with Eleanor, whom she named "Viellard" and referred to by the masculine pronoun. For instance, in a letter to Sarah of September 6, 1794, "I dare say my profligate Viellard is gone off with some new favourite, and I must as usual wait patiently 'till he is pleased to return."[48] This kind of coded game (comparable to some gay men's use of female names and pronouns for one another) appears also in the private life and writings of Michael Field, which I shall examine later in this chapter. The Ladies deliberately adopted a dress that was similar to men's dress. In the actor Charles Mathews's description:

> As they are seated, there is not one point to distinguish them from men: the dressing and powdering of the hair, their well-starched neckcloths; the upper part of their habits, which they always wear, even at a dinner-party, made precisely like men's coats; and regular black beaver men's hats. They looked exactly like two respectable superannuated old clergymen."[49]

Another common motif in the lives of the Ladies and in those of lesbians in the earlier twentieth century is the centrality of animals, who are referred to as members of the household. Although this focus on pets is part of a general trend in England from the mid-eighteenth century onward, it has a special weight of tenderness in the Ladies' writings. Not only their dogs (Sapho, Phillis, Flirt, Rover, Bess, and Gypsey) and cats but even their cows and hens are constructed as tender and affectionate companions, who are to be protected against violence.[50] Most of these animals are female and form part of a female community. For instance, searching for their "poor, faithful hen" on a winter's day in 1788, the agitated Ladies are assaulted by a bull dog and get into an altercation with its master, a weaver, who supports the dog against them. They proceed, fearing that their hen has been killed by a fitchet: "I daresay she thought of, perhaps called on us, but we Alas! heard her not." The next day the headless corpse of the hen is discovered. "The poor woman" from whom they had got the hen comes to condole with them and brings a present of another hen. The Ladies, who describe themselves as acting in a "determined" manner against the "defiant" weaver, are deeply touched by the woman's "kindness," especially since the new hen is "a daughter" of the old one. However, they remain faithful to the memory of the dead hen and declare: "We were grateful for the Intention, sent the Hen to the fowl-yard, but did not nor ever shall behold her as the successor of one who has left no Equal."[51]

Another trope woven into the Ladies' construction of their love is that of the teacher-student relationship. Reading aloud to each other, a common family activity at this time, is inflected by the pleasure of teaching and learning: "Read *Betula Liberata* to my beloved. Explained all the difficult Passages—how delightful to teach her."[52] It is accompanied by images of nurturance. One example from many such journal entries:

> My head which has ached more or less these three weeks grew very bad and My beloved ever Anxious—ever tender Made me take a Mustard Emetic, which Effectually removed my complaint, how could it fail when administered by her. I grew perfectly well and then My beloved and I sat by the Excellent Dressing room fire.[53]

The romantic tone and gesture persist to the end of their lives. Thus, on Christmas day 1819, Eleanor, eighty years old, records, "Beautiful French perfumes from Nightingale Shrewsbury—the gift of my Beloved."[54] In 1824 Wordsworth visited them, and composed the sonnet terming Llangollen "the Vale of Friendship" and celebrating their life: "Sisters in love, a love allowed to climb / Even on this earth, above the reach of Time!"[55] The implicit image here is that of Eden or paradise on earth. Since their lives were rapidly drawing to a close, the sonnet's last line appears to recognize them as a monument, a model of love and friendship. It draws on a long tradition of poetry that celebrates the immortality of a loving couple, for example, poems like Shakespeare's "The Phoenix and Turtle."

Lillian Faderman cites a poem by Sarah Ponsonby to suggest that she distinguished "between sexual love and romantic friendship and identified her own feelings with the latter":

> By Vulgar Eros long misled
> I call'd thee Tyrant, mighty Love!
> With idle fear my fancy fled
> Nor ev'n thy pleasures wish'd to prove.
>
> Condemn'd at length to wear thy chains,
> Trembling I felt and ow'd thy might;
> But soon I found my fears were vain,
> Soon hugged my chain, and thought it light.[56]

I read this poem as evidence of a continuing debate between heterosexual and same-sex erotic love, in which the speaker opts for the latter. She says she feared Love because she was "misled" into thinking that Love was synonymous with Vulgar Eros. The significance of the poem revolves around the connotations of the term *Vulgar Eros*.

John Boswell points out that in Plato's *Symposium* "heterosexual relationships and feelings are characterised as 'vulgar' and their same-sex equivalents as 'heavenly.' "[57] He adds that the Greek word translated as "vulgar" might also be translated as "general."

The *Greek-English Dictionary* "cites this very discussion as the locus for the meaning 'vulgar' " and this "contrast exercised wide influence on subsequent discussions of love."[58] The nineteenth-century terms *Uranian* and *Urning* were derived from the Greek word for "heavenly."[59] *Vulgar* also commonly refers to what is popular and practiced by most people. In the anonymous poem "Don Leon" (1866) the speaker, in the person of Lord Byron, passionately defends homosexual love and says that "the vulgar" extol his song but wage war on his actions, so "I hate the vulgar, and I keep them off."[60] I would therefore read Sarah Ponsonby's poem as saying that she was "misled" by Vulgar Eros into believing that this popular form of Eros was its only form but that she later realized there was another form: heavenly Eros.

The imagery of heaven, Eden, and angels, frequently associated with same-sex love in the nineteenth century, need not indicate the absence of erotic and sexual practice. Its practitioners had this on the best authority—that of Milton's Gabriel. When asked by unfallen Adam. whether angels enjoy erotic love in heaven where there is neither marrying nor giving in marriage, Gabriel, blushing "rosy-red, love's proper hue" (8:619), replies that heavenly spirits enjoy it far more than human beings because they experience total fusion—a claim often made by same-sex lovers on the basis of their greater "likeness" to one another than is the case with heterosexual lovers. That Gabriel refers to homoerotic love is confirmed, perhaps inadvertently, by Milton, when Adam, after the fall, laments that god created women instead of filling the world with men like "angels without feminine" (10:893), so that earth, like heaven, would have been peopled with "Spirits masculine" (890).

If nineteenth-century English literary history is framed by two sets of lovers—the Ladies of Llangollen, who became a literary and romantic monument toward the beginning of the century, and "Michael Field," who represented to the literary world a similar phenomenon toward the century's close, it is significant that the former, living in the heyday of Romanticism, were far more acclaimed than the latter.[61] When Field's first play, *Callirhoe*, appeared in 1884, it was enthusiastically received and its author compared to Shakespeare by more than one reviewer. The enthusiasm changed to a much more mixed response, and even to hostility, when Field was discovered to be two women writing jointly under a pseudonym. One of the women was Katherine Harris Bradley, the other her sister Emma's daughter, Edith Emma Cooper. Katherine Bradley pointed out to Robert Browning, in a letter expressing distress at his having revealed their secret to the press, that the male pseudonym was necessary for them to be able to write freely in a social setup that simultaneously idealized and despised women:

> The report of lady authorship will dwarf and enfeeble our work at every turn. Like the poet Gray we shall never "speak out." And we have many things to say that the world will not tolerate from a woman's lips. . . . we cannot be stifled in drawing-room conventions. . . . you are robbing us of real criticism, such as man gives man. The Gods learn little from the stupid words addressed to them at their shrines: they disguise; meet mortals unsuspecting in the marketplace and enjoy wholesome intercourse.[62]

The mention of the gods is not wholly ironical. Both women had a strong sense of entitlement as poets. They placed themselves squarely in a tradition that extended from the Greek playwrights and lyricists through the medieval balladeers, the Renaissance dramatists and poets, especially Shakespeare, and the Romantics to the Aestheticists.[63] Their writings repeatedly invoke this ancestry. For instance, toward the end of their lives, when a former chairboy of theirs innocently praised them as "learned, clever ladies" who "write Shakespeare and that sort of thing," they laughed but recalled that "it was Robert Browning and not a clerk who apprehended and maintained we 'wrote Shakespeare.' "[64]

An Elizabethan model was available even for their collaboration. In her letter revealing the secret of Michael Field's identity to Browning, Edith wrote: "My Aunt and I work together after the fashion of Beaumont and Fletcher. She is my senior, by but fifteen years. She has lived with me, taught me, encouraged me and joined me to her poetic life."[65] Browning responded with sensitivity to the diffident defiance of that "but": "I . . . am very unnecessarily apprised that difference in age between such relatives need not be considerable. I think the most beautiful woman I ever saw was two years older than myself, and for all that my very Aunt."[66]

The male pseudonym was, however, not just a ruse to forestall male bias. It was also, like the age difference, part of the erotic charge between the two women. They continued to write under this name long after their identity was well-known and used it in private interaction too. Katherine was called "Michael" by Edith and by all their close friends; Edith was called Henry or Hennie, from Heinrich, a name given her by a German nurse who fell passionately in love with her while nursing her through scarlet fever. The name was a reference to Edith's boyish appearance when her hair was cut during this illness. Katherine noted: "She looks very pretty in her short boy's hair and fresh cotton jacket."[67] Katherine also had many other petnames for Edith, the most used ones being Puss, Persian (from Persian cat), Pussie. In her journal entries Edith generally refers to Katherine (in Ladies of Llangollen fashion) as "My Love," or "My own Love," or "Sim," a pet name. Both also occasionally use the masculine pronoun ("he," "him") for each other in the journal. Gordon Bottomley reports the way they picked up and reworked a phrase of male comradeship:

> Either of them would refer to the other in her absence as "My dear fellow": the slight change in the incidence and significance of the phrase turned the most stale of ordinary exclamations into something which suddenly seemed valuable and full of delicate, new, moving music. It seemed said for the first time.[68]

The name Michael Field provided them with the kind of oneness bestowed by a married surname. Thus, friends like Charles Ricketts and William Rothenstein, as well as most commentators, often refer to them as a unit—the Michael Fields, the Michaels, the Fields, Michael (Katherine) and Field (Edith), or, simply, Michael Field. They seem to have reveled in this public announcement of oneness. They had the initials *M.F.* emblazoned on their luggage and used metaphors drawn from marriage to describe their love. In her comparison of themselves to Robert and Elizabeth Browning, Katherine declares that they have outdone this most famous of all Victorian heterosexual romances: "Oh! love. I give thanks for my Persian: those two poets, man and wife, wrote alone; each wrote, but did not bless or quicken one another at their work; *we are closer married*" (emphasis in the original).[69] The word "quicken" introduces the idea of the text as child, *quicken* being the biblical word for the conception of a child. This idea appears clearly in her poem "A Girl," which celebrates Edith's beauty and ends, "our souls so knit, / I leave a page half-writ— / The work begun / Will be to heaven's conception done / If she come to it,"[70] and also in "Unbosoming," which concludes, "And I would give thee, after my kind, / The final issues of heart and mind."[71] The phrase "after my kind" distinguishes their love from the more conventional kind of love and the emotional and intellectual "issues" from the physical "issues." In an 1886 letter to Havelock Ellis protesting against any attempt to dissect their writings and discover who played what part in the collaboration, Katherine used biblical phrasing to figure their union as marriage: "As to our work, let no man think he can put asunder what God has joined."[72] Playing on the word *field* while criticizing the cold pragmatism of the Havelock Ellis wedding, Edith wrote: "This is a true account of the modern sacrament of Matrimony. It is revolting. 'Free love, free field,' is sacreder."[73]

The poets saw themselves as married by nature and celebrated the event in an early poem, which uses the floral imagery common in lesbian writing; the "moist quiet" of the "tender, marshy nook" studded with cowslips may be read as vulval:

Cowslip-Gathering

Twain cannot mingle: we went hand in hand,
Yearning, divided, through the fair spring land,
Nor knew, twin maiden spirits, there must be
In all true marriage perfect trinity.
But lo! dear Nature spied us, in a copse
Filling with chirps of song and hazel-drops,
And smiled: "These children I will straight espouse,
While the blue cuckoo thrills the alder-boughs."
So led us to a tender, marshy nook
Of meadow-verdure, where by twos and threes
The cowslips grew, down-nodding toward a brook;
And left us there to pluck them at our ease
In the moist quiet, till the rich content
Of the bee humming in the cherry tree
Filled us; in one our very being blent.[74]

It is significant that the wedding is accomplished by Nature functioning as presiding goddess and the "true trinity" is thus all-female. Different sorts of trinities and triangles, including that of the two poets and the reader, were to reappear in the poets' writings all their lives. Its centrality to their thinking is evident in their having written what they called "trialogues." Several homoerotically inclined male writers in late nineteenth-century and early twentieth-century England, among them Fitzgerald and Goldsworthy Lowes Dickinson, wrote Platonic dialogues that touched on questions of same-sex love. Michael Field's trialogues are a cross between a play and a dialogue. Their *Stephania: A Trialogue* (1892) deals fairly openly with love between men.

Their writings show a lifelong search for tropes and models of same-sex union. Apart from the trope of marriage, they also use philosophical conceptions of union: Thus, Katherine writes: "Spinoza with his fine grasp of unity says: 'If two individuals of exactly the same nature are joined together, they make up a single individual, doubly stronger than each alone,' i.e., Edith and I make a *veritable Michael*."[75] While the emphasis here falls on the strength of sameness, many other models they use fruitfully develop ideas of difference in union. One of these is that of the older lover and the younger beloved.

Revisiting Cambridge, Katherine wrote: "Sixteen years ago I came to Newnham empty-headed, with vague ambition, vague sentiment . . . I return a poet and possessing a Poet. I look forth on the stars and kneel down and give God thanks."[76] The image of possession appears in many poems, which move easily between the idea of companionate marriage and that of magnetic attraction between a younger childlike beloved and an older nurturing lover. The love poems seem mostly written by Katherine and accepted by Edith in the tradition of the older lover praising the young beloved's beauty. The poems consciously invoke this tradition. For example, "Love's Sour Leisure" reworks the convention of the blazon. Much like Jane Austen's poem to Anna Lefroy, it intellectualizes the physical features, physicalizes the intellectual, and ends with a forthright declaration of the desire to possess the beloved:

> As a poem in my mind
> Thy sweet lineaments are shrined:
> . . .
> But the temple's veined mound
> Is the Muse's sacred ground;
> . . .
> But the mouth! that land to own
> Long did Aphrodite moan,
> Ere the virgin goddess grave
> From the temptress of the wave
> That most noble clime did win;
> Who, retreating to the chin,
> Took her boy's bow for a line,
> The sweet boundary to define,
> And about the beauteous bays
> Still in orbed queenship plays.
> I have all the charact'ry
> Of thy features, yet lack thee;
> And by couplets to confess
> What I wholly would possess
> Doth but whet the appetite
> Of my too long-famished sight:
> Vainly if my eyes entreat,
> Tears will be their daily meat.[77]

Virginity is a necessary condition here for the beloved to become available to the female lover's "possession" and "appetite."[78] Aphrodite is not banished—she shares the territory with Artemis. The word *possession* occurs too in the poem "Vale!": "The withering senses shudder as they lose / Their warm possession; . . . / And if, but from my side, she disappears, / There follows her a piercing *vale* shout / From lips, from eyes, ah most of all from ears / That starve and hope; nor time, nor narrow space / Can give ease to the senses left without / The appeal, the dear temptations of her face."[79]

The extreme pain of separation is a recurrent theme, and the pleasure of union is figured in images inflected with eroticism, as in "Unbosoming," where the speaker's love is compared to an iris, "brimful of seeds" that "push, and riot, and squeeze, and clip, / Till they burst the sides of the silver scrip." An untitled poem ends, "From thee untwined / I shall but wander a disbodied sprite, / Until thou wake me / With thy kiss-warmed breath, and take me / Where we are one."[80] These early poems address the beloved as "Dear," "my love," and "sweetheart," for instance:

> . . . I dare not let thee leave me, sweet,
> Lest it should be for ever;
> Tears dew my kisses ere we meet,
> Foreboding we must sever:
> Since we can neither meet nor part,
> Methinks the moral is, sweetheart,
> That we must dwell together.[81]

A poem that relates how Zeus invented youth and age celebrates their age difference:

> . . . . Had our lives been twinned, forsooth,
> We had never had one heart:
> By time set a space apart,
> We are bound by such close ties
> How sovereignly I'm blest
> To see and smell the rose of my own youth
> In thee.[82]

"An Invitation" eroticizes their intellectual pursuits and invokes a literary ancestry culminating in two writers of homoerotic verse, Catullus and Sappho:

> Come and sing, my room is south;
> Come with thy sun-governed mouth,
> Thou wilt never suffer drouth,
> Long as dwelling
> In my chamber of the south.
>
> . . .
>
> There are myrtles in a row;
> Lady, when the flower's in blow,

Kisses passing to and fro,
From our smelling,
Think, what lovely dreams will grow!

There's a lavender settee,
Cushioned for my love and me;
Ah, what secrets there will be
For love-telling,
When her head leans on my knee!

Books I have of long ago
And today; I shall not know
Some, unless thou read them, so
Their excelling
Music needs thy voice's flow:

Campion, with a noble ring
Of choice spirits, count this wing
Sacred! all the songs I sing
Welling, welling
From Elizabethan spring.

. . .

All the Latins *thou* dost prize!
Cynthia's lover by thee lies,
Note Catullus, type and size
Least repelling
To thy weariable eyes.

And for Greek! Too sluggishly
Thou dost toil; but Sappho, see!
And the dear Anthology
For thy spelling.
Come, it shall be well with thee.[83]

The poems are richly sensuous: images of flowing water, of flowers, of consumption, especially drinking, are recurrent. Edith's mouth, in connection with kisses, figures frequently, for instance, in "A Girl": "A mouth, the lips apart, / Like aspen-leaflets trembling in the breeze / From her tempestuous heart." In contrast to Sarah Ponsonby, who prayed to outlive the older Eleanor, Katherine, figuring herself as nurturer and conceiving the pain of outliving the beloved as greater than the pain of dying, wishes that the younger Edith may die first:

. . . My God, I pray she may die the first,
That I may not leave her!
. . .
Thou must never grow lonesome or old,

Leave me rather to darkness and cold,
O my Life, my Singing![84]

As illustrated in this poem, Field's writing of love combines erotic emotion with tender, nurturant, parental emotion. The blend appears in the journal when the two were in Germany. Edith fell ill, and they were terrified that the hospital authorities would separate them. Edith writes: "I am shut with my beloved in a coach. . . . We clasp each other with an awful weight of anxiety on our hearts, for they may strive to part us and we have no German with which to plead. We make a vow, which neither speaks, that nothing but death shall sever us."[85] Katherine is spouse but also devoted friend and parent. She writes: "How I fought for my young, with how many tongues, with what agony."[86] Earlier, when she rushed into a group of German soldiers and appropriated their food for the hungry Edith, the latter wrote:

> The little German soldiers wonder naturally of what kind this new Orlando comes, who darts on their feast and insists ragingly that necessity must be served. . . . The new Orlando . . . brings the food like a doe to its fawn, unconscious of the regiment's laughter, or of the appearance made by unfastened hair, excited eyes, and the bread, borne along in triumph.[87]

The writers here have a multiplicity of sources to draw on and to put together in new combinations—the model of male friendship as nurturing, even maternal, from *As You Like It*, the implicit model of the Virgin as mystic bride and mother, and, in the reference to wedding vows, the model of the married couple. In each case the model is constructed afresh and changed by its application to these two women in their particular relationship to one another.

Wild Honey from Various Thyme (1908) contains some of Michael Field's most mature poetry. In this collection there develops a triangle between Edith, a person, probably a man, she is attracted to, and Katherine who continues persistently to woo Edith. Mary Sturgeon (who considers Edith the better poet, an estimate with which I do not agree) sees Edith as having "renounced her lover for her fellow."[88] Since Katherine and Edith constantly refer to one another as "lover," it is rather a case of Edith choosing the female lover over the male.[89]

In the first section of the collection Edith expresses her feelings—"I love him"—as well as the intensity of the conflict she undergoes. Here occur some of the very few poems that celebrate male beauty and attractiveness. The male beloved is compared to Pan, to ambergris, and to a camel feeding on myrrh trees. In "Cherry Song" she dreams that she ate cherries with an ungendered lover in a valley. The language is erotic—the fruit is red with sweet juice. She insists, "Our love hath never made presumptuous sally," and that the cherry eating occurred only in a sleep dream.[90] Her language equates the two kinds of emotion, terming them both love, for instance, in "Armour" she represents herself as equipped by

Love for contest and forced to contend with Love itself. "Love: A Lover" begins, "To Love I fled from love / That had so madly charmed me" (29). "Green Lizard Sonnet" marvels at the "transformations" love has given and pleads, "Yet, as thou art a god, interpret wide!" (19).

The sonnet "Sweet-Basil" draws on and reverses Keats's *Isabella*. The man is represented as no more himself but "a symbol" and she wishes that he should leave her and become a memory: "Like that Sweet-Basil of the buried head, / A thing that I might brood and dote upon!" (20). "To the Winter Aphrodite" invokes the goddess—"By Sappho's words hid of thee in a tomb / Pondered of thee where no man passeth by"—and asks her to make of the speaker's heart love's own room (23). The reference to Sappho and the exclusion of men ("no man") suggests an appeal for the protection of her love for Katherine even in a time when it is in abeyance, as if buried in snow but still powerful, like the long-obscured significance of Sappho's poems. The sonnet "Age" argues that old things are more beautiful than young. "Embalmment" tells the lover to keep her like a mummy—"As the Asmonean queen perpetually / Embalmed in honey, cold to thy delight, / Cold to thy touch, a sleeping eremite / Beside thee never sleeping I would be" (26)—and never to reveal the secret of their love.

The meaning of some of these poems is uncertain, since it depends on who is speaking to whom. For instance, "Forever" is a meditation on how love changes when intensity gives way to maturity, the emotional resistance to such change, and the reconciliation to it. "From Baudelaire," with its imagery of "our two spirits in their double shining" and the night "of mystic blue, of rose" spent in a room full of divans, great couches, and "strange blooms" (39), would seem to be about lesbian love. But, given the overall context of Michael Field's work, it is possible that the "strange bloom" is heterosexual love, and the poem ends with a farewell and parting. The untitled poem beginning "I love you with my life" seems to be written in Katherine's style and makes her kind of absolute commitment: "I give you as a ring / The cycle of my days till death . . . / And God may dwell behind, but not above you" (71). This poem is followed immediately by "Chalices," which makes the only direct reference to the third person's also having another tie: "Those twain, each dearer than our liberty, / Of whom Love breaking on us found us fast beloved" (74). Given the abundance of imagery in these poems that is normally considered homoerotic (cherries, violets, lilies, pansies, a shell in the seas, the image of double lights reflected in double mirrors in the poem from Baudelaire), it is possible that the man is attached to another man or even that Edith is in love with another woman figured as a man, much as Katherine was "Michael" and often "he" or "him" in the journal.

In a later section, "Mane et Vespere," the tone becomes much happier, and "Renewal" uses the image of the phoenix (often used in homoerotic contexts to suggest creation that is not reproduction and yet crosses generations) to indicate a new phase of life born from an old: "And I trust myself, as from the grave I may / To the enchanting miracles of change" (120). It would seem that the other lover dies, at least metaphorically or even literally, for "Being Free" begins, "Beloved, I shall speak of thee no more: / It is thy freedom now that thou art dead," and concludes with the idea that the love they dared not trust to speech, may be tasted, "Death standing by" (23). The next section, "The Longer Allegiance," is a series of elegies for Edith's father, who died while climbing in the Alps. Katherine and Edith went together to look for his body. The poems are written by them as joint mourners; they record their anxiety until the body is found and imagine his pain when lost in the forest. This section acts as an interval and brings the poets together for the last section, which celebrates their love.

The last section, "What of This Love?" is essentially a long hymn from Katherine to Edith. All her favorite motifs—the obsession with Edith's profile, the images of gems and flowers, the impossibility of parting, occur in a highly developed form. The image of the pearl had occurred in the early poem "A Girl" ("her soul a deep-wave pearl"). It appears in the epigraph to this section, as an image of their love: "What of this love? Where doth it dwell? / Concentrate and yet harbouring, / Precious against a precious thing—A Pearl within her shell" (165). A whole series of poems celebrates Edith's beauty and particular features of her appearance. "Old Ivories" is about her face, and so is "Her Profile," which compares it to "a dusky pearl" and asks the unanswerable question, "What lips in all the world part as hers part?" (178). "Nightfall" describes her looking up at the evening sky: "The eyes I love lift to the upper pane" (171). "Background" rejoices in Edith's recovering from sickness and "her wonderful, most clear / Clear eyes" (177). "Her Hair" asks the god of the wind, who brushes her "wayward hair" from her temples like the tide from "the silver-golden sands," whether he finds her beautiful and wonders, "And shall I find / The fragrance of a kiss on her lulled eyes, O wind!" (172). A poem written after Edith's death remembers her voice in intimate detail: "The little happenings to thy voice, the drop, / As when the warblings of the linnets stop, / While tiny sounds from twig to twig still hop."[91]

Some of the poems in this section of *Wild Honey* are clearly erotic:

Sweet-Briar in Rose

So sweet, all sweet—the body as the shyer
Sweet senses, and the Spirit sweet as those:
For me the fragrance of a whole sweet-briar
Beside the rose!   (174)

"Festa" uses images of sucking honey and breathing in perfume:

A feast that has no wine! O joy intense,
Clear ecstasy in one white river-room!

> To-night my Love is with me in the bloom
> Of roses—laughing at their redolence:
>
> . . .
>
> Of the wonder that I have of thee, my bride,
> My feast . . .   (176)

This set of poems ends with "A Palimpsest," where shared private memories constitute the safety of a relationship not fully understood by their contemporaries, but committed to future readers:

> The rest
> Of our life must be a palimpsest—
> The old writing written there the best
>
> . . .
>
> Let us write it over,
> O my lover,
> For the far Time to discover,
> As 'mid secret feathers of a dove,
> As 'mid moonbeams shifted through a cloud!   (180)

A few days before her death, Edith read aloud Katherine's love poems to her to their cousin and intimate friend Francis Brookes. She records in the journal that it was only to him she could read what was so "thrilling and sacred to my heart." The poems she mentions are from *Wild Honey*: "The Dear Temptations of Her Face," "Old Ivories," and what she calls "the loveliest nocturne of love created," "Palimpsest," also "Atthis, My Darling" (a poem from the Sappho collection *Long Ago*), and "A Girl." Edith writes, "I am moved to show him my triumph and joy in this lovely praise, and in showing him my so often guarded mood before my glory, I also let my Love understand what her poet's gift has been to me—her poet-lover's gift. . . . It is Paradise between us."[92] She then meditates on their idea that trinity is required for perfect love: as a listener is required to hear the love poems, god is needed to assure the immortality of their love. Katherine's response, also recorded in the journal, images their love and their interaction as erotic and creative: "I find I am listening to Henry's voice—Hennie reading my love poems to her. . . . For a little while I am in Paradise. It is infinitely soft between us. Warm buds open. I feel at least I have merited gems of passionate love. . . . It is an intense moment."[93]

In "Constancy," a sonnet in the *Wild Honey* series, Katherine recounted how Edith said that if she (Edith) were to die, her spell over Katherine would break. Katherine responded: "I confront the charge / As sorrowing, and as careless of my fame / As Christ intact before the infidel" (173). Edith never knew the full extent of Katherine's constancy because Katherine hid from her the fact that she too had developed cancer from grief. She died nine months after Edith, and their friend Charles Ricketts designed their tomb.

The Michael Fields were Aestheticists; they belonged to a circle of men and women that acknowledged the influence of Pater. This Aestheticism was not at all incompatible with commitment to social change. Katherine and Edith were vigorous supporters of women's suffrage and were also active in the antivivisection league. In her youth Katherine had joined Ruskin's Guild of St. George and had carried on a correspondence with him. It ended when Katherine doubted the existence of god and sought to replace him with the love of a dog. Ruskin exploded in rage: "You go on from folly to folly. . . . You think YOUR-SELF abused indeed just now—but that is simply because you thought yourself very clever—and are astonished that I think nothing of your poetry—and less than nothing of your power of thought."[94] Fortunately, she did not follow his advice to "give up dreaming, and writing verses."[95]

In Pater's circle she found more congenial spirits. She and Edith greatly admired Pater's writing, although they deplored his editing it in deference to prudish criticism.[96] They became acquainted with him and his sisters Hester and Clara. At his 1890 lecture on Merimee they met Arthur Symons and Oscar Wilde, both of whom they cultivated. They met Lionel Johnson, who had read all their books and whose feminine delicacy they record with pleasure, comparing him to a dove, a foal, and a little woodland creature. Katherine's first conversation with Wilde took off from their shared admiration for Pater: " 'There is only one man in this century who can write prose.' 'You mean Mr Pater.' " They also agreed that "the whole problem of life turns on pleasure—Pater shows that the hedonist—the perfected hedonist—is the saint." They discussed women writers, and Wilde put forward the theory (very similar to Woolf's as expressed in her essays on the Brontës, especially Charlotte) that "genius spoils a work of art—a work of art that should be intensely self-conscious. . . . Consider the difference between *Jane Eyre* and *Esmond*. Owing to their imperfect education, the only works we have had from women were works of genius."[97]

Katherine's journal comment on Wilde is interesting for the positive womanly qualities she attributes to him:

> What I like about him is the sense of bien-être, of comfort, he conveys to the brain. All that a woman does to a man by her presence on the hearth, or by the tea-table, he does to the brain—neither lulling it nor stimulating it—introducing about it a climate of happiness, so that it is twice itself, freed from the depression of fragility or chill.[98]

They visited his home and, although in 1892 they were offended by what they perceived as his snobbish behavior, he was one of the few who stood by them when *A Question of Memory* was attacked by the press in 1893. He wrote two letters, signing himself their "sincere admirer" and praising the play. Charles Ricketts records in his journal their reaction when the news of Wilde's death reached England:

Dec. 5, 1900. Moore brought to-day the news, some days old, of Oscar's death. I feel too upset to write about it. I know that I have not really felt the fact of his death, I am merely wretched, tearful, stupid, vaguely conscious that something has happened that stirs up old resentment and the old sense that one is not sufficiently reconciled to life and death. Moore had hardly finished giving us the news when a loud ringing was heard and Michael Field arrived, sobbing loudly in the hall.[99]

In their journal Edith recorded their sorrow at Wilde's death and a sort of prose elegy for him that in its rhythms recalls Shakespeare's eulogy by Cleopatra for Antony: "His intelligence was a warm climate. . . . His terrible wit wore white gloves. . . . His face was like a rich yet ungainly fruit and his glance was the light-speck on it. . . . He made folly itself a very big thing."[100]

In 1892 Charles Ricketts and his lifelong companion Charles Shannon had written Michael Field, whom they thought a man, an admiring letter after reading their play *The Tragic Mary* (the title of which was taken from Pater).[101] At this time the Michael Fields were the older, more established, and better-known artists.[102] The two couples soon became close friends and collaborators, referring to each other playfully as "the poets" and "the painters." In 1894 Ricketts set up the Vale Press and announced it to the poets in a letter that said, "May we become rich and grasping, and publish the complete works of Michael Field, Esq."[103] The press published four of Michael Field's tragedies. In 1896 Michael Field contributed poems to the *Dial*, the magazine edited by Ricketts and Shannon. The poets took to submitting their manuscripts to Ricketts for his comments. He also decorated and designed most of their books. In 1888 Ricketts persuaded them to move from Reigate to Richmond, where they lived in a house (which Shannon measured to convince them they could fit in) that was ten minutes' walk from the painters' home. The new house was full of paintings, lithographs, and woodcuts executed by the painters. At this time the two couples met at least once a week. Little gifts—of flowers and ornaments—were constantly exchanged.

A year later Ricketts and Shannon moved to Holland Park, which was not too far away. The Fields set aside every Thursday evening for Ricketts to have dinner with them[104] and bestowed on him such pet names as "Fay," "Fairyman," "Pan," "the Lizard," and "the Basilisk."[105] The two couples had an intimate teasing relationship that lasted twenty years, and after the two women's deaths, Ricketts donated a picture by Rossetti to the National Gallery in memory of his friendship with them. Although Edith was Ricketts's favorite, and he said that after her death he was estranged from Katherine, the two of them continued to correspond. She wrote to him on the morning of her death, and he was one of the chief beneficiaries of her will.[106]

The histories of such friendships and alliances are so little known that they are worth recording in some detail.[107] They are also evidence that Katherine Bradley and Edith Cooper sought out and maintained constant contact with homoerotically inclined men. An awareness of these men's predicament is found in their writings. Like Ricketts and Shannon, they were among the friends of Wilde who retained their sympathy for him through his trial and conviction.[108] They attended a lecture by Verlaine, who was notorious for his openly homosexual poems, and Katherine's journal perceptively comments on his death: "He is half a satyr & half a little child. From Oscar [Wilde] to St Augustine."[109] This suggests that to read the erotic imagery in their love poems as self-aware is not to read lesbian consciousness into a nonerotic romantic friendship.

In an early poem, "Sylvanus Cupressifer," Edith presents a narrative of her friendship with a male homosexual.[110] In a forest the narrator meets a little woodland "half-god creature," It is small and terrified and "for solitude most desolately begs." She befriends him, knows he is "divine," and then is allowed to see his eyes and face. She understands that he is suffering a "woe / Of long ago." He then tells her his name is Sylvan and he once loved a beautiful boy called Cyparissus. This boy loved a red fawn better than he did Sylvan. One afternoon Sylvan shot the fawn by accident and Cyparissus died of grief. Sylvan caused a mourning fir tree to rise up for the boy and has mourned ever since. What is interesting is the way she performs the role of confidante: "I listened to this story hours by hours." After they part she addresses him as a "mourner of obscure and unhoused death." In a context where homosexual men like Simeon Solomon frequently died in homeless obscurity, this phrasing has a similar resonance to that of Wilde's lines from *The Ballad of Reading Gaol*, which were inscribed on his tomb. The poem concludes with the speaker saying she has drawn comfort from Sylvan's story because his sorrow is emblematic of all sorrows: "I too have known, O little, gentle King, / Your comforting— / To hear a sorrow of all sorrows sing: / And I as you can turn / With measured feet afar where boughs are calm."

When Lionel Johnson died in 1901 Edith wrote about him as one of a group that was passing: "We have just read that Lionel Johnson died on Saturday. One by one these young men who were about our way, when we began as Michael, have drifted down the hollow gusts of Fate to piteous graves."[111] They identified themselves with the Pater circle and felt out of place as it disappeared. In 1901 Katherine wrote: "The room was full of faded Victorians, but not my Victorians—mine were of the season before last. . . . One felt that Pater was buried very deep."[112]

Michael Field also participated in the development of a language to celebrate love between men, using the same myths that male poets and painters used at this time, for instance, St. Sebastian, Jesus, and St. John. In *Sight and Song*, the 1892 collection of poems inspired by paintings, there are two poems about St. Sebastian. The poem on Correggio's painting describes the saint's eyes as free although the hands are bound. His eyes look at the child in the Madonna's arms. The imagery suggests thwarted action but a freedom of spirit, the gaze joining two males: "Oh bliss when with mute rites two souls are plighted!"[113] The idea of two souls being married in a silent ceremony is similar to that in the poem quoted earlier about the two women's marriage by Nature. Sebastian is described as having "the peril of a captive's chances." Although he is a captive, the babe looks at him "with soft desire," and he is therefore most fortunate because "No joy is second / To theirs whose eyes by other eyes are beckoned." This idea that to love and be loved is the greatest good fortune possible appears in several other poems, forming the epigraph to *Underneath the Bough*: "Mortal if thou art beloved, / Life's offences are removed. . . . If thou art beloved, oh then / Fear no grief of mortal men" (5). In this poem, too, St. Sebastian's pain is seen as amply compensated for by his persistent love, and the poets explicitly associate their own love with his at the close:

> Though arrows rain on breast and throat they have no power
> to hurt,
> While thy tenacious face they fail an instant to avert.
> Oh might my eyes, so without measure,
> Feed on their treasure,
> The world with thong and dart might do its pleasure!

This seems to me a clear identification of St. Sebastian's persecution with the persecution of those who love against convention, and a declaration that such persecution is ineffective because of the power and persistence of that love.[114]

The other poem, on Antonelli da Messina's St. Sebastian, is different in its emphasis.[115] It figures the saint as an angry rebel who feels unjustly treated even by god. Sebastian is alone and unpitied. He looks in "distress" to heaven, he is "pained, protesting" and "disputes" god's will. He is "sound in muscle," filled with the "acrid joy" of his "manhood," and therefore resents the coming of his last hour. The poets use a phallic image to stress the nature of the deprivation Sebastian feels, which is explicitly described as consisting not in death but in the denial of pleasure:

> At his feet a mighty pillar lies reversed;
> So the virtue of his sex is shattered, cursed:
> Here is martyrdom and not
> In the arrows' sting;
> This the bitter lot
> His soul is questioning.
>
> He, with body fresh for use, for pleasure fit,
> With its energies and needs together knit
> In an able exigence,
> Must endure the strife,
> Final and intense,
> Of necessity with life.

Sight and Song may be read as Paterian art criticism in verse. Field's perceptive readings of St. Sebastian in Renaissance paintings foreground what many art critics have noted, that this saint was a homoerotic icon, providing male painters so inclined with an excuse to portray a beautiful naked young man. Michael Field had a fellow practitioner of this kind of Renaissance criticism in Vernon Lee, also an ardent admirer of Pater. They met Vernon Lee and her lover Anstruther Thompson in Italy in 1901. Lee followed up the implications of *The Renaissance* in her own *Renaissance Fancies and Studies* (1896). She uses Pater's codes and strategies to suggest that readers of any text must seek out their own "affinities" in the past as well as in the present. In the last essay in this collection, entitled "Valedictory," she argues that readers may find in the past "real companionship and congenial activity," especially if the place and time into which they happen to be born does not "fit them to perfection."[116] This is precisely Pater's explanation of why Winckelmann was drawn to the Hellenic world. She defends her Aestheticism against the charges that it represents a "selfish dilettantism" and a "morbid lack of sympathy" (238) with the society we live in by arguing that the past lives within us and this living past "may be a Past of our own making" (239). Approaching it for our own pleasure is similar to travelling in foreign countries where we cannot vote or work but from where we return with wider views and in a happier state of mind. Repeatedly using Paterian phrases ("subtle affinities," "temperament," 240), she stresses that each person will seek out different models from the past:

> Each individual according to individual subtle affinities, certain emotions, ideals, persons, or works of art from out of the Past. For one it will be Socrates; for another St Francis; for every one something somewhat different, or at all events something differently conceived and differently felt: some portion of the universe in time, as of the universe in space, which answers in closest and most intimate way to the complexion and habits of that individual soul. (240)

She insists that readers should not try to appreciate works that are uncongenial to them, and gives the example of Botticelli, pointing out that precisely the features of his work that are so pleasurable to some temperaments will cause "almost discomfort to others" (245). She protests against these temperamental differences being labeled healthy or morbid, "each being, in truth, healthy or morbid just in proportion as it realises its necessities of existence" (245), and, these necessities being different for different persons, each should "cherish to the utmost his natural affinities" (245).

Michael Field's persistent search for their affinities in the past led them through various changes in worldview. In 1887 they saw themselves as rationalists, but in 1897 they declared themselves pagans and their poetry of this time is saturated with Greek mythological imagery. In April 1907 Edith converted to Catholicism. According to Ricketts, when Katherine was told of Edith's conversion she "helplessly exclaimed . . . 'but this is terrible, it means that I too shall have to become a Catholic.' "[117] In May 1907 Katherine was received into the church by Father John Gray, friend and lover of Wilde and possibly the model for Dorian Gray. In her letter to Ricketts announcing this, she stressed what she saw as the inclusive nature of Catholicism: "And you will be glad of this great plunge I have taken into the universal—so that the sun of farthest Ind burns close."[118]

I agree with Mary Sturgeon that there is no great difference between the pagan poems that precede and the Christian poems that follow this conversion.[119] A continuing theme in both is the celebration of the senses and of women's beauty and vitality. The conversion occasions a shift from Sapphic to Marian imagery, but the content does not alter substantially. Michael Field's expansions of Sappho's fragments into lyrics in *Long Ago* (1889) turns out, disappointingly, to focus on Sappho's love for Phaon. Most of the poems are addressed to a male beloved, the masculine pronoun being used for him. There is only one poem clearly addressed to a female beloved ("Atthis, my darling, thou didst stray"). It is as if the poets, though attracted to Sappho for her lesbianism, are too afraid to be open about it in such a context. Their love poems to one another may have been masked for readers by the fiction of their pseudonym. Their poems to Mary and to the female saints free them to celebrate women's beauty uninhibitedly.

In celebrating this beauty, they blend pagan with Christian imagery. Katherine's poems often blend her praise of Edith with that of Mary so that the two are indistinguishable. A poem in *Mystic Trees* (1913) rewrites Sappho's famous fragment, establishing a connection between Sapphic and Marian virginity:

She Is One

> High, lone above all creatures thou dost stand,
> Mary, as apple on the topmost bough,
> The gatherers overlooked, somehow—
> And yet not so:
> Man could not reach thee, thou so high dost grow
> Warm, gold for God's own hand.[120]

Another poem, "The Stillness in Paradise," attributes to Mary an assertive opposition to Christ. Mary lifts herself above Christ and is the real mediator because the crucifixion follows the incarnation that is possible only because of Mary. The phallic image of the cross is replaced by the vulval image of the rose:

> "I, if I be lifted up,
> Will draw all men unto me!"
> Mary did not thus agree—
> Mary opened a flower-cup.

Mary doth herself uplift—
And God looketh on His rose.
As the lovely leaves unclose,
Lo, God giveth unto sinners shrift.   (50)

A series of poems on Mary traces her life through her presentation
as a three year old, the annunciation, the nativity, her visit with the baby
to her parents, the wedding at Cana, her feast day, her grief at Calvary,
and her presence at Pentecost. The series ends with poems on her death,
her assumption, and her enthronement in heaven. The poems on Mary,
here and elsewhere, assert her power and strength. In this they are notice-
ably different from Gerard Manley Hopkins's poems to Mary, which celebrate her as the principle of fertility. For instance, "Another Leadeth
Thee" again shows her as superior to Christ because she is mother of god
: "Behold, / By a woman's hand unrolled / All the mystery sublime / Of thy
ableness through Time!"[121] "Virgo Potens" shows her as a young girl leaping across the hills to visit Elizabeth. The poem celebrates her youthful
energy and fearlessness.[122] Mary is compared to hardy creatures, the goat,
the deer, and the eagle.

Several poems associate Mary and the female saints with Greek
goddesses. "Purissimae Virgini Sacellum" represents the monks on Mount
Carmel praying to Mary in most unlikely terms:

As Pagans by their Virgin of moonlight,
Diana of the Hunter's rocks: so we
Upon the heights, and in the breeze, are seen,
And called the brothers of thy lovely name,
Blest Mary of Mount Carmel.[123]

A poem about SS. Ursula, Kalemire, and Hilary suddenly introduces
Venus, described as "our Venus," as if the poets were talking about their
own personal Venus, and prays that she too be granted grace by Jesus.
The ambiguous mention of the "use" of lips in conjunction with flowers
suggests kisses as well as prayers:

And for Venus—"Jesus, pray
That there fall no shadow grey
On our Venus!"—Lovely blooms,
Growing on the sides of tombs,
Lest our lips fall to disuse![124]

"In the Beginning" visualizes St. John, with his eyes closed, on the breast
of Jesus. The last stanza shows Christ bending above John's "sweet head,"
while John sets his love on "God, his Lord, his Thought, his Lover dear."
The poem ends: "in lapse of silence falling clear, / One heareth only
this— / On the sweet head, a kiss."[125]

Mystic Trees contains poems written when Edith was dying. Some poems fuse her sufferings with that of Christ and her uniqueness to Katherine with that of Mary. Thus, in the midst of many religious poems, "The Only One" suddenly appears. The image of snow that kills flowers suggests Katherine's grief for the untimely death about to overtake Edith:

> I think of her
> As the fastness of hepatica,
> The little fort of blue that held itself so fine,
> So lightsome and so sure,
> In that garden-plot of mine where the snow spread:
> I cannot take anything else, or instead.
> I think of her
> By the plot where I miss my hepatica.[126]

Blue is Mary's color and is used to similar effect in Amy Lowell's poem to her lover, Ada Russell, "Madonna of the Evening Flowers." "Answered Prayer" refers to Edith's refusal to take morphine as a painkiller. She preferred to suffer the pain and retain her mental alertness. Katherine compares her to the nightingale—"my small, grey Bird" singing "from sorrow's springs" in the dark. This image of Philomel, the bird "of the Greeks' choice" carries the implicit idea of early death as rape, as violence.[127] The resentment surfaces in "She is Singing to Thee, Domine" and in the magnificent "Caput Tuum Ut Carmelus," where Katherine's recurrent delight in Edith's profile comes together with an intolerable grief she compares to the grief that caused St. Peter's denial.

The last poem in *Mystic Trees* uses Michael Field's favorite images of flowers and gems, to suggest first death and then the gradual building of immortal bliss. The image of building Jerusalem recalls Blake's "I will not cease from Mental Fight/Nor shall my Sword sleep in my hand / Till we have built Jerusalem / In England's green & pleasant Land."[128] The association of the images of their love with this image of the struggle for a better world inflects the latter with an emphasis on the particular kind of Jerusalem Michael Field and their circle contributed to building:

> Flowers,
> Fall in showers,
> Let go, desist—the winter comes!
> Fall on the ground,
> And spread your lovely strewings round!
>
> Jewels,
> Bickering fuels,
> Harden your sluices and your gums,
> Gem after gem:
> For ye shall build Jerusalem![129]

6

Sapphic Virgins
Mythmaking Around Love Between Women in Meredith, Forster, Hope Mirrlees

The two women, striving against death, devoted in friendship, were the sole living images he brought away; they were a new vision of the world and our life.
—George Meredith, *Diana of the Crossways*

Boys with their tutors. Girls with their mothers.
—Ronald Firbank, *Inclinations*

Romantic anarchism is opposed to violence not only at the political level but also at the familial and interpersonal level. It interrogates men's relations with each other, with women and children, and with the nonhuman world and critiques them as riddled with violence. It finds better models of relating in the mutual nurturance between the apparently powerless—women, children, and nonhuman beings such as animals, birds, and plants. Romanticism is teleological insofar as it insists that the universe is sustained by these loving relations, which will ultimately prove the fittest to survive. In this chapter I shall examine how some late Victorian and early twentieth-century writers integrated this teleology with theories of evolution. In their texts relationships between women, cast in variations of the Marian triangle, constitute the ideal toward which humanity evolves. For instance, in Edward Carpenter's scheme of modified Lamarckian evolution, or "exfoliation," all love relationships, including the heterosexual and the male homosexual, should evolve beyond seeking sex for its own sake. While accepting pleasure as "the natural accompaniment of life," one should never seek it as "the object of life."[1] To thinkers like him, women's way of loving one another seemed closest to such a possibility.

In the first chapter of *Diana of the Crossways* Meredith outlines his idea of human evolution. According to him its distinctive principle is mental growth. As humanity evolves, physical strength becomes less important and mental strength more important. If for Shaw man must evolve to superman, for Meredith the human race must evolve in the direction of the "heroical feminine." His two heroines, Diana and Emma, represent this type. They are new women, intellectuals like Michael Field and many others of Meredith's acquaintance who led movements not only for suffrage and women's education but also in support of pacifism, children's rights, independence for colonized peoples, antivivisection, vegetarianism, male temperance, and chastity. Meredith's Diana is a novelist, and he connects her evolution with that of fiction. If she is, in embryo, the woman of the next century, the fiction women like her write will move away from heterosexual romance toward philosophy. Meredith personifies Fiction, Philosophy, and Nature as women who work together. In this personification of intellectual forces as feminine, Meredith is heir to a long tradition—Plato, Boethius, Christine de Pisan are among his forebears. Philosophy is the "helpmate" of Fiction, "her inspiration and her essence" (14, 16). Having thus replaced the idea of woman as man's helpmate with that of women as each others' helpmates, Meredith advises the reader, addressed as an ungendered "you," to stop looking, in fiction as in life, for such stereotypically feminine virtues as purity and instead to appreciate women's courageous experimentation, in the course of which they have the right to make mistakes.

Diana Merion is an orphan whose closest friend is Emma Dunstane, an older married woman. Emma had nursed Diana as a baby. The two women are parted when Emma marries and goes to India. On her return they are reunited and decide not to part again, so Diana moves into Emma's house. Diana is much wooed by men but has no desire to marry. It is only when Emma's husband, Lord Dunstane, makes advances to her that she is frightened into accepting an unsuitable suitor, Warwick. For fear of wounding Emma, she does not tell her the real reason why she has suddenly decided to marry.

Warwick and Diana are badly mismatched and he wrongly suspects her of adultery. Diana leaves her marital home and sets off to go abroad, hoping that he will sue her for divorce. Emma sends Redworth, one of Diana's suitors, to persuade her to remain in England. Emma's emotional plea works. Diana sets up house on her own and becomes a writer. She is about to elope with a politician, Dacier, when news arrives that Emma is seriously ill and about to undergo surgery. Diana rushes to Emma. Dacier, who was waiting for her at the rendezvous, is first enraged and later admires her fidelity to her friend but changes his mind about the wisdom of giving up his political career for this unrespectable love. His attempts to seduce Diana fail, even though she is still in love with him. When Diana gives away a political secret he had shared with her as a ploy to seduce her, he deserts her and promptly marries Constance Asper, an angel-in-the-house type of woman who will be a political asset. Devastated, Diana nearly starves herself to death, and her life is saved by

Emma's ministrations. Emma persuades Diana to marry the steadfast Redworth. The novel closes with Emma and Diana embracing in a darkened room and Emma hoping for Diana's child.

Diana, named for the virgin goddess of the moon, is endemically "of" the crossways and never moves beyond them—the crossways of the choice between love for women and love for men. At crucial moments of her life she chooses the former, but the circumstances (the woman she loves is already married) prevent this becoming an exclusive life choice.[2] This simultaneous possibility and impossibility constitute the emotional crux of Diana's life and, insofar as the narrator posits her as the type of the new woman, and even of "womanhood" in some wider sense, also the crux of women's predicament in this text. If Diana is a goddess, she must be worshipped also by men—as she is in the novel. Almost every man she meets comes under her spell. As such, her aspirations, including the aspiration for same-sex love, become, for men, a vision of that to which they ought to, but cannot fully, aspire.

The novel develops the ideas of virginity, refusal to marry, and disinterest in heterosexuality as symbols of evolution toward a more human, "higher" life. It also eroticizes the women's relationship through the use of phrases, images, and myths drawn from earlier texts. Thus, Diana's first words in the novel are "Emmy! Emmy! my heart!" (19) The name *Emma* derives from an Old Germanic root indicating the "whole," the "universal."[3] Emma has lost her health in India and is an invalid. She is thus cast in relation to Diana as both nurturer and nurtured. The narrator describes it as "that mutual dependency which makes friendship a pulsating tie" (247). This mutually shifting relation continues throughout the novel and structures the major turning points in the plot.

The first of these turning points is Diana's marriage. In her first conversation with Emma, in chapter 2, Diana says that she can never have any secrets from Emma but that she felt constrained while writing to her in India because she felt she was writing to two people: "He was just a bit in the way. Men are the barriers to perfect naturalness, at least, with girls, I think" (27). While all those around her, including Emma, are plotting her marriage, and most of the men are imagining themselves in love with her, Diana declares herself unattached to any man and the narrator comments: "Diana's unshadowed bright face defied all menace of an eclipse" (27). This comment establishes the idea of marriage as eclipse, an idea that persists to the end of the novel, in much the same fashion as it does in *Middlemarch*, where Dorothea's final "happy" marriage is figured as the best possible option under the circumstances but less than fully satisfying. Dorothea's capabilities remain unexplored and hence, for the reader, more a matter of faith than demonstration; Diana's capabilities are not merely intellectual but also emotional—she lives out extraordinarily passionate and tender feelings for her woman beloved. While she also enters into love relations with men, most of these men are represented as unworthy of her. The novel finally attempts resolution through her marriage to a man whose imitation of what is constructed as woman-woman love (devoted, self-sacrificing, silently sympathetic, proud of and promoting the other's interests and ambitions, anticipating the other's wants) establishes his worthiness. But the resolution remains, as I hope to demonstrate, incomplete.

A metaphor that runs through the novel is that of the hunt. Diana the huntress is forced into the position of the hunted. This metaphor, common in this period (it is equally powerful in Hardy's *Tess*), is rewritten in *The Well of Loneliness*. Emma's husband's attempt to hunt Diana when they are riding together in the woods precipitates Diana's entrapment in marriage. In the course of their first conversation, Diana had told Emma: "Be sure I am giving up the ghost when I cease to be one soul with you, dear and dearest! No secrets, never a shadow of a deception, or else I shall feel I am not fit to live" (27). This speech is crucial to my reading of the novel. Diana draws here on the idea of the double soul and of the beloved as one's likeness, an idea that both women repeatedly invoke throughout the novel. Keeping a secret from Emma appears to her intolerable, even suicidal, but she is forced to do this, and the rest of the novel is enacted under that shadow. Unwilling to continue living in Emma's house, she cannot explain to her why she must leave and so takes the only route available, that of marriage. This marriage is a form of death. When Emma's husband seizes her hand and waist, she finds it nearly impossible to believe what is happening: "Even then, so impossible is it to conceive the unimaginable even when the apparition of it smites us, she expected some protesting absurdity, or that he had seen something in her path— What did she hear? And from her friend's husband!" (45). She feels "profoundly humiliated," and unaccountably guilty, and is forced to "lock up her heart" from Emma (45, 46). The house becomes a "hostile citadel" to her (45).

Up to this point Diana had refused all offers of marriage, declaring that a husband would appear "a foreign animal" in her "kingdom" and that "the idea of a convent was more welcome to her than the most splendid marriage" (43–44). Her letter announcing her engagement is received by Emma like an assault: "It . . . fired its shot like a cannon with the muzzle at her breast" (53). Unable to give any explanation for her acceptance, Diana merely says "it is the wisest thing a waif can do" (53). Male heterosexual aggressiveness functions to turn Diana from a queen with a "kingdom" to a "waif." The letter says nothing about the man and its only expression of emotion is for Emma herself, with regard to whom it virtually makes a wedding vow: "I write in haste, to you first, burning to hear from you. Send your blessing to yours in life and death, through all transformations,—Tony." (53). Trying to decode the letter, Emma realizes that "it bore a sound of desperation" (53) but lacks the clue that would enable her to understand the source of that desperation. Hurt by Tony's lack of openness, she replies carefully and coldly. She is disappointed: "Her brilliant beloved Tony, dazzling but in beauty and the gifted mind, stood as one essentially with the common order of women. . . . Diana was in eclipse full three parts. The bulk of the gentlemanly official she had chosen obscured her" (54). The phrasing suggests that to Emma Diana was an exception, not only because of her beauty and intelligence but because of her "Diana-ness," that is, her separateness from women interested only in men and marriage. When she loses that status, she loses it for ever, as the narrator's account of the wedding underlines: "Diana Antonia Merion lost her maiden name. She became the Mrs Warwick of our footballing world" (56). When Diana enters the emotional world where cross-sex relations are considered primary, she loses some possibilities and even memory: "Why she married she never told. Possibly in amazement at herself subsequently, she forgot the specific reason" (56). That heterosexual molestation may frighten a woman into heterosexual marriage and that she may subsequently bury the connection in her memory are important insights. Meredith here advances the serious (as opposed to the more common pornographic) study of molestation begun by Shelley. The rest of the novel, in the course of which the reader is repeatedly reminded by the narrator of this initial defining incident, is an account of the hunt of a wounded creature. It recounts the two women's attempt to retrieve fragments from the wreck.

The second turning point occurs when Emma sends Redworth to stop Diana from leaving the country. Writing to tell Emma of her decision to leave, Diana pours out a flood of endearments and protestations: "My beloved! my only truly loved on earth! . . . I long for your heart on mine, your dear eyes. . . . My beloved! . . . Write your whole heart. It is not compassion I want, I want you. . . . I kiss this miserable sheet of paper" (69). Kissing and repeatedly rereading the letter, Emma divines that Diana will visit her girlhood home, the Crossways, before she leaves the country. The empathy of what is here termed "a classic friendship between women, the alliance of a mutual devotedness men choose to doubt of" (70) functions to reverse the direction of the hunt.[4]

Meredith invokes a Shakespearean model of friendship between women by comparing Diana to Hermione and, implicitly, Emma to Paulina. By alluding to *The Winter's Tale*, in which the two women spend sixteen years of their lives with each other, Hermione returning to her husband only in order to meet her daughter, the text participates in constructing a literary ancestry for love between women. Emma tells Redworth, Diana's silent admirer: "You have seen the hunted hare. . . . 'By this, poor Wat far off upon a hill.' . . . She is one of Shakespeare's women. Another character, but one of his own: another Hermione!" (73). Listening uncomprehendingly, Redworth "was heated by these flights of advocacy to feel that he was almost seated beside the sovereign poet thus eulogised" (73). Emma, an inspired reader of Shakespeare to her own ends (like the Ladies of Llangollen, Anna Seward, and Michael Field), becomes the one who rewrites him. In her letter pleading with Diana to come to her, Emma threatens to die if Diana refuses and fuses the tropes of mother and lover to make her appeal: "You break your Emma's heart. . . . I shall not survive it. . . . It is my life I cry for . . . like the mother seeing her child on the edge of the cliff. Come! This is your breast, my Tony!" (74).

Figured as a fatherless child with a mother-lover, Diana is also the wronged Mary. Finding her where Emma had expected her to be ("Oh, marvel of a woman's divination of a woman," 83), Redworth sees her as "a Madonna on an old black Spanish canvas" (84). Diana refuses to return but gives in when Redworth tells her Emma will die of shock and adds: "Friendship, I fancy, means one heart between two" (91). Redworth's sympathy is suggested in the way he uses words that they have used between themselves: "His unstressed observation hit a bell in her head, and set it reverberating. She and Emma had spoken, written, the very words. She drew forth her Emma's letter from under her left breast, and read some half-blinded lines" (91). Heterosexual relationships tend to drive Diana out of England, but the relationship with Emma makes England home. She tells Emma: "Any road that leads me to you is homeward, my darling!" (104). British society is represented as hatefully conservative and misogynist; the only hope for the country's future is symbolized by the relationship between the two women. This looks forward to Forster's vision of England in *Howards End*.

The third turning point occurs two-thirds of the way through the novel, when Diana is about to elope with Dacier. When Dacier stands on the railway platform and Diana fails to turn up, his reactions indicate the absence of empathy that Emma has in such abundance. Instead of fearing that some disaster may have occurred, he proceeds to revile Diana and all women. He thinks her a coquette, and a Shakespearean allusion once more places the situation: "The idea of his being a puppet fixed for derision was madly distempering. He had only to ask the affirmative of Constance Asper to-morrow! A vision of his determining to do it somewhat comforted him" (233). Dacier's emotional inadequacy emerges here in his egotistic self-pity. Like Othello, he thinks of his honor while Diana, like Shakespeare's Emilia, thinks of her beloved.

While Emma's husband wallows in sentimentality, Diana holds Emma through the ordeal of the surgery and emerges looking like Keats's Moneta or Eliot's Maggie borne along by the flood:

> He [Dacier] was petrified by Diana's face, and thought of her as whirled from him in a storm, bearing the marks of it. Her underlip hung for short breaths; the big drops of her recent anguish still gathered on her brows; her eyes were tearless, lustreless; she looked ancient in youth, and distant by a century, like a tall woman of the vaults, issuing white-ringed, not of our light. (241–42).

Although the plot moves toward the closure of marriage, the novel's symbolism points beyond the story line. Meredith suggests possibilities that are not followed through. One such symbolic moment occurs in Dacier's memory of this moment: "The two women, striving against death, devoted in friendship, were the sole living image he brought away; they were a new vision of the world and our life" (243).

The structure I have been reading in this novel proceeds from an initial separation between the two women caused by the marriage of one, to their partial union following the marriage of the other, and a more complete union following the thwarting of a heterosexual romance. When the romance with Dacier ends with his engagement to Constance, accompanied by the Hardyesque irony of the death of Diana's husband, the symbolic pattern is worked out through Emma's saving Diana's life as Diana had helped save hers. In this chapter, the Diana-Emma relationship is posed against the institution of marriage into which Dacier and Constance are about to enter. Ironically entitled "Is Conclusive as to the Heartlessness of Women with Brains," the chapter opens with a sarcastic celebration of matrimonial preparations and a meditation on heterosexuality as that which unites apparent enemies, including the two sexes: "Marriages are unceasing. Friends do it, and enemies; the unknown contractors of this engagement, or armistice, inspire an interest. It certainly is both exciting and comforting to hear that man and woman are ready to join in a mutual affirmative, say Yes together again. It sounds like the end of the war" (323–24). Although Meredith ends the novel with such an armistice, thus colluding in the societal fiction that marriage is the "end of the war," his merciless and unqualified dissection of it here, very similar to Samuel Butler's dissection in *The Way of All Flesh*, indicates the "crossways" of thought from which the novel derives its energies. The first half of the chapter is about the wedding that Emma's husband attends, praises, and weeps at but that Emma refuses to attend; the second half details Emma's visit to Diana.

Diana's devoted maid, Danvers, informs Emma that Diana has been lying in a dark cold room without eating for nearly three days and will die if not persuaded to eat. She finds Diana apparently lifeless: "Hateful love of men! Emma thought, and was moved to feel at the wrist for her darling's pulse. He has killed her! the thought flashed" (330). Diana recognizes the touch of her hand and says, "It is Emmy," to which Emma replies, "My Tony" and "It is Emmy come to stay with you, never to leave you" (330). The idea of Emma's being cold rouses Diana to say, "My dear will be cold," (330) and Emma is thus enabled to light the fire. The image of the flame sheltered by the hand, which will appear again in Woolf's *Mrs. Dalloway*, appears here, as Emma holds Diana's hand: "Over this little wavering taper in the vaults Emma cowered, cherishing the hand, silently hoping for the voice" (330). The flame is figured here as simultaneously embodying Diana's life and as warming Emma. She warms Diana's feet by holding them to her breast, lies beside her, holding her in her arms, and tells her: "You are in Emmy's arms, my beloved." Diana's pain grows "lax" and "neighbours sleep" like her "pleasure," her eyes closing under the "sensation" (331) of closeness to Emma, and the day passes in this fashion.

The ritual of sleeping together is followed by that of eating together, and the images are drawn from those of a wedding. These rituals are found, too, in Michael Field's poems envisioning women's togetherness, which I shall examine in the last chapter. The romantic motif of saving the beloved's life is assimilated to the narrative of love between women. Emma says she is hungry and that she will get food and "be mistress of the house" (331). Sipping at the bouillon she has had prepared, she says, " 'Pledge me' is a noble saying, when you think of humanity's original hunger for the whole. It is there that our civilizing commenced, and I am particularly fond of hearing the call. It is grandly historic. So pledge me, Tony. We two can feed from one spoon; it is a closer bond than the loving-cup" (332). The first reference here is to the definition in Plato's *Symposium* of love as the original hunger for the whole. It alludes too to Aristophanes' myth, recounted in the same text, of lovers, whether heterosexual or homosexual, striving for fusion into the one whole they originally were. The reference to the loving cup invokes the ritual of marriage when bride and groom drink from one cup. The pledge of love and friendship, also taken in a common cup, and often in a same-sex context, for instance, in the Catullus poem translated by Ben Jonson as "Drink to me only with thine eyes," is here premised as a "closer bond" than that of marriage and also as "grandly historic."[5] If Western civilization is constructed, as it was in Meredith's England, as having commenced in Plato's Athens, the closest bond historically conceived may be not that of heterosexual marriage but that of the marriage of true minds as envisioned in the *Symposium*. The image of the two women as lovers is once more inflected by that of mother and child:

> Tony murmured, "No." The spoon was put to her mouth. She sighed to resist. The stronger will compelled her to move her lips. Emma fed her as a child, and nature sucked for life.
>
> The first effect was a gush of tears.
>
> Emma lay with her that night, when the patient was the better sleeper. But during the night, at intervals, she had the happiness of feeling Tony's hand travelling to make sure of her. (332)

To feed and to be fed emerges as a powerful metaphor of love between women in texts of this time, for instance, in Christina Rossetti's *Goblin Market*. Opposed to it is the metaphor of hunting, with its implicit suggestion of killing to eat. Drinking from one cup and nursing at the breast suggest one kind of feeding; hunting to capture, kill, and consume suggests quite another. Nourishment and nurturing are posited against consumption and devouring.

The ambivalence of the text's resolution emerges in its use of the imagery of hunting in relation to heterosexuality. Redworth is from the start the one among Diana's many suitors who is favored by Emma. This is because she sees him as "the one man known to me who can be a friend of women" (74). Yet, immediately after she has described him thus, Redworth, discussing with Emma his chances of succeeding in stopping Diana's flight, uses the image of the hunt, causing Emma to wince. He says, "One break in the run will turn her back," and the narrator continues: "The sensitive invalid felt a blow in his following up the simile of the hunted hare for her friend" (74). The image continues in the account of Redworth's ride across the downs. He "pursue[s] the chase" (77), and, as Diana yields, the chapter ends with a surprisingly violent image when we are told that she "felt as a quivering butterfly impalpably pinned" (91). The butterfly image recalls Wordsworth's memory of himself as a child, "a very hunter" pouncing on the butterfly, while his more sensitive sister, "God love her! feared to brush / The dust from off its wings." The hunting imagery revives again toward the end of the novel. Diana's suitor Westlake is termed a "pursuer" and his "primitive ardour of courtship" an "effort to capture" (358).

Redworth, through his long and silent devotion and his role as mediator and messenger on Emma's behalf, may seem to fall in a different category, like the suitor of Diana's maid who is compared to a woman friend: "A maid of mine had a 'follower.' She was a good girl; I was anxious about her and asked her if she could trust him. 'Oh yes, ma'am,' she replied, 'I can; he's quite like a female.' I longed to see the young man, to tell him he had received the highest of eulogies" (265). But Redworth remains, nevertheless, a "manly man," even a "patriarch," as Diana terms him when she admires his cricket playing and thinks him the kind of man who would "lock up his girls in the nursery" (Emma disputes this, telling Diana to remember his "heterodox" views on women's education, 361). His schemes to give Diana pleasure, such as his buying her house, the Crossways, and filling it with all her furniture and other possessions, also bought up at the sale of her goods, are simultaneously signs of his sympathy and of his wish, in her phrase, to rob her of liberty: "The Crossways had been turned into a trap" (364).

The narrator is similarly divided, for the content of the last chapters apparently invites the reader to rejoice in a wedding that the chapter titles figure as the capture and taming of a wild creature.[6] Chapter 42 is titled "The Penultimate: Showing a Final Struggle for Liberty and Run Into Harness"—here Emma bullies Diana into accepting Redworth. Diana agrees, saying: "I am going into slavery to make amends for presumption. Banality, thy name is marriage!" to which Emma replies, "Your business is to accept life as we have it" (385). The narrator here terms Diana's fate "her common-place fate" (385). The last chapter is titled "Nuptial Chapter: And of How a Barely Willing Woman Was Led to Bloom with the Nuptial Sentiment." Diana, courting Redworth's proposal, is described as wishing him "to make one snatch at her poor last small butterfly bit of freedom, so that she might suddenly feel in haven, at peace with her expectant Emma" (387). If the first marriage was undertaken to find a refuge and to maintain Emma's peace, the second is undertaken for not entirely different reasons. "Haven" is a significant diminution of "heaven." The women's togetherness is no longer Edenic; it is only a refuge for the hunted. Diana's relinquishing of her independence is conceived as inevitable under the circumstances, a husband being required to protect her from other men. So the "return to the wedding yoke received sanction of grey-toned reason" (392). Diana is "dominated" and "submits" to Redworth's sexual passion but is "not enamoured"; the narrator compares them to hawk and fowl (389, 392–93). After all this the description of Diana's feeling for Redworth as "the return to mental harmony with the laws of life" (396) and of their marriage as "the perfect mating" (397) rings somewhat hollow.

The novel closes not with the married couple but with Emma and Diana and Emma's wish for Diana's child who will be her godchild. The prototype implicitly invoked in these last two chapters is that of Ruth and Naomi—the younger woman accepting, even finally courting, a quiet, older male suitor, solely on the advice of the older woman to whom she is devoted, and the child of the younger woman being hailed as the child of the two women. The end repeats the climactic scene of Diana's sickness in chapter 36. Again, the two women are alone in a dark room: "Emma's exaltation in fervour had not subsided when she held her beloved in her arms under the dusk of the withdrawing redness. They sat embraced, with hands locked, in the unlighted room" (397). Woolf may be alluding to this moment when, in *A Room of One's Own*, she images women's liking for one another as an unlighted chamber where nobody has yet been and mentions *Diana of the Crossways* as an exceptional attempt to represent that liking. Emma tells Diana that she prays to live long enough to be a godmother, and the last line is: "There was no reply: there was an involuntary little twitch of Tony's fingers" (398).

Diana's silence here is emblematic of the unresolved dilemma she embodies. The novel participates in mythmaking around love between women, an ongoing enterprise in turn-of-the-century texts. Meredith suggests that love between man and woman, embroiled in "nature," "mating," and complementarity, which is also inequality, may be necessary for continuance of the race but, if the life of the body is less important than the life of the spirit, heterosexual love is less important than the love between women.

The two women's feminist intellectual aspirations are emblematic of progress, they stand for the future. The subtext suggests that their love, too, stands for the future.[7] Toward the close of the novel, shortly before she accepts Redworth, Diana remarks that "all life is a lesson that we live to enjoy but in the spirit" (348). After the wedding (and after an extended discussion by the narrator of Redworth's sexual passion and Diana's submission to it), Emma asks her if she is hopeful and happy. Diana replies that she spent the previous night thinking of Emma and realized that while the senses bring despair, thought always brings hope: "I heard you whisper, with your very breath in my ear, *'There is nothing the body suffers that the soul may not profit by.'* That is Emma's history. With that I sail into the dark" (emphasis in the original, 396). Emma takes this as a sign that Tony's mind is working "sanely," that she is happy, loves her husband, and is in harmony with the laws of life. As a motto for marriage, the sentiment is certainly unconventional. Heterosexuality and reproduction may entail suffering for the female body but mainstream nineteenth-century fictions rarely acknowledge this so explicitly. The pain is more often glossed over, the wedding sentimentalized, and childbirth invisibilized.

E. M. Forster's *Howards End* (1910) is a successor to *Diana of the Crossways* in the way it foregrounds the pains of heterosexuality and the rewards of love between women.[8] It closes with dead or dying (rather than triumphant) husbands and flouts the crucial institution of legitimacy. It figures the self-destruction of the patriarchal family and the emergence of a Marian triangle, a matrilineal unit of mothers and children, as England's future. This idea of tyranny self-destructing and love between women triumphing may be drawn from Shelley's *Prometheus Unbound*, whose utopian act 4 figures a female earth and heaven in fruitful union. Forster's first novel, *The Longest Journey*, was influenced in its critique of marriage and monogamy by Shelley from whose *Epipsychidion* the novel's epigraph and title were drawn:

> I never was attached to that great sect,
> Whose doctrine is that each one should select
> Out of the crowd a mistress or a friend,
> And all the rest, though fair and wise, commend
> To cold oblivion, though 'tis in the code
> Of modern morals, and the beaten road
> Which those poor slaves with weary footsteps tread
> Who travel to their home among the dead
> By the broad highway of the world, and so
> With one chained friend, perhaps a jealous foe,
> The dreariest and the longest journey go.

Epipsychidion posits the beloved as a sibling as well as a partner, addressing her as "Spouse! Sister!"

Another possible influence on *Howards End* is Shelley's "Rosalind and Helen: A Modern Eclogue" (136–51).[9] Like Forster's novel, this verse dialogue has two female protagonists who form an intimate dyad as young women, are parted by the marriage of one of them, are reunited after the death of the men in their lives, and then proceed to live together with their children. In both narratives it is Helen who reproaches the other woman for abandoning her and it is Helen who has a child out of wedlock. Rosalind and Helen are Englishwomen exiled in Italy, and nostalgia for their childhood home and for the natural beauty of England is an important emotional element in their reunion. The poem traces their conversation through one night in a ruined temple in a forest—like Margaret and Helen's night together at Howards End. Nature presides over Rosalind and Helen's reunion and they decide to live together in Helen's house. They are represented as having aged through sorrow, and Rosalind dies young, although she lives to see her daughter grow up and marry Helen's son. Although the bulk of the narrative is taken up with the two women's recounting to one another their lives with their male partners, it is framed by their friendship. Rosalind's name recalls Shakespeare's heroine, especially as Helen addresses her in the opening line, in Celia-like terms, as "my sweet Rosalind." Helen's son Henry, repeatedly described as a "gentle boy" and "gentle child," is drawn to Rosalind when he sees her and tells his mother: "Bring home with you / That sweet strange lady-friend." He then runs home but "stopped, and beckoned with a meaning smile, / Where the road turned." The two women decide to take a new turn in the road when they set up house together in "a lonely dwelling" described in terms that recall Rosalind and Celia's house in the forest. Apart from the marriage of their children, their union too is figured in terms of marriage when Helen tells Rosalind : "Sweet, we will not part / Henceforth, if death be not division," phrasing that again echoes Celia's "Shall we be sunder'd / Shall we part, sweet girl?" At the end of the poem, when both women are dead, the narrator promises that death does not divide them: "And know, that if love die not in the dead / As in the living, none of mortal kind / Are blessed as now Helen and Rosalind."

Howards End is structured around several triangles. In chronological terms the first of these is that of Margaret, Helen, and Tibby. The eight-year age difference between the sisters is carefully foregrounded. If, in one sense, Margaret plays mother to her younger siblings ("She had brought up a charming sister, and was bringing up a brother"),[10] in another sense, the two girls are partners raising a boy child (they remember and discuss Tibby's childish tantrums like two fond parents). The structure of Leonardo's painting—with the older and the younger woman in loving relation to one another and the male child at a slight angle to both—is repeated. It is reconstructed at the end of the novel, when Helen's child takes Tibby's place. Helen, like the Madonna, has a child out of wedlock. A reference to Mary is the only hint offered the reader of Helen's condition before she leaves England. When Tibby mentions the Basts, Helen looks "like a frightened animal" (252) and her expression haunts him until it is "absorbed into the figure of St Mary the Virgin, before whom he paused for a moment on the walk home" (252). Though Leonard is posited as the father, most commentators have experienced a sense of incredulity at this fatherhood. The incredulity is engendered by the novel itself, which invisibilizes the sexual relationship and makes it utterly unconvincing. Although Forster came to see this unconvincing quality as a flaw, it is possible to read it as an important part of the novel's effect. Closely corresponding to it is the unconvincing quality of Margaret's love for Mr. Wilcox. If Helen's horrified reaction is shared by many readers, it is surely because the narrator is at pains to construct Mr. Wilcox as intellectually, emotionally, and sexually a most unsuitable partner for Margaret.

In contrast, the Helen-Margaret relationship comes across as completely convincing. The text leads the reader to endorse the "inner life" over the "outer," primarily by identifying the former with the Helen-Margaret (and the Margaret-Mrs. Wilcox) relationship and the latter with heterosexuality (Leonard-Jacky, Mr. and Mrs. Wilcox, Charles-Dolly, Margaret-Mr. Wilcox, Leonard-Helen). Love between women comes across as infinitely more satisfying than any of the varied examples of heterosexuality, all of which are deeply imbalanced and based on concealment as deceit.[11]

Forster constructs the relationships between women in this novel, especially the Margaret-Mrs. Wilcox relationship, in terms of hiddenness and with Paterian phrasing and imagery. Margaret and Helen live in a Michael Field-type household. It is not only feminine but also Aestheticist. They support women's suffrage and other causes of the day, they move in a circle of intellectuals and artists, they go regularly to classical music concerts, they prize conversation, personal relations, and art. Their tastes in art are indicated in passing when Margaret declares herself willing to lose all their apostle spoons but not their little Ricketts picture. This is a surprising evaluation because the former would be much more expensive than the latter. Charles Ricketts clearly represents to Margaret something more than monetary or even strictly aesthetic value. Pater's favorite words—"strange" (62, 65), "subtle" (6), "curious" (69), "sympathy" (6, 62)—are summoned to suggest the quality of women's relationships with one another.[12]

Chapter 8 opens: "The friendship between Margaret and Mrs Wilcox, which was to develop so quickly and with such strange results, may perhaps have had its beginnings at Speyer, in the spring" (62). The tone of tentativeness assumed by the narrator is similar to Pater's when he speculates about the lives of Renaissance artists. In both cases it suggests the importance of noninstitutionalized relationships, the possible emotional centrality of the socially marginal. We are told of Mrs. Wilcox: "Perhaps it was she who had desired the Miss Schlegels to be invited to Howards End, and Margaret whose presence she had particularly desired. All this is speculation: Mrs Wilcox has left few clear indications behind her" (62). The nature of the speculation, with the twice-repeated "desire," is similar to Pater's speculations about dead spiritual ancestors: "Beneath the Platonic calm of the sonnets there is latent a deep delight in carnal form. . . . He often falls into the language of less tranquil affections. . . . He . . . had not been always, we may think, a mere Platonic lover."[13] Forster too uses *affection* to indicate same-sex love and to suggest something stronger than what is normally understood by affection: "The affections are more reticent than the passions, and their expression more subtle. If she herself should ever fall in love with a man, she, like Helen, would proclaim it from the house-tops, but as she only loved a sister she used the voiceless language of sympathy" (6). The episodic nature of falling in love is here posited against the continuous condition of loving, and the biblical allusion may suggest that what is at present silent or hidden will one day be proclaimed from the house tops.

If we follow the narratorial hint that Mrs. Wilcox had "desired" Margaret's presence at Howards End, the Helen-Paul episode becomes, from Mrs. Wilcox's point of view, an unexpected interruption in a narrative that should have opened with herself and Margaret. Her first conversation with Margaret when they do meet alone can be read from this angle. The two women overtly talk at cross-purposes, although they reach a covert sympathy. In the first paragraph of chapter 8, after saying that Mrs. Wilcox has left few clear indications behind her, the narrator immediately continues: "It is certain that she came to call at Wickham Place a fortnight later" (62). Mrs. Wilcox thus pursues the relationship she desires with Margaret, after the Helen-Paul interruption is sorted out. Margaret's letter constructs the relationship as between two families rather than two individuals, "You have been good enough to call on us," and she signs it, formally, "M.J.Schlegel" (64). The reply is couched in singular (as opposed to plural) pronouns, "You should not have written me such a letter. I called to tell you that Paul has gone abroad," and signed "Ruth Wilcox" (64). Mrs. Wilcox's significant first name is revealed for the first time in the novel.

Mrs. Wilcox is visually constructed like a Leonardo painting interpreted by Pater when Margaret visits her in her London apartment and is "shown straight into Mrs Wilcox's bedroom" (65). She is sitting up in bed, writing letters: "The light of the fire, the light from the window, and the light of a candle-lamp, which threw a quivering halo round her hands, combined to create a strange atmosphere of dissolution" (65). The idea of "strange . . . dissolution" will recur later, when Margaret thinks of the dead Mrs. Wilcox as a consciousness that encompasses everything, a vision very similar to that suggested to Pater by La Gioconda: "the fancy of a perpetual life, sweeping together ten thousand experiences."[14] These Paterian images recur at the end of the chapter in the cluster—darkened chamber, flickering light/flame, shadows, hiddenness—that Woolf uses in *A Room of One's Own* in connection with love between women. The word *strange* is replaced by *curious*: "Then the curious note was struck again. . . . There was a long pause—a pause that was somehow akin to the flicker of the fire, the quiver of the reading-lamp upon their hands, the white blur from the window; a pause of shifting and eternal shadows" (69–70). Earlier, Mrs. Munt had termed Margaret and Helen "odd girls." "Strange," "curious', "odd"—these words place the women's relationships, as does the word "normal" when Margaret's and Mrs Wilcox's conversation is interrupted by a maid: "They were interrupted, and when they resumed conversation it was on more normal lines" (67).

What are the less normal lines into which the conversation twice slides? When Margaret tells Mrs. Wilcox that Helen has gone to Germany, "She gone as well," murmured the other. "Yes, certainly, it is quite safe—safe, absolutely, now" (65). Margaret takes this to mean that Mrs. Wilcox is worried lest Helen meet Paul again. Mrs. Wilcox, however, knows that Paul frequently flirts with women and that nothing will come of it even if they do meet. What is it that she considers "safe" then? In my reading, it is her own relationship with Margaret that she can now safely pursue without interruption. She uses Margaret's phrase "an instinct, which may be wrong" (66) to entirely different ends. Margaret used it to indicate her feeling that the two families, including herself and Mrs. Wilcox, should not meet. Mrs. Wilcox did not agree with this. She merely felt that Helen and Paul should not meet, but with them safely out of the way she wished to meet Margaret, and she repeats the phrase again when questioned: "An instinct which may be wrong." At this point, as we learn later, Mrs. Wilcox knows she is seriously ill but has kept this hidden from her family. So she may be worrying, not, as Margaret thinks, about Paul and Helen but about her own attraction to Margaret, an instinctive attraction that she follows but is not entirely sure of. Margaret questions her, "You aren't sure?" and Mrs. Wilcox is "uneasy" (66), uncertain.

In this annunciationlike visit, when Margaret, angel-like, appears to Mrs. Wilcox in her bedroom, there are two major topics of conversation: marriage and Mrs. Wilcox's girlhood home. Mrs. Wilcox's voice "quickens" only when she talks of the latter; her account of her son's wedding is expressionless and bores Margaret, who drops the framed photo of Dolly and smashes the glass. This action echoes that of Leonard, who smashes his wife Jacky's "likeness" (51). The fragility of the frame of marriage, of what Forster, describing Margaret's wedding, ironically calls "the glass shade . . . that cuts off married couples from the world" (255), is suggested through these two incidents of the smashing of bridal pictures. The spouse is an inadequate and easily breakable likeness.

At parting, Mrs. Wilcox, holding Margaret's hand, hesitantly asks whether she ever thinks about herself. She calls Margaret a "girl" (70). Margaret is a little annoyed by the diminutive, at which Mrs. Wilcox smiles and asks if she has been rude. The diminutives "girl" and "boy" have a long history of functioning, as Boswell has pointed out, in same-sex relationships, as in heterosexual ones, as an endearment.[15] They certainly do so in many of the nineteenth-century texts I have examined. Margaret fills in the gaps of Mrs. Wilcox's speeches and Mrs. Wilcox accepts her readings, but these incomplete speeches are capable of other readings as well. Thus, explaining her terming Margaret a "girl," Mrs. Wilcox says, "I only meant that I am fifty-one, and that to me both of you . . . " (70). Margaret interprets this to mean that Mrs. Wilcox thinks her inexperienced and proceeds to give a speech on the subject. Mrs. Wilcox's response to this speech suggests that she may also have in mind the idea of Margaret as her younger self: " 'Indeed, you put the difficulties of life splendidly,' said Mrs Wilcox, withdrawing her hand into the deeper shadows. 'It is just what I should have liked to say about them myself' " (70). This closing line indicates that Margaret represents much that Mrs. Wilcox would have liked to be. "Splendid" is an epithet Mrs. Wilcox uses again in the next chapter to describe Margaret's articulateness. Although Margaret reads this as a snub, Mrs. Wilcox insists that she means what she says.

Mrs. Wilcox is described as having a "personality" (74). *Personality*, like *temperament*, is a word used by both Pater and Wilde to indicate homoeroticism. In that light Mrs. Wilcox"s remark "We never discuss anything at Howards End" (74) is significant. Margaret reads the "We" to refer to the Wilcox family. But this is not what Mrs. Wilcox has in mind, for she follows it up with "I sometimes think that it is wiser to leave action and discussion to men" (74). If men, which would include the Wilcox men, are to be consigned to discussion and action, then the "We" of Howards End are women. At the end of the novel Howards End is constructed as a matrilineal home inhabited by a community of women. The witchlike and powerful Miss Avery, who refused to marry a Wilcox, who gives Evie an expensive present because she is her mother's daughter, and who guards the house in order to hand it over to Margaret, knows what she wants and pursues it willfully without discussion. She refurnishes the house, convinced that Margaret will stay there, even though Margaret insists she will not.

Margaret reads Mrs. Wilcox's idea of leaving action and discussion to men as an antifeminist desire to keep women back while men "move forward" (75). But Mrs. Wilcox, who is not making a definite statement ("I sometimes think"), is suggesting an emotional separatism from the public world of male-dominated institutions, including institutions of government and learning. Her statement gropes toward Woolf's doubts in *A Room of One's Own* as to whether women should join institutions such as the academy and government and play men's power games for the rewards of money and status. Woolf doubts the efficacy of a feminism that leads women to join men's races in which they will continue to be handicapped while apparently "equal." Privileging liberty over equality, in the tradition of romantic anarchism, she argues that women should form an outsiders' society wedded to poverty and chastity. Woolf's political strategy here looks back to such thinkers as William Godwin, who argued that "truth dwells with contemplation," and Pater, who remarked that the end of culture is not rebellion but peace.

The debate over the merits of the contemplative life versus the active life has a long history and is linked to the debate over the merits of celibacy and same-sex community versus those of marriage. When Meredith advises the reader to stay away from the male monster of politics and cling to the skirts of philosophy, he too identifies action with male violence and contemplation with the mental evolution of humanity through women. Margaret's feminism is limited, both in her statement of it and in her attempted acting-out of it in her marriage: "Whether, since men have moved forward so far, they [women] too may move forward a little now. I say they may" (75). Her model assumes that men are ahead of women and that women must try to catch up. In the space of Howards End, Mrs. Wilcox and Miss Avery suggest that women who explore their own vision of freedom are better off than those who strive for equality in partnership with men. Margaret and Helen follow the route from the second to the first possibility.

Mrs. Wilcox is not constructed as a figure of wisdom and all-knowingness, although this is how she appears at times to Margaret and Helen. On the contrary, she is constructed, like Mrs. Moore in *A Passage to India*, as a woman who, at the end of her life, doubts the principles on which she has lived that life. She is in a state of questioning and uncertainty. Her reply to Margaret's remarks about women is "I don't know, I don't know" (75). The act of leaving Howards End to Margaret completes a series of acts that reverse the direction of her entire life as a wife and mother. This is figured in her putting Margaret's name "at the top of the page" (78) of her Christmas list. Christmas being a family festival, the names of spouse and children should top the list. During the shopping expedition her mind is not on the gifts (the choice of which she leaves to Margaret) or greeting cards (which she does not order) but on Margaret's future. Their return to the carriage "by devious paths" (80) figuratively expresses Mrs. Wilcox's approach to Margaret. Margaret's failure to understand this approach is evident even before she refuses Mrs. Wilcox's "queer and imaginative" (82) invitation to Howards End. Mrs. Wilcox makes perhaps her most important (and "out-of-character") speech in relation to Margaret's having to leave Wickham Place, but this speech is also an analysis of the institution of virilocal marriage that uproots women from their own homes:

> Then she said vehemently: "It is monstrous, Miss Schlegel; it isn't right. I had no idea that this was hanging over you. I do pity you from the bottom of my heart. To be parted from your house, your father's house—it oughtn't to be allowed. It is worse than dying. I would rather die than—oh poor girls! Can what they call civilization be right, if people mayn't die in the room where they were born? My dear, I am so sorry—" (81)

Margaret's inadequate response to this radical analysis is that Mrs. Wilcox must be overtired and hence "inclined to hysteria" (81). Parting from the parental house is an ordeal suffered by girls in the nineteenth-century novel and on this parting patriarchal civilization rests. Mrs. Wilcox's questioning of "civilization" rests on her identification of marriage with death or worse than death. The "poor girls" of her exclamation are not only Margaret and Helen but all girls who must go through this process of transplantation. In several women's novels the process does equal death. One thinks of the pregnant and dying Catherine Earnshaw leaning from the bedroom window of Thrushcross Grange and longing for the freedom of her girlhood at Wuthering Heights or Maggie Tulliver turned away from the door by her brother. Mrs. Wilcox does not die in the room where she was born because her family, pretending to concur in her wish to return to Howards End, tricks her and takes her to a hospital. The terse note she scribbles on her deathbed signals her feeling that what is called civilization is not "right." This civilization demands that her house, as her property, should be inherited by her husband and children. Dying, Mrs. Wilcox attempts to remake her life by leaving her house, her only major possession, to a same-sex friend chosen late in life but, nevertheless, definitely chosen. She seeks also to empower the Schlegel sisters in their singleness together, for fear of homelessness is often, as in Diana Merion's case, an inducement to marriage.

The narratorial commentary underlines the political significance of this action by which "all the conventional colouring of life had been altered" (96).[16] The meaning of Mrs. Wilcox's note, if fully faced by her family, "would have driven them miserable or mad" (96). For, as Mr. Wilcox remarks, the will does not represent an act of philanthropy—Margaret is not a poor woman. It represents an act of love, and Forster's language foregrounds this. The note was written "under the spell of a sudden friendship" (96). It was "contrary to her very nature, so far as that nature was understood by them" (96). "Contrary to nature" was a phrase often applied to same-sex relationships (as in Huysmans's *A Rebours*). The idea of falling under a spell is more commonly applied to falling in love, for which friendship may operate as a euphemism when the love is between members of the same sex. Margaret is a "spiritual heir" because "no bond of blood" (96) is involved. Yet the word *passion* is used: "Has the soul offspring? A wych-elm tree, a vine, a wisp of hay with dew on it— can passion for such things be transmitted where there is no bond of blood?" (96). The idea of spiritual offspring from a marriage of true minds between same-sex "friends" dates back to Plato and Shakespeare's *Sonnets*, an ancestry repeatedly claimed by such writers on homoerotic themes as Pater, Wilde, Carpenter, Symonds, Samuel Butler. The idea of the artist's perception of a curious inner landscape being passed on "to us in a chain of secret influences" is central to Pater's essay on Leonardo. Mrs. Wilcox is figured as a practitioner of what Wilde termed "the art of life" and she transmits her passion for a way of life—the way of life in a women's community represented by Howards End—to Margaret who is already living an approximation to such a life.

In *A Room of One's Own* Woolf calls on women to be "traitors" to the system of marriage and property into which they are born, to opt out of it and form an "outsiders' society." She may have been recalling Forster's characterization of Mrs. Wilcox as "treacherous to the family, to the laws of property, to her own written word" (97). Evie uses the word *outsider* to refer to Margaret and assumes that ancestors are only biological: "Mother believed so in ancestors too—it isn't like her to leave anything to an outsider, who'd never appreciate" (97). By leaving her house, the abode and sign of ancestry, to an outsider, Mrs. Wilcox constructs herself as an outsider and refigures the significance of ancestry.[17] The next chapter repeats the word *strange* for Mrs. Wilcox's action: "Miss Schlegel had never heard of his mother's strange request" (100). That Margaret at this stage of her life would not have understood Mrs. Wilcox's action is indicated by the narrator: "By her also it would have been rejected as the fantasy of an invalid" (100).

Margaret follows Mrs. Wilcox's journey through heterosexuality in order to reach the same conclusion. Reflecting on her dead friend, Margaret thinks that "Mrs Wilcox had escaped registration" (100–1). In *The Longest Journey* Rickie had wished that there were a registry office for friendships so that they could be given the public sanction that marriage receives. Rejecting the ceremonies of baptism, marriage, and funerals as "clumsy devices," Margaret envisions the possibility of other human aspirations: "Truer relationships gleamed. Perhaps the last word would be hope—hope even on this side of the grave" (101). *Hope* is a key Shelleyan word; it concludes *Prometheus Unbound*: "to hope till Hope creates / From its own wreck the thing it contemplates." For Forster the possibility of a happy ending involving two same-sex partners seemed very remote; he wrote *Maurice* to imagine such an ending but could not publish it in his lifetime. Here he figures a happy ending for England as a connection between women.

The novel's epigraph, "Only connect . . . " has generally been read as referring to the Wilcox-Schlegel, that is, the heterosexual, and therefore the "inner-outer" connection. I read it as referring to the woman-woman and, therefore, the inner-inner, hidden connections. Feeling at peace in the house, Margaret "forgot the luggage and the motor-cars, and the hurrying men who know so much and connect so little" (202). Knowledge as information, the knowledge of Woolf's "educated men," is posed against the wisdom of the uneducated women of Hilton, women like Miss Avery and Mrs. Wilcox. These women's relations with one another are suggested by the image of the house and the tree, described in feminine terms. The tree and the vine in conjunction are old images of erotic relationship, and Forster's idea of "comradeship" as expressing the spirit of England alludes here to Keats's image in the "Ode to Autumn" of the mossed cottage trees bending with apples and the vines running round the thatch eaves. These are symbols of comradeship rather than sexuality—Autumn is "close bosom friend" of the sun. "Comradeship," generally used by turn-of-the-century writers to refer to homoerotic relations between men, is used here to refer to such relations between women. The tree is "a comrade." It has both "strength" and "tenderness" as it bends over the house. It resists being encompassed by men. The heterosexual image of the woman's waist spanned by the man is refused: "the girth, that a dozen men could not have spanned, became in the end evanescent, till pale bud clusters seemed to float in the air" (203). Although we are told that to compare house or tree to man or woman is to dwarf the vision, the nonsexual comradely relation between the two is imagined in female terms (resistance to spanning by men, bud clusters) and anticipates the novel's closure in comradeship between two women and two boy children. Margaret notes that the tree and the house stand for a human comradeship: "Yet they kept within limits of the human. Their message was not of eternity, but of hope on this side of the grave. As she stood in the one, gazing at the other, truer relationships had gleamed" (203).

Margaret's relations with Mr. Wilcox are triangular from the start. Initially, a triangle is formed with Leonard, which Forster calls the "triangle of sex" and compares to two cocks and a hen in a barnyard (144). This is soon replaced by a more serious triangle, that of Margaret-Helen-Mr. Wilcox, and this triangle persists. The morning after their unpleasing first kiss, Margaret and Mr. Wilcox meet when she is with Helen, and "she took him by one hand, retaining her sister in the other" (184). The chapter begins with Margaret's heroine-appropriate and absurd intention to reform Mr. Wilcox, "to help him" acknowledge his emotions and become capable of love (183). The narrator tersely remarks of this intention: "But she failed" (184). The measure of her failure is not primarily Mr. Wilcox's unchanged behavior but her own decimation. The chapter ends with her succumbing to his bullying and agreeing to cut short her stay at her aunt's house. The next chapter opens with her giving Helen "a thorough scolding" (191) for daring to confront Mr. Wilcox over the wrong advice given to Leonard. The Margaret-Mr. Wilcox relationship thus commences with Margaret's betraying the women of her own family in order to play wife to Mr. Wilcox. She pursues this course of action through the rest of the novel up to the point of the crisis at Howards End. Her finally taking women's side against men is preceded by a long course of taking men's side against women. She labels Jacky "no good" (238) and sees Henry as "the only hope" to save Helen from being "so queer" and growing "queerer" (278).

What saves Margaret from Dolly's fate or even Ruth Wilcox's is her indifference to reproduction. Forster's narrative splits heterosexuality and reproduction, assigning one to each sister. The Wilcoxes as a family stand for the two principles in inseparable conjunction. The narrator's sardonicism regarding the process, "A short-frocked edition of Charles also regards them placidly; a perambulator edition is squeaking; a third edition is expected shortly. Nature is turning out Wilcoxes in this peaceful abode, so that they may inherit the earth" (182), concurs with Miss Avery's, who remarks that "they breed like rabbits" (271). Survival through reproduction is a characteristic of less intelligent and weaker species in Darwin's evolutionary scheme; the narrative suggests that Schlegels, who stand for women and womanlike men, will survive through the life of the mind. They will inherit despite interruptions from the Wilcoxes. This utopian vision is invoked when Margaret in the penultimate chapter thinks, "There were truer relationships beyond the limits that fetter us now" (327). The Wilcoxes stand not just for men versus women but for heterosexuality, family, and reproduction versus same-sex love, friendship, community, and creativity. In this divide Schlegels, including the dead father who submitted to the young Margaret's decision making, Tibby, however inadequately, and Helen's son are on "women's side" and for the latter syndrome.

When Miss Avery remarks that Mrs. Wilcox ought to have married a soldier, the reference is perhaps not so much to martial as to intellectual warfare. It is Miss Avery who hangs up Mr. Schlegel's sword, thus making it available to Charles, who uses it to kill Leonard and destroy himself. In this action the Wilcox men self-destruct, much in the fashion of Shelley's tyrannical Jupiter in *Prometheus Unbound*. Although the narrator invites readerly tenderness for Leonard, his removal too seems required for the women-only ending to be possible. Reproduction without heterosexual encumbrance is possible only by legitimizing the illegitimate. This constitutes the crux of Margaret's final battle. The legal "illegitimacy" of Helen's child is also a trope for the illegitimate idea of a child raised by two women, for feminine kinship as "holy family." If, in *Maurice*, Forster, as John Fletcher has suggested, erases himself,[18] the intellectual Clive-like homosexual, in *Howards End* he endorses his own upbringing in a household of women, by the powerful "mothers" who are often blamed by psychoanalysts for the "creation" of homosexual men. The novel's last scene visualizes the women and children very much in the fashion of a Leonardo painting—the Madonna with the Christ child and infant St. John, in the company of St. Anne or an angel.

At certain crucial moments in the text the apparent situation seems to carry a weight larger than itself. Such is the moment when Margaret resolves to defend Helen against Mr. Wilcox and the doctor. Mr. Wilcox describes Helen as "Musical, literary, artistic, but I should say normal" (286). The three initial epithets were encoded words often used to refer to homosexual men and are found, for instance, in Havelock Ellis's questions to and descriptions of the homosexual men and women he examined. The familiar images of the "hunt," "the chase" (281), the "capture" (279) occur, with the interesting variation that the civilized pursuers are compared not to foxhunters but to "the wolf-pack" (279). In this context the violence of Margaret's reaction, sliding into the present tense of narratorial comment, seems to gesture toward the sexologists' scientific labeling of homosexuality:

> How dare these men label her sister! What horrors lay ahead! What impertinences that shelter under the name of science! The pack was turning on Helen, to deny her human rights, and it seemed to Margaret that all Schlegels were threatened with her. Were they normal? What a question to ask! And it is always those who know nothing about human nature, who are bored by psychology and shocked by physiology, who ask it. However piteous her sister's state, she knew that she must be on her side. They would be mad together if the world chose to consider them so. (286)

The closure of *Howards End* functions symbolically as the completion of the interrupted relationship between Margaret and Mrs. Wilcox. After she has refused Mrs. Wilcox's invitation, Margaret realizes that Mrs. Wilcox's wifehood and motherhood are irrelevant to the main intensity in her life, the Paterian exquisite "passion" for her house, and that Margaret has been invited to "share this passion," her "only one passion" (83). Watching Mrs. Wilcox ascend to her apartment in the lift, Margaret has "the sense of an imprisonment" (83). The image of glass figures the invisible barrier of marriage:

> Margaret watched the tall lonely figure sweep up the hall to the lift. As the glass doors closed on it she had the sense of an imprisonment. The beautiful head disappeared first, still buried in the muff; the long trailing skirt followed. A woman of undefinable rarity was going up heavenward, like a specimen in a bottle. And into what a heaven—a vault as of hell, sooty black, from which soots descended! (83)

The marital home, ironically figured as heaven, is also a hell in which Mrs. Wilcox has lain buried all her life, and the images also gesture toward her imminent death. Determined to break through the barrier, Margaret follows Mrs. Wilcox to the railway station and buys a one-way ticket to Howards End. The two women are about to journey together to the house where Mrs. Wilcox says Margaret is "coming to sleep . . . coming to stop." She addresses Margaret, for the first time, as simply "dear" (84). She refers to an undifferentiated "them," the people (the women?) of the village whom Margaret will join: "I dare say they are sitting in the sun in Hertfordshire, and you will never repent joining them." The "them" cannot be the Wilcoxes, who are not at Howards End. Margaret responds, "I shall never repent joining you," and is told, "It is the same" (84). Their walk down the platform is interrupted by the appearance of the Wilcoxes, and Mrs. Wilcox betrays Margaret, using Margaret's own inadequate phrase "Another day" (84). Margaret is "left alone. No one wanted her" (85). The action is repeated when Margaret joins Mr. Wilcox against Helen. She makes reparation when she gives Helen and her child Howards End as Mrs. Wilcox gave it her.

It is Helen, sitting in "the sun" (286), whom she finally joins at Hertfordshire. In contrast to the bridal pictures framed in glass that can be smashed, Helen, Margaret's true likeness, is "framed in the vine, and one of her hands played with the buds. The wind ruffled her hair, the sun glorified it" (286). The image of the halo, associated with Mrs. Wilcox, is transferred to Helen here. The night they spend together is a full-moon night and is presided over by the virginal Miss Avery. *Virginal* is a word applied to Margaret by the narrator: "She was, in her own way, as masterly [as Mr. Wilcox]. If he was a fortress she was a mountain peak, whom all might tread, but whom the snows made nightly virginal" (179). One may compare here Clarissa Dalloway who has "a virginity preserved through childbirth."

Although Mr. Wilcox is alive and "more like a woman" (325) at the novel's close, and the triangle is resolved by being stabilized ("I wanted you; he wanted you; and everyone said it was impossible, but you knew" Helen says, 336), yet his death is imminent. Howards End embodies the terrifying virginity of Diana who kills the men who look upon her. Margaret says of the house, "It kills what is dreadful and makes what is beautiful live" (297), and the persons either literally or metaphorically killed there are Leonard, Charles, and Mr. Wilcox.

Leonard, beginning his journey from London to Howards End where he will die, is represented as being lured by the moon. The image of the drop sliding into the sea, a common image for the soul merging with the universe at death, suggests that he is moving toward his doom like Medusa's victims. The image of the snake also appears in his nightmares, but his fears disappear as he gazes at the moon:

> Why had he been afraid? He went to the window, and saw that the moon was descending through a clear sky. He saw her volcanoes, and the bright expanses that a gracious error has named seas. They paled, for the sun, who had lit them up, was coming to light the earth. Sea of Serenity, Sea of Tranquillity, Ocean of the Lunar Storms, merged into one lucent drop, itself to slip into the sempiternal dawn. And he had been afraid of the moon! (319).

Of the three men "killed" by the matrilineal house, Leonard is the only one allowed this kind of vision, but the word *tranquilly* is also applied to Mr. Wilcox at the very end, when he is telling Margaret of Mrs. Wilcox's having left the house to her (340). In this utopian narrative men quietly consent to die in order that women together may evolve a new world.[19] Helen, trying to explain her disinterest in heterosexual love, suggests, in an incomplete sentence, how it does not compare with her love for Margaret: "How nothing seems to match— how, my darling, my precious—" (335).[20] The novel's last lines link Margaret with Mrs. Wilcox in an erotic female image. When she is told of the legacy, "Something shook her life in its inmost recesses, and she shivered" (340).

In his myth for the salvation of England, Forster invests women's love for one another with his most dearly held values—the inner life, personal relations, and the ability to say "I," an ability that Charles Wilcox, in his most sympathetic moment, inarticulately wishes he had been given in childhood, so that as an adult he might have comforted his father. These values, central to the Romantic lyric and to the genre of the personal letter, move *Howards End* beyond the Victorian novel, overlaying its plot structure with a fluid lyrical open-endedness from its opening line: "One may as well begin with Helen's letters to her sister" (1).

While eroticism may seem to be evaded in the Margaret-Helen relationship by their biological sisterhood, one may read the taboos on homosexuality and incest as simultaneously challenged here, a pattern found in Romantic texts. Many real-life relatives, like Michael Field, were erotically involved with one another. If Vanessa and Virginia Stephen were, as is often suggested, the models for Margaret and Helen, the erotic charge between them may well have suggested a similar charge between the fictional heroines. From Virginia's letter to Vanessa on the eve of the latter's wedding, and from *Moments of Being*, it is possible to argue that Virginia would have liked a lifelong "marriage" with Vanessa as a living arrangement. Forster may be seen as fulfilling this fantasy—in 1910 he could not have been sure that Virginia would marry a "Leonard"!

One of the best-known Victorian precedents for such a pattern of closure is Wilkie Collins's *The Woman in White* (1860), whose conventionally good and beautiful heroine, Laura Fairlie, is eclipsed by her brilliant "ugly" half-sister, Marian Halcombe. While Marian's courage, intellect, and outspokenness, repeatedly characterized as "manly," win her the unreserved admiration of both hero and villain, Laura is her only love object. When forced into her first marriage, Laura insists on Marian's living with her, and when Laura finally marries the hero Hartright, Marian chooses to remain unmarried and live with them. Marian's name is significant, as are most names in this novel. There is an interesting contrast between the very sympathetic portrait of this Sapphic woman and the highly unsympathetic portrait of Mr. Fairlie, a neurotic elitist aesthete. This eccentric bachelor, who lives in seclusion surrounded by male servants and collections of objets d'art, makes a spirited and amusing protest against the way married people inflict their problems on single people. He is a fairly obvious caricature of the emerging male homosexual type romanticized by Huysmans, Pater, and Wilde. The novel's endorsement of women's love for each other may be rendered safe by its containment in the legitimate domesticity that Fairlie finds intolerable.

The avoidance of overt sexuality in the elaborate myths worked out in such fictions as Meredith's and Forster's is critiqued in Hope Mirrlees's *Madeleine: One of Love's Jansenists*, a novel that openly invokes Sappho and Mary together. Reading it to review it, Mirrlees's friend Virginia Woolf wrote to Clive Bell, "It's all sapphism so far as I've got—Jane and herself."[21]

Her review stresses Mirrlees's choice of psychological rather than material reality as her subject, "It is the inner world that matters," and praises the novel as "difficult and interesting." She points out that for the protagonist to go insane at the end is "generally an evasion on the part of the artist" but that Mirrlees has managed this with considerable success, so that the reader encounters the ending with a "little shock of emotion."[22]

I am interested in the way Mirrlees constructs an ancestry and a series of models for her sixteenth-century French heroine Madeleine, especially by fusing Sapphic and Marian myths. Although Madeleine considers her passion for her namesake, the novelist Madeleine de Scudéry, spiritual, its erotic and even sexual dimensions are made fairly evident via a number of strategies. Mirrlees's device of giving both women the same name suggests the self yearning for fusion with its likeness. Narcissus, Hylas, and Sappho are invoked in various chapter titles. Madeleine is about twenty years younger than her beloved but perceives herself as the active pursuer and wooer. Although Madeleine despises her womanizing father and is deeply attached to her mother, the narrator suggests that her sexual energies are inherited from him, and she herself comes to believe that the course of her romance will parallel that of his extramarital liaison. Madeleine is a Precieuse and therefore an emotional separatist who is convinced "that the perfect *amitie tendre* can exist only between two women"[23], a conviction that is strengthened when her male suitor, Jacques, first tells her about the life and poetry of the Greek Sappho. Her yearning for a "radiant, transfigured world" (34) is embodied in her desire for a passionate friendship with Madame de Scudéry, "the modern Sappho."[24]

That this is not merely an adolescent phase is indicated by her having been "spellbound" by a beautiful little girl, Jeanne, at the age of seven. The adult Madeleine integrates her Jansenism with Sapphism, believing that the love of her female beloved will lead her to the love of a feminized Christ.[25] She derives this interpretation of Jansenism from a conversation she overhears between two young men who say that Christine of Sweden was told that the Precieuses are the Jansenists of love.[26] Throughout the novel Madeleine prays earnestly to the Virgin Mary to grant her desire for friendship with her beloved. She visits a Carmelite convent to pray to her name saint Magdalene, whom she terms the Christian Venus. On another occasion she visits the Abbaye of Port-Royal, a convent of Cistercian nuns that was the main centre of Jansenist resistance to papal authority in France. Looking at the portraits of women who were benefactors of the abbey, she imagines a portrait of herself and her beloved also hanging there:

> Some day would another drawing be added to the collection? A drawing wherein would be portrayed a plain, swarthy woman in classic drapery, whose lyre was supported by a young fair virgin gazing up at her, and underneath these words—Madeleine de Scudéry and Madeleine Troqueville, twin-stars of

talent, piety and love, who, in their declining years retreated to this House that they might sanctify the great love one bore to the other by the contemplation of the love of Christ. (157)

In contrast to Dorian brooding over his biological ancestors' portraits, Madeleine here claims members of a women's community as her spiritual ancestors.

Madeleine's fantasies of her ideal courtship of "Sappho" are scattered through the novel in smaller type. They culminate in a final fantasy where she boldly declares her passion, "A flame has long burned me" (249), quotes the Greek Sappho's ode ("That man seems to me greater than the gods") to strengthen her case, evokes St. Sebastian pierced by arrows, and describes her feelings as "Platonic" (252): In Madeleine's definition a Platonic feeling exists between two women and leads "down the slope of Inclination straight into the twilight grove of l'Amitie Tendre" (253). She describes the inner landscape of this love as follows:

> . . . so charmed is its atmosphere, so deep its green shadows, so heavy its brooding peace. For all round it is traced a magic circle across which nothing discordant or vulgar can venture . . . the Grecian Sappho . . . discovered hundreds of years ago the charm by which the magic circle can be crossed . . . it is merely this . . . take another maiden with you. . . . Madame, shall we try the virtue of the Grecian Sappho's charm?'
> And Sappho murmurs "yes." (253–54)

Madeleine sacrifices her suitor Jacques (whose friendship she enjoys but whose caresses bore her) to her love for Sappho, yet this love remains unexpressed in real life. She dislikes and is competitive with Madame de Scudéry when she meets her. Her attempts to attract the older woman's admiration succeed only in annoying her. The object of Madeleine's passion is not the real "Sappho" but "the Sappho of her dances" (258), that is, an idea in her head.

Toward the close, the narrator remarks that happiness would be much easier if "we were never visited by these swift, exclusive passions, which are so rarely reciprocal" (267). The end figures Madeleine's love as absurd, "grotesque," and "sick" and even suggests that she is being punished for spurning Jacques's love (274). But the epilogue, with its epigraph from the writings of the anthropologist, Jane Harrison, Mirrlees's lover, is more ambiguous. The epigraph reads: "Art springs straight out of the rite, and her first outward leap is the image of the god" (275). Drawing on the Shakespearean conflation of lover with lunatic and poet, Mirrlees dignifies Madeleine's Sapphic love by figuring her as an artist. In the epilogue, titled "The Rape to the Love of Invisible Things" (275), a group of wits, observing the insane Madeleine in the lunatic asylum, refer to her as "the Pseudo-Sappho" (275) because she imagines that she is "Sappho," that is, Madeleine de Scudéry. The wits remark that just as in ancient religion the worshipper became the god, so the true ending of a romance should be the lover becoming the beloved. What at one level is an insane delusion may at another level be a fusion more complete than is possible in sane everyday reality.

Mirrlees suggests that spiritual and mystical lesbianism may be dangerous and even a form of insanity. Conversely, she may also suggest that mysticism, with its transcendence of the visible reality of heterosexuality, may be consonant with art and with the impossible and invisible love between women. Mysticism, especially when the deity or the universal whole is figured as female, as, for instance, in Marian mysticism, works as an ecstatic interaction between two female entities, since the soul or spirit is usually figured as female. Thus Evelyn Underhill, in her 1910 classic *Mysticism*, although she subtitles it *A Study in the Nature and Development of Man's Spiritual Consciousness* and tends to use the male noun and pronoun for "the mystic," slides into using "she" and "her" for the self and the soul or spirit, as also for the personified ultimate reality—Beauty or the idea of the beautiful, the true, the good. Female images are used, too, for both— she quotes Plato, who compares the self to an oyster in its shell. The oyster containing a pearl is also a metaphor for the Virgin Mary in medieval poetry.[27] She uses female tropes for the ideal reality—the bride, the grail, the mystic rose. Underhill stresses the "ardour of unsatisfied love" as generative of the mystic quest.[28] In the early twentieth century, when samesex love, especially lesbian love, was figured as the love of the impossible and unattainable, and as more likely to be unsatisfied than satisfied, it could, paradoxically, be celebrated as consonant with, and perhaps even definitive of, the classic discourse of mysticism that informs much of the greatest Western and Eastern lyrical poetry. Underhill quotes medieval, Renaissance, Romantic, and Sufi poetry as illustrative of the mystic impulse of love.

The same tropes were often used both for mystical love and for erotic love. An example is that of the pearl and oyster. Used to refer to Mary and to Christ—the "pearl without price" generated in an enclosed interior space—this image was associated with purity and immortality. This is the way it figures in the medieval "Pearl," an elegy for a little daughter who is finally seen as absorbed into Mary's band of virgins. However, two Victorian magazines devoted to erotica were named the *Pearl* and the *Oyster*. I would term these magazines erotic rather than pornographic. Women were active participants rather than passive victims in almost all the stories. The erotic practices described range from couple and group sex—heterosexual and homosexual—to sadomasochism—heterosexual, homosexual, and lesbian—to sodomy and tribadism, all very sympathetically portrayed. The last story in the last issue of the *Pearl* narrates the conversion of an elderly man who was shocked by male homosexuality and wished to prosecute it as a criminal activity but decided, after reading the *Pearl*, that all pleasure is legitimate. In the *Oyster*, erotic narratives are interspersed with serious essays on women's rights.

The fusion of mystical and erotic Sapphism as a model for male homosexual love is found in G. L. Dickinson's 1893–1894 sonnet sequence addressed to a male beloved. Explicitly protesting against the body-mind dualism espoused by his beloved, which prevents the physical consummation of their love, Dickinson uses the trope of souls as feminine to suggest that in some better future they may be able to embrace. While Dickinson thought, in the terms of the time, of himself as a woman-soul trapped in a man's body, what is interesting is the figuring of the male beloved's soul as also feminine, a "sister-soul."[29] In this figuring Dickinson goes beyond the inversion syndrome wherein a homosexual man always falls in love with a manly man. He uses female homoeroticism as the symbol for physically and spiritually fulfilled love, the kind of love that he aspires to but that is thwarted by the prejudices of his beloved. Sonnet 4 figures Dickinson's soul as "knocking" for "entrance" but prevented because the beloved's "eyes are guarded with a crystal pane" and his "lips" too "straitened . . . to let her in." The thwarted soul "wanders like a ghost," defeated by the beloved's resistance. Dickinson hopes that with the passing of many years the time may come when she attains by patience what can never be attained by force: "And unimpeded clasp the sister-soul / That rounds her broken crescent to a whole." The image of the moon figures this love between men as Sapphic. Sonnet 2 suggests that "sisters" can and do embrace in ways that "brother's love" is not permitted to. The dedicatory poem commits the consummation of his love to some unknown future, perhaps to a fusing like that described by Milton's Gabriel, perhaps to other lovers in some happier future age: "Perhaps on that to-morrow / When we are counted dead, / By some diviner passion / It will be perfected."

The turn-of-the-century texts considered in this chapter explore the idea of a search for one's likeness through the genre of semibiography or historical fiction. This use of the genre derives from Pater. The covert tensions of the major Victorian novels become overt in these "other Victorian" texts. Thus the figure of the same-sex friend or sibling that was a marginal source of unease in the major Victorian novels comes closer to the center in these turn-of-the-century fictions. Samuel Butler's *The Way of All Flesh* is another such fiction where the hero's male mentor is ultimately recognized as his most congenial companion, and marriage as happy ending is displaced by divorce, freeing the hero for male friendship, which constitutes the happy ending.

That Meredith's *Diana* is based on Caroline Norton, Forster's Schlegel sisters on the Woolf sisters, and some of Mirrlees's characters on historical figures is not fortuitous. As in Pater's and the other texts examined in earlier chapters, the historical, biographical, and mythological elements are important for the sense of ancestry they bestow on a metaphorically orphaned homoeroticism. By relating same-sex friendships to Sappho, Mary, Diana, Demeter, Greek or Renaissance artists, the

Precieuses or the Romantics, these writers suggest the ideal character of these friendships, their highly evolved nature, their relationship to achievement in life and in art, their iconographic value, or their universality and inevitability. In all cases a sense of dignity, worth, and integration with civilization rather than exclusion from it is achieved through these tropes and textual strategies.

7

Biography as Homoerotic Fiction
Freud, Pater, and Woolf

Of all literature (yes, I think this is more or less true) I
love autobiography most. In fact I sometimes think only
autobiography is literature—novels are what we peel off
and come at last to the core, which is only you or me.
—Virginia Woolf

A Man's life of any worth is a continual Allegory. . . .
Shakespeare led a life of Allegory; his works are the
comments on it.
—John Keats

To suggest that undeniably "great" figures from the past—Plato, Socrates, or even the Greeks generally, Shakespeare, Leonardo, or Renaissance writers and artists generally—were homoerotically inclined was a way of legitimizing such inclinations in Victorian England, where the idea of genius had come to be widely accepted. Pater developed the fictionalized biographical portrait as a genre inflected by this suggestion. His portraits held up their subjects as desirable models for imitation by the reader and hinted at an autobiographical element via the writer's identification with his subject. The genre was further developed by Symonds, Wilde, Carpenter, and others. Freud's intervention tended to pathologize the genre. Woolf and writers of her generation inherited and mediated between the Aestheticist and the psychoanalytical ways of approaching homoeroticism through biography.

Victorian biography leaned in one of two directions: Carlyle's, who in the 1840s had defined history as the biography of great men, and Leslie Stephen's, who believed that the lives and opinions of many little-known people constitute history. Stephen's aim in his monumental *Dictionary of National Biography* was to compile the achievements of the less than great, by whose consensus the better known were ultimately adjudged great or otherwise.[1] The Carlylean model of struggling genius provided a useful starting point for writers like Pater and Wilde who wished to write deviance into the idea of greatness. Arguing that the poet and the prophet penetrate the divine mystery of the universe, Carlyle asked: "What are faults, what are the outward details of a life; if the inner secret of it, the remorse, temptations, true, often-baffled, never-ended struggle of it, be forgotten?"[2] He even went on to say that it was from these silent struggles that great work emerged and he gave the example of Shakespeare's struggles as expressed in the *Sonnets*:

> How much in Shakspeare [sic] lies hid; his sorrows, his silent struggles known to himself; much that was not known at all, not speakable at all: like *roots*, like sap and forces working underground! . . . Doubt it not, he had his own sorrows: those *Sonnets* of his will even testify expressly in what deep waters he had waded, and swum struggling for his life;—as what man like him ever failed to have to do?[3]

Taking a cue from Carlyle, Pater in *The Renaissance* and Wilde in *The Portrait of Mr. W. H.* suggested that homoerotic experience constituted that secret life of the artist from which great art arose. Many turn-of-the-century fictions, such as those by Michael Field, Meredith, Butler, Forster, pursued the implications of this suggestion, constructing homoerotic experience as crucially definitive of Western civilization. One of the ways they did this was to connect such experience with historical and mythological periods and figures already considered great and to endorse this greatness, even while rereading it in startling ways.

Foucault argues that the ideas of homosexuality and the homosexual personality were invented by sexologist, psychoanalytic, and other such discourses of perversion and inversion and that homosexual self-construction began only as a " 'reverse' discourse," a talking back.[4] I will attempt to demonstrate precisely the opposite process through a reading of Pater's 1873 essay on Leonardo da Vinci and a comparison of it with Freud's essay on the same artist. Freud's essay is an anxious rewriting of Pater's. Pater constructs and celebrates the homoerotic personality as active, self-conscious, wise, and knowledgeable. Freud's project is to reverse this discourse and analyze the homosexual personality as repressed, unhappy, and lacking in self-knowledge. Freud draws many of his crucial ideas from Pater, without acknowledgment, but omits three elements of Pater's art of biography: the focus on social and historical atmosphere, the assumption that fulfillment rather than repression/sublimation makes for creativity, and the narratorial stance of "appreciation" rather than analysis.[5]

Freud presents his essay on Leonardo as different from other biographies of this artist insofar as he dares to suggest that Leonardo was a repressed homosexual. Freud claims that most biographers would not even hint at such a possibility in relation to a great man. Although he makes two references to Pater's essay, nowhere does Freud acknowledge that Pater had indicated Leonardo's homoeroticism in a way that was understood by Pater's contemporaries and had celebrated Leonardo's love for a boy. Freud's claim to be the first to write of Leonardo's homoerotic inclinations is simply not true.

Pater's essay, "Leonardo da Vinci," in *The Renaissance* is written in the mode of "appreciation"—his next collection of essays is entitled *Appreciations* (1889). The essay begins by referring to Vasari's representation of Leonardo as an unconventional thinker who appeared mysterious to his contemporaries. Pater then outlines his own project: "A lover of strange souls may still analyse for himself the impression made on him by those works, and try to reach through it a definition of the chief elements of Leonardo's genius" (64). Pater casts himself as a "lover" whose analysis arises from love. He presents his essay as an analysis not of Leonardo but of the impression that Leonardo's works makes on Pater. The subjectivity of the enterprise is fully acknowledged, in accordance with his critical dictum in the preface:

> What is this song or picture, this engaging personality presented in life or in a book, to *me*? What effect does it really produce on me? Does it give me pleasure? and if so, what sort or degree of pleasure? How is my nature modified by its presence, and under its influence? The answers to these questions are the original facts with which the aesthetic critic has to do. (xxix, emphasis in the original)

Throughout the essay Pater places himself, and the reader, in the receptive position and "Leonardo" in the active position. To Leonardo is attributed the "art of going deep" (66); he lived "in a world of which he alone possessed the key" (68); he "penetrated into the most secret parts of nature" (70); he "plunged also into human personality" (71). A series of active verbs endow Leonardo with power, knowledge, and self-consciousness. Simultaneously, a series of adjectives ("strange," "curious," "subtle," "secret," "exotic," "exquisite," "hidden") encode this power as imbued with homoeroticism. Leonardo's works, filled with this power, "become, as it were, the receptacle of them, and pass them on to us in a chain of secret influences" (74). Leonardo is our spiritual ancestor, and his art is, in Pater's reading, "perfect." Homoeroticism contributes to this perfection: "Out of the secret places of a unique temperament he brought strange blossoms and fruits hitherto unknown; and for him, the novel impression conveyed, the exquisite effect woven, counted as an end in itself—a perfect end" (75).

Freud's essay constructs himself as an "investigator," approaching Leonardo in order to demonstrate that everyone is "subject to the laws which control the normal and morbid actions with the same strictness."[6] In this self-representation Freud claims to be conducting not an analysis of the impression made on him by the artist's work but an application of objective "laws" to the artist and his work. Freud omits to point out that the "laws" are invented by himself. The purpose of his project is to "subject" Leonardo to these laws. He then introduces Leonardo as an artist who is "injured," "suppressed" (29), the object of a wounding. Freud cites evidence to the effect that Leonardo was a happy, sociable, and pleasure-loving person. Against this evidence he introduces his own speculation: "It is quite possible that the conception of a beaming, jovial, and happy Leonardo was true only for the first and longer period of the master's life. . . . It is possible that the luster of his disposition became pale" (30–31). Phrased in this way, the speculation is unobjectionable, as the opposite, it is quite possible that this was not so, remains valid. However, here, as at every stage of his argument, Freud's speculations ("perhaps," "may," "seem") slip into assumptions.

A striking instance of this slippage soon appears. After noting that the accusation of homosexuality was brought against Leonardo and that he surrounded himself with beautiful young men, Freud goes on:

> Without sharing the certainty of his modern biographers, who naturally reject the possibility of a sexual relation between himself and his pupils as a baseless insult to this great man, it may be thought by far more probable that the affectionate relationships of Leonardo to the young men did not result in sexual activity. Nor should we attribute to him a high measure of sexual activity. (38–39)

The first part of the first sentence exonerates Freud from the prudishness of other biographers, but the second part, attributing speculation to some unspecified subject ("may be thought"—by whom?), hastily defines the relationships as affectionate and not actively sexual. Between these two possibilities—desire and affection—love disappears. It is precisely love that is foregrounded in Pater's account of the relationships:

> But among the more youthful heads there is one at Florence which Love chooses for its own—the head of a young man, which may well be the likeness of Andrea Salaino, beloved of Leonardo for his curled and waving hair . . . and afterwards his favourite pupil and servant. Of all the interests in living men and women which may have filled his life at Milan, this attachment alone is recorded. And in return Salaino identified himself so entirely with Leonardo, that the picture of St. Anne, in the Louvre, has been attributed to him. (74)

Pater speculates in the direction of imagining a life for Leonardo full of human interests and a love that is reciprocal and fulfilling. Conversely, when Freud proceeds to analyze Leonardo's attitude to love, he reads Leonardo's comment, "For verily, great love springs from great knowledge of the beloved object, and if you little know it, you will be able to love it only little or not at all" (40),[7] as evidence that Leonardo replaced love by investigation—"and it seems that in his case it was really so. His affects were controlled and subjected to the investigation impulse. He neither loved nor hated" (41). From "it seems" the argument has proceeded to an absolute statement of an extraordinarily sweeping nature.

Freud's first reference to Pater is in a footnote where he quotes one sentence: "But it is certain that at one period of his life he had almost ceased to be an artist" (35, note). Freud quotes this sentence to back up his claim that Leonardo's slowness in painting (which Pater attributes to his striving for perfection) was "a symptom of his inhibition" (35). In its context Pater's sentence leads on to an entirely different suggestion. In Pater's account this period of Leonardo's life occurred during his visit to Milan. According to Pater, Leonardo went there as a player on the harp and exercised a "fascination" (69) on those around him. Pater describes the life of Milan as "a life of brilliant sins and exquisite amusements" (70). Immersed in this life, "Leonardo became a celebrated designer of pageants; and it suited the quality of his genius, composed, in almost equal parts, of curiosity and the desire of beauty, to take things as they came" (70). In Pater's reading Leonardo is not obsessed by painting but is equally good at other arts. The period at Milan is represented as a time spent by Leonardo enjoying himself and fascinating others. Freud draws from Pater, without acknowledgment, his emphasis on Leonardo's curiosity. But whereas Freud sees this inquisitiveness as replacing the ability to love, and contributing to Leonardo's unfulfilled love life, Pater sees it as fruitful: "Curiosity and the desire of beauty—these are the two elementary forces in Leonardo's genius; curiosity often in conflict with the desire of beauty, but generating, in union with it, a type of subtle and curious grace" (70). The choice of erotic words removed from their conventional heterosexual context (*desire, union, generating*) places Leonardo's genius as of the "type" Pater selects in all his essays, the Platonic type that generates beautiful works of art, not children.

Freud's second citing of Pater is in connection with what Pater describes as "that unfathomable smile . . . which plays over all of Leonardo's work" (79). Freud quotes Pater's remark : "Besides, the picture is a portrait. From childhood we see this image defining itself on the fabric of his dreams; and but for express historical testimony, we might fancy that this was but his ideal lady, embodied and beheld at last" (79). Freud says that this remark "deserves to be taken literally" (90) and proceeds to his analysis, concluding that the ideal lady is Leonardo's mother, the smile was her smile, and that his homosexuality is therefore really repressed heterosexuality: "When as a lover he seems to pursue boys, he really thus runs away from women who could cause him to become disloyal to his mother" (75).

But Pater reads the smile quite differently, in the preceding and succeeding passages that Freud does not quote. He suggests that "the germinal principle, the unfathomable smile" (79) was drawn by the boy Leonardo from his master Verocchio's folio of drawings, which he copied many times when under training. The childhood memory is not an infantile unconscious one, but derives from "the elder, by-past master" (79). The second suggestion Pater makes is that the smile was found by Leonardo in a material reality—in the actual woman he painted, and that it was induced to remain on her face by the playing of music. Pater throughout connects Leonardo with the life of his times and suggests that

Leonardo's images of female homoeroticism derive from "the living women of Florence" (78). Pater's image of the "germinal principle" passed from male teacher to student stresses the older lover-younger beloved element in learning: what Leonardo gets from Verocchio he passes on to Andrea and others, and to "us in a chain of secret influences." Pater points out that this smile "plays over all of Leonardo's work" and that the same smile appears on the face of his John the Baptist. Freud describes it as "on the lips of all his feminine figures" (85), and his analysis concentrates on the smiling women, identified as "nothing else but reproductions of Caterina, his mother" (90), and the beautiful children's heads who are "reproductions of his own childish person" (90).

Where Pater's description of the St. John and Bacchus strongly suggests their "profane" homoerotic quality, "one of the few naked figures Leonardo painted—whose delicate brown flesh and woman's hair no one would go out into the wilderness to seek, and whose treacherous smile would have us understand something far beyond the outward gesture or circumstance" (75–76), Freud coyly dismisses these pictures in one paragraph, as androgynous (rather than homoerotic), "It is possible that in these forms Leonardo disavowed and artistically conquered the unhappiness of his love life, in that he represented the wish fulfillment of the boy infatuated with his mother in such blissful union of the male and female nature" (96). In Pater's reading the picture "would have us understand" its secret; in Freud's, "These pictures breathe a mysticism into the secret of which one dares not penetrate" (96). Given that Freud's project is precisely to penetrate secrets and that "mysticism" is not one of his major assumptions as a possible source of secrets, why does he not dare penetrate this secret? Perhaps because what he describes as "the mysteriously triumphant" (96) gaze of these beautiful boys contradicts the thesis of Leonardo's unhappy love life and "sexual inactivity" (119), upon which Freud's entire argument regarding the sublimation of homosexuality here rests.

Freud's disregard of the material and cultural differences between Leonardo's world and Freud's own are nowhere more evident than in his question regarding representations of feminine power, "the psychological riddle, namely, that the phantasy of men takes no offense at the fact that a figure which was to embody the essence of the mother should be provided with the mark of the masculine power which is the opposite of motherhood" (67). He proceeds to explain the riddle by an account of a universalized "male child" (67) who discovers that girls have no penis.

The "psychological riddle" is why Freud should think that power is the opposite of motherhood. In the Protestant and Judaic worldviews to which Freud was exposed as a child, this may have been the case, but it was by no means the case to the same extent in the Catholic Italy where Leonardo grew up, surrounded by images of the power of Mary. Freud reviews androgynous and hermaphroditic deities like Mut who possess the phallus and breasts in order to explain, in a far-fetched fashion, the origin of Leonardo's fantasy of the bird that struck his mouth with its tail. But he ignores completely the simple fact of thousands of representations of Mary (with breasts and without phallus) as a powerful goddess figure, to which Leonardo was exposed. Attempting to explicate the acknowledged power of Leonardo's female figures, Freud's narrative works to disempower women, reducing these figures to reproductions of the "poor, forsaken" Caterina (95).[8]

Freud claims that "the genitals were originally the pride and hope of living beings; they enjoyed divine worship" (70), but then a slippage occurs whereby "genitals" are replaced by "maternal penis" (71) so that "primitive forms of genital worship" (71) become assimilated to phallus worship, completely eliding the worship of womblike and vaginal icons in many ancient cultures. Leonardo's reworking of the Mary in the lap of St. Anne figure is ascribed to his memory of his mother, stepmother, and grandmother, all conjured up by Freud in such phrases as "his father's mother who, we will assume, was not less tender to him than grand-mothers are wont to be" (93). The female homoerotic power of the picture, suggested by Pater, is completely displaced. In Freud's reading, the women are concentrating on the Leonardo/Christchild, and their youth and beauty arises from the latter's childhood memory, not from his adult perception of two women in relation to one another.

Freud's displacement of the Virgin by a patriarchal god occurs in an interesting passage where Leonardo's mental daring in repudiating ancient authorities is attributed to his deprivation of a father and hence of an authority figure in his early years. "Psychoanalysis," Freud declares, "has taught us the intimate connection between the father complex and belief in God, has shown us that the personal God is psychologically nothing but an exalted father" (103). In this family scenario the mother is only "kindly nature" (103), but is not powerful. That a personal goddess may be an exalted parent figure and that in many representations of the Virgin Mary she is an autonomously powerful figure, with no father figure around, is forgotten. The polytheistic ambience of Catholicism and the matrilineal possibilities of kinship are replaced by the Protestant and Judaic religions and nuclear family structure of Freud's own world, in which the authority figure can only be male and where there is an absolute division of gender roles between "tender mother" (72) and powerful father. These assumptions make possible Freud's extraordinary statement casually thrown off as unquestionable: "Whoever works as an artist certainly feels as a father to his works" (100), and his even more extraordinary attribution of Leonardo's pleasure-loving and nonaccumulative attitudes to "the compulsion to copy his father and to excel him" (100).

Freud's omission of atmosphere is part of his project of constructing Leonardo as a lonely genius. For instance, that challenging ancient authorities was an exercise in which many Renaissance thinkers engaged to different degrees is not acknowledged. Pater's essay on Leonardo draws much of its power from being placed in a series of essays that build homoeroticism into the atmosphere in which Italian Renaissance artists lived and worked. Pater chooses to write not about the English but the Italian Renaissance. The one German he writes about, Winckelmann, goes to Italy and converts to Catholicism in order to come closer to the Hellenic ideal suitable to his "temperament," his desire for an ideal love between men. Pater focuses on a series of Catholic images and a series of images of homoerotic love. Both sets of images caused excitement, or unease, among readers, depending on the extent of their commitment to Victorian Protestantism and its ideal of marriage as a union between complementary unequals. Pater's attraction to Catholic Italy was doubly disturbing in that it appeared to be for him a route to approach a pagan world that did not stigmatize homoerotic interaction and also to romanticize what Wilde in a different context was to call "a passionate celibacy."

That Leonardo could not have been aware of his inclinations and could not have acted upon them is crucial to Freud's project. Freud acknowledges Leonardo's multifaceted knowledge, investigative capacities, and unbounded curiosity. That such a man should have been aware of his own sexual preferences seems not very far-fetched. But to suggest this would be to suggest that homosexuality is not always, everywhere, and for everyone a source of misery, that it may even be a source of joy, such as the joy manifested in Leonardo's paintings. This is precisely what Pater's text suggests, a suggestion intolerable to Freud. One of Freud's quotations from Leonardo can be read as a statement of Leonardo's conscious aversion to heterosexuality and of his idea that heterosexuality is constructed, not natural: "The act of procreation and everything that has any relation to it is so disgusting that human beings would soon die out if it were not a traditional custom, and if there were no pretty faces and sensuous dispositions" (37). What Freud terms Leonardo's "cool sexual rejection" (37) of women is read by Freud as abnormal and requiring explanation, since Freud takes heterosexuality as a given. In Leonardo's statement of the case, however, it is heterosexuality that requires explanation.

Throughout Freud's text the active, often sexually suggestive, words metaphorically ascribed by Pater to Leonardo are appropriated by Freud himself and an undifferentiated "us," which may mean psychoanalysts or readers who agree with Freud but certainly does not gesture, as Pater's "us" does, to homoerotically inclined readers. Thus Freud's "biographical effort really endeavors to penetrate the understanding of the psychic life of its hero" (37); "we break up an infantile phantasy" (62); "we. . . force" Leonardo's phantasy to "give up" its "sense" (65); we have "the key to his character" (40). By transforming the amazingly active, energetic Leonardo into a homosexual with a "stunted sexual life" (114), running away from the love of a dominant mother, the text confers on Freud's royal "we" an almost godlike power. Leonardo may have known that the sun does not move, but he didn't know that he was a homosexual repressing desire for his mother and rivalry with his father—Freud knows this and reveals it to us.

A. A. Brill, who translated Freud's essay into English in 1947, uneasily moves through the same "roll of honor" that Pater, Wilde, Symonds, and Carpenter had canvassed—Michelangelo, Marlowe, Shakespeare, Montaigne, also Damon and Pythias and David and Jonathan. He adds an American—Melville. However, his purpose in citing all these names is to deny that these men were sexually "abnormal" (26) or that they ever sought "any sensual gratification" (26) from the men they "revered" (a very odd word for the passionate feelings expressed toward younger men by some of them). He is particularly anxious about Leonardo because of the trial for homosexual practices. Brill decides: "There is no doubt that the accusations were based on some facts which were evidently misinterpreted" (26). Freud's anxiety to exonerate Leonardo from active homosexuality, which provides Brill with the formula to similarly exonerate a whole range of artists, seems to me a response to the repeated suggestion by Pater and his followers that homoeroticism was the conscious and primary erotic choice of such men. The twentieth-century "modern" scientists are much more uneasy with the idea of homosexuality than the Victorian writers.

A touching moment occurs toward the end of the essay, when Freud seems to acknowledge part of his motivation: "I succumbed to the attraction which emanated from this great and mysterious man, in whose being one seems to sense forceful and impelling passions, which nevertheless evince themselves in a remarkably subdued manner" (117–18). The sentence reverses the mode of the essay and places Freud as receptive, succumbing to an attraction emitted by Leonardo. It apparently endorses Pater's estimate that "Leonardo's nature had a kind of spell in it" (69). It suggests, too, that much of the analysis of Leonardo may more fruitfully be read as self-analysis and that it is Freud who displaces his attraction into investigation: "One remains beyond love and hatred. One has investigated instead of having loved" (42–43).

The importance of the decisive shift from the Paterian to the Freudian mode of biography and art criticism consists in the shift from a receptive to an analytic pathologizing mode. Pater's mode moves toward appreciation, not toward the establishment of laws into which, like a Procrustean bed, the other is to be fitted. Freud's mode sets itself up as scientific and offers the satisfactions of asserting power over the investigated other. This satisfaction is enhanced when the other is a "great" achiever. It works by covering up slippages in logic with rhetoric and gaps in knowledge with speculation masked as "law." This shift is not engineered only by Freud, nor are practitioners of this sort of criticism restricted to followers of Freud—arguably, it has become the dominant form of literary criticism practiced today.[9] Where Pater's mode of criticism blurs the lines between science and art, critical commentary, and literary writing, Freud's mode sharpens them.

Pater's kind of suggestive biographical writing was neither more nor less fictionalizing than Freud's. Although Freud acknowledges in one sentence toward the close that his essay may be a "psychological romance," the whole tenor of his argument is to assert his "scientific" stance. Because Pater refrains from making such claims, his mode of fictionalizing becomes more influential for constructions of homoerotic and literary ancestries in experimental writing that blurs the boundaries of fiction and critical writing. Among women Aestheticist practitioners of this kind of writing are Vernon Lee, Michael Field, and H.D. Describing the effect the statue of the Delphic charioteer had on her, H.D. wrote, echoing Pater's title *Appreciations* : "There is no trouble about art, it is the appreciators we want. We want young men and women to communicate with the charioteer and his like."[10]

In this chapter and the next I will examine how these two kinds of fictionalized biography affected the biographical fictions of Virginia Woolf.[11] Woolf, writing, as her father did, the biography and history of persons not considered great, draws on Pater's impressionist fictionalizing strategies to suggest that intensity in life as in art may be achieved by ordinary women and men, those whom Pater had invoked in the conclusion. Like Pater, she uses homoerotic experience as a trope for unconventional intensities.

The common language I have traced in texts by late-nineteenth-century men and women writers writing homoeroticism was received by Woolf and complicated by her historical context wherein same-sex attachment and community had come to be labeled and stigmatized.[12] Woolf's fictions combat this stigmatization by drawing on the language evolved since Romanticism to valorize such attachment.

Virginia Stephen grew to adulthood in an atmosphere Barbara Fassler has memorably described:

> Suffering was . . . every homosexual's daily portion in a nation with the most repressive laws and the most hostile public opinion in Europe. Sublimation, too, was a strong current in the ethic and life-style of many homosexuals . . . . A good many quietly anguished souls . . . followed an ethic of devotion, loyalty, romantic sentiment, and abstention from overt sexual acts.[13]

Goldsworthy Lowes Dickinson, E. M. Forster's mentor, was a living example of this kind of lifestyle, and Woolf more than once commented on his sufferings in her letters.[14] On the other hand, Edward Carpenter, also a mentor of Forster's, had established a cult of joyful homosexual comradeship in an atmosphere of simple living and high thinking, wedded to principles of pacifism, feminism, and anti-imperialism. The paradoxical blend of these two facets of homosexuality, hopeless devotion and joyful eroticism, was to be found in Woolf's intimate friend, Lytton Strachey, who, for all his openness about his homosexuality and mischievous delight in shocking the respectable, was in many ways a romantic at heart, "throughout his life always hopelessly in love or hopeless at not being in love."[15] The dominant note in the love lives of Strachey, Dickinson, E. M. Forster, and indeed of Woolf herself, was one of anguish induced by unrequited or partially requited love, often for persons who chose heterosexuality after experimenting with homosexuality in their youth.

Bloomsbury inherited from the Romantics and Aestheticists the aspiration to a chosen community of friends and lovers. Crucial to this chosen community was the sharing of unconventional sexual preferences, especially homosexual preferences. These friends shared a sense of being not so much outcasts—though that too was a word they used—as outsiders. In one sense an elite, they were, in another sense, threatened and embattled, suffering too from continuing exclusion, even oppression. Woolf's alliances with her male homosexual friends and her writing of such alliances into her fictions are of vital importance to her construction of love between women.

Feminist critics like Madeline Moore who read Woolf as an emotional separatist fail to take into account the depth of her nonsexual love for her male friends. Far from representing a misogynist conspiracy, as Phyllis Rose and others accuse them of doing, their acceptance of their homosexuality was a crucial factor in their easy acceptance of women as equals and confidantes. It is surely not accidental that Bloomsbury was perhaps the first and only literary constellation in England to have been presided over and represented to the world by two women.

Early in 1909 Virginia accepted Lytton Strachey's marriage proposal, which was withdrawn the day after it was made. In 1924 she characterized her feelings for him thus: "Oh I was right to be in love with him 12 or 15 years ago. It is an exquisite symphony his nature when all the violins get playing as they did the other night; so deep, so fantastic"[16]. Over the years she repeatedly stressed the uniqueness of their intimacy and noted how she hoarded up thoughts to share with him. Lytton too had a strong desire for a life with Virginia. While she was on her honeymoon, he wrote: "I saw you for such a short time the other day; it was tantalizing. I should like to see you every day for hours. I have always wanted to. Why is it impossible? Why is everything that is satisfactory in this life impregnated with unsatisfactoriness?"[17] In one of her many appreciative comments in her diary on the nature of her relationship with Lytton, she wrote: "Intimacy seems to me possible with him as with scarcely anyone; for besides tastes in common, I like & think I understand his feelings."[18]

On the one hand, she found distasteful the deliberately cultivated effeminate appearance and mannerisms of the younger generation of male homosexuals, like Eddie Sackville-West, remarking fastidiously: "They paint and powder, which wasn't the style in our day at Cambridge."[19] Remarkably, despite her feminist rage at exclusion from Cambridge, she here identifies with its homoerotic ambience: "our day." Yet the qualities she most appreciated and praised in men were those normally associated with women—gentleness, shyness, modesty. She paid Lytton the compliment of calling him "a female friend"[20], describing him as "so true, gentle, infinitely nimble, & humane."[21] She tended to oscillate between mockery of "the pretty and ladylike" young men and appreciation of them as "gentle youths."[22] Her initial ridicule of Eddie Sackville-West, for instance, gave way to liking: "I like Eddy: I like the sharpness of his spine; his odd indivualities [sic] and angles."[23] Their friendship developed to the point where she could tease and argue the question with him, even acknowledging herself, in a letter to Ethel Smyth, to be irrationally prejudiced: "Yes, I am afraid I do agree with you in thinking it silly. But I suspect we are wrong. I suspect the ramrod and gunpowder of our East Indian grandfathers here influences us. I think we are being provincial and petty. When I go to what we call a Buggery Poke party, I feel as if I had strayed into the male urinal; a wet, smelly, trivial kind of place. I fought with Eddy Sackville over this; I often fight with my friends. How silly, how pretty you sodomites are I said; whereat he flared up and accused me of having a red-nosed grandfather."[24]

In contrast, her revulsion from the "normal" was often forthrightly expressed and not retracted. Carolyn G. Heilbrun, recognizing the centrality of "freedom from conventional sexual ideas" to Bloomsbury, yet sees Woolf's androgynous vision as simultaneous with "admiration for virility, pleasure in the contemplation of it." It is not at all clear how she concludes that Woolf recognized the "attractions of virility," for this word almost always occurs in Woolf's writings as a pejorative.[25] Commenting on Ralph Partridge's love for Dora Carrington, she wrote, "We have had a mad bull in the house—a normal Englishman in love; and deceived. . . . I don't like the normal when it is at 1000 horse power. . . . It was the stupidity of virility that impressed me—& how, having made these convenient railway lines of convention, the lusts speed along them, unquestioning."[26] If she laughed at Eddie's and Lytton's homosexual love affairs, she was often repulsed by her brother-in-law Clive's heterosexual ones.

She sometimes betrays a startlingly virulent revulsion against male heterosexuality and reproduction, for example, shortly after her breakdown in 1915: "Sydney Waterlow . . . proposes to live next door to us at Richmond and there copulate day and night and produce 6 little Waterlows. This house for a long time stank to me of dried semen."[27] Years later, in a calm and happy frame of mind, she wrote to Vanessa "I am not a judge of the masculine form" and again, " You will never succumb to the charms of any of your sex—What an arid garden the world must be for you! . . . Greatly though I respect the male mind . . . I cannot see that they have a glow worms worth of charm about them."[28] On one occasion she fused her distaste for egotism and for male sexuality in a striking image: "The state of reading consists in the complete elimination of the ego; and its the ego that erects itself like another part of the body I dont dare to name."[29] Egotism interfered with reading and writing, in Woolf's poetics. The elimination of the ego recalls Pater's and Wilde's emphasis on the receptivity of reading, which draws on Keats's idea of negative capability.

Woolf was conscious that many of her friendships with men were built on a shared homoeroticism: on the death of G. L. Dickinson she remarked that she had had with him "the same sort of intimacy I had with Lytton and some others; though of course not nearly so close as with Lytton."[30] In 1921 she had written to Roger Fry about G. L. Dickinson:

> I do my best to make him jump the rails. He has written a dialogue upon homosexuality which he won't publish, for fear of the effect upon parents who might send their sons to Kings: and he is writing his autobiography which he won't publish for the same reason. So you see what dominates English literature is the parents of the young men who might be sent to Kings.[31]

In 1928 Woolf and Forster coauthored a letter to the editor of the *Nation* protesting the banning of *The Well of Loneliness*: "The subject matter of the book exists as a fact . . . novelists in England have now been forbidden to mention it. . . . Although it is forbidden as a main theme, may it be alluded to . . . ? Perhaps the Home Secretary will issue further orders on this point."[32]

Both in her letters and in her fictions, talking about male homosexuality was the route whereby Woolf was able to approach her desire for a Sapphic relationship. The languages of male homoeroticism developed in the Victorian male communities at Oxford and Cambridge proved a useful legacy. Talk of "buggery" and of Plato's *Symposium* was the first spoken language of homosexuality that she encountered as a girl. In a January 1924 letter to Jacques Raverat she first openly expressed her desire for Vita Sackville-West via comments on male homosexuality:

> Have you any views on loving one's own sex? All the young men are so inclined, and I can't help finding it mildly foolish. . . . Then the ladies, either in self-protection, or imitation or genuinely, are given to their sex too. My aristocrat . . . is violently Sapphic, and contracted such a passion for a woman cousin, that they fled to the Tyrol. . . . I can't take either of these aberrations seriously. To tell you a secret, I want to incite my lady to elope with me next.[33]

The disowning of "these aberrations" clearly emerges as a blind for her own strong feelings. Pater, Wilde, Samuel Butler, E. M. Forster were among those who had reworked the mainstream English novel by foregrounding in it a critique derived from Romantic poetry. Woolf is the first major woman novelist to integrate herself into this tradition of fiction writing.

From her first novel onward, Woolf explores the alliances between homoerotically inclined men and women.[34] St. John Hirst in *The Voyage Out* has a literary ancestor in Forster's Ansell of *The Longest Journey*. The first half of the novel oscillates between presenting Hirst as a pompous misogynist and placing his hostility to Rachel and to women in the context of his emotional isolation as a homosexual. This unsympathetic portrayal of Hirst gives way to an almost wholly inward and sympathetic depiction in the second half. Hirst emerges as a rebel who breaks social codes to which the putative hero, the heterosexual Hewet, conforms. In his rebellion Hirst finds allies in unconventional women, a pattern that recurs in Woolf's last novels. It is to Helen, not to Hewet, that Hirst confides the story of his life and his love for men. In a less serious way he finds an ally in Mrs. Flushing, a type of aristocratic freedom of spirit. When he surreptitiously reads in church Swinburne's translation of Sappho's "Ode to Aphrodite" (a significantly chosen constellation), she eagerly joins him. Hewet, however, "quarrel[s]" with him about it.

The development of the friendship between Hirst and Helen parallels the mutual gravitation of Rachel and Hewet. Helen and Hirst are both depressed, fearing an impending emotional loss. Helen's feelings are conveyed through a striking image, which suggests the phallic entrance of Hewet into her Edenic love for Rachel: "Her sense of safety was shaken, as if beneath twigs and dead leaves she had seen the movement of a snake."[35] The image is repeated a few pages later, this time by Hirst, when Helen tries to dissuade Rachel and Hewet from taking the walk in the forest that is to decide their future: " 'Good-bye!' cried Rachel. 'Goodbye. Beware of snakes,' Hirst replied" (277). Rachel's last words in the novel are a vehement protest against being displayed as an engaged woman, and her last conscious wish is for aloneness. Hewet's desire for oneness, which is in fact a desire to absorb Rachel into himself, stands in contrast to Hirst's desire for the sight of Helen that revives him despite, even because of, distance: "It was asking a good deal of Hirst to tell him to go without waiting for a sight of Helen. These little glimpses of Helen were the only respites from strain and boredom, and very often they seemed to make up for the discomfort of the day" (343–44).

The novel ends with Hirst's vision, and this figure looks forward to much that is significant in Woolf's work. In *Jacob's Room* Bonamy's love for Jacob is the closest approach to a romantic depiction in an otherwise very unromantic novel. As Ian Young has suggested, "Gay novels . . . have been among the last remaining examples of Romantic literature" because they deal with "the struggle to discover, create or sustain personal values in the face of social hostility."[36] Depicting this love rooted in a Forsterian university-based friendship, Woolf uses the image of the spaniel, which was to recur in her work, at greatest length in *Flush*, as an image of unrequited homosexual love. Heavily loaded and encoded words and images surround this love when the narrator muses on what is valuable in life: "A strange thing—when you come to think of it—this love of Greek, flourishing in such obscurity, distorted, discouraged, yet leaping out, all of a sudden . . . always a miracle."[37] Clearly, more is at stake here than the love of a classical language! And, again, "Plato and Shakespeare continue" (106). Woolf was the daughter of a man whose friends and acquaintances participated in this encoding, which gave the term *Greek love* a special significance. The contemporary of a flourishing circle of influential homosexual litterateurs, Leslie Stephen was himself a resolute exemplar of rigidly patriarchal heterosexuality. Or was he so rigid, after all? *To the Lighthouse* suggests the fascinating possibility that he too may have had "university friendships" of the kind Jacob has, although he may have refused to acknowledge their meaning.

Woolf said she wrote *To the Lighthouse* to exorcise her parents' ghosts. Mr. and Mrs. Ramsay are modeled on her parents Leslie and Julia Stephen. The homoerotic nature of the painter Lily Briscoe's attraction to Mrs. Ramsay has been examined by many commentators. The relation this love bears to homoeroticism between men in the same text has not been noticed. I suggest that Woolf here acknowledges both her biological and her literary ancestors, the eminent and the "other" Victorians.

Woolf's portrait of the artist as a Sapphist inclines to the Paterian rather than the Freudian mode insofar as Lily is conscious of her attraction to Mrs. Ramsay. Her expression of homoerotic emotion in her painting is not the result of repression but of conscious transmutation. In her eroticization of an older woman, Lily is squarely in a late-Victorian Sapphic tradition; the painting as the offspring of her love connects her to the Platonic tradition as well. Though Lily's love, like that of many Victorians, remains unconsummated, and causes as much pain as joy, it enriches her inner life. She fits the Carlylean mold of the poet as hero and is also one of the modern "men and women" whom Pater had invoked in his conclusion. In her, Pater's men of genius are rewritten as a woman whose gift may not be recognized but who shares with those ancestors a "vision" of same-sex love illuminating the world.

William Bankes and Augustus Carmichael visit the Ramsay household much as homoerotically inclined men like J. A. Symonds and Henry James visited the Stephen household. William Bankes makes his first appearance in the novel in chapter 4, through Lily's consciousness, at a moment when she is reflecting on the "absurdity" and "impossibility" of revealing to Mrs. Ramsay her feelings for her. She feels under immense stress, compelled as she is to "control her impulse to fling herself . . . at Mrs Ramsay's knee" and declare these feelings for which, however, she cannot find appropriate names.[38] At this moment William Bankes enters her consciousness as a person with whom she can wordlessly share her suppressed feelings:

> One could not say what one meant. So now she laid her brushes neatly in the box, side by side, and said to William Bankes: "It suddenly gets cold. The sun seems to give less heat," she said, looking about her, for it was bright enough, the grass still a soft deep green, the house starred in its greenery with purple passion flowers and rooks dropping cool cries from the high blue. But some-

thing moved, flashed, turned a silver wing in the air. It was September, after all, the middle of September, and past six in the evening. (23–24)

The imagery here suggests the passing of life and a sense of passion missed—the alluring green, purple, blue, and silver are countered by the growing cold and the sun losing its heat on an autumn evening. As Lily and William Bankes set out for their walk, the imagery becomes more and more strongly suggestive of a guarded and suppressed erotic desire that they cannot express:

> So off they strolled down the garden in the usual direction, past the tennis lawn, past the pampas grass, to that break in the thick hedge, guarded by red-hot pokers like braziers of clear, burning coal. . . .
>   They came there regularly every evening drawn by some need. It was as if the water floated off and set sailing thoughts which had grown stagnant on dry land, and gave to their bodies even some sort of physical relief. (24)

The sight they "watch" and "wait for" as a "delight" is a Coleridgean "fountain of white water" that "spurted irregularly" (24). The fountain in *To the Lighthouse* is an erotically charged image, appearing most famously when Mrs. Ramsay's "fountain and spray of life" is aggressively "plunged" into by the phallic "beak of brass, barren and bare" (44). Here, its orgasmic quality does not link Lily and Bankes or even emanate from them; they stand apart from one another and at a distance from the fountain. What they share is the sight, the vision of it. They are observers, and their "common hilarity" gives way to "some sadness—because the thing was completed partly" (25).

The sense of distance and of unfulfillment or partial fulfillment is linked not with heterosexual but with homosexual feeling, as is evident from the narrative's immediately sliding into Mr. Bankes's memories of his youthful relationship with Mr. Ramsay, which was broken off by the latter's marriage:

> Looking at the far sand hills, William Bankes thought of Ramsay: thought of a road in Westmorland, thought of Ramsay striding along a road by himself hung round with that solitude which seemed to be his natural air. But this was suddenly interrupted, William Bankes remembered . . . by a hen, straddling her wings out in protection of a covey of little chicks, upon which Ramsay, stopping, pointed his stick and said "Pretty—pretty," an odd illumination into his heart, Bankes had thought it, which showed his simplicity, his sympathy with humble things; but it seemed to him as if their friendship had ceased, there, on that stretch of road. After that, Ramsay had married. After that, what with one thing and another, the pulp had gone out of their friendship. (25)

Bankes feels let down by Mr. Ramsay's unexpected and "odd" appreciation of domesticity and parenthood; however, his own feelings remain unchanged, and Woolf's characterization of these feelings reveals them as erotically charged:

> But in this dumb colloquy with the sand dunes he maintained that his affection
> for Ramsay had in no way diminished; but there, like the body of a young man
> laid up in peat for a century, with the red fresh on his lips, was his friendship,
> in its acuteness and reality laid up across the bay among the sandhills. (25)

The language emphasizes the physicality of his feeling for Mr.
Ramsay and its untimely but only partial death occasioned by the latter's
marriage. This metaphorical "death" recalls many similar moments in
Woolf's work, for instance, the death of Evans associated with Septimus's
marriage, and the death of Clarissa's erotic self with her marriage. Here
the death appears to be in the nature of a burial alive, rather like the
mock-deaths of such figures as Snow White and Shakespeare's Imogen.
Although buried, the young man's body remains "fresh," "acute," and
"real." The terms in which it is conceived (red-lipped youth) recall such
celebrations of male beauty as Shakespeare's *Sonnets* and the poet's
promise that his verse will keep the beloved ever young and fair even after
his death and entombment. Bankes's feeling is that his attraction to
Ramsay is alive and beautiful, although buried, and that, by marrying,
Ramsay betrayed both the friendship and his own potential: "as if he had
seen him divest himself of all those glories of isolation and austerity
which had crowned him in youth to cumber himself definitely with flut-
tering wings and clucking domesticities" (27).

Remembering the youthful dynamism of the friendship, Bankes is
forced to acknowledge its current stagnation: "Repetition had taken the
place of newness. It was to repeat that they met" (25). He also feels
acutely sensitive to his own exclusion from the world of passion symbolized by the flower: "Mr Bankes was alive to things which would not have
struck him had not those sandhills revealed to him the body of his friendship lying with the red on its lips laid up in peat—for instance, Cam . . .
would not 'give a flower to the gentleman' as the nursemaid told her" (26).

Cam (who bears the name of the river flowing through Cambridge,
site of so many male attachments) by her refusal triggers off in Bankes an
awareness of society's condemnation of him, its devaluation of his
"wrong" loyalty to the buried friendship: "And Mr Bankes felt aged and
saddened and somehow put into the wrong by her about his friendship.
He must have dried and shrunk" (26).

Describing the sensibility of the woman artist in *A Room of One's
Own*, Woolf had used the image of burial: "It ranged too, very subtly and
curiously, among almost unknown or unrecorded things: it lighted on
small things and showed that perhaps they were not small after all. It
brought buried things to light and made one wonder what need there had
been to bury them"[39]. Bankes's friendship, buried in the landscape of his
mind, is described in an odd phrase as "laid up in peat for a century" (25).
The mention of a century suggests that more is involved than one lifetime
or one relationship. If Woolf is rewriting her father's youth, this goes back

to the mid-nineteenth century; however, from the perspective of Bankes himself, a century would take the phenomenon back to at least the beginning of the nineteenth century. I would like to suggest a possible historical source for the figure of William Bankes, a buried thing that Woolf brings to light.

William Bankes, who died in 1855, appears in *The Dictionary of National Biography*, edited by Leslie Stephen, as "the eldest surviving son of Henry Bankes of Kingston Hall, Dorsetshire . . . educated at Trinity College, Cambridge. . . . Byron, his contemporary, describes him as the leader of the set of college friends which included C. S. Matthews and Hobhouse. Bankes was Byron's friend through life."[40]

Woolf would have come across Bankes in *Lord Byron's Correspondence*, a collection of about 350 until then unpublished letters, which arrived from Mudie's on February 18, 1922, and which she declared herself eager to read immediately.[41] She was also familiar enough with Moore's *Life, Letters, and Journals of Lord Byron* (published in two volumes in 1830 and reprinted in 1832) to refer to it in a reading note on Beau Brummell.[42] Moore's collection contains several admiring references by Byron to Bankes. Byron describes Bankes as "my collegiate pastor, and master, and patron."[43] There are a total of nine letters to Bankes here, spanning a period of well over a decade. Byron confides his sorrow for two deceased male lovers: "the only beings I ever loved, females excepted; I am therefore a solitary animal, miserable enough."[44] Bankes, in turn, makes claims on Byron's affections, complains of neglect on account of Byron's "superabundance of friends," and bids Byron "farewell" since the latter does not write frequently enough.[45] Byron responds reassuringly. The letters are pervaded by a tone of deep intimacy. For instance, in a highly flirtatious letter of February 19, 1820, inviting Bankes to Ravenna, Byron writes, "Neither dangers nor tropical heats have ever prevented your penetrating wherever you had a mind to it, and why should the snow now? . . . All your evenings, and as much as you can give me of your nights, will be mine."[46]

What *The Dictionary of National Biography* carefully refrains from mentioning is that this Dorset MP and lifelong friend of Byron was twice arrested for homosexual offenses—once on June 7, 1833, and again in 1841. On the first occasion he was with a soldier, Private Flower, in a public lavatory in Westminster, at ten at night, and the soldier's breeches were unbuttoned. The Duke of Wellington, the Earl of Ripon, and the Master of Harrow stood as character witnesses at Bankes's trial, and he raised three thousand pounds bail and was acquitted. The second arrest was for the same kind of offense.[47] Whether or not Woolf was aware, from Bloomsbury's active interest in the history of homosexuality, of these incidents so reminiscent of episodes in Forster's stories such as "Arthur Snatchfold," she would certainly have decoded the Bankes-Byron letters, whose language is not substantially different from that of Strachey's or Forster's letters.[48]

William Bankes's case, then, was a signal case of the status of male homosexuality in Victorian England. His class position rescued him from the final disgrace that Private Flower and, later, Wilde, suffered. Difference in class accounting for differential treatment of homosexuals is commented upon by Forster in the terminal note to *Maurice*, where he perceives it as a continuing phenomenon.[49] The primary emotional reality of Bankes's life remained invisible in literary history, as monumentalized by such biographers as Woolf's father. He was included in *The Dictionary of National Biography* as a writer and amateur archaeologist "known to the literary world by his travels to the East. He . . . translated from the Italian in 1830 an autobiographical memoir of Giovanni Finati, with whom he travelled in Egypt and the East. In 1815 he discovered an ancient Egyptian obelisk in the island of Philae" (1044). The *Dictionary* reduces his choice of singleness to sterility, noting that (like Woolf's Bankes) he died (interestingly, in Venice!) "leaving no issue."

The unusual spelling of the surname *Bankes*, instead of *Banks*, strengthens the possibility that Woolf commemorates and rewrites a chosen "ancestor" in *To the Lighthouse*.[50] Her rewritten fictional Bankes stands in relation to Mr. Ramsay somewhat as the historical William Bankes stood in relation to Leslie Stephen. If Leslie Stephen rewrote Bankes by suppressing his homosexuality, Bankes has his revenge in Stephen's daughter's book, where he collaborates with Lily Briscoe to critique Mr. Ramsay's intellectual dishonesty, characterized by Lily as "blindness" and "narrowness" and by Bankes, less charitably, as "hypocrisy" and "concealment":

> His little dodges deceived nobody. What she disliked was his narrowness, his blindness, she said, looking after him.
> "A bit of a hypocrite?" Mr Bankes suggested, looking, too, at Mr Ramsay's back, for was he not thinking of his friendship, and of Cam refusing to give him a flower? (54)

If Cam turns out to be her father's daughter at the end of the book, her refusal of the flower to Mr. Bankes connects up in his mind with Ramsay's denial of the full meaning of their friendship.[51]

In the *Dictionary* the "nameless" loves of William Bankes cannot be mentioned. In *To the Lighthouse* it is Mr. Ramsay who literally and metaphorically has no name. We are never told the first name of either Mr. or Mrs. Ramsay—the personal identity is swallowed up by the couple identity. In his philosophical explorations of the nature of reality Mr. Ramsay reaches "Q" but is at that point interrupted by the sight of "his wife and son, together, in the window. They needed his protection: he gave it them. But after Q? What comes next? . . . A shutter, like the leathern eyelid of a lizard, flickered over the intensity of his gaze and obscured the letter R. . . . He would never reach R" (40). One irony here is that his wife and son are in no need of his protection and in fact experience his presence as an intrusion; the other irony is that R is his own initial. Domesticity and patriarchal imperatives prevent self-knowledge. A few pages later we are told "even his own name was forgotten by him" (52). This forgetfulness, contrasting as it does with Bankes's acute memory of the past, is ascribed to emotional fearfulness:

> He had not done the thing he might have done. It was a disguise; it was the refuge of a man afraid to own his own feelings, who could not say, This is what I like—this is what I am; and rather pitiable and distasteful to William Bankes and Lily Briscoe, who wondered why such concealments should be necessary. (53)

Lily has mixed feelings about both Mr. Bankes and Mr. Ramsay and is critical of both, for very different reasons, yet it is with the former that she enters into alliance, sharing as she does with him the condition of singleness and solitude. It is with him that she chooses to share the painting containing her hidden love, her "vision," of Mrs. Ramsay:

> If it must be seen, Mr Bankes was less alarming than another. But that any other eyes should see the residue of her thirty-three years, the deposit of each day's living, mixed with something more secret than she had ever spoken or shown in the course of all those days was an agony. At the same time it was immensely exciting. (61)

The language here strongly suggests the sharing of homoerotic feeling. At first, Mr. Bankes is not a perceptive viewer, but he takes in "complete good faith" (62) her explanation and she concludes: "This man had shared with her something profoundly intimate" (63). Lily thanks Mr. and Mrs. Ramsay's "world" for making possible this sharing, yet she chooses to share not with either of them but with William Bankes. In the heterosexually defined world, the homosexually inclined man and woman share their buried secrets and develop a lifelong alliance. In the closing section of the book Lily reflects: "Indeed, his friendship had been one of the pleasures of her life. She loved William Bankes" (200).

Lytton Strachey and E. M. Forster were among the readers of most importance to Woolf; she always anxiously awaited their reactions to her new books.[52] To Lytton she wrote in 1919, "I don't suppose there's anything in the way of praise that means more to me than yours."[53] Despite her moments of aversion to male homosexuality and Forster's to lesbianism, she and he continued to talk "of sodomy, & Sapphism, with emotion."[54] It is important that the conversation continued, with an acknowledgment of the irrational nature of the aversion. In 1925 she counted Strachey and Forster among the half-dozen most important people in her life: "But then if 6 people died, it is true that my life would cease. . . . Imagine Leonard, Nessa, Duncan, Lytton, Clive, Morgan all dead."[55]

The idea of this kind of sharing is repeated in "The Lighthouse" section, where Mr. Carmichael takes Mr. Bankes's place as Lily's secret sharer. At this point, unlike Mr. Ramsay, who is overwhelmed with sympathy from all quarters when he loses his wife, and demands such sympathy, Lily is not even perceived by others as a mourner: "No one had seen her step off her strip of board into the waters of annihilation. She remained a skimpy old maid, holding a paint-brush on the lawn" (205). She conquers her pain and absorbs it into her "ordinary experience," but it recurs (as did Mr. Bankes's pain over his lost friendship) since it is part of that experience, both past and present: " 'Mrs Ramsay! Mrs Ramsay!' she cried, feeling the old horror come back—to want and want and not to have. Could she inflict that still?" (229). The phrasing indicates that Mrs. Ramsay inflicted this pain on Lily during her lifetime too.[56] The pain of mourning a death now merges with the pain of mourning a love made impossible and, as it were, killed, by marriage. Lily organizes her anguish and also completes her understanding of Mrs. Ramsay through the painting. It is therefore appropriate that she shares the completed painting with Mr. Carmichael as she had shared the half-finished painting with Mr. Bankes. As Bankes's half-complete friendship with Mr. Ramsay paralleled Lily's incompletely realized relationship with Mrs. Ramsay, so Carmichael's transmutation of his loss of Andrew Ramsay parallels Lily's transmutation of her loss of Mrs. Ramsay.

The Carmichael-Andrew relationship is an exquisite little cameo traced as if with invisible ink beneath the surface of the text. It is first indicated by Mrs. Ramsay, who, feeling that Carmichael disapproves of and shrinks from her, notices "how devoted he was to Andrew, and would call him into his room, and, Andrew said, 'show him things' " (111). The other meaning of the word "thing" would be evident to any careful reader of Shakespeare's *Sonnets*, its most famous and explicit use being in the master-mistress sonnet: "By adding one thing to my purpose nothing."

In "The Lighthouse" section, Lily recalls

> that when he had heard of Andrew Ramsay's death (he was killed in a second by a shell . . .) Mr Carmichael had 'lost all interest in life.' What did it mean—that? she wondered. . . . She did not know what he had done, when he heard that Andrew was killed, but she felt it in him all the same. (221)

What Mr. Carmichael "had done" is indicated in the "Time Passes" section. Chapter 6 of that section has four parenthetic insertions of which the first two relate to Prue Ramsay's marriage and death. The third and fourth tell of Andrew's death and suggest Carmichael's response:

> A shell exploded. Twenty or thirty young men were blown up in France, among them Andrew Ramsay, whose death, mercifully, was instantaneous. . . .
> Mr Carmichael brought out a volume of poems that spring, which had an unexpected success. The war, people said, had revived their interest in poetry. (153)[57]

The process of mourning, loss, and recuperation through art is viewed externally and from a distance in the case of Carmichael, in Lily's case with excruciating inwardness, but they have been through a similar experience: "They had not needed to speak. They had been thinking the same things and he had answered her without her asking him anything" (237), we are told.

Two years after *To the Lighthouse*, Woolf wrote *A Room of One's Own*, in which she chose to name the woman author of Sapphic fiction Mary Carmichael.[58] "Mary" is the name of the virgin who produces without the intervention of a man; it is also the name of the Queen of Scots beloved by many women writers, among them Jane Austen and Michael Field; it is also the name of the feminist who chooses not to marry in *Night and Day*. The unusual surname must link to Woolf's earlier use of it.[59] If *To the Lighthouse* is about chosen ancestors, spiritual and literary, as much as about biological ancestors, is Augustus Carmichael, author of elegiac love poems for a man, the "parent" of Mary Carmichael, author of a novel about Chloe who liked Olivia?

8

The Wilde-ness of Woolf
Evading and Embracing Death in
Orlando and The Waves

For he who lives more lives than one
More deaths than one must die
—Oscar Wilde

Death was defiance. Death was an attempt to
communicate. . . . There was an embrace in death.
—Virginia Woolf

Woolf inherited two types of narratives of same-sex love from her Victorian ancestors. One constructed the protagonist as a misunderstood martyr, either driven to Sapphic suicide or heroically transmuting unexpressed love into art. This is the narrative rewritten as twentieth-century myth by Forster in *The Longest Journey*, Woolf in *To the Lighthouse*, and Radclyffe Hall in *The Well of Loneliness*. The other type of narrative constructed the protagonist as a joyful outlaw reveling in Edenic sensuality, marveled at but not fully comprehended by conventional society. Wilde's own life could be read as an enactment of both narratives. In *Orlando* Woolf attempted to rewrite the second type of narrative (as Forster had in *Maurice*), but in her next novel, *The Waves*, she reverted to the first type. I shall examine Woolf's dialogue in these texts with the fictions of Pater, Gautier, and Wilde.

If *Orlando* is, as Perry Meisel says, "the consummate Paterian portrait," it is also Wildean in the personal note it strikes.[1] Like Basil's picture of Dorian, it is simultaneously a work of art and a reflection of and tribute to a beloved person. Homoeroticism is the encoded subtext both in *The Picture of Dorian Gray* and in *Orlando*. Where Wilde foregrounds an ancestry, constructed as homoerotic, Woolf buries that part of this ancestry which is closest to her own time. Two important phases of the English literary history through which Woolf's protagonist passes are missing— the Romantic and the Aestheticist. Orlando moves straight from the "eighteenth century" of Pope and Swift to the Victorian era, and the "other Victorians" are absent from her social world. In my reading this absence is the defining presence, as is the other absence, that of Woolf, the lover, from the life of Vita, the beloved.

Perry Meisel has argued that Pater was a major influence on Woolf, although one she sought to repress and deny, because the school of thought he represented had come to be discredited as antisocial, anarchist, and immoral.[2] Bloomsbury's antagonists were quick to point out the connection: Wyndham Lewis clearly stated that "there is a very much closer connection than people suppose between the aesthetic movement presided over by Oscar Wilde and that presided over in the first post-war decade by Mrs Woolf."[3] Meisel argues that "as a second-generation Wilde, Woolf, too, becomes a witting disciple of Pater, although in her case the discipleship is a veiled and secret one."[4] Meisel does not explore the influence of Wilde, although he points out that it is even more repressed, "Wilde's name appearing even less often than Pater's in the works, diaries, letters and memoirs of members of Bloomsbury."[5] Meisel points out how intensively the young Virginia Stephen read Pater and that she was tutored by his sister Clara, on whom the central figure in her Sapphist story "Slater's Pins Have No Points" is based.

It is worth detailing some of the close connections between the worlds of Oscar Wilde and Virginia Woolf to demonstrate how integrated traditions of homoerotic creativity were and how invisibilized they are in *Orlando*. Madge Vaughan, one of the first women Virginia Stephen fell in love with, was the daughter of J. A. Symonds. Common acquaintances of Woolf and Wilde included Yeats, Max Beerbohm, Andre Gide, Edward Carpenter, Bernard Shaw, and Laurence Housman (brother of the poet and a campaigner for women's rights). Woolf's close friend Roger Fry was a friend of Ricketts and Shannon, J. A. Symonds and Rothenstein, and had met Michael Field. Jacques Emile-Blanche, with whom Woolf carried on an intimate correspondence, was a friend and admirer of Wilde's to whom he had introduced Proust, of whose work Woolf was an ardent admirer. Ethel Smyth, whom Woolf had admired from a distance long before she became her intimate friend, had been briefly engaged in her youth to Wilde's brother, Willie.[6]

The connections were not just social but intellectual and ideological as well. When in 1939 Marie Stopes presented a petition to the prime minister asking for a civil list pension for Lord Alfred Douglas, Virginia Woolf was the only other woman, apart from Stopes, who signed.[7] Among the women (and lesbian) writers who were Woolf's contemporaries and whom she knew or knew of, several had been influenced by Wilde. Natalie Clifford Barney had sat on his lap as a little girl and attributed her decision to become a writer to this experience.[8] Elizabeth Robins, the American actress and feminist, pioneer of Ibsen on the London stage, was a friend of Leslie and Julia Stephen and also of Wilde and, in later years, of the Woolfs. Katherine Mansfield, who had a strong and in many ways unique affinity with Virginia Woolf, had, as a young woman, "an obsession . . . with the image and writing of Oscar Wilde."[9] Her biographer, Jeffrey Meyers, writes: "The numerous quotations from *Dorian Gray* in Katherine's journal of 1906–08 reflect the overwhelming influence of Oscar Wilde. . . . Like Wilde, she claimed the sexual and intellectual freedom of the artist and felt intensity was the touchstone of experience."[10]

The belief in freedom, intellectual and sexual, and the notion of life as a process in which "moments of being" are distinguished by their intensity, are central to Bloomsbury thought. These ideas, as also the idea of love and art as ends in themselves, were transmitted from the Romantics by Pater and Wilde to Bloomsbury. J. K. Johnstone notes that "Bloomsbury's main contribution to twentieth-century thought may prove to have been that they regained a considerable degree of respect for the creed of art for art's sake at a time when it had fallen into disrepute."[11] J. E. Chamberlin, in his study of Wilde's thought as centrally definitive for the literature of his times, argues that Wilde revived the legacy of the Romantics and transmitted it to Yeats, Joyce, and Woolf.

Although this legacy remained largely unacknowledged by Bloomsbury, there was one occasion when a member, E. M. Forster, publicly acknowledged what Pater or Vernon Lee would have called an "affinity" with Wilde. This was in the lecture "Art for Art's Sake" delivered before the American Academy of Arts and Letters, New York, in 1949. In an obvious reference to Wilde's lecture tour of the United States in 1882, Forster began:

> I believe in art for art's sake. It is an unfashionable belief and some of my statements must be of the nature of an apology. Sixty years ago, I should have faced you with more confidence. A writer or a speaker who chose "Art for Art's Sake" for his theme sixty years ago could be sure of being in the swim, and could feel so confident of success that he sometimes dressed himself in aesthetic costumes suitable to the occasion . . . and carried a poppy or a lily in his medieval hand.[12]

Thus quoting in a half-amused, half-affectionate tone from Gilbert and Sullivan's song on Wilde, Forster goes on to say that his distance from Wilde's mode and manner springs not from any objection to them but from an accident of history: "Times have changed. Not thus can I present either myself or my theme today." Without naming Wilde, Forster acknowledges him as an ancestor. As early as 1905, when the reverberations of the Wilde scandal were only a decade old, Virginia Stephen's brother Thoby had dared defend the so-called Decadents and their values in terms that would have provided grist to Wyndham Lewis's mill:

> The decadents are simply those who in a society that is ruled by convention possess independence of thought, and still care for art at a time when for most men it has ceased to exist. That the reflections of such minds should be some-

what melancholy is inevitable, and that they should desire to express what they feel I take to be evidence rather of candour than of perversity."[13]

What follows is a reading of *Orlando* and *The Waves* as drawing on and attempting to rewrite nineteenth-century traditions of homoerotic writing.

Recent feminist criticism has tended to canonize *Orlando* as Woolf's breakthrough in the writing of Sapphism. Following Joanne Trautmann's pioneering study, lesbian feminist criticism has made it impossible for the Virginia-Vita relationship to be ignored or trivialized as it often was before.[14] After Sherron E. Knopp's reading of *Orlando* as primarily a Sapphic fiction, most commentators tend to follow her celebratory tone, which shadows Woolf's own.[15] Louise DeSalvo seeks to demonstrate that "one of the most compelling experiences in Sackville-West's life during these years could not find expression in fiction. Woolf had solved the problem by creating the form of Orlando to contain her love for Sackville-West." Madeline Moore places *Orlando* at the center of the Woolf canon, arguing that Woolf wrote "openly about women's passion . . . in the context of her fanciful biography."[16] I agree, however, with Suzanne Raitt that "*Orlando* was bound up with Woolf's experience of loss, as well as of power," that there is a sense in which it is Woolf's revenge for her lover's infidelity and even manifests a desire for that lover's death.[17]

In 1931, three years after the publication of *Orlando*, Woolf stated that she felt obstructed in some intangible way from writing about her "own experiences as a body" and that this obstruction was the one major problem she, as a woman novelist, had not been able to solve.[18] *Orlando* may be the "most charming love letter" in the English language, but it does not heal the love/sex, heart/body, and, most important, the married/homosexual split it inherits. That it mutes the anguish of that split rather than foregrounding it does not render the anguish less real.

One of the dilemmas of the enterprise of *Orlando* is that it is a public tribute to a living beloved, carrying photographs of her and dedicated to her by name. Partly because of this, perhaps, Woolf attempts to exclude not only the compelling and searing emotions the relationship generated in her but also the relationship itself. In erasing Romanticism and Aestheticism from Orlando's biographia literaria and, implicitly, from her own, Woolf, in a characteristic modernist gesture, disowns what had come to be seen as the melancholy personal exhibitionism, the sentimentality, of nineteenth-century texts. She associates her subject with a past (Renaissance, eighteenth century) valorized as joyful, self-assertive, and guilt-free.[19] Her overt project, like Forster's in *Maurice*, is to insist on a happy ending, on the possibility of a joyful liberated eroticism. *Orlando* refuses the options of Sapphic suicide and Romantic anguish that *The Waves* embraces. Orlando goes through mock-deaths and emerges as a survivor. Although a homoerotically inclined artist, she refuses to be romantic martyr or tragic hero. She is not an Oscar Wilde or a Stephen

Gordon. She makes a successful marriage and is also a successful writer. *Orlando*, however, is a text at war with itself—at one level it celebrates the success that at another level it critiques. It works out these contradictions through its dialogue with Victorian ancestors.

Woolf's celebration of her protagonist's insouciance draws on Théophile Gautier, who was one of Wilde's favorite writers, but her critique resonates with Wilde's own in *The Picture of Dorian Gray*. Richard Ellmann points out that Gautier's *Mademoiselle de Maupin* (1836) "nonchalantly presents a heroine with bisexual tastes, which in the end she lavishly gratifies. The theme of variable sexuality was set by Gautier's heroine for the rest of the century" (85). That the novel continued to be controversial even in the early twentieth century is indicated by the fact that shortly before unsuccessfully suing *The Well of Loneliness* in the United States, the Society for Suppression of Vice had taken *Mademoiselle de Maupin* to court in that country, seeking to have it banned.

Gautier's novel is remarkable for its critique of male domination and for its simultaneous celebration of male and female homosexual love, with primacy given to the latter. Madelaine, the title figure, like so many Elizabethan heroines, engineers her own "sex change" by sallying into the world in male attire. She does this because she is unwilling to marry or love any man unless she is sure he is worthy of her and she knows that men do not reveal their lives and opinions to the girls, leading sheltered lives, whom they mean to marry. Disguised as a man, Madelaine sees men, as it were, unveiled. She is violently repulsed by their brutality, hypocrisy, coarseness, and vulgar licentiousness, and particularly by the fact that from all-male conversation "there emerged a deep, true feeling of utter contempt for women."[20] Madelaine is already inclined to passionate friendships with women. Her narrative is structured, in Richardsonian fashion, as a correspondence with her friend Graciosa whom she addresses as "the person I love best in the world" (261). When a beautiful young woman called Rosette falls in love with her, under the impression that she is a man, Madelaine, although she tries to resist, finds herself compelled by "an invincible attraction" (284). As time passes Madelaine's doubts crystallize. She laments the fact that she can only have a man as a lover, because she is now convinced that women are not only physically more beautiful than men but also mentally and emotionally superior and that no man can love as a woman can—or can even understand a woman's love.

The other narrator in the novel is the Chevalier d'Albert, an aspiring poet and aesthete. He has a liaison with Rosette but does not love her, although he wrongly imagines that she loves him. He desires an ideal love, but defines it primarily in terms of physical beauty. He is dedicated to beauty as the supreme value in life but is completely conventional in his stereotyping of women. He holds their minds in contempt, valuing only their physical beauty. This is the main difference between him and

Madelaine, for, while she too is keenly appreciative of women's beauty, she is clear that

> what I wanted most of all was not physical beauty, it was beauty of soul, it was love. . . . Oh, how often I've wished I were really a man, as I appeared to be! How many women whom I'd have understood, whose heart would have understood my heart! . . . What sweetness, what delights! All the sensitive plants in my soul would have flowered freely without being forced to contract and close up all the time at some rough touch! (317, 321)

The Shelleyan image of the woman as sensitive plant seems to distinguish women's way of loving from men's, and to suggest the near impossibility of a happy heterosexual love for a woman. A complication is introduced when d'Albert falls in love with the disguised Madelaine. This love proves to be a humanizing experience for him. Initially horrified by what he thinks is an "unnatural" predilection in himself, he gradually comes to realize that the love of beauty is never immoral and images his new love as "a flourishing tree" (200), thus suggesting that it is a natural growth. He realizes, too, that women and men are not two distinct species, as he had earlier believed: "I no longer know who I am, or what others are, I wonder if I'm a man or a woman " (181). He begins to see that love is not biologically generated and becomes more comfortable with the idea of loving a man:

> What is remarkable is that I hardly think about his sex any more, and that I love him with perfect confidence. Sometimes I try to persuade myself that this love is abominable, and I tell myself so as harshly as I can, but I speak only with my lips, it is an argument which I create for myself and do not feel. It really seems to me that it's the simplest thing in the world, and that anyone else in my place would feel the same. (197)

Orlando retains and expands Gautier's feminist agenda but does not fully incorporate the idea of same-sex love as a humanizing force that heals the love/sex split. Woolf shifts the focus from sexuality (desire for a man or a woman or both) to gender (whether a person is a man or a woman or both or neither). Because Orlando is both man and woman, she can desire both sexes. Desiring both sexes (not being both sexes) was a possibility Madelaine had dreamed of:

> My dream would be to have each sex in turn, and to satisfy my dual nature: man today, woman tomorrow. . . . My nature would then be completely fulfilled, and I should be perfectly happy, for true happiness is to be able to develop freely in all directions and to be everything that you can be. But such things are impossible and one mustn't think of them. (330)

The physical beauty of the two protagonists is described in similar androgynous terms—Orlando's—'No human being since the world began has ever looked more ravishing. His form combined in one the strength of a man and a woman's grace" (86)—and Madelaine's—

"Everything was united in the lovely body that posed before him: delicacy and strength, form and colour" (342). Their nature, which cannot be contained in the gender roles ascribed to "man" and 'woman," is similarly analyzed. Madelaine says of herself:

> It often happens that the sex of the soul is not the same as that of the body and this contradiction cannot fail to produce a great deal of confusion. . . . I like horses, fencing, all violent forms of exercise, I like to climb and run about here and there like a young boy. . . . I don't like obeying in the least, and the words I most often say are "I will." (273)

If Gautier here anticipates the invert theory and describes a personality similar to Stephen Gordon's, he does not conceive it as negative, physically anomalous, or "wounded." His celebratory tone is closer to those who conceived of the Uranian, or Urning, as capable of higher things than other people:

> In truth, neither sex is really mine: I don't have the foolish submissiveness, the timidity or the pettiness of women; I don't have the vices of men, their disgusting debauchery and their brutal tendencies. I belong to a third sex, a sex apart, which has as yet no name; higher or lower, inferior or superior; I have the body and soul of a woman, the spirit and strength of a man. (329)

The narrator of *Orlando* concludes—and the difference is crucial— that all human beings are a mixture of both sexes. Woolf's positing of universal bisexuality is different from Gautier's celebration of Madelaine's conscious choice of a bisexual life for herself. The Platonic idea of a composite androgynous being is present in both texts, but where Plato's model allows for three categories—men and women who love each other, men who love men, and women who love women, Gautier's posits men (who love women), women (who love men) and a third nameless sex (of bisexual persons). Woolf's posits all human beings as having a shifting bisexuality, sometimes more male (more given to loving women) and sometimes more female (given to loving men):

> In every human being, a vacillation from one sex to the other takes place and often it is only the clothes that keep the male or female likeness, while underneath the sex is the very opposite of what it is above. Of the complications and confusions which thus result everyone has experience. . . . Whether, then, Orlando was most man or woman it is difficult to say. (118)

Gautier's narrator makes a tongue-in-cheek pretense at being baffled by what finally happens between Madelaine (referred to as Rosalind when she acts the part of Shakespeare's heroine and emerges in women's dress) and Rosette:

> Instead of going back to her room, she went to Rosette's. What she said there, what she did there, I have never been able to discover. . . . But a chambermaid of Rosette's informed me of this singular circumstance: . . . the bed was rumpled

and disturbed, and it bore the imprint of two bodies. . . . I confide this observation to the sagacity of the reader, and I leave him free to draw whatever conclusions he likes from it; as for me, I've made a thousand conjectures about it, each more preposterous than the other, and so far-fetched that I really don't dare to write them down, even in the most suitable periphrased style. (344–45)

In *Orlando* the only account suggestive of sex between women is placed in the context of Orlando's meeting with a group of prostitutes. The women drink, converse, and tell stories. Even if we read this as suggestive because of the encoded word *impossible*, it pluralizes Orlando's possible lovers as "women" rather than any one woman:

So they would draw round the punch-bowl . . . and many were the fine tales they told . . . when women get together—but hist—they are always careful to see that the doors are shut and not a word of it gets into print. All they desire is—but hist again—is that not a man's step upon the stair? . . . Women have no desires, says this gentleman . . . let us . . . merely state that Orlando professed great enjoyment in the society of her own sex, and leave it to the gentlemen to prove, as they are very fond of doing, that this is impossible. (136)

In the next paragraph we are told less equivocally, "For the probity of breeches she exchanged the seductiveness of petticoats and enjoyed the love of both sexes equally" (138). The words *petticoat* and *love* occur together again in a later passage, which denies that Orlando "loved" in the sense of making love. Here, however, the phrase "enjoyed the love" points clearly to sexual love.

The two novels close in very different ways. Madelaine sleeps with both her male and female admirers before riding off into the dawn. We are not told what becomes of Ninon, the young girl with whom she has a powerful erotic and emotional relationship. She had rescued this girl from a threatened life of prostitution and had disguised her in male attire as her page. It can only be assumed that she takes her with her at the end. Much is made of the age difference between the two, of Madelaine's nurturing role, and of Ninon, in her adolescent delicacy, being in relation to Madelaine as a woman is to a man.

Where *Mademoiselle de Maupin* is open-ended, *Orlando* is not, because Orlando marries and has a son, and the novel ends with her reunion with her husband. Woolf suggested that her fictions should be called elegies, and the elegiac note is not altogether missing even from this playful fiction. Marriage functions as a kind of death. When Orlando, as a man, marries Rosina Pepita, he falls into a deathlike trance and awakens as a woman. When as a woman she marries Shelmerdine, this does not resolve the anguish of her buried-but-still-living-love for Sasha. As a woman she never encounters Sasha. This is linked to the text being subtitled "a biography." As an account of Vita's life, it has to record Vita's marriage and, more important, Virginia's feelings about that marriage, which were inevitably connected with her feelings about her own marriage. These feelings are diffused, in the elegiac tone of the text, but are nowhere represented. Woolf herself does not make an appearance in Vita's "vita," as constructed here, so her love, like Basil Hallward's worship of Dorian, remains the hidden subtext.

It is possible to read *Orlando* as rewriting *The Picture of Dorian Gray*, replacing pain with joy, guilt-ridden with guilt-free sexuality. But this would be too simple a picture. Wilde's text echoes through Woolf's, countering the lighthearted adventurousness of Gautier's. If Woolf celebrates Vita Sackville-West's life, she also writes trauma into it: Vita's trauma at parting with Violet and Woolf's own trauma in pursuit of a love that remained at one level unattainable.

Like *The Picture of Dorian Gray*, *Orlando* is about the experiments with life of a beautiful aristocratic youth who is miraculously endowed with unaging youth and beauty. Woolf follows Wilde, audaciously taking on the mantle of Basil Hallward, to write the biography of a beloved who refuses to grow old. That Orlando lives through four centuries also makes her/him a trope for a homoerotic sensibility constructed as going back to the Renaissance. The sex change may suggest, among other things, that bisexuality as a lifestyle for women became possible in the eighteenth century when writers like Aphra Behn first began to write for a living.

Orlando apparently recasts Wilde's tragedy as comedy. But comedies may be read as tragedies of another kind. More important, what might be comedy when it happens to someone else may be tragedy when it happens to oneself. Marriage may entail the killing of certain feelings, possibilities, relationships, and it characteristically does so, both in English drama and in Victorian mainstream novels. Marriage entails the marginalizing of same-sex relationships. By naming her protagonist Orlando, Woolf irresistibly recalls *As You Like It*, a play central both to *Mademoiselle de Maupin* and to *The Picture of Dorian Gray*. In Shakespeare's text the marriages at the end entail the silencing of women. Celia, who engineered the flight to Arden solely for love of Rosalind, speaks not a word in the last act, once she has committed herself to a man, and Rosalind too is silenced in the last seventy lines, while her person and property are being exchanged between men. The intensely romantic love between the two women and the potential homoeroticism of Orlando himself are firmly "barred" as "confusion" and as "strange events" by Hymen, the male god of marriage. The other famous Orlando is Ariosto's, who goes mad for love. Woolf's Orlando is saved from madness by a sex change and, ultimately, by marriage. This kind of salvation in *Mrs. Dalloway* involves a loss of emotional fulfillment. Septimus Smith, clinging to the memory of his love for Evans, is unable to act the good husband, goes mad, and kills himself; Clarissa, having sacrificed her love for Sally to marriage, feels that she has committed emotional suicide.[21]

Both Wilde's and Woolf's texts begin with the beloved's beauty. Woolf attempts to heal the mind/body split that is central to the anguish generated in *Dorian Gray*. Virginia's appreciation of Vita's beauty was evident from the start of their relationship and remained central to it. She set a very high value on beauty, a value she shared with Lytton: "And that's what I adore in him—his enthusiasm for beauty."[22] In describing Vita she returned again and again to the celebratory tone, using words suggestive of light ("glow," "incandescence," "luminous") both physical and visionary: "I like her & being with her, & the splendour—she shines in the grocers shop in Sevenoaks with a candle lit radiance, stalking on legs like beech trees, pink glowing, grape clustered, pearl hung."[23]

It is significant that Vita's expressions of affection for Virginia are not worded in comparably physical terms or images. Virginia constructed in Vita the figure of the ideal youthful beloved (there was a ten-year age difference between them), drawing on several traditions of homoerotic writing, such as Sappho's praise of young maidens in her odes, Plato's *Symposium* (the text was one of her early favorites, in innocent canvassing of which she shocked society on an occasion amusingly described in "22 Hyde Park Gate"), and Shakespeare's *Sonnets*. Influential too are Pater's and Wilde's idea of the beautiful friend who inspires the artist's best work and G. E. Moore's notion of the ideal friend who "must be not only truly beautiful, but truly good in a high degree."[24] Virginia's recurrent descriptions of Vita's beauty in terms of light are related to this last idea—Vita's inner beauty (simplicity, modesty, unselfishness, generosity, honesty) radiates outward in the visible beauty that "dazzles" and enchants Virginia. Vita may write "with a pen of brass" but "is always such gold—pure to the heart."[25] Appearing in the humdrum world of fishmonger's or grocer's shop, she transfigures it, endowing small everyday details with significance, in Romantic epiphanic fashion.

Animal images became primary after the establishment of their intimacy. Before that, however, she linked Vita to Greek and Elizabethan models: "Dear Vita has the body and brain of a Greek God";[26] "And Vita Nicolson, more than ever like a Guards officer in bearskin and breeches. Very Elizabethan too."[27] She is an indigenous version of Diana, the virgin huntress: "Her real claim to consideration is, if I may be so coarse, her legs. Oh they are exquisite—running like slender pillars up into her trunk, which is that of a breastless cuirassier (yet she has 2 children) but all about her is virginal, savage, patrician."[28] If she refers to Vita as a "virginal" Amazon, she also sees her as Sapphic. A brief diary entry records of Vita: "She looked like Sappho by Leighton, asleep."[29]

Attraction between men is represented in Wilde's text as contingent on the split between mind and body. Dorian loses the simplicity and beauty attributed to his nature by Basil when he begins to think about and respond to the sexual attraction that his physical beauty evokes. Lord Henry says: "Beauty, real beauty, ends where an intellectual expression begins. . . . The moment one sits down to think, one becomes all nose, or all forehead, or something horrid."[30] The idea that ideal beauty must be divorced from the intellect is based on an objectification of the youthful beloved, against which, as I shall demonstrate later, Dorian himself protests. This idea is teasingly echoed and refuted at the start of *Orlando*: "But, alas, that these catalogues of youthful beauty cannot end without mentioning forehead and eyes. . . . Directly we glance at eyes and forehead, we have to admit a thousand disagreeables which it is the aim of every good biographer to ignore" (10).

The chief source of Dorian's misery is that he is unable to live up to Henry's unreal ideal of beauty devoid of thought. Before his "fall," he is described as having in his face "all the candour of youth . . . as well as all youth's passionate purity. One felt that he had kept himself unspotted from the world" (27). The Christian idiom used here recurs throughout the narrative, reinforcing Dorian's guilt. That Dorian retains his appearance of purity after he is no longer technically "pure" causes him triumph but also anguish. In *Orlando* the notion of purity is mocked and dismissed through the absurd figure of Our Lady of Purity, while candor, far from being linked to purity, is opposed to it (Truth, Candor, and Honesty attend the sex change and compel the banishment of Purity, Chastity, and Modesty). It is therefore possible for Orlando to look and feel innocent despite his/her sexual escapades and for the narrator to endorse this feeling: "There was a serenity about him always which had the look of innocence when, technically, the word was no longer applicable" (16).

Woolf attempts to rewrite *The Picture of Dorian Gray* in a vein of joy. She endorses the Greek-Renaissance traditions Basil Hallward invokes against the Protestant-Judaic traditions that infuse Wilde's narrative with a sense of sin and guilt. What Dorian does in mortal terror, Orlando does with pleasure, thus fulfilling Wilde's prophecy that "the sin we had done once, and with loathing, we would do many times, and with joy" (56). Dorian had desired to "live out his life completely . . . give form to every feeling, expression to every thought, reality to every dream" (29); Orlando actually does so. *Orlando* demonstrates the thesis of Wilde's text that "man was a being with myriad lives and myriad sensations" (76) by presenting a hero who is not one but many, who has "a great variety of selves to call upon" (193). Orlando never regrets any of her/his actions. Living by Lord Henry's "new hedonism," she exemplifies the "harmony of soul and body" that is the inspiring principle of Basil Hallward's art. Orlando's youth and beauty are even more outrageously long-lived than Dorian's; they last through centuries instead of decades, yet they trouble her not at all. Orlando at the end of the novel is thirty-six, and Dorian is not more than forty. It is as likely that Dorian's retaining his youthful good looks is natural as it is that Orlando's retaining hers is magical.

The difference between the self-acceptance of Orlando and the self-hatred of Dorian emerges through the use of the mirror image in each text. Dorian at first exults in contrasting the face he sees in the looking glass wth the distorting mirror that is his picture. But by the end of the novel he hates both the self he sees in the mirror and the self he sees in the painting. If Basil's mirror ideal disgusts him as an "unjust mirror, this mirror of his soul" (166), he is also repulsed by the sight of his unchanging beauty reflected in a mirror that is the gift of Lord Henry. He flings it to the floor and crushes it "into silver splinters beneath his heel" (165). This self-hatred "kept him awake at night" (166). Echoing this passage (through the words *mirror, splinter,* and *sleep*), Orlando hopes for a happier ending that will conduce to the Keatsian vision of "a sleep / Full of sweet dreams, and health, and quiet breathing":

> Hail happiness, then, and after happiness, hail not those dreams which bloat the sharp image as spotted mirrors do . . . dreams which splinter the whole and tear us asunder and wound us and split us apart in the night when we would sleep; but sleep, sleep so deep . . . prone let us lie on the sand at the bottom of sleep. (184)

Orlando is able to look at herself with appreciation at the end: "She took out a little looking-glass. Honestly, though she was now thirty-six, she scarcely looked a day older. She looked just as pouting, as sulky, as handsome, as rosy . . . as she had done that day on the ice" (189).

Dorian tries to deny his homoerotic impulses and escape them through marriage to Sibyl. After abandoning her, he returns home and falls into a long sleep. When he wakes it is to a willed but unreal remorse. His feelings emerge through the unwilled miracle of the change in the painting. When Orlando returns home after losing Sasha, he too falls into a long sleep. When he wakes, having forgotten his past, the question, full of Paterian and Wildean echoes (through such words as *strange, penetrate, secret*), is asked: "And then what strange powers are these that penetrate our most secret ways and change our most treasured possessions without our willing it?" (42–43). That the sex change is a stand-in for homosexuality is suggested by the coded language. Even before it Orlando has "something out of the common . . . hid beneath her duffle cloak" that women sense and are "eager to come at the truth of" (19). The invocation to Truth at the moment of the sex change is also phrased in such terms: "You flaunt in the brutal gaze of the sun things that were better unknown and undone; you unveil the shameful, the dark you make clear" (85).

If Dorian is too frightened to respond to love—not only Sybil's but even Basil's or Lord Henry's love—it is partly because these loves do not offer him the support he needs. They are of the nature of worship or admiration rather than understanding. He tells Lord Henry, "Your voice and the voice of Sybil Vane are two things I shall never forget. . . . each of them says something different. I don't know which to follow" (51). Although he thinks he is following Henry's voice, he is soon unable to communicate with Henry. In the subtly written final conversation, Henry, whose wife has left him, reveals his feelings for Dorian, saying that he (Dorian) can never change for him (Henry), and speaks nostalgically of the month they met when lilacs (a flower connected with homosexual love) were in full bloom. The conversation is noncommunicative: when Dorian virtually tells Henry that he is the murderer of Basil, Henry refuses to believe this, and Dorian too fails to respond to Henry's appeal: "I have sorrows, Dorian, of my own, that even you know nothing of" (162). The failure of communication makes Henry's invitation to Dorian to ride in the park, and to lunch with various women whose clever conversation he describes as tiresome, sound far from hedonistic, in fact, the very epitome of conventional routine. Dorian responds with exhaustion: "He was tired of hearing his own name now" (164). The text is inward with Dorian as it is not with Lord Henry. Several unstressed moments indicate that Dorian is looking for more than pleasure, more than admiration—that he is looking for love.

Dorian's initial wish that the portrait might grow old instead of himself is triggered by his bitter perception that Basil cares only for his beauty and will cease to adore him when that beauty fades. In a crucial conversation he tells Basil: "You like your art better than your friends. I am no more to you than a green bronze figure. Hardly as much, I dare say" (34). In protest against objectification and his own entrapment in it, Dorian prophesies: "When I find that I am growing old, I shall kill myself" (35). Later, at the moment when Dorian is about to reveal to Basil the secret of the painting, Basil declares his feelings for Dorian but is unable to use the word *love*. The mind-body dualism that Lord Henry's Romantic Paterian philosophy seeks to combat splits Basil's discourse so that he can describe his feelings only in pejorative terms: "idolatry," "intolerable fascination," "mad worship" (94). In response, Dorian makes one of his most perceptive comments. " 'My dear Basil,' said Dorian, 'What have you told me? Simply that you felt that you admired me too much. That is not even a compliment' " (95). Dorian has many willing and unwilling admirers but no "lovers"; no one who can be said to love him.

The word *love*, so frequent in Wilde's other writings, is conspicuous by its relative absence from this text. Yet it is that absence Dorian pursues. Like the narrator of Solomon's *Vision*, he is unsatisfied by the pursuit of desire and desperately seeks love. On the two occasions outlined above he makes an attempt to communicate his secret to his two friends; on both he is preempted by the other's declaration of admiration, which does not quite amount to love because it dares not openly use the word. The text suggests that Dorian's "sin" (and perhaps also Lord Henry's and Basil's) is not unnatural love but an unnatural inability to acknowledge love; not self-love but self-hatred. The love that dares not speak its name may be inhibited not just by social pressure but also by self-devaluation. In *De Profundis* Wilde represents himself as having thought, at the time of his greatest pain and isolation, "At all costs, I must keep love in my heart" (898). Dorian's defeat does not represent the failure of the new hedonism. It represents Dorian's failure to live by that philosophy.

Most commentators dismiss Sybil Vane as a weakly written and sentimental element in the text. She is, however, the only figure represented as sure of what she wants and as able to carry out actions on which she decides. In this sense she illustrates the duchess's remark to Lord Henry: "Courage has passed from men to women" (150). Most actions in this text are unintended. They are either the result of accident or contradict the stated intention of the agent. Lord Henry's marriage is in stark contradiction to his philosophy, yet he regrets its end. Dorian regrets almost every one of his actions and is haunted by them. The killing of Basil is not planned; the killing of Sybil's brother is accidental; the final death of Dorian himself is not intended. This last action is almost a parodic imitation of Sybil's decisive suicidal action. Like Sybil, Dorian is found stretched out on the floor of an upstairs room. It is Sybil who commits the grand tragic and romantic action. Like Chatterton, the hero of the Romantics and the Aestheticists, or like Septimus Smith in *Mrs. Dalloway*, she refuses to compromise. She makes the characteristic gesture of the romantic artist as martyr, a figure central to typical same-sex love narratives. Such figures die young, either literally or metaphorically, at their own hand or at that of a persecutor. This death represents both a refusal to compromise and the narrative's elegiac response to the unfulfillment of homoerotic love, besieged by unpropitious social circumstances. In this context her name is important, constructing her as wise, powerful, and prophetic. Her action is more prophetic for Dorian than are Lord Henry's failed prophecies.

It is in Dorian's death wish, his pursuit of his death, that most readers have located the homoerotic significance of the narrative. Toward the end, Dorian's revulsion against hunting signals his own identification with the hunted animal in a way that looks forward to Stephen Gordon's similar identification: "The consciousness of being hunted, snared, tracked down, had begun to dominate him." He cries out when he sees the hare: "Don't shoot it, Geoffrey. Let it live" (152), and later tells Henry that he wishes hunting were stopped for ever because it is "hideous and cruel" (153). His death is both suicide and murder. Like Sybil's, or like Sappho's in the legend, it is a protest, a choice of death over a loveless life. It is significant that the text represents a woman as the model for this gesture.

Dorian refuses to make a loveless marriage; he also finds his loveless life an unbearable anguish. Orlando marries twice (as a man, he marries Rosina Pepita; as a woman, Shelmerdine) and apparently finds marriage no obstacle to bisexual affairs. Anguish is erased. This may be be read as a determined paean to joy; it may also be read as avoidance or as self-erasure. Woolf had written on October 14, 1927: "If you've given yourself to Campbell, I'll have no more to do with you, and so it shall be written plainly, for all the world to read in Orlando."[31] And so it is, with a significant shift. After Orlando marries, she has "no more to do" with women. She no longer leads the double life she led in the eighteenth century. In compensation, the narrative gives her a son and glimpses of the ghost of Sasha. Where Dorian ends up having sex without love, Orlando ends up having love without sex. This is related to her continuing tendency to split the two.

The archduke/duchess Harry/Henrietta represents the clearest homosexual possibility in the book and may be a parody of Lord Henry (in another parodic possibility, Orlando as hostess is termed "our modern Sibyl"). He falls in love with Orlando as a man but Orlando, although also attracted, flees in terror because he sees the attraction as the white bird, love, who suddenly turns around and reveals its black alter ego, lust. Confronted by, and herself constructing, this classic split between love and sex, heart and body, Orlando flees England. On her return to England she resolves the split by leading a double life—one by day, dressed as a woman, another at night, dressed as a man. After her marriage she replaces the double life with writing, thinking, dreaming, and we are told that she does not indulge in "slipping off [her] petticoat and—" (242) engaging in what "male novelists" term love. This is generally and rightly read as a critique of compulsory heterosexuality. However, unfortunately or fortunately, lesbian sex would also involve "slipping off one's petticoat" (242).

Does Woolf take her revenge for Vita's abandonment of her for other women by her tongue-in-cheek admission that Orlando, while kind, generous, "faithful to friends" (242), does not "love"? At one level, she defines Orlando as lesbian by this statement, since she explicitly states that the "love" Orlando does not engage in is love as male novelists like Lawrence define it, that is, heterosexual intercourse. At another level, she may be commenting on Vita's promiscuity. In her initial announcement to Vita that *Orlando* might be an account of "you and the lusts of your flesh and the lure of your mind," Woolf had pointed to the split in Vita's way of loving: "(heart you have none, who go gallivanting down the lanes with Campbell). . . . I should like to untwine and twist some very odd, incongruous strands in you: going at length into the question of Campbell."[32]

Toward the end of the book Orlando asks herself what matters in life and concludes that it is not fame or worldly success that matters but rather success as Pater (and following him, Wilde) defined it: "It is not articles . . . nor eight-hour bills nor covenants nor factory acts that matter; it's something useless, sudden, violent . . . something rash, ridiculous . . . ecstasy, it's ecstasy that matters. . . . So she repeated: 'Ecstasy, ecstasy', as she stood waiting to cross."[33] On the last page of the book the word is repeated: " 'Ecstasy!' she cried, 'ecstasy!' " (204).

This passage clearly echoes Pater's formulation that had become Wilde's central tenet: "To burn always with this hard gem-like flame, to maintain this ecstasy, is success in life." The narrator supports Orlando's insight here, insisting on Romantic hedonism and Gautier-Pater-Wildean self-realization as the aim of life. Drawing on Wilde's vision of anarchist

"Pleasure is Nature's test, her sign of approval. When man is happy, he is in harmony with himself and his environment,"[34] the narrator invokes desire and happiness:

> Hail! natural desire! Hail! happiness! divine happiness! and pleasure of all sorts
> . . . and anything, anything, that interrupts and confounds the . . . forging of
> links and chains, binding the empire together. . . . Hail, happiness . . . and all
> fulfilment of natural desire . . . hail! in whatever form it comes, and may there
> be more forms, and stranger. (184)

This invocation attempts a triumphant reversal of the prescriptive use of the word *natural*. But this invocation occurs at the moment of the birth of Orlando's son, an event that can hardly be deemed evidence of "strange desire." Although Madeline Moore argues that the son is conceived without heterosexual intercourse having taken place, this argument is a little like that which rages around whether or not there is time for Othello's marriage to be consummated. Strange desire is not foregrounded in *Orlando*, as it is, for instance in *The Well of Loneliness* or *Maurice*. It is smuggled in by narrator and by protagonist, and the narrator is at pains to define the process as smuggling.[35] The image of smuggling suggests that Orlando breaks the law but does so surreptitiously; she does not defy it or alter it. Like Wilde in his famous encounter with a customs official, she declares her genius and camouflages her sexuality. While the Wilde trial, like the Radclyffe Hall trial, became an emblem of the inextricability of genius and sexuality, even perhaps of genius and homosexuality, no such explosion disturbs Orlando's triumphal progress.

The smuggling image occurs at the point when Orlando returns to writing poetry after marriage. The four lines Woolf quotes from Vita's poem *The Land*, deal, as Barbara Fassler has noted, "with the lesbian passion she both gloried in and feared."[36] What has not been noticed is that these lines draw directly on Lord Alfred Douglas's poem "Two Loves," which defined homosexual love as "shame" and as "the love that dare not speak its name." Vita's lines, quoted in *Orlando*, are "And then I came to a field where the springing grass / Was dulled by the hanging cups of fritillaries, / Sullen and foreign-looking, the snaky flower / Scarfed in dull purple, like Egyptian girls." Douglas's poem describes the flower in almost exactly the same terms: "snake-like fritillaries / Scarce seen for the rank grass."[37] In Orlando the censoring power is uncomfortable with the passage and asks: "Girls? Are girls necessary? You have a husband at the Cape, you say? Ah, well, that'll do" (166). This is followed by the passage that describes the spirit of the age as a customs officer who allows a traveler to smuggle in cigars. The comparison to cigars places Vita's interest in "girls" as a luxury she is allowed because she has compromised with the spirit of the age by marrying and by refraining from overt rebellion:

> She was extremely doubtful whether, if the spirit had examined the contents of
> her mind carefully, it would not have found something highly contraband for

which she would have had to pay the full fine. . . . She had just managed, by some dexterous deference to the spirit of the age, by putting on a ring and finding a man on a moor, by loving nature and being no satirist, cynic or psychologist—any one of which goods would have been discovered at once—to pass its examination successfully. (166–67)

The metaphor of "the full fine" (which recurs in *Flush*) recalls the price such men as Wilde and Solomon and such women as Radclyffe Hall paid. The passage is self-reflexive—Woolf performs exactly the smuggling action she describes and is enabled to do so by casting her text as "a biography" of a woman whose life provides the camouflage required.[38] The lines following those that Woolf quotes are a good example of Vita Sackville-West's "dexterous deference to the spirit of the age." "Egyptian girls" stand for lesbian passion and the poet-speaker sees them as "staining the waste / With foreign colour, sulky, dark and quaint, / Dangerous." The danger lies in their power to imprison. The Egyptian girl is described as "throwing a net, soft round the limbs and heart, / Captivity soft and abhorrent, a close-meshed net . . . A gypsy Judith, witch of a ragged tent." Terrified, the speaker says "I shrank from the English field of fritillaries, / Before it should be too late, before I forgot / The cherry white in the woods, and the curdled clouds."[39] Though the fritillaries are English, they and the homoerotic passion they symbolize are exoticized in the speaker's fascinated gaze as non-English aliens, in contrast to the "white" cherry. The act of "loving nature" to which Woolf ascribes Orlando's success in evading the "full fine" is not an acceptance of all desire as "natural" but a terrified flight from desire to the love of what is societally defined as acceptably "natural." It is sealed and signified to the world by the act of getting married and putting a ring on her finger. It can hardly be said to be in opposition to the "forging of links and chains, binding the empire together" (184).[40]

The schism between "English" and "Egyptian" in Sackville-West's poem quoted by Woolf corresponds to the schism between her public life as wife and mother and her hidden life as lover of women. If Orlando does, in her hidden life, maintain the "ecstasy" that Woolf's narrator, following Pater, defines as "success in life," the text is nevertheless shot through with an uneasy awareness that Orlando has also, like Clarissa Dalloway, "schemed and pilfered," has "wanted success" of another, nonecstatic kind. The awareness introduces, at least for this reader, "an emptiness at the heart of life" into the text's project of celebration. By figuring the subject of her biography as one who makes crucial compromises with a stultifying, conventional society, Woolf criticizes her much as Strachey criticized his eminent Victorians. The absence of the risk-taking Romantic and Aestheticist writers from Orlando's literary ancestry may be part of this critique.[41]

Ecstasy, valorized by the narrator, disappears from Orlando's life, and from the text, with Sasha. Some part of Orlando dies with the disappearance of Sasha as some part of Vita died with the disappearance of Violet and some part of Virginia with what she called "the defection of Vita." With the erasure of Sasha from Orlando's conscious memory, pain, jealousy, and erotic triangles also vanish. Orlando's conflicts from that time onward are primarily external. Woolf seems to suggest that with the loss of Violet Vita loses the capacity to love and to suffer or anaesthetizes it.

Throughout her life Virginia expressed, with varying degrees of intensity, a sense of unrequitedness and loss vis-à-vis her women friends. This has often been read as a search for a mother substitute. It is equally possible to read it as a need for an everyday intimacy with a woman that the structuring of her life prevented.[42] Whereas her letters to women constantly express jealousy of other women and men and demand reassurance, her letters to men almost never express any such jealousy and are full of reassurances that she loves the man concerned. Both she and Vita frequently expressed jealousy vis-à-vis each other's husbands. Perhaps the most poignant expression of this feeling of exclusion is Vita's account of a dream she had at a time when her involvements with other women were causing Virginia to go into a "rage of jealousy":

> I dreamed last night that you and Leonard had never been really married, and that you decided it was high time to hold the ceremony. . . . You did not invite me to the wedding. So I stood in the crowd, and saw you pass on Leonard's arm.
>
> For some reason or reasons (not far to seek) this dream made me extremely miserable, and I woke in tears, and have not yet thrown off the effect of it.
>
> Will you tell your bridegroom that I sent back the proofs of King's Daughter to Mrs Cartwright last week?[43]

King's Daughter was a collection of poems to another woman of whom Virginia was extremely jealous. The letter clearly places Virginia's inaccessibility, Vita's grief and exclusion, and her relationship with the other woman in relation to one another. If Vita's nightmare was Virginia's marriage, Virginia's was Vita's promiscuity. In her diary she recorded a dream in which Vita "had gone off with someone, very markedly, at a party, in a small house whose room I was about to make into my study by knocking down a wall—I still see it; I hear Nessa saying she's tired of you: then my teeth broke; then as I say Vita went off triumphantly with somebody, being sick of me."[44]

If Vita was not "faithful," it perhaps had much to do with the fact that marriage prevented her relationship with Virginia developing into a life-sustaining one. After Virginia's death Vita repeated the lament that both women had always voiced when away from one another in grief or sickness: "I still think I might have saved her if only I had been there." The editors comment, "Vita was probably right."[45] Virginia had recorded in her diary the growing distance between them as a cause for her depression in her last years: " I could here analyse my state of mind these last 4 months, & account for the human emptiness by the defection of Vita; Roger's death; & no-one springing up to take their place."[46]

A quotation from an elegy in a letter to Vita is revealing: "But now my porpoise no longer crowns the fishmongers shop—thats a quotation from the Scholar-Gypsey. . . . And how I miss you! You wouldn't believe it. . . . But you don't want me."[47] The editor's explanatory note reads: "Matthew Arnold—but of course it was not a quotation." The dismissal is too hasty. The reference to "crowning" recalls Arnold's "Thyrsis," his Keatsian elegy for Arthur Clough. The poem is a continuation of "The Scholar Gypsy." A particular tree on a hilltop was a symbol to the two friends of their shared vision and ideals. The poem ends: "the light we sought is shining still . . . Our tree yet crowns the hill." But this hopeful note is preceded by lamentation for the departure of Clough, for the alterations in the flower-filled landscape they loved that have "put by / The coronals of our forgotten time," and, most important, the loss of the poet's youthful joy in life. It is from this part of the poem that Woolf quotes, jokingly linking it to her erotic pet name for Vita ("porpoise in the fishmonger's shop"):

> Yes thou art gone! and round me too the night
> In ever-nearing circle weaves her shade,
> I see her veil draw soft across the day,
> I feel her slowly chilling breath invade
> The cheek grown thin, the brown hair sprent with grey;
> I feel her finger light
> Laid pausefully upon life's headlong train;—
> The foot less prompt to meet the morning dew,
> The heart less bounding at emotion new,
> And hope, once crushed, less quick to spring again.

Woolf quotes from a Victorian poem of same-sex love to articulate her feelings of loss and grief, feelings connected with the onset of old age. In an early love letter she had written to Vita: "You don't see, donkey West, that you'll be tired of me one of these days (I'm so much older)."[48] The Platonic, Sapphic, and Marian models of older lover and younger beloved generate anxiety and grief when the institution of heterosexual marriage obstructs them and no equally powerful institution upholds them. It is in the subdued elegiac quality of *Orlando* that I would locate its participation in traditions of writing homoeroticism. In *The Waves* Woolf took on these traditions more directly, acknowledging her Romantic and Aestheticist heritage and examining the meaning of their attraction to suicide as metaphor.

Orlando (1928) was followed by *A Room of One's Own* (1929) and *The Waves* (1931). Rhoda in *The Waves* is a portrait of a Victorian Sappho. Articulating her attraction to women in a language drawn from the Romantics, especially Shelley, she leaps to her death by drowning, as Sappho did in legend and as Woolf was to do in reality a decade later. In *The Waves* Woolf comes fully to terms with her Romantic and Sapphic heritage. As Charles Schug says, "If Virginia Woolf strove to write novels that were poetic in form, the kind of 'poetry' she wrote, we can now say, was Romantic poetry."[49] *The Waves* represents Woolf's breakthrough in terms of form, a successful experiment in developing her own kind of stream-of-consciousness novel, quite different from Dorothy Richardson's or Joyce's. Equally, it represents a breakthrough in terms of content, containing her first celebratory portrait of male homosexuality and a portrait of Sapphism painted with the suggestive colors inherited from Romantic and Aestheticist ancestors. In her later fictions these themes are developed with increased fearlessness and suggestive power.

In *A Room of One's Own* (as in *Orlando*) Woolf had argued that male novelists' explicit descriptions of heterosexual intercourse were repetitive and "dull" because they lacked "the power of suggestion" (105). In contrast, she had remarked that Coleridge's writing "explodes and gives birth to all kinds of other ideas, and that is the only sort of writing of which one can say that it has the secret of perpetual life" (105). Woolf never subscribed to the quasi-Freudian, Lawrentian view that explicitness equals liberation. She remarked in 1932 of a lesbian novel that it was "all about Sapphism, so dull, so improper."[50] In contrast, when in 1931 she conceived of a "new book . . . about the sexual life of women," she exclaimed, "Lord how exciting!"[51] If the excitement lies not in the subject matter alone but in the suggestive power with which she writes it, the strategy of suggestion depends on a dialogue with the reader through a commonly inherited literary language.

Of the six speaking voices in *The Waves*, only two marry—Bernard and Susan. Louis and Jinny live lives of promiscuous heterosexuality. I shall consider Neville, the homosexual poet, and Rhoda, the thwarted Sapphic poet, as "doubles," secret sharers, much like Clarissa Dalloway and Septimus Smith. The first name that Rhoda mentions is Neville's: "Neville is gone."[52] That they share certain urges is indicated by their use of words in the first section. Rhoda is the first of the six voices to use the word *freedom*. She defines her aloneness as freedom when she is playing her game of sending flower petal boats on an imaginary voyage. Neville is the first to use the word *solitude*; and also the first to use the words *liberty, imagination,* and *in love*. All these words occur in his thoughts at church, as he pits his Hellenic life-affirming vision against the life-denying worldview of Christian religious authority in which Louis "rejoices." To Neville and Rhoda, too, first come intimations of mortality. While Rhoda imagines a drowning sailor whom she tries to rescue, Neville reflects on the meaning of death.

Neville comes closest to representing Bloomsbury's Romantic anarchist values, with his resistance to establishment norms, distrust of authority, devotion to art, and to the idea of friendship, his conviction that of all things in the world, "love came a long way first." The association with him of the symbols of Greece, the rose, and Shakespeare's

Sonnets establishes a link between him and Septimus Smith, in whose thoughts these were recurrent homoerotic motifs. His critique of a religion that outlaws pleasure and beauty is set firmly in a Romantic tradition: " 'The brute menaces my liberty,' said Neville, 'when he prays. Unwarmed by imagination, his words fall cold on my head' " (24). As a male, Neville can mask his nonconformity in the apparent conformity of the university world. He is modeled on men like Walter Pater, A. E. Housman, G. L. Dickinson, even E. M. Forster, who escaped the pressure to marry by taking shelter at the university and leading double lives. Since such institutions are unavailable to Rhoda, she has to survive by a literary tradition that provides inadequate sustenance on its own, unaided by external mechanisms.

Neville first discovers himself and his place in the world when he goes to school; for the girls, school is the place where the process of destruction and anguish begins. School grooms them only for heterosexual love and marriage. But Rhoda does manage to find in the library Shelley's poem "The Question." It encodes for her the questions about love to which life denies her an answer. In contrast, Neville discovers not only an intellectual tradition that openly celebrates the kind of love he desires but also the spaces where such love can be enacted:

> I come, like a lord to his halls appointed. . . . a library, where I shall . . . pronounce the explicit, the sonorous hexameters of Virgil, of Lucretius, and chant with a passion that is never obscure or formless the loves of Catullus, reading from a big book, a quarto with margins. I shall lie too, in the fields among the tickling grasses. I shall lie with my friends under the towering elm trees. (21)

That his passion for Catullus's love poetry is not "obscure" or "formless" suggests his awareness that Catullus's loves, like his own, were male. "Too" is so placed as to mean that, apart from reading Virgil and Catullus, he will lie in the fields. It also means that, like Virgil and Catullus, he too will lie in the fields with his friends. This second meaning is fraught with the biblical double entendre contained in "lie" and with the fact that Virgil's homoerotic love poetry is pastoral.

The study of Greek and Latin, from which Rhoda is excluded, provides Neville with models for his unconventional loves. This was an experience common to many young Englishmen in the nineteenth and early twentieth centuries. For instance, Lytton Strachey, in his diary at school, reassured himself thus about the legitimacy of his attraction to a schoolfellow: "I may be sinning but I am doing so in the company of Shakespeare and Greece."[53] Neville's suffering springs from what may be called "a lover's quarrel with the world," experienced in microcosm in his love for the conventional Percival, but also extending to his relationship to conventional society.

The men who take against Neville react favorably to Bernard, even though the two have been educated in the same way. This is because

Bernard's aims as an artist are not diametrically opposed to those of society. Shakespeare's *Sonnets* become a medium for expressing the difference. For Bernard they are a place to store up memories like dead flowers: "O friendship, I too will press flowers between the pages of Shakespeare's sonnets!" (60). For Neville, they are a living inspiration; phrases from the sonnets unconsciously creep into his speech. "You are you. That is what consoles me for the lack of many things" (122) echoes sonnet 84: "You are you." Similarly "I am one person—myself" (59) echoes sonnet 121, which Wilde quoted in *The Portrait of Mr W. H.*: "I am that I am."[54] Shakespeare and Plato are part of Neville's "system," the intellectual history and ancestry he and his community construct: "Thus we spin round us infinitely fine filaments and construct a system. Plato and Shakespeare are included, also quite obscure people, people of no importance whatsoever. . . . To follow the dark paths of the mind and enter the past" (121).

The word *love* occurs most frequently in Neville's monologues. Ethel Smyth, who found *The Waves* "profoundly disquieting," the saddest book she had ever read, felt that the characters lacked "something necessary to the human equipment and the best of them all is Neville because he was anyhow capable of love."[55] Neville organizes his world around his vision of love, which includes the acceptance of pain: "Love makes knots; love brutally tears them apart. I have been knotted; I have been torn apart" (145). Conversely, Neville is Woolf's first and fullest portrait of a homosexual man as self-assured, unashamed, successful both in love and professionally. For this reason, perhaps, he excites a surprising degree of homophobia in commentators much more sympathetic to such figures as Septimus Smith who are agonized and suicidal as a result of their homosexuality. Thus Beverly Anne Schlack castigates Neville at length in predictable terms as an ivory tower snob who is "alienated from the natural world, which neither notices nor conforms to his predilections" and a "spiritually impoverished sensationalist."[56]

Unfulfilled desire for love is at the center of Rhoda's life. She has often been read as Woolf's self-portrait, especially because her suicide by drowning anticipates Woolf's own. Woolf's elegiac novel echoes Shelley's prophecy in *Adonais* of his death by drowning. The subterranean quality of Rhoda's emotions is conveyed through a cluster of images associated with lesbianism in Woolf's fictions. As Woolf writes Sapphic difference, it coheres around the active pursuit of love. Like Austen's *Emma*, Rhoda does not wait passively to be pursued. In her aspiration to assume the active role Rhoda differs radically from Jinny, whose sexuality, although apparently nonconformist in its promiscuity, is actually well within the mold of woman as the one sought after and pursued. Where Rhoda indirectly competes with men in her dream of being the active pursuer, Jinny competes with women for male attention. Hence the greater social acceptability of Jinny: "One man will single me out and will tell me what he has told no other person. He will like me better than Susan or Rhoda" (37).

It is the absence of a possible beloved that diminishes Rhoda's sense of self, leaves her faceless: "There is no single scent, no single body for me to follow. And I have no face" (88). Her fears arise from this absence, which also distinguishes her predicament from Neville's. Her monologue in the fourth section opens with a direct echo from Neville's. Neville says:

> I came quickly and directly, *here*, to sit by the person whom I love. . . . I am never stagnant; I rise from my worst disasters, I turn, I change. Pebbles bounce off the mail of my muscular, my extended body. In this pursuit I shall grow old.
>
> "If I could believe," said Rhoda, "that I should grow old in pursuit and change, I should be rid of my fear." (87)

Rhoda falls in love with her teacher Miss Lambert. The "purple light" of Miss Lambert's ring appears to her "an amorous light." She cherishes her beloved's face as one of her imagined "curious treasures" under her dress (22–23). Purple is the color of passion and recurrently so in Woolf's writings. Lily represents her beloved Mrs. Ramsay as a "triangular purple shape," "a purple shadow," and, while working on *To the Lighthouse*, Woolf wrote to Vita Sackville-West: "We're still talking, you'll be surprised to hear, about love. . . . Then Morgan says he's worked it out and one spends 3 hours on food, 6 on sleep, 4 on work, 2 on love. Lytton says 10 on love. I say the whole day on love. I say its seeing things through a purple shade."[57] *Curious* is a coded word drawn from Pater and Wilde.

Neville experiences reciprocal relationships that enable him to speak in the lyric dialogic voice ("I" and "You"): "But when you come everything changes. . . . There can be no doubt, I thought, pushing aside the newspaper, that our mean lives, unsightly as they are, put on splendour and have meaning only under the eyes of love" (120). Rhoda's sentiments are exactly the same, but she can only speak about a "she," not to a "you": " 'When Miss Lambert passes,' said Rhoda, ' . . . everything changes and becomes luminous. . . . Only her purple ring still glows, her vinous, her amethystine ring' " (30).

In the eighth section Neville's "softness" is contrasted with Susan's "hardness." Rhoda, like Neville, is "soft"; like him, she experiences the world as fluid; the images of the flame, of luminosity, and of orgasmic melting liquescence appear: "When Miss Lambert passes, she makes the daisy change . . . even my body now lets the light through; my spine is soft like wax near the flame of the candle. I dream; I dream" (30–31).

Neville confides in Bernard and can speak of a "we," where Rhoda, deprived of any sense of community, always uses "I." Rhoda moves from dream to fantasy. Her fantasy involves attracting the beloved's attention by feats of martyrdom. Woolf appropriates to Rhoda the male homo-erotic image of St. Sebastian pierced by arrows and connects it with Marian devotion; like Radclyffe Hall, she reclaims a Sapphic icon and erotic symbol—the lesbian as martyr. Since Rhoda is in a girls' school, the ungendered "immaculate people" who spend their holidays at

Scarborough are girls, and the face that makes her choke with emotion is identified as belonging to a "she":

> I choose out across the hall some unknown face and can hardly drink my tea when she whose name I do not know sits opposite. I choke, I am rocked from side to side by the violence of my emotion. I imagine these nameless, these immaculate people, watching me from behind bushes. I leap high to excite their admiration. At night, in bed, I excite their complete wonder. I often die pierced with arrows to win their tears. If they should say, or I should see from a label on their boxes, that they were in Scarborough last holidays, the whole town runs gold, the whole pavement is illuminated. (29)

This passage is indebted to Mirrlees. Madeleine's fantasies are often accompanied by her "leaping" and dancing round the room, and to win her beloved's "admiration" is her main aim, since she is told that admiration is the route to love. Like Rhoda's, her feats remain imaginary and the beloved is unaware of her love.

This is followed by Rhoda's third and centrally defining fantasy, described at greatest length. It recurs again toward the end of the book when she is moving toward death. This fantasy is about transforming love into art. It springs from her reading of Shelley's "The Question," a poem about the desire to love, to offer one's heart, and about the lack of a beloved to accept that offering. *The Waves* quotes the poem at some length, especially its brilliant evocation of "visionary flowers" growing in a spring landscape. The flowers are transparent symbols of erotic desire and emotion, and the lush landscape is one of the feminized homoeroticized landscapes I considered in chapter 2. The ungendered speaking voice makes a bouquet of the flowers and the poem concludes: "I hastened to the spot whence I had come, / That I might there present it!— Oh! to whom?"

Woolf's construction of lesbian experience through Shelley's verse demonstrates that Romantic lyrical discourse makes available a language for this experience, as Greek and Latin literature had made available a language for male homoeroticism. Rhoda identifies herself with the speaking voice of Shelley's poem: "Here is a poem about a hedge. I will wander down it and pick flowers, green cowbind and the moonlight-coloured May, wild roses and ivy serpentine" (38). All of these descriptions of flowers are direct quotes from the poem. She continues by adding a detail of her own—she imagines bringing these flowers into the schoolroom: "I will clasp them in my hands and lay them on the desk's shiny surface" (38). Still quoting the poem, she imagines herself gazing into the water in a Narcissus-like gesture. Rhoda suddenly feels impeded in this self-contemplation. The images here are very close to those in the passage in Woolf's essay "The Pargiters," where the woman novelist is figured as a fisherwoman whose imagination is obstructed by her reason when she brings up from the subconscious mind, figured as water, some submerged truth about women's bodies and passions. Rhoda goes through exactly this experience. She quotes Shelley to describe eroticism and artistic self-expression as simultaneously thwarted:

> I will sit by the river's trembling edge and look at the water-lilies, broad and bright, which lit the oak that overhung the hedge with moonlight beams of their own watery light. I will pick flowers; I will bind flowers in one garland and clasp them and present them—Oh! to whom? There is some check in the flow of my being; a deep stream presses on some obstacle; it jerks; it tugs; some knot in the centre resists. Oh, this is pain, this is anguish! I faint, I fail. (38)

The first sentence quotes several phrases from "The Question" but the last sentence quotes Shelley's "The Indian Serenade," where the narrator arises from dreams of the beloved and pleads for love but ends with a vision of death:

> Oh lift me from the grass!
> I die! I faint! I fail!
> . . . My heart beats loud and fast;—
> Oh! press it to thine own again,
> Where it will break at last.   (380)[58]

Faint is a favorite Shelleyan word; it occurs in contexts where the poet is reaching out for a dream that cannot be fulfilled. This unfulfillment together with the ungendered and feminized *I* makes Shelley's verse a space eminently available to homoerotic self-construction in a heterosexist society. "The Question" uses the stream as an image of a longed-for embrace that cannot be completed in life and that the speaker can scarcely imagine completing even in a dream: "a shelving bank of turf, which lay / Under a copse, and hardly dared to fling / Its green arms round the bosom of the stream, / But kissed it and then fled, as thou mightest in dream." Ungendering takes place through the two partners in the embrace being natural objects—stream and copse. This figuring removes it from definitive heterosexuality. Woolf picks up the image of the stream and links it with the earlier image of the orgasmic liquescence of Rhoda's body and being:

> Now my body thaws; I am unsealed; I am incandescent. Now the stream pours in a deep tide fertilizing, opening the shut, forcing the tight-folded, flooding free. To whom shall I give all that now flows through me, from my warm, my porous body? I will gather my flowers and present them—Oh! to whom?
>
> Sailors loiter on the parade, and amorous couples; the omnibuses rattle along the sea front to the town. I will give; I will enrich; I will return to the world this beauty. I will bind my flowers in one garland and advancing with my hand outstretched will present them—Oh! to whom? (38–39)

Here the sailors are an image of the life Rhoda seeks and is denied; earlier the drowning sailor was an image of her concern with that which lay submerged. The image of the drowning or drowned sailor had appeared more than once in the musings of Septimus Smith in *Mrs. Dalloway*. Septimus sees himself as "a drowned sailor on a rock," one who has been dead yet is somehow alive, similar to his lost beloved Evans. The drowned sailor as a homoerotic image had occurred in Wilde's poem "Charmides." It is a development of the Narcissus figure who falls in love with his mirror image in the water, and pursues it to his own undoing, and also of the Sapphic figure who drowns herself from unfulfilled love. It is suggestive of that which is destroyed but not buried, that which may rise to the surface to shock and horrify. To Septimus the image also brings a sense of liberty, contingent upon accepting outcast status:

> . . . now that he was quite alone, condemned, deserted, as those who are about to die are alone, there was a luxury in it, an isolation full of sublimity. . . . Even Holmes himself [the psychiatrist] could not touch this last relic straying on the edge of the world, this outcast, who gazed back at the inhabited regions, who lay, like a drowned sailor, on the shore of the world. (83)

Rhoda experiences a very similar sense of isolation, and repeatedly dreams of death by drowning. In the seventh section, anticipating her suicide, she recalls all her fantasies, and the only one that accompanies her into death is the one drawn from "The Question":

> So terrible was life that I held up shade after shade. . . . Harrogate, perhaps, Edinburgh, perhaps, was ruffled with golden glory when some girl whose name I forget stood on the pavement. But it was the name only. I left Louis; I feared embraces. . . .
> . . . who then comes with me? Flowers only, the cowbind and the moonlight-coloured May. Gathering them loosely in a sheaf I made of them a garland and gave them—Oh, to whom? we launch out now over the precipice. . . . I touch nothing. I see nothing. . . . The sea will drum in my ears. . . . Rolling me over the waves will shoulder me under. Everything falls in a tremendous shower, dissolving me. (138–39)

Noteworthy here is the link between the inaccessibility of the female beloved and Rhoda's choosing to leave Louis because she fears the embraces he represents. More significant is the fact that in her fantasy Rhoda sees herself in the position and posture traditionally assumed by the male lover—as the one who presents a bouquet or garland to a female beloved. This gesture of presenting the poem to a woman is the male lover's both in Petrarchan and anti-Petrarchan conventions. Rhoda seeks to be, like Neville, the pursuer, the active lover, the one who performs heroic feats and is martyred for love, the one who offers all the dangerous flowers of body, mind, spirit. As opposed to her determined portrait of the bisexual woman as "successful" in the biographical *Orlando*, Woolf here presents an autobiographical portrait not so different from Renee

Vivien's or Radclyffe Hall's. To do so, she reads Shelley's poetry much as Carpenter and Barnefield read it, the yearning being figured as homoerotic in quality.

Like the younger Romantics' and like Stephen Gordon's, Rhoda's desire for love is integral to the desire for self-expression. There is a strong suggestion that she is an incipient artist, thwarted in her creativity because she is deprived of a muse. A phrase like "I will return to the world this beauty" evokes the activity of the artist. Carolyn Heilbrun, in her introduction to May Sarton's *Mrs. Stevens Hears the Mermaids Singing*, a novel about the woman poet as lesbian, in which Sarton suggests that women as poets are always "lesbians" because the muse is female, comments:

> Hilary's concept of the muse is important because, as a lover of women, Hilary cannot possibly assume that women can achieve art through passivity, fecundity, or the avoidance of their own anger. Each time the muse appears to Hilary, it is Hilary who acts, Hilary who loves, Hilary who rages and pursues and writes the poem. . . . We remember Lily Briscoe who refused to solace Mr. Ramsay's soul, and we see why the givers of solace are never painters or poets, and never can be.[59]

Rhoda's tragedy is that while she refuses the feminine role of solace giver to men, she is unable to find in her environment sustenance to develop as a poet and lover of women. By having Rhoda leap to her death by drowning, Woolf eschews the myth of Judith Shakespeare and replaces it with that of Sappho. For Shakespeare's sister, in Woolf's myth, is always and only a victim. She dies in childbed, a victim of biological and socially constructed womanhood. Woolf endows Rhoda with agency through the metaphors of Shelleyan vision and Sapphic suicide. The combination of unfulfillment in life and heroism in death brings Rhoda close to Thomas Chatterton, the ultimate Romantic icon of the artist at odds with an unjust society. The power of Chatterton as a symbol arises from the paradox that though he is in one sense murdered by society he yet refuses to be simply a victim when he chooses suicide. Stephen Gordon occupies just such a paradoxical position. Under the pressures of a heterosexist society, Mary's love has wilted, but, before Mary can leave, Stephen assumes agency by forcing her to leave. The defiant assumption of agency in a situation that seems to leave no space for anything but victim status constitutes the move from pathos to tragedy. Musing on Septimus's suicide, Clarissa Dalloway reads it as Sapphic, a protest against being deprived of love: "Death was defiance. . . . Closeness drew apart; rapture faded; one was alone. There was an embrace in death."[60]

While much feminist criticism tends to read suicide as negative, disempowering, life denying, it is also possible to read it as the ultimate gesture of taking control of one's own existence. In several traditions, including one powerful Romantic tradition, it signifies protest against stultifying conventions, self-construction in resistance to oppressive stereotypes. In other traditions, such as those adumbrated in some Indian texts, it signifies the achievement of serenity, a decision that life and the life work are complete and can be brought to a dignified, even aesthetic, closure.[61] Sappho's and Woolf's deaths can be read as drawing on and constructing such enabling myths—the myth of the great woman poet whose life and death become an empowering narrative.

Robert Campin, *Triptych of the Annunciation*, central panel (without frame), oil on wood. The annunciation as an ideational moment: Mary in intercourse with herself and the book, the angel an embodiment of the idea in her mind. *Metropolitan Museum of Art, the Cloisters Collection, 1956 (56.70)* See chapter 1, p. 23

Murillo, *The Virgin and St. Anne*. Mother and daughter as teacher and student: a humanized model for ordinary women. *Alinari/Art Resource NY (S0061759 16696)* See chapter 1, p. 32

Rembrandt, *The Holy Family*, Hermitage, St. Petersburg, Russia. Mary's continuing symbiotic relationship with the book, even after she becomes a wife and mother. *Scala/Art Resource NY (S0001870 K100087)* See chapter 1, p. 32

Fra Angelico, *Crucifixion*, detail, Museo di San Marco, Florence, Italy. Mary's posture duplicates that of Christ on the cross, signaling her role as coredemptrix through her sharing of his passion. *Scala/Art Resource NY (S0061758 K101451)* See chapter 1, p. 25

Master of King Albrecht, *The Virgin in Armor*, Vienna, Austria. One of the representations of Mary as a powerful figure in her own right. An interesting model for women like St. Joan and a forerunner of cross-dressed women warriors in Renaissance texts, like Belphoebe and Britomart. *Foto Marburg/Art Resource NY* (S0062373 65718) See chapter 1, p. 24-25

Leonardo da Vinci, *The Virgin and Child and St.Anne*, Louvre, Paris, France. A Sapphic Virgin. *Alinari/Art Resource NY (S0021802 AL23262)* See chapter 1, p. 28, and chapter 3, p. 65

Gerard Davis, *The Virgin Amongst Virgins*, Musée des Beaux-Arts, Rouen, France. Mary as inspirer of learned female communities such as that envisaged by Christine de Pisan in *The Book of the City of Ladies. Giraudon/Art Resource NY (S0061765 18623)* See chapter 1, p.33

Simeon Solomon, *Righteousness and Peace Have Kissed Each Other,* wood engraving, from Simon Reynolds, *The Vision of Simeon Solomon* (Stroud: Catalpa,1984). A Sapphic version of a Judeo-Christian theme.
Courtesy Simon Reynolds.
See chapter 3, p. 75

9

Dogs, Phoenixes, and Other Beasts
Nonhuman Creatures in Homoerotic Texts

> For mystery matched with eccentricity
> Provides the grist for great publicity,
> And myths of flexible dimension
> Are apt to call forth less dissension.
> —Vikram Seth, *Beastly Tales*

The late Victorian definition of homosexuals as a third sex was based on the idea that gender is socially constructed and was therefore not far from Monique Wittig's theory that lesbians are not women. If a woman is socially defined as one who is attracted to a man and must complement him, while a man is socially defined as one who is attracted to a woman and must play certan roles in relation to her, then those who are attracted to members of their own sex do not fit either category.[1] Lytton Strachey gestured toward the possibility of the future erosion of gender in his 1904 dialogue "He, She and It." This dialogue speculated that once women were admitted to all the same professions as men, heterosexual romance, since it is based largely on artificially tailored psychological differences between men and women, would be eroded. Since difference is as necessary to romantic attraction as is sameness, men would in future be attracted to boys and women to girls. Strachey's use of the word "It" in his title suggests the erosion of the meaning of "He" and "She" in a situation where age difference rather than gender difference becomes the basis for attraction. Virginia Woolf often expressed the feeling that she was neither man nor woman: "Poor Billy [Virginia] isn't one thing or the other, not a man nor a woman, so what's he to do? run up the ladies skirts."[2] Here she expresses her sense of otherness through the figures of a goat and a mouse.

Since an animal cannot speak, it is a perfect symbol for "the love that dares not speak its name." As a trope, it is multifariously suggestive:

of domesticated yet natural instinctive life, of that which is despised as beastly and fleshly but may also be read as peculiarly innocent, of the oppressed victim who cannot protest, and of sexuality outside social law. Keith Thomas has demonstrated that eighteenth-century England saw the spread of sentiments against cruelty to animals and a shift away from a complacently anthropocentric view of nonhuman life.[3] Some of these sentiments derived from Greek and Christian debates on vegetarianism and Christian traditions such as the Manichaean and the Franciscan. In the 1780s a series of translations of Indian philosophical and literary texts introduced ideas and images of the oneness of all life that made a major impact on the literary scene, especially on Romantic writers.[4]

Romantic writings on animals move beyond the sentimental tradition of eulogizing pets. In these writings respect for nonhuman life becomes crucially integrated with respect for human life and basic to a radical critique of establishment Christianity. The male god who demands bloodshed in atonement is replaced by nature as mother goddess, of whom Wordsworth says in "Hart-Leap Well," after the description of the hunted hart's pain: "One lesson, Shepherd, let us two divide, / Taught both by what she shows and what conceals; / Never to take our pleasure or our pride / With sorrow of the meanest thing that feels."[5] This worldview that replaces rationality with the capacity to suffer as the highest value is perhaps most powerfully expressed in Coleridge's "Rime of the Ancient Mariner," where, as in Valmiki's *Ramayana*, human grief and poetic speech arise from the slaying of a bird. More significant even than the rewriting of crime and punishment in nonanthropocentric terms is the identification of salvation with the ability to joy in nonhuman forms of life, even reptilian forms, when the mariner acknowledges the failure of his distinctively human capacity for speech in the presence of the water snakes: "O happy living things! no tongue / Their beauty might declare: / A spring of love gushed from my heart, / And I blessed them unaware" (198). The redirection of the biblical language of worship from a father god to living creatures springs from a pantheistic impulse. The millenarian vision of such poets as Milton and Cowper, deriving from the Edenic idea, where "All creatures worship man, and all mankind / One Lord, One Father,"[6] is replaced by Shelley's nonpatriarchal and nonhierarchical vision, privileging love over fear: "All things are void of terror; man has lost / His desolating privilege, and stands / An equal amidst equals."[7]

Animals were stand-ins for the love object in both heterosexual and homosexual love poetry much before the nineteenth century. I am interested in the ways in which the new discourses against cruelty to animals, intersecting with other antioppression discourses, facilitated explorations and defenses of homosexual experience. I shall examine how animal tropes operate in some homoerotic texts to express the irreducible value of the radically other.[8] Some texts use dangerous animals like lions or tigers to emblematize the reader's fears of the homoerotic. Domestic creatures, especially that quintessentially English pet, the dog, suggest how close to home the feared eroticism really is. And birds evoke the established Romantic significations of flight, freedom, song, and immortality but also, especially in the case of a mythical bird like the phoenix, self-renewal, self-transformation, and miraculous survival powers.

In an early poem, "Caenis Caeneus," Michael Field had drawn out the implications of a Greek myth about a sex change and a species change. In Ovid's account the girl Caenis is raped by Neptune and then asks him to transform her into a man so that she may never be humiliated in that way again. By removing the incident of the rape in their account, the Fields make Caenis's discontent with heterosexuality emblematic of all women's, not only raped women's, discontent. As a man, Caeneus remembers his earlier life and shrinks from heterosexuality as, the poets indicate, women tend to: "And when he wooed the girl whom he would kiss / Oft deemed he shared her shrinking from her bliss."[9] This agitation comes to a head when the centaurs rape the Lapith women and Caeneus fights the rapists. They kill him and he is turned into a bird, the Caenis, which soars above their heads. When the bird dies Caenis's soul in Hades is once again that of a girl. The existence she longs for is now neither that of man nor of woman; she sobs, "Ah, would I were a bird!" (50). This longing suggests the desire to be freed of gender imposed by human society.

In a 1929 letter to Quentin Bell, Virginia Woolf, describing a spring day, expressed a similar appreciation of nonhuman creatures' freedom from convention: "Beauty shines on two dogs doing what two women must not do."[10] In Woolf's writings dogs become symbols of joyful eroticism despised by society; they are also associated with singleminded intense devotion, pathetically coupled with dumbness, loyalty, and humility. In 1935 she wrote of their cocker spaniel: "We've bought a dog who is at once passionately in love with Leonard. Its a curious case of hopeless erotic mania—precisely like a human passion."[11] The paradoxical blend of these two facets of homosexuality was to be found in Lytton Strachey of whose life and biographical style Woolf intended *Flush* to be an affectionate parody. When he died she wrote: "I nibble at Flush . . . the point is rather gone, as I meant it for a joke with Lytton and a skit on him."[12] Much earlier, in 1919, in response to Lytton's criticism of the sexless atmosphere of *Night and Day*, she had told him: "I take your point about the tupping. . . . I've an idea for a story where all the characters do nothing else—but they're all quadrupeds."[13] Strachey had used animal images to evoke the innocence of eroticism in his 1913 epistolary novelette *Ermyntrude and Esmeralda*. In this highspirited romp two young women friends learn about sexuality by observing their brothers, servants, and family friends.[14] The girls refer to the male genitals as "bow-wows," to the female genitals as "pussies," and to arousal as "pouting." They learn from their observations and experiences that it is just as possible for two bow-wows or two pussies to pout for one another as it is for a bow-wow and a pussy to pout for one another.

Dogs, to Woolf, symbolized the untamable nature of eroticism. When Pinker, the spaniel given to the Woolfs by Vita Sackville-West, died, Virginia wrote to Ethel Smyth: "We were both very unhappy—This you'll call sentimental—perhaps—but then a dog somehow represents— no I can't think of the word—the private side of life—the play side."[15] "Gipsy, the Mongrel," a short story she wrote in late 1939 or early 1940, is about a dog who, despite her promiscuous and lawless behavior, exerts an "indescribable charm" over her owners.[16] She is explicitly compared to a lovely woman friend, the mention of whom calls up the memory of Gipsy—both woman and dog had lovely smiles and both finally vanish without a trace. When Gipsy's owner tells her story, trying to hide his emotion, the narrator remarks: "It was a love story he was telling" (274).

Woolf developed a similar language to express her own erotic emotions. In her letters to close friends she referred to herself by a number of pet names, some bestowed by others, some self-chosen, that identified her with various animals: squirrel, sparroy, goat, dog, worm, mandrill, mole. She also gave them animal names—Leonard was addressed as "mongoose," Vanessa as "dolphin," and Vita as "insect," "porpoise," and "dolphin." Vita was also variously compared to a dog, a donkey, a pony, an oyster. "Little moles being born" was Woolf's image for the flaring up in her of sexual feelings for Vita. Oysters or winkles were symbols of women's genitals and of lesbian passion.

Vita's extravagant fondness for dogs was well known. Early in their friendship she presented Virginia with a spaniel, Pinker, and Virginia playfully accused her of having led the Woolfs into "dog worshipping."[17] In the first flush of their romance, Virginia expressed her happiness by calling herself a "mole," a "badger, nocturnal, secretive," a "nestling . . . lively squirrel." But the most recurrent image is that of the dog: "Remember your dog Grizzle and your Virginia, waiting you [*sic*]; both rather mangy; but what of that? These shabby mongrels are always the most loving, warmhearted creatures. Grizzle and Virginia will rush down to meet you—they will lick you all over."[18] Through this image she also voiced her doubts and fears: " 'Esteem' is a damned cold word—(yours for me). Still I accept it, like the humble spaniel that I am."[19] She asks teasingly: "Tell me what you are feeling? Are you aching? And if you were asked, do you like Canute [Vita's elkhound] or Virginia best, what would you say?" Feeling that Vita had not enough time for her, she wrote: "I feel like a nice puppy, wandering about under a dinner table and now and then you give it a titbit off your own plate."[20]

Around this time Virginia also invented Bosman's Potto, a lemur. Potto takes shape as a small hairy animal with furry paws. He (always referred to as a male) functions both as Virginia's alter ego, a great many letters being signed "Potto" or "Virginia and Potto" or "V and P," and also as a symbol of the erotic love between her and Vita. Much after Virginia had told herself in her diary that the passionate side of the friendship was over, she continued to express in her letters to Vita wild desire, dependence, need, and jealousy, all attributed to Potto.

As a young girl Woolf had expressed her physical love for women through dog images, for instance, to Violet Dickinson: "How did you sleep, I wonder, after the sudden revelations I made you . . . I think with joy of certain exquisite moments when Rupert [the chow] and I lick your forhead [sic] with a red tongue and purple tongue; and twine your hairs round our noses."[21] When her hopes for a life with her sister Vanessa were belied by the latter's marriage to Clive Bell, the twenty-five-year-old Virginia used similar images to articulate her despair. In 1904 the two sisters and their brother Adrian had moved out of their father's house at Hyde Park Gate into their own lodgings at 46 Gordon Square, Bloomsbury. They had enjoyed less than three years of their new freedom together when Vanessa married. Not only did Virginia suffer the pain of losing her precious companion, but the pressure on her, from her women friends, to go and do likewise, increased considerably. The dual pressure is evident in her letter of January 3, 1907, to Violet Dickinson:

> I did not see Nessa alone, but I realise that that is all over, and I shall never see her alone any more; and Clive is a new part of her, which I must learn to accept . . .
>
> If either you or Kitty ever speak of my marriage again I shall write you such a lecture upon the carnal sins as will make you fall into each others arms; but you shall never come near me any more. Ever since Thoby died women have hinted at this, till I could almost turn against my own sex![22]

The kind of marriage Virginia at this point would have preferred is indicated in her letter written to Vanessa on February 6, 1907, the day before Vanessa married Clive. Since this important letter, with its playful use of animal images to speak the unspeakable has received little attention from biographers, it is worth reproducing in full:

> Address of Congratulation
> to our
> Mistress
> on her
> Approaching Marriage

> Dear Mistress,

> We the undersigned three Apes and a Wombat wish to make known to you our great grief and joy at the news that you intend to marry. We hear that you have found a new Red Ape of a kind not known before who is better than all other apes because he can both talk and marry you: from which we are debarred.
>
> We have examined his fur and find it of fine quality, red and golden at the tips, with an undergrowth of soft down, excellent for winter. We find him clean, merry, and sagacious, a wasteful eater and fond of fossils. His teeth are sharp, and we advise that You keep him on Bones. His disposition is Affectionate.

We therefore commend your marriage, and testify that you will make an excellent Mistress for any Ape or Wombat whatsoever. You are very understanding of Apes, loving and wholesome, vigilant after fleas, and scourging of all Misdoing.

We have been your humble Beasts since we first left our Isles, which is before we can remember, and during that time we have wooed you and sung many songs of winter and summer and autumn in the hope that thus enchanted you would condescend one day to marry us. But as we no longer expect this honour we entreat that you keep us still for your lovers, should you have need of such, and in that capacity we promise to abide well content always adoring you now as before.

> With Humble Obeisance to our Mistress
>   We sign ourselves,
>   Her devoted Beasts
>   Billy
>   Bartholomew
>   Mungo
>   and
>   Wombat

The Sixth of February
nineteen hundred and seven,
Year of our Lord.[23]

The tradition in which Virginia hoped for a successful outcome of her "wooing" of Vanessa looks back to the lives of such "wedded" sisters as Jane and Cassandra Austen. The parodic tone of her letter is very similar to that of the adolescent Jane Austen's in her dedication of "The Beautifull Cassandra" to her sister:

> Madam
>
> You are a Phoenix. Your taste is refined, your Sentiments are noble, and your Virtues innumerable. Your Person is lovely, Figure elegant, and your Form magestic. Your manners are polished, your Conversation is rational and your appearance singular. If therefore the following Tale will afford one moment's amusement to you, every wish will be gratified of
>
> > your most obedient
> >   humble servant
> >   The Author[24]

Virginia's letter simultaneously projects such a marriage as not impossible ("in the hope that you would one day condescend to marry us") and forbidden to her ("from which we are debarred"). That she continued to "adore" as promised is clear from letter after letter to Vanessa. For example, over a year later: "Shall you kiss me tomorrow? Yes, Yes, Yes. Ah, I cannot bear being without you. I was thinking today of my greatest happiness, a walk along a cliff by the sea, and you at the end of it."[25] Twenty seven years later, the tone is strikingly unchanged: "Oh dear when shall I see you? Never. . . . But you don't mind. I mean nothing to you, as Ethel says, Except what Pinka [dog] means. . . . Please kiss Quentin as you won't kiss me."[26] Sometimes her tone was more serious, as in a diary entry the same year, 1928: "She is a necessity to me—as I am not to her."[27]

Since *Orlando* was a fantasy biography of Vita, on February 23, 1929, Virginia playfully asked if she intended to reciprocate the favor: "Is your new novel to be all about Potto? He thinks so. He is willing to help you in any way he can. His past is full of adventure, he says; moreover the Bosman's were great people in their way, Sackvilles after a kind."[28] In September 1931 Woolf began writing *Flush*, which starts off by tracing Flush's ancestry. The title may involve wordplay—Woolf had used the word *flush* to describe Vita's way of life: "I felt the spring beginning, & Vita's life so full and flush."[29] *Flush* can be read as a parallel to *Orlando*: a fantasy biography of "Potto," of that hidden self that was neither man nor woman.[30]

The same syndrome reappears in *Flush*. The description of the physical and mental affinity between Miss Barrett and Flush is resonant with the homoerotic idea of seeing oneself mirrored in the beloved. The notion of the "likeness" from which the self is sundered, and that completes it, appears:

> Heavy curls hung down on either side of Miss Barrett's face; large bright eyes shone out; a large mouth smiled. Heavy ears hung down on either side of Flush's face; his eyes too were large and bright; his mouth was wide. There was a likeness between them. . . . Broken asunder, yet made in the same mould, could it be that each completed what lay dormant in the other?[31]

With such a likeness, it is possible to be both single and double, alone and together: "Flush felt that he and Miss Barrett lived alone together in a cushioned and firelit cave" (25). The female image of an interior space being lighted up occurs also in *A Room of One's Own* to describe the illumination of relationships between women by the woman novelist of the future: "If Chloe likes Olivia, and Mary Carmichael knows how to express it, she will light a torch in that vast chamber where nobody has yet been." The dim radiance of firelight was connected by both Virginia and Vita, in their letters, with their intimacy. For instance, when an American gentleman wrote to inquire whether *Orlando* was inspired by Virginia's affair with Vita, Vita wrote to her: "I have a secret pride in the thought that 'your affair with V.S-W' should enable you to write with authority. Would it? There is much to be said on the subject, but perhaps it would be better said by firelight on a winter evening when one had omitted to turn on the lights."[32]

There is also evidence in *Flush* of the kind of playful parallelism that is all-pervasive in *Orlando*. Thus one of the differences between Miss Barrett and Flush is the difference in age and health. Virginia was ten years older than Vita. Like Elizabeth Barrett, Virginia was often ill, while

Vita, like Flush, was robust. Flush lies on a rug at Miss Barrett's feet or on the sofa with her while she strokes his head. Vita's favorite posture was sitting on a rug at Virginia's feet, Virginia stroking her hair. Vita described the scene to Harold: "She sat in the dusk in the light of the fire, and I sat on the floor as I always do, and she rumpled my hair as she always does."[33]

Licks and kisses are fused when the interaction between Flush and Miss Barrett is described: "Once he had roused her with a kiss" (47) and "Did the bearded god himself press his lips to hers?" (28). The fusion of licks and kisses is found scattered through Virginia's letters to Vita: "A soft, wet warm kiss from poor Potto" or "Please Vita dear don't forget your humble creatures—Pinker and Virginia. . . . Every morning she jumps on to my bed and kisses me, and I say thats Vita."[34]

Miss Barrett lives in a world of words; Flush is dumb and uses the language of kisses to express love: "Flush . . . pressed closer to Miss Barrett and kissed her 'expressively.' *That* was real at any rate" (32). This resonates with Woolf's oft-repeated idea that women need to devise a new language to express those areas of their experience that have remained silent and obscure. She often accused Vita of "dumbness," of not expressing emotions and endearments in words: "A very nice dumb letter from you this morning."[35] Vita argued that dumbness was a sign of intense emotion and that Virginia's "undumb letters" and "exquisite phrase[s]" concealed feelings less profound.[36] Virginia disagreed: "Yes, I miss you, I miss you. I dare not expatiate, because you will say I am not stark, and cannot feel the things dumb people feel. . . . Good-bye, dearest shaggy creature."[37] This opposition emerges through the interaction of Miss Barrett and Flush when the silent intensity of homoerotic love is powerfully conveyed though a series of coded terms:

> Do words say everything? Can words say anything? do not words destroy the symbols that lie beyond the reach of words? . . . Then suddenly a hairy head was pressed against her; large bright eyes shone in hers. . . . For a moment she was transformed; she was a nymph and Flush was Pan. The sun burnt and love blazed. (28)

Blazed is a word Woolf used to evoke love between women, for example, at the end of what she called her "nice little story about Sapphism," "Slater's Pins Have No Points": "Julia blazed, Julia kindled. . . . Julia kissed her on the lips."[38] The image of the nymph had a similar resonance. She wrote to Vita in November 1933: "When shall I see you? Oh but that isn't an end is it—what was once a grove of flowering trees, and nymphs walking among them through the daffodils."[39] The confusion of Flush with Pan recalls the homoerotic resonance of Pan in Michael Field's Arcadian / Edenic poems. The effect of Vita's advent on Virginia's life was Edenic—blissful but only temporarily so. While for Vita the relationship was one among many, for Virginia it was perhaps the only one in which she fully acted out her desires. As Vita moved on to other lovers,

Woolf transferred to Potto the "dumbness" she had earlier attributed to Vita. In a letter of March 6, 1928, after a quarrel over Vita's new affairs had been made up, Woolf wrote: "My mind is at your service if you can use it. And Potto has a large warm heart, but then he can't write and its Virginia who writes."[40]

Many of the metaphors and phrases normally associated with romantic love and marriage are pressed into service to evoke the relationship between Miss Barrett and Flush:

> Between them, Flush felt, more and more strongly, as the weeks wore on, was *a bond*, an uncomfortable yet thrilling tightness. . . . She loved Flush, and Flush was worthy of her love. It seemed as if nothing were to break *that tie*—as if the years were merely to compact and cement it, and as if those years were to be *all the years of their natural lives.* (26–33, emphasis mine)

Because Woolf is not writing about any dog and any woman but about Elizabeth Barrett Browning, whose romance is arguably the most famous heterosexual romance of the Victorian literary world, the delineation of Flush's illusion is doubly ironic. The reader, because of historical hindsight, knows that the "tie" will be broken. This hindsight functions as the ironic parallel of that powerful literary tradition which works to assure the reader that the woman-woman tie is only an interlude and that, in the end, "Jack shall have Jill." Yet the intensity of the language describing Flush's emotion imbues the assurance with more sorrow than consolation. Also, the fame of the Barrett-Browning romance divests it of suspense for the reader, allowing interest to be more fully concentrated on Flush's emotions.

When Miss Barrett's correspondence with Robert Browning begins, Flush feels threatened without knowing why, and the buried echo from *Macbeth* barely suggests tragedy: "Flush heard a bell rousing him from his sleep; warning him of some danger; menacing his safety and bidding him sleep no more. Miss Barrett . . . too slept no more" (35). Such is their empathy that Flush, without any knowledge of what causes her agitation, feels in himself every tremor she experiences. The emotional quality of this empathy that isolates is evoked in the ironic repetition of the phrase that once expressed their intimacy: "They waited, alone together" (37). When Browning finally makes his appearance at the door, Flush, unlike, surely, any dog that has ever lived, does not spring to his feet or look at the intruder, but looks, instead, at Miss Barrett, feels her reaction: "Flush, watching Miss Barrett, saw the colour rush to her face; saw her eyes brighten and her lips open" (37). This moment may be compared with that in *The Voyage Out* when Hewet approaches and "Helen could not see who it was, but keeping her eyes fixed upon Rachel observed something which made her say to herself, 'So it's Hewet' " (268).

The introduction of Robert Browning is followed by the most intense passages in the book. Flush's extreme sensitivity, his "even excessive appreciation of human emotions" (12) make him a symbol. Through him is expressed an erotic emotion that is simultaneously sensual and spiritual, encompassing passion and the sympathy of friendship. He becomes a Sapphic metaphor and is compared to traditional Sapphic metaphors like the pearl beyond price: "He was of the rare order of objects that . . . because they typify what is spiritual, what is beyond price, become a fitting token of the disinterestedness of friendship" (14).

Woolf's most intense exploration of jealousy is found in *Flush*, an intensity matched only in some of her letters to Vita Sackville-West. A comparison of passages from the two texts demonstrates the similarity:

> What was horrible to Flush, as they talked, was his loneliness. (38)

> *

> You being away—I . . . feel lonely, like something pitiable which can't make its wants known. How you have demoralized me.[41]

> *

> He shifted his position . . . she took no notice. He whined. They did not hear him. At last he lay still in tense and silent agony. . . . Flush touched her. . . . Then she laughed pityingly; as if it were absurd—Flush, poor Flush could feel nothing of what she felt. He could never know what she knew. Never had such wastes of dismal distance separated them. He lay there ignored; he might not have been there, he felt. Miss Barrett no longer remembered his existence. (38–39)

> *

> Yes, I must really write to you because I want to know what is happening. But that said, I've nothing to say. That's because you're in love with another, damn you! . . . I said to myself, no wonder Vita no longer loves you, because you bore her and if there's one thing love won't stand, it's boredom. . . . Shall you be in London this week? Shall you come and see me? I only ask: even a dog can do that. . . . I may be windswept into the sea. But what would Vita care. . . . She'd bury me under, wouldn't she, Vita?[42]

The passages in *Flush* carry a weight of irony that moves them beyond the syndrome of unrequited love. The arrogance of humans toward animal emotions acts as a metaphor for the arrogance of heterosexuals toward homosexual emotions. Miss Barrett's assumption that Flush can never "feel" and "know" what she does is undercut by the text's conveyance of Flush's emotions as more intense than hers. Whether this arrogance expresses itself as contemptuous pity or as well-meant kindness, its effects are torturous: "It was easy enough for Mr Browning to be magnanimous, but that easy magnanimity was perhaps the sharpest thorn that pressed into Flush's side" (43). The device of this strange triangle—dog, mistress, male lover/rival—allows Woolf to glance obliquely at another triangle— that of two women and a man—also conventionally considered strange, "as if it were absurd." The latter kind of triangle she described more directly in "Geraldine and Jane," her sympathetic sketch of the Victorian feminist novelist Geraldine Jewsbury's love for Jane Carlyle and jealous rages against Carlyle and other men.

When Flush capitulates and makes the best of the situation, Woolf emphasizes the complete silence in which the inner conflict is conducted and resolved. Her language fully "humanizes" his predicament:

> As he lay there, exiled, on the carpet, he went through one of those whirlpools of tumultuous emotion in which the soul is either dashed upon the rocks and splintered, or, finding some tuft of foothold, slowly and painfully pulls itself up, regains dry land, and at last emerges on the tip of a ruined universe to survey a world created afresh on a different plan. . . . The outline only of his dilemma can be traced here; for his debate was silent. (46)

Flush is described as progressing from illusion to reality. *Illusion* was a word Woolf used to refer to erotic enchantment. Thus she wrote to Vanessa that the male sex illuded her as the female illuded Virginia. Shedding the illusion that he is Miss Barrett's primary love object, Flush comes to what he thinks is the realistic conclusion that his attempt to kill Robert Browning failed because both of them love Miss Barrett. The reader knows that a spaniel cannot kill a man and that Flush's attempt was absurd. But what is absurd at one level passes into profound seriousness at another: "Looking up at her as she lay, severe and silent, on the sofa, he knew that he must love her for ever. Things are not simple but complex. If he bit Mr Browning, he bit her too. Hatred is not hatred; hatred is also love" (46). Around the time she began to write *Flush*, Woolf also put Potto through a process of death and rebirth similar to the spiritual death and rebirth Flush undergoes. On July 25, 1931, she wrote to Vita:

> Potto is dead. For about a month (you have not been for a month and I date his decline from your last visit) I have watched him failing . . . Last night it was clear that the end was coming. . . . I just caught . . . the following words—'Tell Mrs Nick that I love her. . . . She has forgotten me. . . . I die of a broken heart.' He then expired.[43]

However, a few days later, she wrote, in response to Vita's protest: "You're right—he's not dead. . . . He stirred yesterday. . . . Yes yes I am still unfortunately attached to the woman I never see; the vision in the fishmongers shop."[44]

Woolf's use of the dog fantasy in her letters to Vita is her way of making possible the "impossible." If a dog can write, can speak, can love, then so can a woman love a woman, contrary to all expectations and to what is considered normal and natural. Thus she writes to Vita:

> I will just have my little fling, since your letter was such a nice one, like a beautiful Borzoi, Queen Alexandra's favourite dog, writing with an eagles quill. Did you ever see a Borzoi write a poem? A sextet? Well, if you haven't you've missed

Flush's despair springs from an existential dilemma. He cannot be what Elizabeth needs and wants. By virtue of his biological existence, he is excluded from the primary intimacy he desires. The difference in species between dog and human functions as a metaphor for the social gap created between members of the same gender who are conditioned to downgrade their intimacy as not capable of primacy. Richard Ellmann has shown how the roles of lover and beloved in Wilde's stories such as "The Happy Prince" are enacted by "members of different species," thus casting light on the homosexual love that Wilde termed "the love of things impossible."[46]

Woolf places the despair in a social context. Flush is described as longing for the day "when" he too will write and speak as Elizabeth does. The twice-repeated use of the word "when" rather than "if only" hints that what is considered impossible is actually within the realms of the possible. But, the narrator continues, "truth compels us to say that in the year 1842–43, Miss Barrett was not a nymph but an invalid; Flush was not a poet but a red cocker spaniel; and Wimpole Street was not Arcady but Wimpole Street" (28–29). The stress on specific time and place suggests that although, here and now, the longing and the desire are not realizable, they may be realizable in some other time and place. This links up with one of Septimus's "revelations" in *Mrs. Dalloway*. At the point when he feels that his "marriage [is] over" and he is alone and free, he has revealed to him the truths that trees are alive, that there is no crime, and that there exists "love, universal love." These truths need "an immense effort to speak out." Then, two of his revelations are fused to suggest that in a future that accepts love as no crime what has been considered subhuman or beastly will be accepted as human. The trope for this fusion is that of a dog which "snuffs his trousers" suddenly being transformed into a man. Septimus is terrified by this transformation:

> No crime; love; he repeated, fumbling for his card and pencil, when a Skye terrier snuffed his trousers and he started in an agony of fear. It was turning into a man! He could not watch it happen! It was horrible, terrible to see a dog become a man! At once the dog trotted away. . . . Why could he see through bodies, into the future, when dogs will become men?[47]

The episode of Flush's abduction, imprisonment, and maltreatment serves symbolically to underline the fact that love between man and woman against the wishes of the woman's father was not the only form of love under attack in Victorian England. Woolf writes an ironic subtext into the grand romance of defiant love, unfolds the footnotes of Victorian biography and history. The inhabitants of Wimpole Street live in "submission to the laws of God and man" (15);[48] consequently, the passion Flush symbolizes is tolerated only as long as it is kept within the "limits of decorum and respectability" (50). But if one is foolish enough to let it get out of hand, one pays the price—imprisonment, torture, risk to life—that Wilde had paid: "The only safe course for those who lived in Wimpole Street and its neighbourhood was to keep strictly within the respectable area and to lead your dog on a chain. If one forgot, as Miss Barrett forgot, one paid the penalty as Miss Barrett was now to pay it" (52).

The image of impulsive passion as an animal under restraint occurs several times in the writings of Vita Sackville-West. In *Seducers in Ecuador* (a novel in semifarcical style, dedicated to Virginia Woolf), she wrote: "It is . . . the purpose of this story to demonstrate . . . the danger . . . of contracting in middle age a new habit liable to release those lions of folly which prowl about our depths, and which it is the duty of every citizen to keep securely caged."[49] In *Heritage*, a novel about suppressed and late-realized passion, she comments that most people's system of philosophy is "inimical to natural, inconvenient impulse. It obeys us as a rule, like a tame lion doing its tricks for the lion-tamer. A terrifying thought truly, that we are shut up for life in a cage with a wild beast that may at any moment throw off its docility to leap upon us."[50] In *The Garden* she admonishes herself: "Quiet you down, you troubled soul, lie down / As patient dog when bidden, in a corner; / Forget those days when you could not control / Something that rose unbidden and unknown."[51] Her fears regarding her relationship with Virginia Woolf may have related more to herself than to her lover. As she wrote anxiously to Harold: "She has never lived with anyone except Leonard, which was a terrible failure, and was abandoned quite soon. So all that remains an unknown quantity; and I have got too many dogs not to let them lie when they are asleep."[52]

Flush pays the penalty for being unchained. He is imprisoned and tortured. He is on the wrong side of the law, and so will Miss Barrett be if she attempts to pay the dog stealers and rescue him. When she determines to rescue Flush, her whole family is against her, "All Wimpole Street was against her. . . . But worst of all—far worse—Mr Browning himself threw all his weight, all his eloquence, all his learning, all his logic, on the side of Wimpole Street, against Flush." (59). Defying Browning's opinion in her determination to save Flush's life, she places his love for her and Flush's love for her on the same plane, asking him what he would do if she were abducted and threatened with mutilation. In drawing this analogy she challenges the notion that Flush's love is of a lower order and lesser value than the love between her and Mr. Browning.[53]

When Flush is rescued, he develops an awareness of the hypocrisy of respectable men: "He shrank away from Mr Kenyon and Mr Browning. He trusted them no longer. Behind those smiling, friendly faces was treachery and cruelty and deceit. Their caresses were hollow" (66). His bond with Miss Barrett survives because "she alone had not deserted him." (66). Woolf draws an analogy between two sets of criminals—dog stealers and character stealers. She implicitly compares Flush, the victim of the first set, to those "wretches who cut their throats or fly the country (60) when victimized by blackmailers. Setting off for the continent, that haven of nineteenth- and twentieth-century English homosexuals and other outcasts and rebels like Byron, Shelley, and Wilde, Flush feels himself in league against the powers that be in England: "They were escaping; they were leaving tyrants and dogstealers behind them. . . . let us leave Wimpole Street and Whitechapel behind us" (70).

After the Barrett-Browning marriage, the book suffers a falling-off. Although the tie between Flush and Miss Barrett, like that between Geraldine and Jane, can "stretch and stretch indefinitely without breaking,"[54] the marriage does result in an emotional parting. Woolf herself felt the novel was "too long—got out of hand—."[55] Perhaps this is because, after the marriage, the relationship betrays "only repetition—not newness," like the Ramsay-Bankes relationship after Ramsay's marriage. Thus Flush's initial hatred and later acceptance of Mrs. Browning's baby are repetitions of his earlier reactions to Robert Browning.

Toward the end of the book, both Flush and Mrs. Browning live in memory. Flush's death, like the death of an emotion, brings about no visible change in the external world: "He had been alive; he was now dead. That was all. The drawing room table, strangely enough, stood perfectly still" (102). On March 11, 1935, Woolf acknowledged in her diary, "My friendship with Vita is over. Not with a quarrel, not with a bang, but as ripe fruit falls. . . . But her voice saying 'Virginia' . . . was as enchanting as ever. Only then nothing happened. . . . And there is no bitterness and no disillusion, only a certain emptiness."[56]

The tropes Woolf uses in *Flush* derive their power from earlier uses in homoerotic texts. Michael Field's collection of elegies for their dog, *Whym Chow: Flame of Love*, is, as Leighton points out, remarkable for its distance from Victorian sentimental pet poems like Elizabeth Barrett Browning's poems on her dog Flush. The distance arises from the complete conviction in Michael Field's poems that there is no difference between the love of a dog and any human love. This absence of distinction functions as a marker for the absence of distinction between homosexual and heterosexual love. The only criterion they acknowledge is intensity. The poems' force springs from an unapologetic passion, related to an unashamed declaration of love between the two women, and moves the expression of both beyond sentimentality. If, in *Flush*, the dog's point of view is separated by a "dismal distance" from the woman's, here women's and dog's points of view are constructed as very close.

The dog is, in much of English literature, a domestic symbol par excellence. The element of buried wildness in the dog that Woolf and Sackville-West suggest altogether displaces domesticity in Field's poems. At the symbolic level homoerotic passion, safely domesticated in much Victorian literature, is here glorified in its uncontainable intensity. Whym Chow is addressed as a "Bacchic Cub," an "Eastern Prince," an "Asian

Bacchant," and repeatedly compared to Christ.[57] He is a regal and divine creature who submits only to the power of love, and to no other power, giving "of love as Kings give of their grace" (46). He is described as "blazing," "dancing," "fierce," "wild," "beautiful . . . with desire's exceeding smart" (24), as "full of the passions nurtured in the wild / And virgin places of the world" (55). His love is an "ecstasy," "inviolate," a "perpetual adoration." He is compared to the elements—the sun and the sea and to powerful wild creatures—lions, tigers, and hawks. The joy of embracing wildness, outside conventional domesticity, is crucial to this construction. One may contrast Katherine Mansfield's 1919 poem "Friendship," where the relationship between two girl friends is imaged as a tiny fluffy kitten that grows into a tiger as they grow into women. The speaker is terrified of the tiger, but the friend "with placid brow, / Cries 'This is our Kitty-witty! / Why don't you love her now?' "[58] What was acceptable to the speaker as a romantic friendship becomes terrifying as a devouring adult passion.[59] Michael Field's poems blend both dimensions of love in an unterrified manner.[60]

Whym Chow is repeatedly evoked in terms associated with homoeroticism—imaged as a flame, a fountain, a shell, a series of gems, a star, and flowers, especially rose and lily. "Fur for Mandarins" brings together the images of gems, flowers, and the tiger:

> Tiger and the tiger-lilly,
> Flower of broom and flower of gilly;
> Gems of every mine and valley
> That have gold and red to rally . . .
> Where the marigold scowls lusty,
> Though its coat be dun and dusty:
> Where all haunt of colour burneth
> With such glow as never turneth
> From its tropic . . .   (29)

Katherine's poems explicitly link her love for Edith with Edith's and Whym Chow's love for each other. The dog's distress at being left alone, which leads Edith to give up trips to stay with him recalls an early poem, "Second Thoughts," by Katherine in which Edith is imaged as a tamed wild creature whom she finds it impossible to leave:

> I thought of leaving her for a day . . .
> I lifted her face in my hands to kiss, . . .
> But at sight of the delicate world within
> That fox-fur collar, from brow to chin,
> At sight of those wonderful eyes from the mine,
> Coal pupils, an iris of glittering spa,
> And the wild, ironic, defiant shine
> As of a creature behind a bar
> One has captured, and when three lives are past,

May hope to reach the heart of at last,
All that, and the love at her lips, combined
To shew me what folly it were to miss
A face with such thousand things to say . . .
For the shining lamps, for the clash of the play—
O madness; not for a single day
Could I leave her! I stayed behind.[61]

The choice of a life "alone together" in preference to a social life privileges the pleasures of private intimacy over those of public glitter ("the play" suggests the literary world and the fame their own plays could have achieved if they had been more active in that world). The poem "Sleeping Together" figures these private pleasures as sensual and bodily, Whym Chow being the partaker with the coupled poets writing in the plural first person. The activities of "Sleeping together . . . Eating together . . . Breathing together . . . Loving together . . . Joying together" are fleshed out in description and in erotic imagery including the mention of "our bed" (42–45).

Several of Edith's poems address the unique connection between herself and Whym Chow, describe her senses as bereft, her arms as empty, and him as her "eternal attribute," like St. Jerome's lion (51). Katherine's poems, such as "Trinity," explicitly make of Whym Chow a "symbol" of her union with Edith:

I did not love him for myself alone:
I loved him that he loved my dearest love.
O God, no blasphemy
It is to feel we loved in trinity.
To tell Thee that I loved him as Thy dove
Is loved . . .   (15)

This daring reconfiguration of the divine erotic triangle simultaneously transforms its gender from male (God-Christ) to female (Katherine-Edith) and also imbues the mother-daughter-female-lover-beloved syndrome with the eroticism of the father-son-eros-eromenos syndrome. Katherine published this book in 1914 after Edith's death. Her poem "My loved one is away from me" describes how she and Whym used to wait for Edith in "anguish" and "terror" whenever she was away. The intensity of their "yearning" and the pining of their "senses" for "our sole possession," she says, "seemed madness." What seems to the heterosexual eye excessive in the love of a woman for a woman is for Katherine as uncontrollable and beyond conventional rationality as the dog's violent and unembarrassed pining for its mistress. It is not clear whether this poem was written after Edith's death, but it ends by describing Katherine's aloneness:

My loved One is away—my cry!
. . . O Chow, my little Love, you watch above her;
Watch still beside me, be with me her lover!   (23)

It is interesting that in both Woolf's and Field's texts the animal symbolizing erotic love between women is a male dog. Lytton Strachey's novelette is more conventional in figuring the female genitalia as "pussies" and the male as "bow-wows." Its relative conventionality regarding lesbianism is also evident: heterosexual and male homosexual passions are reciprocated and consummated in his text but lesbian passion is one way and is refused consummation by its object. Woolf, in her remark about herself as being "neither man nor woman" with which I opened this chapter, goes on to gender herself as male: "what's *he* to do—run up the ladies' skirts" (emphasis mine). This figuring, like the assumption of male dress, pet names, and pronouns, has much to do with the conventional association of the male with active sexuality in terms of courting, pursuing, and lovemaking rather than waiting and submitting. It is never confused with the desire to be a man—the love is explicitly between women, and female erotic imagery (gems, flowers, shells) coexists with maleness displaced onto an animal symbol.[62]

In *The Well of Loneliness*, too, the hunted fox, the wounded warhorse, and, at the end, the dog David, as "dumb" and anguished as Stephen herself, are compared in their victimization to persecuted homosexuals. Yet animals also function as tropes for the joy of same-sex love. To begin with, they are substitutes for the beloved denied to Stephen by society. This is literally so in the case of her first pony Collins, whom she names for the dismissed housemaid on whom she had a crush, and implicitly so in the case of her adored horse Raftery, with whom she communicates "in a quiet language having very few words but many small sounds and small movements, which to both of them meant more than words."[63] She meets Angela through Tony, the terrier, and Angela's first letter ends, " 'Tony says please come Stephen!' " (141). Angela's jealous husband hits out at Tony, making him "stand proxy for Stephen" (151).

Flush is closest to *The Well* in the symbolism of contained wildness, imaged as a dog taking walks in parks. Like Flush, David longs for wild forests and feels confined in the parks; he yearns for "the smell of wild things which a dog might hunt and yet remain lawful" (345), but is denied them. When spring comes and he is forbidden to dig up flowers or chase pigeons, he feels, "Why was there nothing really exciting that a spaniel might do and yet remain lawful?" and pleads, " 'Just this once let me sin for the joy of life, for the ancient and exquisite joy of sinning!' " but is told that "nice dogs" never do such things (418–19). Woolf may well have retained a memory of this cluster of images for, though she condemned *The Well* as dull and unreadable, she did read it. "I . . . have already wasted hours reading it" she wrote to Ottoline Morell in early November 1928.[64]

The play with animal images continued to be among the most creative dimensions of homoerotic texts. From a simple encoding to the triggering of complex philosophical meditations on the nature of being, it proliferates in many directions. An example of the former is found in Vita

explicit, use of dog images demonstrates that the code was consciously
understood by at least some writers and readers. This novel, which has an
alsatian's head on its cover, as *Flush* had a spaniel's, makes little sense as
straightforward "realist" fiction but much more sense as symbolic narrative.

The protagonist, Sir Walter, a brilliant, middle-aged lawyer, is married, but he and his wife Rose have remained celibate at his wish. This
arrangement is supposedly related to his pessimism regarding the human
race, but it soon emerges that it is actually related to his revulsion from
heterosexuality. The "secret love" of his life is Svend, an alsatian.
Realizing that Rose has for years suppressed her love for Walter, his
brother Gilbert, a brain surgeon, decides to help her by making Walter
suffer and thus grow more sensitive to her suffering. To this end, he asks
Walter to give him Svend as an object for vivisection. After some equiv-
ocation, Walter is forced to acknowledge his emotions: " 'He loves me,'
said Walter. After a pause he added, 'And I love him.' "[65] Gilbert then lies,
saying Svend is going to go blind in six months' time and will in any case
have to be put to sleep. At this, Walter agrees to give him up. The imagery
of chaining, imprisoning, and rebelling now comes into play. When
Svend is for the first time put into a lead, Walter says, " 'There is your pris-
oner . . . chained and numbered' " (169). Walter's mask of unemotional
rationality breaks down in Rose's presence, and she declares her love for
him, to which he does not respond. That night he has a dream:

> He had dreamt that he was given a lioness as a pet, but although her head was
> huge and hairy, in the normal way, she had no hide on her body, which was just
> raw red meat, sloppy when he patted it. He felt obliged to pat it, for she kept
> rubbing herself affectionately against his thighs, filling him with disgust,
> although he was ashamed of being disgusted and felt that he ought to be sorry
> for her and even fond of her. (172)

The lioness, the devouring female, is connected with repulsive
flesh and mandatory affection and contrasted with the attractive male
Svend who must be imprisoned and killed. Interestingly, the author
makes the beloved dog a male and the repulsive animal a female. The
apparently straightforward relation to male homoeroticism is perhaps
not so direct, however. For the raw, red, hairless and hideless large
expanse of meat rubbing itself against the thighs suggests a penis experienced as disgusting, and the male dog, as I have demonstrated, is frequently a symbol for female homoeroticism. Is Walter a cover for the lesbian's masculine persona, and Svend for lesbian eroticism, the dream
lioness representing heterosexuality? That the dream was one the author
herself had makes this reading (and an identification of Sackville-West
with Walter) more likely.[66]

Sackville-West knew that her contemporary, Forster's and Woolf's
friend, the homosexual writer J. R. Ackerley had lived out the drama of a

passionate devotion to his female dog Queenie. He had described his
book *We Think the World of You* as "autobiographical, of course; I have no
creative ability; and the heroine is a dog who becomes substitute love for
a boy, and through whose senses the homosexual part of the book is
described. Terribly, terribly Freudian."[67] Sackville-West's novel also contains her first open portrait of a homosexual man, Walter's nephew Robin,
and ends with Walter and Svend reunited.

Constraints of space do not permit me here to continue tracing the
uses of animal imagery in later homoerotic texts, but I will briefly consider two Indian poets writing in English today, to suggest the relatively
unbroken nature of this tradition, before returning to an overview of it
and linking it with themes discussed earlier.

Vikram Seth and Suniti Namjoshi use many beasts, mythical and
real, as tropes to suggest crossings of the boundaries of race, gender, culture, and sexual preference.[68] Less containable than human beings in categories of nationality and gender, animals, as they have figured in
Western and Eastern mythologies and literatures, often reveal the surprising commonalty of apparently distinct traditions, a commonalty of
life that frequently questions rigid distinctions even between species.

In Suniti Namjoshi's writings the protagonist generally speaks as
"Suniti," the Sanskrit first name functioning in English as a marker of
strangeness, or she assumes the persona of a nonhuman creature. Suniti
constantly consorts with nonhuman creatures. These creatures are often
rendered even stranger by unexpected attributes, as with the wise blue
donkey or Bhadravati, the intelligent lesbian cow. The strangeness cuts
both ways—the donkey is supposed to be a stupid beast but is the only
one who speaks in the Bible and is also chosen by Christ for his triumphal
ride into Jerusalem. The cow in modern Western parlance connects with
contempt for women ("stupid cow") as well as for Hindus ("cow worshippers"). Contesting the British reading of cow worship as barbaric idolatry,
Mahatma Gandhi insisted that the cow was a symbol of all nonhuman
creatures. In his reading, cow worship was a ritualized acknowledgment
of the dignity of nonhuman beings and of human responsibility to treat
them as fellow creatures. Namjoshi's lesbian cow yokes together two
apparent irreconcilables—wittily focusing on the invisibility and "impossibility" of Indian lesbians both in Indian and in Western contexts.

In one preface Namjoshi connects her choice of a beastly persona
with her questioning of gender stereotyping and also with her pantheistic Hindu background wherein a beast is not inherently inferior to a
human being because the same spirit may in various reincarnations
inhabit both human and nonhuman bodies. She concludes this meditation by asking, "But what sort of beast was I?"[69] Hindu gods and goddesses
generally have particular animals or birds as their companions. Some gods
like Ganesh are themselves a compound of human and animal. Animals,
birds, reptiles, and even insects are worshipped in their own right and

thereby protected from violence. Ancient Hindu myths often turn centrally on friendships between human and nonhuman creatures and legends of medieval Hindu mystics and poets, both male and female, often include such friendships. In the context of my reading of many Christian mystics and saints as symbolic opters-out of gender and of heterosexual structures, their association with beasts as attributes (St. Agnes and her lamb, St. Scholastica and her dove, St. Francis and his wolf, St. Jerome and his lion) presents an interesting parallel. Namjoshi playfully inserts herself into these traditions in the title of her recent book, *Saint Suniti and the Dragon.* Her writings choose this trope as a takeoff point for exploring the changing nature of the self and of others and for experimenting with new types of relationships between human beings and the universe.

In her poem "Homage to Circe" different animals express different facets of eroticism. The beloved, who evokes these facets, is adored as capable of transforming the lover (rather than, as in the myth, condemned for bestializing the lover). The speaker says, "I am all animals to you," and thanks Circe for "the continuous feast" she offers all her adoring animals (33–34). Carnivorous beasts often symbolize the dominant culture. In "Among Tigers" the "lordly race" from whom the speaker keeps her distance could be Europeans, men, or heterosexuals.[70] But, on the whole, nonhuman creatures inhabit worlds of joy and play in Namjoshi's writings and are capable of happy interaction with women. She acknowledges Woolf as an ancestor in this strain of writing in "By the River: For Virginia Woolf." This fable, about a beautiful mare and a beautiful woman disporting in the forest, alludes to Woolf's comment that Chloe has rarely liked Olivia in mainstream fiction or criticism. Namjoshi concludes, "An observer might have said that they were both beautiful. An observer might have added that they were both desirable. But would he have noted that they liked one another?"[71]

Namjoshi acknowledges a male ancestor in "Beauty Incarnate and the Supreme Singer: For Oscar Wilde," a rewriting of Wilde's "The Nightingale and the Rose." Wilde's story can be read, in the terms I have suggested, as an evocation of the Romantic Sapphic lyrical dialogue, since both nightingale (Philomel) and rose are female symbols, and as a representation of that dialogue being appropriated by heterosexuals to utilitarian ends. Namjoshi's comic rewriting shows two nonsymbolic and therefore "ordinary" female protagonists, the wren and the iris, appropriating the dialogue. The poetic wren insists that "in order to sing you have to suffer" and begins her plaint despite the iris's anxious protests (84–85).

Although she questions the Sapphic narrative's privileging of unrequitedness and grief as the sources of poetry, Namjoshi's powerful sonnet sequence "The Lion Skin" elaborates precisely that narrative.[72] The speaker's assumption of an animal persona allows her to approach and fantasize about an unresponsive beloved. The speaker dreams that she is a lion walking with her lady through a wood. This Spenserian dream remains inconclusive because "I've never had the courage to dream the dream through, / but I think she says, 'You be me, and I'll be you.'" The next two sonnets imagine the lady flaying the lion, thus dispensing with "disguise," and the two women becoming lovers. The fantasy is interrupted, however, because this La Belle protests against being made an object of fantasy, and then vanishes, leaving the speaker alone, clutching her dream. In the next sonnet the poet meditates on the Sapphic theme of unrequited love and describes how she contents herself with fantasy: "I tell myself that the dream is made of such stuff / that to dream is best and the dream enough." The process of converting the dream into poetry that may provide the beloved with "mirth and holiday" is figured as chopping the "tough skin" of the lion and making balls out of it. This violent image suggests the pain, even the death, undergone by the poet-lover, but, unlike Keats's knight-at-arms, she is "content" because her experience is "real, and still real, again and again, / whenever you choose." The "muse" makes possible a transaction that, although not the sexual one the poet hoped for, gives "pleasure" and is "of use."

The old idea of a faithful animal who dies for a beloved human is reworked here in conjunction with the equally old idea of unrequited love. The resultant narrative of sacrifice—even suicide—recalls many earlier homoerotic narratives. The figural nature of the lion's "death" in Namjoshi's sonnet sequence casts light on the metaphoric nature of the deaths in some of those earlier narratives. The suicide with which so many homosexual narratives end may be read not as simply literal but as a metaphoric intensification of Sappho's cry: "Since she left, I have had no word from her / Frankly, I wish I were dead." Death, as in Andersen's fairy tale "The Little Mermaid," confers tragic and artistic status on the homosexual lover and immortalizes him/her outside of the routinely conventional marriage that the prince and princess achieve. Death is the poem, the "swan song" that the homosexual lover writes, thus becoming paradoxically fully awake and aware. The little mermaid deliberately chooses love and death; the married prince and princess, conversely, are asleep at the end of the story. Their sleep is a metaphor for lack of self-consciousness, for the conformist "unexamined life" that is not worth living.

Vikram Seth's collection of narrative poems, *Beastly Tales from Here and There* captures these two traditions of the homoerotic narrative—that of death and that of survival.[73] Each of the ten poems is named for two creatures of different species, for instance, "The Eagle and the Beetle," "The Goat and the Ram." Thus, the contents page embodies difference—the exciting asymmetry of unconventionally matched pairs. Five of the stories end in death; five in survival of one kind or another. With the exception of "The Hare and the Tortoise" and "The Rat and the Ox," both of which are about competition, all are stories of friendship and its conflicts, either internal or against the world. In only two stories does the friendship survive and triumph.

One of these, "The Cat and the Cock" is about a same-sex friendship "founded on a rock" (43). The friends share a house and dance and sing together. Eroticism is suggested in the camp phrase "Handsome fur and fancy feather" (43). Both cat and cock are male, but the cat wanders by day while the cock keeps house. The cat warns the cock not to "trust other carnivores" (43). The cock disregards this warning when he succumbs to the blandishments of a female fox posing as a male ("the postman"). The fox, who is a widow, intends to feed the cock to her children, whom she warns not to step out of the house. The cat flaunts his gay charms (the code phrase "musical temptation" is used) to serenade and seduce each of the fox's four daughters and her son, imprisoning them all in his sack. The opposition between housekeeping that reproduces and housekeeping based on friendship is suggested in the cat's repeated refrain as he captures each child: "in the end / I will surely free my friend. / I will surely save his life / From the pot and kitchen-knife" (49). However, the cat, being kinder than the fox, finally sets the little foxes free. The other story of survival is about a greedy goat and ram. The clever female goat takes the lead throughout, giving orders to the timid male ram. Although the pair survive, their living happily ever after is signally devoid of the cat and cock's joyfulness. The story ends: "They never argue, never fight / They never have bad dreams at night. / With moderation and accord / They pass their days, serenely bored" (61).

In two stories, "The Louse and the Mosquito" and "The Frog and the Nightingale," a heartless male destroys his female friend and collaborator. In "The Crocodile and the Monkey" the same-sex friendship between crocodile and monkey is disrupted by the crocodile's wife and in "The Eagle and the Beetle" the female beetle takes revenge for the slaughter of her friend, the male hare, by destroying the murderous eagle's eggs. Friendship proves stronger than the reproductive impulse protected by divinity, for when the eagle lays her eggs in Zeus's lap, the beetle, by aiming its dung at the god, compels him to inadvertently break the eggs.

The most poignant and explicit of the tales is "The Mouse and the Snake." Two female mice enter a granary where their activities are thus described: "unpoliced / Broke in and began to feast / And their laughter fell and rose" (15). The suggestive imagery of feasting, laughter, and unpoliced illicit activity combines with that of the mouse, an old female erotic image, and is disrupted by a phallic snake "Gold and shiny, vicious, long, / Venom-fanged, hypnotic, strong—" (15) who hisses "obscenely" and swallows one of the mice. The other fights back heroically and forces the snake to cough up the corpse of her companion. The event is framed by the poet in a dialogue between male friends. Mr. Yang, who witnesses the event, narrates it to his friend, the poet Chang, who composes an elegy, "The Faithful Mouse," to "prove that shock and pain, / Death and grief are not in vain" (17). The poet remarks that the mice never read this poem, so the "bitter tears" of the "bereft" mouse are not erased or compensated for by the commemoration (16).

In "The Elephant and the Tragopan," however, which is the last and longest tale, the tragopan's death does seem to boost the animals' cause. Although the tale appears to transparently write that cause as environmental, the male friendship around which it revolves suggests that another cause may be what the narrator refers to as "a minor missing link," when he notes that "myths of flexible dimension / Are apt to call forth less dissension" (93). Certainly, the two quasi morals, that "you never know / Just when your luck may break, and so / You may as well work for your cause / Even without overt applause" and that "you'll find friends / In the most unexpected places," apply equally to both causes (93).

In these tales the relationships are between animals, humans appearing only as remote eulogizers or direct enemies. But Seth's libretto, *Arion and the Dolphin* (1994), is about a human-nonhuman friendship. Rewriting a Greek myth, Seth shows human love as cowardly, fickle, and self-seeking (the captain loves Arion but betrays him from fear and for gold) and the dolphin's love as selflessly devoted. Animal love emerges as more than conventional fidelity; it is troped as romantic and passionate. Having saved Arion's life, the dolphin chooses to die rather than be parted from him. The dolphin's fatal approach to human shores leads to his capture, display as a performing animal, and death from exhaustion and despair. Thus the nurturing lover dies for the dazzling beloved who ends up singing his elegy.

The idea that a homoerotically inclined individual is neither fish nor flesh or, in Woolf's phrase, "neither a man nor a woman," has made the mermaid an apt symbol for narratives about the forging of such individuality and inclination. The unavailability of the mermaid for heterosexual and reproductive purposes coexists in legend with her disturbing eroticism. She is often conflated with the siren who lures men only to destroy them. Andersen's fairy tale reverses the syndrome of unavailability by making the mermaid, as stand-in for the gay male, cross-dress as a woman, at the cost of losing her voice. Her dumbness is an obvious trope for the love that dare not speak its name. In this nineteenth-century parable, gay love is misread by its object as filial. The prince treats her as a little sister. Freedom, the ability to live in a watery underworld, can only be regained by killing love, which the gay protagonist is unable to do.

"The Little Mermaid" is a good example of the process I have traced, of gay male narratives using lesbian tropes, for the mermaid is conventionally female. T. S. Eliot's lines suggest the lesbian quality of her femaleness that excludes the heterosexual male: "I have heard the mermaids singing each to each / I do not think that they will sing to me." Namjoshi's poem "Playboy" uses this idea to mock the heterosexist notion that women's sexuality is always displayed for men and appeals only to them.

The male onlooker initially thinks the mermaids are "surging and sighing" and "baring their bosoms" for his pleasure; however, their seeming obliviousness to him next convinces him that they are trying to bait him. He descends into the sea, which spurns and overturns him, while the mermaids continue to sport and display themselves, "unaware of my rage, undisturbed in their ecstasy."[74] The poem may not be as simple as this reading suggests. The speaking "I" is not gendered and, in the overall lesbian context of Namjoshi's writing, where the speaker is almost always female, the title may refer to an attitude rather than to a male. In that case, the mermaid may stand for the element of unrequitedness in all desire, which is central to Sapphic narratives.

The mermaid appears and vanishes, sings and inspires singing, but does not remain, cannot be domesticated, and, as such, is an image for the evanescence of the lyrical impulse. In *Mrs. Stevens Hears the Mermaids Singing* the mermaid is conflated with the muse. The Muse is always female in Sarton's schema, and, for a lyric poet, is always "incarnate." Thus, implicitly, every woman lyric poet is a lesbian, on the model of the first Lesbian lyricist. In the Canadian lesbian film "I've Heard the Mermaids Singing," too, the protagonist's experience of love for a woman is inseparable from the experience of unrequitedness, grief, and exclusion. Nevertheless, the protagonist's experience does enable her to share her art of photography, just as Mrs. Stevens's unfulfilled lesbian loves enable her to write poems and Lily Briscoe's love enables her to complete her painting.

The fabulous creature (unicorn, mermaid, phoenix), being "created" rather than "creaturely," generally symbolizes creativity. The unicorn with its phallic horn is a symbol of the male lover and seems to be generally a heterosexual symbol; on the other hand, the mermaid and the phoenix, one female, the other androgynous, recur in homoerotic literary contexts. In medieval and Renaissance texts the phoenix, arising from its ashes, is a common symbol both for the resurrection of Christ and for Mary. It suggests the virgin birth and also the immaculate conception of Mary by Anne. Carol Falvo Heffernan has demonstrated how both Mary and the phoenix are linked to the female symbols of the fountain and the garden. "Mary opens the closed gate of heaven" and, like the phoenix singing as it flies toward the sun, rejoices in her creativity when she sings the Magnificat.[75] Like the phoenix, she is both as old as the universe and eternally young. Heffernan quotes a reading that is used at the Mass of the Immaculate Conception:

> From eternity, in the beginning, he created me,
> and for eternity I shall remain . . .
> I have grown tall as a palm in Engedi,
> as the rose bushes of Jericho;
> as a fine olive in the plain,
> as a plane tree I have grown tall.

I have exhaled a perfume like cinnamon and acacia,
I have breathed out a scent like choice myrrh . . .
(Ecclesiasticus 24:9–20)

The parthenogenetic and nonheterosexual birth of the virgin is cel-ebrated here in conjunction with her exaltation as powerful ("I have grown tall") and beautiful. Heffernan remarks that "presumably the church—and, therefore, Mary as archetype of the Church—here sees her origins in her relationship to Wisdom before the Creation."[76] If this is the case, the primal creation is envisaged here as occurring by and between two female forces. Wisdom, or Sophia, is female and asserts that she was from the beginning and before the creation of the universe. The Virgin, visually often represented as floating above the universe, her feet on the crescent moon, her head encircled by twelve stars, like pagan moon god-desses, is doubly empowered by being linked to Wisdom, an emotional to an intellectual force. The conventional female emotion/male reason and female body/male mind opposition breaks down in this combination, which, I would argue, is everywhere present in Western literary and visual traditions.

The phoenix, like the Virgin, is connected with many of the para-doxes I have explored as constitutive of constructions of homoerotic love. Both self-destructive/suicidal and self-generative, old and yet ageless, eternally young and beautiful, creative not biologically but artistically (it sings as it builds a nest/pyre on which it burns itself), solitary yet possess-ing an unbroken ancestry in itself, neither male nor female as those cate-gories are heterosexually constructed in society, the phoenix is paradisal, primal, Edenic. It represents both death and survival, thus combining the impulses of Sapphic and Marian narratives. The phoenix has been one of the most ubiquitous and recurrent images in homoerotic texts since Romanticism.[77] It usually stands for the ability to heal and regenerate one-self and, as such, appears alone, often identified with the narrating voice.

An exception to the figuring of the phoenix as alone is found in Shakespeare's elegy "The Phoenix and Turtle," which sets a pattern for subsequent odd couplings of different species. Shakespeare in general conceives of the phoenix as female, for example, in sonnet 19 the pro-noun *her* is used. The turtledove, too, is, in general, female or, as in the case of the holy spirit as dove, neutral. A paradigm of love between females is here, as in later texts, such as Donne's "The Canonization," a model to which other loves aspire. In Donne's poem the phoenix is the "one neutral thing" to which "both sexes fit." Although Shakespeare's poem uses the pronoun *his* for the dove, the interspecies coupling and the overall avoidance of gendered pronouns suggest something out of the way, as does the air of amazement that pervades the poem. It draws sub-textually on the idea of the Virgin Mary as phoenix and the holy ghost as dove, which adds to the suggestion of something miraculous.

Shakespeare's poem stresses the love as likeness model found in his *Sonnets* and thus by implication is homoerotic. The birds are not complementary, as the ideal heterosexual couple was supposed to be. They are inseparable even though they retain individuality: "Two distincts, division none." The phrase "Either was the other's mine" is the same as that in sonnet 134 where the beloved is "that other mine," an other self. The image of the "mutual flame" invests the love with eroticism.

Keats's rewriting of Shakespeare's elegy returns the model to its Marian origins. The Grecian urn's final message clearly derives from Shakespeare's last stanza, as the urn itself recalls the phoenix and turtle's funerary urn. The Grecian urn fixes heterosexual love narratives in states of permanent unfulfillment ("never, never shalt thou kiss") and itself remains a virgin, fostered by and wedded to ungendered forces (quietness, silence, time). It is definitively female, both in its symbolic shape and through epithets such as "bride," and refuses to yield its secret to men, including the male poet. Itself a historian and excelling the male poet in expressiveness, it remains "a friend [not lover] to man, to whom" it gives an incomplete and ambiguous message and whom it shuts out from paradise ("that is all / Ye know on earth"). I would argue that the "ye" is addressed explicitly to the "man" thus shut out.

If Keats's questions are not fully answered, this may have something to do with the poetic ancestor with whom he is in dialogue. Shakespeare's poem closes with an ungendered collectivity of readers who are invited to approach the funerary urn containing the ashes of the phoenix and turtle. The characterization "To this urn let those repair / That are either true or fair" (instead of "true *and* fair") suggests that the visiting pairs or individuals are conceived of as either lovers ("true") or beloveds ("fair").[78] The birds thus become love's martyrs and their tomb, like the legendary tomb of Iolaus, a site for commemoration and the taking of vows. That the poem is an elegy and the celebration is of dead, not living, lovers, is significant. Writing at a time, when, as John Boswell has demonstrated, the possibility of public recognition of same-sex unions or spiritual marriages was disappearing, Shakespeare fixes this historical memory with his poem, setting up a model to which later lovers can aspire, even as they mourn its passing. The moment of death is particularly powerful as a trope because, in the terms of the poem, it fixes the perfection of a Marian spiritual marriage and simultaneously builds into it the death wish of Sapphic yearning. The later lovers who "repair" to the tomb of the phoenix and turtle, that is, later readers of the poem, are placed in a posture of hopeless desire toward what the couple represent, for they are definitively told, "Truth and beauty buried be."

Inserting himself into these traditions of yearning, Wilde, in his sonnet "The Grave of Keats," surrounds his ancestor with a cluster of homoerotic images—"Fair as Sebastian," "gentle violets," and dubs him Sappho's heir: "O sweetest lips since those of Mitylene!" He then constructs himself and others like him as the lovers of this male beloved: "And tears like mine will keep thy memory green, / as Isabella did her Basil-tree."[79] In *The Ballad of Reading Gaol* the image of the urn as preserver of the memory of ancestors recurs in lines that were inscribed on Wilde's tomb: "And alien tears will fill for him / Pity's long-broken urn, / For his mourners will be outcast men, / And outcasts always mourn."[80] It is a long way from the construction of same-sex lovers as among those that are "either true or fair" to defining them as "outcast men." I have tried to demonstrate that the earlier construction and self-view continued to coexist with the later, which never entirely displaced it. Since this book is largely about the claiming of ancestry, I may as well conclude with the ancestor whose "powerful rhyme" was among the most enabling forces for the writers I have considered:

> Property was thus appalled,
> That the self was not the same;
> Single nature's double name
> Neither two nor one was called.
>
> Reason, in itself confounded
> Saw division grow together,
> To themselves yet either neither,
> Simple were so well-compounded:
>
> That it cried, "How true a twain
> Seemeth this concordant one!
> Love hath reason, Reason none,
> If what parts, can so remain.
> (William Shakespeare, "The Phoenix and Turtle")

Notes

Introduction: Imagined Ancestries

1. Terry Castle, *The Apparitional Lesbian: Female Homosexuality and Modern Culture* (New York: Columbia University Press, 1993), 19. Janice Raymond, *A Passion for Friends: Toward a Philosophy of Female Affection* (Boston: Beacon, 1986), argues similarly that feminists have tended to focus on women's oppression rather than women's empowerment and that "feminist theory must take into account the forces maintaining the survival of women as well as those forces maintaining the subordination of women" (22).

2. Teresa de Lauretis, *The Practice of Love: Lesbian Sexuality and Perverse Desire* (Bloomington: Indiana University Press, 1994), 75, 308. Some of the confusion in de Lauretis's model may arise from her conflation of late twentieth-century American cultures with "Western cultures," past and present. Christine Downing, *Myths and Mysteries of Same-Sex Love* (New York: Continuum, 1990) sets out "to discover in male homosexuality some of the lineaments more often associated only with lesbian love—that is, to reverse the more familiar approach, which interprets female experience on the basis of a male model" (11). Her argument, however, while tracing parallel patterns in male and female homoerotic models, only briefly touches on lesbian models for male homoerotic imaginings (166–67).

3. Paula Bennett, "Critical Clitoridectomy: Female Sexual Imagery and Feminist Psychoanalytic Theory," *Signs: Journal of Women in Culture and Society* (1993), 18(2):235–59. In this indispensable essay Bennett shows how "feminist theorists have maintained a singular silence regarding this little organ. The clitoris, which for two millennia before Freud was viewed as (to quote one mid-nineteenth-century gynecologist . . .) the "prime seat" of female erotic sensibility if never the only one, remains

effectively erased in their work" (237). A quick glance through the index of most recent queer theory texts will demonstrate the continuing nature of the bias in this work too. For example, Jonathan Dollimore's *Sexual Dissidence: Augustine to Wilde, Freud to Foucault* (New York: Oxford University Press, 1991) suggests through its title that sexual dissidence was exclusively male through the ages. Despite its brief sections on lesbianism (a dozen pages out of 355, citing only twentieth-century examples), it is pervaded by discussions of anality, sodomy, and buggery but does not mention the clitoris even once.

4. John Boswell, "Categories, Experience, and Sexuality," in Edward Stein, ed., *Forms of Desire: Sexual Orientation and the Social Constructionist Controversy* (New York: Garland, 1990), 133–74. Boswell points out that insofar as *homosexuality* is a construct, so are *heterosexuality, marriage,* and *family,* yet social constructionists do not object to the use of the latter three terms as modified universals. Therefore their strong objections to the use of terms like *homosexual* to describe same-sex preferences in earlier societies would seem to be fueled by homophobia rather than simply by antiessentialism. Boswell also demonstrates that the idea of lifelong preferences for same-sex or cross-sex eroticism is present in Plato's *Symposium* (and hence available to all its later readers), in Aristophanes' story, which posits such preferences (men-men, men-women, women-women) as having existed ever since human beings have existed.

5. On Kinsey's scale a person of exclusively heterosexual experience is a 0, a person of exclusively homosexual experience is a 6, a person of equal experience of both kinds is a 3. A 1 is a person whose experience has been predominantly heterosexual, only incidentally homosexual, and so on. See Alfred Kinsey, Wardell Pomeroy, and Clyde Martin, *Sexual Behavior in the Human Male* (Philadelphia: W. D. Saunders, 1948), 638–41.

6. Judy Grahn, *Another Mother Tongue: Gay Words, Gay Worlds* (Boston: Beacon, 1990 [1984]), 270.

7. I was glad to discover via Stephen Greenblatt's recent paper, "What Is Literary History?" which he sent to a conference on "The Renaissance: Text as Event," held at Jadavpur University, Calcutta, in January 1996, that he now thinks the canon is not constructed by what he calls "professorial will" alone but also by large numbers of nonacademic readers and by the power of literary texts, which, he acknowledges, cannot be wholly deconstructed and is not reducible to the contexts of textual production and dissemination.

8. See Downing's reading of the Aristophanic myth in Plato's *Symposium*, as accounting for all love, homosexual and heterosexual, in terms of a primal wounding. Contra Freud, this longing is not for a lost mother or parent but for a lost other self, the finding of whom is such a rare chance that most people are left "longing for an impossible fusion" (244–45).

9. See John Boswell's exploration of "the ideal of nonbiological, fostering love" (239) in classical and in Christian mythology and literature and in such concepts as the Roman "alumnus" and the Christian godparent, in *The Kindness of Strangers: The Abandonment of Children in Western Europe from Late Antiquity to the Renaissance* (New York: Vintage, 1990 [1988]). Such concepts and practices of nonbiological kinship were available as avenues for expressions of homoerotic feeling.

10. See Eve Kosofsky Sedgwick's brilliant reading of aunts and uncles as representing "alternative life trajectories" (63) for children in "Tales of the Avunculate: Queer Tutelage in *The Importance of Being Earnest ,*" *Tendencies* (Durham: Duke University Press, 1993), 52–72.

11. Philippa Levine, *Feminist Lives in Victorian England: Private Roles and Public Commitment* (Oxford: Basil Blackwell, 1990). Levine accepts Lillian Faderman's model

of nongenital romantic attachments between women until the "invention" of lesbianism by the sexologists. See Faderman, *Surpassing the Love of Men: Romantic Friendship and Love Between Women from the Renaissance to the Present* (London: Women's Press, 1981). Consequently, she downplays the importance of lesbian desire, and insists on the cosy coexistence of happy marriages and attachments between women even when the material she quotes seems to contradict it (70–71). She reads male friendship as a rejection of the private sphere and an embracing of masculine identification (68–69); consequently, she has nothing to say about homosexual men as feminists. Supportive feminist men occur only as fathers, husbands, and lovers of women.

12. Harold Bloom, *The Anxiety of Influence: A Theory of Poetry* (New York: Oxford University Press, 1973).

13. Virginia Woolf, *A Room of One's Own* (London: Harcourt Brace, 1929), 79.

14. Camille Paglia, *Sexual Personae: Art and Decadence from Nefertiti to Emily Dickinson* (New York: Vintage, 1991 [1990]) attempts a reading of Western civilization based on this assumption.

15. Eve Kosofsky Sedgwick, *Between Men: English Literature and Male Homosocial Desire* (New York: Columbia University Press, 1985).

16. Although aware of Boswell's work, Foucault makes the claim that "the Middle Ages had organized around the theme of the flesh and the practice of penance a discourse that was markedly unitary," thus reinforcing an untenable stereotype. See Michel Foucault, *The History of Sexuality* (New York: Vintage, 1990), 1:33. His survey of sexual discourses ends with the second century A.D. and starts over in the seventeenth.

17. In chapter 2, "Varieties of Female Friendship: The Nun as Loose Woman," Raymond, *A Passion for Friends*, which has heavily influenced my argument.

18. E. Johnson, ed., *The Colloquies of Erasmus*, trans. N. Bailey (London: Reeves and Turner, 1878 [1524]), 231.

19. Raymond, *A Passion for Friends*, 104.

20. Ibid., 107.

21. While the effects of the Marian myth would be specific to the Christian imagination, there are numerous, very similar, ideas of virgin goddesses in other cultures. That the cult of Mary grows out of earlier goddess cults such as that of Diana of Ephesus is widely acknowledged. See, for example, Stephen Benko, *The Virgin Goddess: Studies in the Pagan and Christian Roots of Mariology* (Leiden: E. J. Brill, 1993), 256.

22. De Lauretis refutes Bennett by making the argument that "insofar as the clitoris functions in representation like a penis (that is, with the same attributes and function in sexual arousal and pleasure, if without the symbolic valence of the paternal phallus), it too cannot assume the role of privileged or absolute signifier of lesbian desire" (*The Practice of Love*, 235). This argument seems to me based more in an unwillingness to displace the penis (and the father, Freud) than in experience or representation, for the clitoris does not penetrate or ejaculate and the penis is not capable to the same extent of continuing excitation as is the clitoris, a fact that, I shall argue, colors Romantic and Aestheticist representations of continuing ecstasy (rather than goal-directedness) as a desirable condition. If one did not begin with the assumption of the primacy of the father, one could as easily say that the penis functions like a clitoris "in sexual arousal and pleasure" although it does not have the symbolic valence of the maternal clitoris.

23. Castle insists on "the connection between lesbian experience and human experience as a whole" and that "lesbians are indeed 'everywhere' and always have been" (*The Apparitional Lesbian*, 18).

24. Marina Warner, *Alone of All Her Sex: The Myth and the Cult of the Virgin Mary* (New York: Knopf, 1976), and Julia Kristeva, "Stabat Mater" in Susan Rubin Suleiman,

ed., *The Female Body in Western Culture: Contemporary Perspectives* (Cambridge: Harvard University Press, 1986). See also de Lauretis's trenchant critique of Kristeva's "homophobic, heterosexist subtext" (*The Practice of Love*, 163–202).

25. The idea of impossibility crops up repeatedly in discourses of same-sex love. In Sidney's *Arcadia* a woman who desires another woman despairs because she thinks such desire impossible to put into action. Andrew Marvell's poem "The Definition of Love" describes his most likely homoerotic love as "begotten by despair / Upon impossibility."

26. Emmanuel Cooper, *The Sexual Perspective: Homosexuality and Art in the Last One Hundred Years in the West* (London: Routledge, 1986), 6.

27. See Jeffrey Weeks, "Inverts, Perverts, and Mary-Annes: Male Prostitution and the Regulation of Homosexuality in England in the Nineteenth and Early Twentieth Centuries," *Journal of Homosexuality* (Fall 80–Winter 1981), 6:113–34. See also Judy Grahn's remarks on the Spanish gay slang words, *marimacha, maricona, maricoa, mariachi*, which relate gay men and lesbians to Mary, the Mother (*Another Mother Tongue*, 106).

28. This point is often missed by those who think that a biased history and model such as Foucault's can be accepted as a history and model of male sexuality and supplemented by women's histories and models. A history of men that excludes women is an inadequate history even of men, and vice versa.

29. Sedgwick, *Between Men*, 2–3.

30. Ed Cohen, *Talk on the Wilde Side* (New York: Routledge, 1993), quotes the newspaper account of mob violence toward the men arrested in the Vere Street sodomy case, 1810: "The mob, particularly the women, had piled up balls of mud to afford the objects of their indignation with a warm reception. . . . [When they were in the pillory] upwards of 50 women were permitted to stand in the ring, who assailed them incessantly with mud, dead cats, rotten eggs, potatoes, and buckets filled with blood, offal and dung" (248).

31. As Richard Dellamora, *Masculine Desire: The Sexual Politics of Victorian Aestheticism* (Chapel Hill: University of North Carolina Press, 1990), points out, nineteenth-century homosexual male writers' criticism of male-female relations is often directed at "conventional courtship and marriage" (169), in which those relations are most frequently embodied. Many feminist theorists simplistically equate such criticism with misogyny, on the heterosexist assumption that the Puritan post-Reformation model of companionate marriage was liberating for women and that a critique of marriage, especially by a man, must necessarily be antiwomen.

32. Dennis Proctor, ed., *The Autobiography of Goldsworthy Lowes Dickinson* (London: Duckworth, 1973), 90.

33. G. J. Barker-Benfield, "The Spermatic Economy: A Nineteenth-Century View of Sexuality," in Michael Gordon, ed., *The American Family in Social Historical Perspective* (New York: St. Martin's, 1978).

34. In the present study I restrict these claims to English texts and to English Romanticism.

35. The strategy of ungendering speaker and addressee has often been forced on those writing of homoerotic love. This compulsion may have been a blessing in disguise, insofar as it moved their writing away from stereotyped and unreal masculine-feminine categories and made it accessible to many more readings.

36. Monique Wittig, "The Mark of Gender" (1985) in *The Straight Mind and Other Essays* (Boston: Beacon, 1992), 80.

37. Perry Meisel, *The Absent Father: Virginia Woolf and Walter Pater* (New Haven: Yale University Press, 1980), 45.

1. In what follows I make extensive use of material drawn from Hilda Graef, *Mary: A History of Doctrine and Devotion* (New York: Sheed and Ward, 1963), and other cited sources.

2. As Eileen Power puts it, "In this matter the people ran away from the church, which followed panting in their rear; and the medieval Virgin is essentially their creation, a figure of popular folklore even more than a figure of doctrinal devotion." "Introduction," in Johannes Herolt, *Miracles of the Blessed Virgin Mary*, trans. C. C. Swinton Bland (London: George Routledge, 1928), xviii–xix.

3. For example, Stephen Benko, *The Virgin Goddess: Studies in the Pagan and Christian Roots of Mariology* (Leiden: E. J. Brill, 1993), remarks, "The fact that popular piety developed the ideas of the 'perpetual virginity' and 'immaculate conception' was a positive contribution to the life of the church because it rescued a crucial part of religion which Christianity nearly lost, namely, the feminine aspect of the divine" (205–6).

4. Walter L. Arnstein, *Protestant Versus Catholic in Mid-Victorian England: Mr. Newdegate and the Nuns* (Columbia: University of Missouri Press, 1982), 42.

5. Charles Stephen Dessain, *John Henry Newman* (London, 1966), suggests that the social prejudices confronted by a convert to Catholicism in the mid-nineteenth century were greater than those faced by a convert to communism in the mid-twentieth (79). This may account for the relatively small number of conversions in England and the larger number of dropouts from Catholicism. Arnstein, *Protestant Versus Catholic*, 215–16.

6. Arnstein, *Protestant Versus Catholic*, 185.

7. Peter B. Neckles, *The Oxford Movement in Context: Anglican High Churchmanship, 1760–1857* (Cambridge: Cambridge University Press, 1994), 186.

8. Both quoted in Neckles, ibid., 186.

9. That one of Catholicism's strengths is its assimilation of pagan practices is, paradoxically, a fact the Catholic Church cannot acknowledge, given that assimilation went hand in hand with the stamping out of such practices in their non-Christian forms. Eileen Power quotes Briffault, who notes that the statue of Mary at the site of ancient Enna at Castrogiovanni holds a divine girl child because the statue was that of Ceres and Proserpine taken over by Christians.

10. Neckles, *The Oxford Movement*, 75.

11. "Introduction," in E. R. Norman, ed., *Anti-Catholicism in Victorian England* (London: George Allen and Unwin, 1968), 32–33.

12. Ibid., 171.

13. Ibid., 106.

14. Norman, *Anti-Catholicism*, 108.

15. Arnstein, *Protestant Versus Catholic*, 46–47.

16. Ibid., 47.

17. Ibid., 89.

18. D. G. Paz, *Popular Anti-Catholicism in Mid-Victorian England* (Stanford: Stanford University Press, 1992), 69. See Alan Bray, *Homosexuality in Renaissance England* (London: Gay Men's Press, 1982), 19, for more references to the papacy as Sodom. Bray remarks that Protestantism thus "adapted to its own use the identification of sodomy with heresy that the Catholic Church had itself constructed during its confrontation with the heresies of the twelfth century" (19).

19. Arnstein, *Protestant Versus Catholic*, 186.

20. In 1876 there were only 299 monastic communities in England; by 1900 there were 600 communities of women but the average convent contained no more than a dozen women. Arnstein, *Protestant Versus Catholic*, 215–16.

21. Arnstein quotes popular texts as well as texts by E. B. Browning and Walter Scott, representing the walling-up of a nun by priests as punishment for rebellion.

22. Ibid., 62, 135.

23. Robert Bruce M'Combie, quoted in Arnstein, *Protestant Versus Catholic*, 182, and Chief Justice Cockburn, warning the jury against anti-Catholic prejudice in the Mary Saurin case, quoted, ibid., 119.

24. Arnstein, *Protestant Versus Catholic*, 108.

25. Quoted, ibid., 136.

26. Quoted, ibid., 137–39.

27. Quoted, ibid., 216–17. Florence Nightingale, using a phrase that anticipates Woolf's in *Three Guineas*, remarked that "the petty, grinding tyrannies of the good English family" far surpassed those of the convent (222).

28. Paz, *Popular Anti-Catholicism*, 20.

29. See Eamon Duffy, *The Stripping of the Altars: Traditional Religion in England, 1400–1580* (New Haven: Yale University Press, 1992), 256–65.

30. It is interesting that "Mary," unlike Miss Muffet or Curlylocks, is a fearless young lady in nursery rhymes and generally gets her own way.

31. Leigh Hunt, "Specimens of British Poetesses," part 3, in *Men, Women, and Books: A Selection of Sketches, Essays, and Critical Memoirs* (New York: Harper, 1847), 125–26.

32. Walter Pater, "A Study of Dionysus," in Charles L. Shadwell, ed., *Greek Studies: A Series of Essays* (New York: Macmillan, 1901 [1894]), 30–31. Some of the associations of "Mary" are linked with popular English flower names. Eileen Power points out, "Her name was sown in wild flowers over the fields, and in England country children plucked Lady's Slippers and Lady's Fingers and Virgin's Bower, watched the 'winking Mary-buds begin to ope their golden eyes.' " Power, *Miracles*, ix.

33. Eric Trudgill, *Madonnas and Magdalens: The Origins and Development of Victorian Sexual Attitudes* (New York: Homes and Meier, 1976), 257.

34. Trudgill traces some of these in chapter 10, "The Rise and Fall of the Madonna," *Madonnas and Magdalens*, 248–76. For an account of the Pre-Raphaelites' use of Madonna imagery, see Jan Marsh, *Pre-Raphaelite Women: Images of Femininity* (New York: Harmony, 1987), esp. the chapter "Holy Virgins."

35. Quoted in Arnstein, *Protestant Versus Catholic*, 95.

36. The Protestant Evangelical Mission and Electoral Union denounced the sisterhoods as "Popish establishments" that practiced "Mariolatry," Arnstein, *Protestant Versus Catholic*, 156–57.

37. Victor and Edith Turner, "Postindustrial Marian Pilgrimages" in James L. Preston, ed., *Mother Worship: Theme and Variations* (Chapel Hill: University of North Carolina Press, 1982), 145.

38. Virginia Woolf, "Nancy Stair," *Guardian*, May 10, 1905, in Andrew McNeillie, ed., *The Essays of Virginia Woolf, 1904–1912* (London: Hogarth, 1986), 40–41.

39. Theodore Roosevelt, "National Duties," in *The Strenuous Life* (New York: Century, 1905), 281. Admittedly, these are extreme statements of the case. The middle classes had a strong conception of companionate marriage, but this companionship was seen as ideally cemented by parenthood. Nor was the English aristocracy, despite its greater tolerance of difference, unaffected by powerful middle-class propaganda such as that in Tennyson's *The Princess*.

40. Graef, *Mary: A History*, 117–18.

41. Virginia Woolf, *A Room of One's Own* (New York: Harcourt Brace, 1929), 53–54.

42. As Jean Guitton comments, on Leonardo da Vinci's "Virgin of the Rocks": "I find here in this ambivalent painting . . . all of the themes which have so frequently occupied our contemporaries: the idea that . . . angel and man belong to the same ambiguous race; that the difference of sexes vanishes in the androgyne; that the active thought is the beginning and the end of everything." Jean Guitton, *The Madonna* (New York: Tudor, 1963), 94.

43. Benko, *The Virgin Goddess*, 220.

44. Interestingly, this lyric does not mention either Eve ("Adam lay i-bounden . . . And all was for an appil, / An appil that he tok") or Christ, so that the Fall is ascribed to a man and the restoration to a woman.

45. Bellegambe, *Anne Conceiving the Virgin* (Giraudon), Musée de Douai.

46. The widespread Protestant misconception that "the immaculate conception" refers to Mary's conception of Jesus suggests the power of the original inversion.

47. Thomas Stehling, "To Love a Medieval Boy," in Stuart Kellogg, ed., *Essays on Gay Literature*, 151–70. These two poems were addressed to earthly women.

48. See Graef, *Mary: A History*, 266–69, 198–201, 243–44, 258, 292–97. The focus on Mary's sufferings at the cross in such hymns as the Stabat Mater and in numerous paintings, especially those, like Fra Angelico's *Crucifixion* that show her in a crucified position, outstretched arms supported by others, stress this theme of equality.

49. Graef, *Mary: A History*, 266–70.

50. Ibid., 315–18.

51. Benko, *The Virgin Goddess*, 222.

52. By Prince Puckler Muskau. See Mrs. G. H. Bell, ed., *The Hamwood Papers of the Ladies of Llangollen and Caroline Hamilton* (London: Macmillan, 1930), 1.

53. For a summary of nineteenth-century antimasturbation writings, see Ed Cohen, *Talk on the Wilde Side* (New York: Routledge, 1993), 35–68. Paula Bennett, "Critical Clitoridectomy: Female Sexual Imagery and Feminist Psychoanalytic Theory," *Signs* (1993), 18:235–59, argues, following Thomas Laqueur, "Orgasm, Generation, and the Politics of Reproductive Biology" in Catherine Gallagher and Thomas Laqueur, eds., *The Making of the Modern Body: Sexuality and Society in the Nineteenth Century* (Berkeley: University of California Press, 1988), 1–41, that knowledge of the clitoris's importance was deliberately lost in the course of the nineteenth century. However, even Freud acknowledges the clitoral orgasm when he argues that it has to be displaced by the vaginal in order for a girl to turn into a heterosexual woman. Sheila Jeffreys demonstrates how early twentieth-century sexologists feared that women accustomed to clitoral pleasure might prefer it to vaginal penetration by a man. See *The Spinster and Her Enemies: Feminism and Sexuality, 1880–1930* (London: Pandora, 1985), 171–72.

54. In the section entitled "The Necessary Ordeal" Trudgill adduces some of the reasons I have outlined to argue that Victorian women's disinterest in marital sex was "by no means purely mythical" (58). See *Madonnas and Magdalens*, 56–64. He even points out that "private sexual pleasure in fantasy and masturbation could easily coexist with a fastidious distaste for conjugal relations" (58).

55. The translation of the Hebrew *alma* (young girl) as *Parthenos* links Mary with the powerful warrior-maid Athena whose title it was. In some "gender-bending" paintings Mary appears as warrior. For example, in the Master of King Albert's Retable's *The Virgin in Armor* (circa 1410) she is clad in full armor including a hatlike helmet with only her long hair (like Spenser's Britomart's) betraying her sex. More common are paintings of Mary battling and trampling on the devil, represented as male.

56. Some of the stories told by the early fathers to teach the doctrine of Mary's perpetual virginity parallel stories told today in lesbian magazines. Female seagulls

nesting together is an example of the latter; Basil of Caesarea (d. 379) tells a story of birds producing fertile eggs without copulating. Graef, *Mary: A History*, 63.

57. The mid-second-century *Protoevangelium* of James tells the story of Mary's life. It represents her as dancing in the Temple, an idea that undoes the otherwise sinful associations of the dancing woman (Herodias's daughter) in the New Testament. Later enormously popular works such as the thirteenth-century *Mariale Super Missus Est* elaborated and commented on these stories.

58. During a presentation of this argument at the Society for the Humanities, Cornell University, it was suggested to me that this shift of emphasis functions in an anti-Semitic way to deny Jesus's Judaic ancestry. It seems to me that such a reading reflects a tendency to identify ancestry with fatherhood, which is combated by orthodox Jewish insistence that only one born of a Jewish mother is a Jew. William of Newburgh's twelfth-century Marian exegesis of the Canticle, *Explanatio Sacri Epithalamii in Matrem Sponsi*, argues that the Virgin's prayers for her own people remind her son that he has taken "his flesh from them" and that they should therefore share in his "spiritual goods" and be saved. See Graef, *Mary: A History*, 257–59.

59. For a 1901 English version of a French lesbian Mary-Anne-Elizabeth community (Marie Antoinette, her lover Marie-Louise, and her sister-in-law Elizabeth) see Terry Castle's account of "Catherine Hyde's" narrative. Castle, *The Apparitional Lesbian* (New York: Columbia University Press, 1993), 136–40.

60. We should not assume too easily that nineteenth-century writers had "lost" all knowledge of medieval writing. As I shall argue later, Leigh Hunt, Oscar Wilde, and many others were well-informed about Renaissance and later women writers whom twentieth-century feminists have assumed were "lost." John Audeley's fifteenth-century "Carol to St. Anne" is an example of the inscription of this figure in English verse.

61. For example, A. Vogtlin, ed., *Vita Beatae Virginis Mariae et Salvatoris Rhythmica* (Tubinen, 1888). Janice Raymond uses the term *marriage resister* to suggest the political importance of such a refusal.

62. Victorian scholarship made these lives popularly available, for example, Mrs. Arthur Bell's turn-of-the-century three-volume study *The Saints in Christian Art* (London: George Bell) devotes one volume to English saints and considerable space to such women as St. Marina, who lived for years disguised as a monk and brought up a boy she was falsely accused of having fathered, St. Godelieve of Flanders, who was murdered by her husband because she refused to sleep with him, as well as to such better-known Englishwomen as St. Hilda. Perhaps most interesting is St. Wilgefortis, who miraculously grew a beard and moustache to get rid of a suitor and was worshipped by women under the name of St. Uncumber because they hoped she would uncumber them of husbands.

63. Benko's account of the pagan festivals celebrated by women points to their lesbian dimension. At the celebration honoring Dionysus and Demeter in Athens "the celebration, restricted to women, eventually developed into an all-night orgy where women shed all standards of decency." *Virgin Goddess*, 67. This dimension persisted in early Christianity. Thus the second-century Montanist cult in Asia Minor encouraged spiritual, sexless marriage, and one Montanist prophetess had a vision that Christ came and slept with her "in the shape of a woman" (153). Benko suggests that the prophetess transformed a local goddess into a Christ-as-woman figure (154).

64. For examples, see Herolt, *Miracles of the Blessed Virgin Mary*.

65. Janice Raymond makes this point, following Simone de Beauvoir who attributes the repugnance some men feel for old virgins to their fear of these women's power.

66. Elizabeth Raikes, *Dorothea Beale of Cheltenham* (London: Archibald Constable, 1908), 232.

67. Annie E. Ridley, *Frances Mary Buss and Her Work for Education* (London: Longmans, Green, 1896), 387–88.

68. Nuns and nunneries appear as figures for women's autonomy and lesbian feelings in several of Woolf's texts. In *Mrs. Dalloway* Clarissa is compared to a nun just before she retreats into her room and recalls her youthful passion for Sally Seton, contrasting it with her nonpassionate marital feelings. Her "virginity preserved through childbirth" is troped directly on the idea of Mary. "A Women's College" explicitly compares the college, where Angela discovers her passionate feelings for her friend Alice, to a nunnery.

69. The way Mary's life came, in her legends, to be structured around various visionary apparitions, as did many of the lives of the saints, suggests that Terry Castle's idea of the apparitional lesbian may have even deeper cultural roots than those Castle explores.

70. See David Hilliard, "Unenglish and Unmanly: Anglo-Catholicism and Homosexuality," *Victorian Studies* (1982), 25(2):181–210, for an account of how "Anglo-Catholic religion within the Church of England has offered emotional and aesthetic satisfactions . . . to members of a stigmatised sexual minority" (181). Hilliard deals only with male homosexuals. Conversely, Joanne Glasgow, "What's a Nice Lesbian like You Doing in the Church of Torquemada? Radclyffe Hall and Other Catholic Converts," in Karla Jay and Joanne Glasgow, eds., *Lesbian Texts and Contexts: Radical Revisions* (New York: New York University Press, 1990), 241–54, argues that lesbians were attracted to Catholicism because lesbian sexuality "did not exist as a Catholic reality" (242). Glasgow's argument is unconvincing to me because it does not account for the equal attraction of homosexual men (often friends of the women concerned) to Catholicism, which she ignores. For a French parallel, see Karla Jay, *The Amazon and the Page: Natalie Clifford Barney and Renée Vivien* (Bloomington: Indiana University Press, 1988). Jay shows how Barney and Vivien claim Sappho (and also Plato and Shakespeare) as ancestors, attempt to rewrite the Virgin Mary as a lesbian model, and use the word *virginity* to signify lesbian resistance to heterosexual enslavement.

71. Herolt, *Miracles of the Blessed Virgin Mary*. Power stresses "the Virgin's predilection for the disreputable" (xxiv).

72. Sandra L. Zimdars-Swartz, *Encountering Mary: Visions of Mary from La Salette to Medjugorje* (New York: Avon, 1992 [1991]), 266–67.

73. Zimdars-Swartz, ibid., argues that nineteenth- and twentieth-century devotees of Marian apparitions understand intercession as "a dramatic interaction between God, who in the person of the Father and the Son represents the divine law, and the Virgin, who represents divine mercy" (247).

74. John Donne, *The Complete English Poems*, ed. A. J. Smith (Harmondsworth: Penguin, 1971), 306.

75. Guitton, *The Madonna*, 76.

76. The transactions conducted in these texts are much more open and fluctuating than is suggested by Eve Kosofsky Sedgwick's model of homosocial triangulation. See *Between Men: English Literature and Male Homosocial Desire* (New York: Columbia University Press, 1985), 21–27. Terry Castle, while accepting Sedgwick's model as paradigmatic for "the canon of eighteenth- and nineteenth-century English and American fiction" (*The Apparitional Lesbian*, 73), thinks it is challenged by female countertriangulation only in "lesbian novels" (74).

77. The term *Mariolatry* is used by Protestants to denounce what they perceive as Catholic "idolatry," which, in Christian terms, is necessarily infidel. Catholics like

Graef defer to papal authority in condemning what they see as the Mariolatric excesses of Marian cults. I use the term nonpejoratively. I see many positive features in idolatry as it functions within polytheistic civilizations such as the ancient Greek and the Hindu. I do not concur with the Christian, Islamic, Judaic, and secular denunciations of it. Nor do I see any virtue in "iconoclasm," whether in its violently physical or its intellectual, but equally intolerant, variants.

2. The Sapphic Sublime and Romantic Lyricism

1. As many recent commentators have demonstrated, "there is a continuity from the English romantic era to our own." See Allan Chavkin, ed., *English Romanticism and Modern Fiction* (New York: AMS, 1993), 1. Modernism, despite its anti-Romantic postures, is the heir of Romanticism. In different ways the novels of James, Hardy, Meredith, Forster, Woolf, Conrad, Joyce, Lawrence rewrite Romanticism, as Charles Schug argues, into "the modern spirit," for "what we find in the modern novel is a work of literature closely resembling in its formal and structural attributes the great romantic poems of the early nineteenth century." See *The Romantic Genesis of the Modern Novel* (Pittsburgh: University of Pittsburgh Press, 1979), 18–19.

2. See Bruno Snell, *The Discovery of the Mind* (New York: Dover, 1982). Sandra M. Gilbert and Susan Gubar, *The Madwoman in the Attic: The Woman Writer and the Nineteenth-Century Literary Tradition* (New Haven: Yale University Press, 1979), argue that women have been excluded from writing lyric poetry because the genre demands a strong "I." I disagree, since Sappho, one of the creators of the Greek lyric, has a very strong "I," and several nineteenth-century women poets excelled in the lyric, for example, Emily Brontë, Emily Dickinson, Christina Rossetti, and Michael Field.

3. As Eva Stehle Stigers puts it, "Sappho was 'abnormal,' perhaps, in being unusually open to romantic impulse, unusually aware of the human urge for union and the inevitable separateness. . . . Lesbian love offered the most receptive setting for romantic *eros*. Escape to a realm of beauty, illusion of perfect union, inevitability of parting, these could be expressed through union with another woman because . . . the other woman could seem to . . . make the emotional connection far more easily than a man; and because separation, if only by virtue of the inevitability of marriage, was inevitable." See "Romantic Sensuality, Poetic Sense: A Response to Hallett on Sappho," *Signs* (1979), 4(3):465–71, 467.

4. I shall not enter into the futile debate over whether or not Sappho was a "lesbian." Those who set out to prove that she was not are generally inspired by thinly disguised homophobia, as, for example, Andre Lardinois, "Lesbian Sappho and Sappho of Lesbos," in Jan Bremmer, ed., *From Sappho to De Sade: Moments in the History of Sexuality* (London: Routledge, 1989), 15–35. Whether or not the historical Sappho engaged in sexual relations with women is irrelevant to my purposes; that the texts ascribed to her express passionate erotic longing for women with all the concomitants of such passion—jealousy, grief, joy, praise of beauty, desire for togetherness—and that they were perceived as expressing such longing in the period I examine are the relevant facts.

5. The process of self-feminization is read by Anne Mellor, *Romanticism and Gender* (New York: Routledge, 1993), as an appropriation arising from "a gender ideology which subtly denies the value of female difference" (29). Although she denies that she endorses gender difference as inescapably given, her entire argument is based on such an assumption. The unacknowledged heterosexism of her framework leads her to argue that Wollstonecraft's and other women writers' positing of "the egalitarian family" as an ideal was a "truly revolutionary political program, one in which gender and class dif-

ferences could be erased" (38). How "husband and wife [who] regard each other as equals" (38) would erase gender and class differences remains unexplained.

6. This implies that some (not all) of the qualities that women have been compelled to develop as a result of gender-based division of labor are desirable and should be imitated by men in order to develop different kinds of human beings and to do away with that division of labor, while, on the other hand, next to none of the qualities developed by men (as men) are similarly desirable, and therefore these should be shed. In my reading this feminization does not entail, as it does in Kaja Silverman's Freudian and Lacanian framework, man's "becom[ing] the one who is penetrated, and, in the process, feminized." See Silverman, *Male Subjectivity at the Margins* (New York: Routledge, 1992), 174. The idea that to be wounded and penetrated is to be feminized is a heterosexist one. If women's sexuality in Romantic texts is clitoral rather than vaginal, then to be feminized is to become aware of the possibilities of autonomous, pleasure-giving, and nonpenetration-centered, orgasmic sexuality.

7. Diane Long Hoeveler, *Romantic Androgyny: The Women Within* (University Park: Penn State University, 1979), sees the process as resulting in the absence of any "fully believable or real or 'round' " (1) women characters in Romantic poetry. I would argue that there are scarcely any "round" male characters either in Romantic poetry, while there are such characters, both male and female, in Romantic drama and fiction, for the very good reason that Forster's notion of "round" character may work in the genre of fiction but not of the lyric. Hoeveler assumes throughout that sexual = heterosexual and finally terms "severe psychological shortcomings" a list of impulses that includes "homosexual impulses" (176).

8. Wayne Koestenbaum, in a brilliant essay, "The Marinere Hath His Will[iam]: Wordsworth's and Coleridge's *Lyrical Ballads*," in *Double Talk: The Erotics of Male Literary Collaboration* (New York: Routledge, 1989), explores the homoeroticism of what Paul Magnuson has termed the "lyrical dialogue" between the two poets.

9. Virginia Woolf, *A Room of One's Own* (New York: Harcourt Brace, 1929), 5.

10. Woolf assumes that Rossetti is "respond[ing]" (15) to the male poet's call. But while *Maud* genders lover and beloved, Rossetti's "My heart is like a singing bird," avoids doing so. The difference is crucial to my argument about the Romantic lyric.

11. Milton is quoted when the narrator considers "the thought of that one gift which it was death to hide" (38), Shelley in the reference to the eagle or vulture that eats at the breasts of powerful men (38), Gray in her musings on the thwarted woman writer as "some mute and inglorious Jane Austen" (51).

12. The tendency of H.D.'s Paterian essay, "The Wise Sappho," in *Notes on Thought and Vision* (San Francisco: City Lights Books, 1982), in contrast to Woolf's, is to recognize Sappho's importance as a cultural force and literary influence, but unfortunately this essay had no comparable influence.

13. Typical of such reading are Judy Grahn, *The Highest Apple: Sappho and the Lesbian Poetic Tradition* (San Francisco: Spinsters' Ink, 1985) and Jane McIntosh Snyder, *Sappho*, in the Lives of Notable Gay Men and Lesbians series (New York: Chelsea House, 1995).

14. Elaine Showalter, ed., *The New Feminist Criticism: Essays on Women, Literature, and Theory*, 4. The titles of books such as Showalter's *A Literature of Their Own* (1979) and Patricia Meyer Spacks's *The Female Imagination* (1975) indicate the powerful tendency toward exalting difference in Anglo-American feminism. French feminism, with the exception of Wittig, is imbued with perhaps a more extreme version of the same tendency.

15. Dorothy Allison, *Skin: Talking about Sex, Class, and Literature* (Ithaca: Firebrand, 1994), 175.

16. Angela Leighton, *Victorian Women Poets: Writing Against the Heart* (Charlottesville and London: University Press of Virginia, 1992), 35. Christine Downing, *Myths and Mysteries of Same-Sex Love* (New York: Continuum, 1990), 8, and Snyder, *Sappho*, 36, also take this view.

17. It is often assumed, following Foucault, that if sexologists thought an active female sexuality was impossible or that all sexuality was penetrative or that lesbians used dildos everyone else necessarily thought so too; see Downing, *Myths and Mysteries*, 7–10. Similarly, Judith P. Hallett, "Sappho and Her Social Context: Sense and Sensuality," *Signs* (1979), 4(3):447–64, assumes that because English dictionaries begin to ascribe homosexual meaning to the words Sapphist and Lesbian only after 1890 the words did not have these meanings before. But see Terry Castle, *The Apparitional Lesbian* (New York: Columbia University Press, 1993), 131, for Hester Thrale's 1789 diary reference to Marie Antoinette and her friends as "Sapphists." In "Don Leon," a powerful poem in defense of male homosexuality, published in 1866, purportedly written by Byron but probably written by his friend George Colman, there are two lines referring to an affair between two women: "A pair of breeches S . . . n and W . . . k shock / They ask no joys beyond each other's smock". The author in a note explains that the two ladies were Lady Strachan and Lady Warwick. He goes on to quote Sappho's ode as addressed to a woman and states unequivocally that in Rome "females addicted to these modes of mutual gratification were called *tribades* and *fricatrices*." He quotes Lucian's *Dialogues Between Courtesans*, in a translation where *tribade* is used as a noun for a woman who prefers women. The annotator also refers to "these lesbian practices" in France. This is an example of the use of words both as adjectives and nouns and also of an ascribing of lesbian identity through history. See Bernard Grebanier, *The Uninhibited Byron: An Account of His Sexual Confusion* (New York: Crown, 1970), 340–41.

18. Longinus, *Longinus's On the Sublime*, ed. D. A. Russell (Oxford: Clarendon, 1964), ix.

19. T. R. Henn, *Longinus and English Criticism* (Cambridge: Cambridge University Press, 1934), and M. H. Abrams, *The Mirror and the Lamp: Romantic Theory and the Critical Tradition* (Oxford: Oxford University Press, 1953), esp. 72–78 and 132–38.

20. William Smith, *Dionysius Longinus on the Sublime, Translated from the Greek, with Notes and Observations and some Account of the Life, Writings and Character of the Author* (London: J. Watts, 1739).

21. Leonard Welsted, *Epistles, Odes andc. written on Several Subjects with a Translation of Longinus's Treatise on the Sublime* (London: J. Walthoe, 1724).

22. Castle comments on this attraction, but not on Sappho as a model for Byron. *Apparitional Lesbian*, 103–4.

23. Susan J. Wolfson, "Feminizing Keats," in Hermione de Almeida, ed., *Critical Essays on John Keats* (Boston: G. K. Hall, 1990), 317–56, demonstrates how Keats's poetical practice blurred gender boundaries and how this was perceived as unmanly, effeminate, or feminine in the nineteenth century.

24. "Keats Reading Women, Women Reading Keats," *Studies in Romanticism* (1990), 29:341–370, p. 368.

25. Hermione de Almeida, "Introduction: Intellectual Keats," 8n3, in Hermione de Almeida, ed., *Critical Essays on John Keats*.

26. Fern Farnham, *Madame Dacier: Scholar and Humanist* (Monterey: Angel, 1976), 82.

27. Alexander Chalmer, ed., *The Works of the English Poets* (London: J. Johnson, 1810), 20:375.

28. John Donne, *John Donne: The Complete English Poems*, ed. A. J. Smith (Harmondsworth: Penguin, 1971), 127–29.

29. John Keats, *The Letters of John Keats: 1814–1821*, ed. H. E. Rollins (Cambridge: Harvard University Press, 1958), 1:163–65. To John Hamilton Reynolds, September 21, 1817. "Sappho" was a popular pen name among women poets at this time. Mellor, who, unlike Keats, apparently sees no difference between the poetic merits of Philips's and Elizabeth Montague's poetry, ascribes his criticism of the latter to his "discomfort with being aligned with the feminine" and his applause of "passionate female friendship" to his exclusion from it; see *Romanticism and Gender*, 180. Despite Keats's celebration here of a woman's creativity that has nothing to do with reproduction, Mellor insists that Keats associates "poetic creation . . . with female biology . . . the creative [read, reproductive] power of women" (184).

30. Percy Bysshe Shelley, *The Letters of Percy Bysshe Shelley*, ed. Frederick L. Jones (Oxford: Oxford University Press, 1964), 1:343–44. To Clio Rickman, Dec. 24, 1812.

31. William Blake, letter to William Hayley, November 26, 1800, in G. E. Bentley, ed., *William Blake's Writings* (Oxford: Oxford University Press, 1978), 2:1548*n*1.

32. Samuel Taylor Coleridge, *The Complete Poetical Works of Samuel Taylor Coleridge*, ed. Ernest Hartley Coleridge (Oxford: Clarendon Press, 1912), 353.

33. Lord Byron, *Byron's Letters and Journals*, ed. Leslie A. Marchand (London: John Murray, 1973), 1:124–25. To Elizabeth Pigot, July 5, 1807.

34. Carol Falvo Heffernan, *The Phoenix at the Fountain: Images of Woman and Eternity in Lactantius's Carmen de Ave Phoenice and the Old English Phoenix* (Newark: University of Delaware Press, 1988).

35. H.D. "The Wise Sappho," brings together all these images—rose, violet, lily, star, moon, jewel, shell, purple, to imagine Sappho and her world. In her 1919 "Notes on Thought and Vision," too, these images occur, but the central image is that of oyster and pearl, for the body that makes and remakes the spirit.

36. Robert Southey, *New Letters of Robert Southey*, ed. Kenneth Curry (New York: Columbia University Press, 1965), 1:24–25, to Grosvenor Charles Bedford, June 1, 1793.

37. Leigh Hunt, *The Poetical Works of Leigh Hunt*, ed. H. S. Milford (London: Oxford University Press, 1923), canto 3:73–74, 269–70.

38. William Wordsworth, *The Poetical Works of William Wordsworth*, ed. Thomas Hutchinson (London: Henry Frowde, 1906), 109.

39. All references to Keats's poems are to John Keats, *The Poetical Works and Other Writings of John Keats*, ed. H. Buxton Forman (New York: Phaeton, 1970).

40. Quoted in Margaret Goldsmith, *Christina of Sweden* (New York: Doubleday, 1935), 11.

41. Hoeveler, *Romantic Androgyny*, insisting that Keats is making himself "heir to a . . . literary patriarchy," reintroduces the Miltonic Adam whom Keats leaves out: "He eats the fruit left from the last meal of Adam and Eve" (245).

42. Mellor, *Romanticism and Gender*, points out that contemporary characterizations of Keats as a masturbatory poet feminized him by implicitly linking him with "female masturbation and other lesbian acts" (173).

43. Mario L. D'Avanzo, *Keats's Metaphors for the Poetic Imagination* (Durham: Duke University Press, 1967), details these images but reads them as indicative of "sexual union" between man and woman (130), despite the absence of phallic images.

44. Jack Stillinger, *The Hoodwinking of Madeline and Other Essays on Keats's Poems* (University of Illinois Press, 1971).

45. Mellor, *Romanticism and Gender*, 175.

46. Alan Bewell, "Keats's Realm of Flora," *Studies in Romanticism* (1992), 31:71–98, is a sensitive and scholarly elaboration of how Keats's use of the language

of flowers endeared him to women and to male homosexual readers but drew the wrath of reviewers on his head. Bewell does not comment on the oral, nonpenetrative connotations of this imagery or its Sapphic resonances and sees it as gendered, male, and opposed to autoeroticism. He argues that Keats was frightened by reviews into disowning the feminine language of flowers, especially its relation to female autoeroticism.

47. Hoeveler, *Romantic Androgyny*, 65. Typical of such heterosexist misreading of oral eroticism as infantile and narcissistic is Barbara A. Schapiro's discussion of it in *The Romantic Mother: Narcissistic Patterns in Romantic Poetry* (Baltimore: Johns Hopkins University Press, 1983). She reads the lines "We rest in silence, like two gems upcurl'd / In the recesses of a pearly shell" (*Sleep and Poetry* 120–21) as expressing "the desire to retreat into an ideal maternal world" (35) as if clitoral and vulval imagery must always be maternal and escapist.

48. Castle, *Apparitional Lesbian*, 100.

49. All references to Shelley's poems are to the Cambridge edition, Percy Bysshe Shelley, *The Poetical Works of Shelley*, ed. Newell F. Ford (Boston: Houghton Mifflin, 1975).

3. Ecstasy in Victorian Aestheticism

1. For instance, Alan Sinfield, *The Wilde Century: Effeminacy, Oscar Wilde, and the Queer Moment* (New York: Columbia University Press, 1994) assumes that homoerotically inclined women and men in the nineteenth century inhabited different worlds, literal and literary.

2. Linda Dowling, *Hellenism and Homosexuality in Victorian Oxford* (Ithaca: Cornell University Press, 1993).

3. As Peter B. Neckles points out, "The Oxford Movement formed a chapter in the intellectual history of nineteenth-century Europe, and was in tune with such deep cultural currents as Romanticism." Neckles, *The Oxford Movement in Context* (Cambridge: Cambridge University Press, 1994), 324.

4. Mrs. Arthur Bell, *Lives and Legends of the English Bishops and Kings, Mediaeval Monks, and Other Later Saints* (London: George Bell, 1904), 107. David Hugh Farmer, ed., *The Oxford Dictionary of Saints*, 3d ed. (Oxford: Oxford University Press, 1992) recounts a version wherein he later repents and she restores his sight.

5. Farmer, *The Oxford Dictionary of Saints*, adds that her double monastery became the nucleus of the town of Oxford. She was formally adopted as patron of the university in the fifteenth century; her shrine was despoiled by Henry VIII's commissioners, restored under Mary Tudor, desecrated in 1558 by Calvinists out to suppress her cult, has been partially reconstructed from remains discovered in a well at Christ Church, and is still visited by pilgrims (189–90).

6. See, for example, the essays in Laurel Brake and Ian Small, eds., *Pater in the 1990s* (Greensboro: University of North Carolina Press, 1990), esp. Billie Andrew Inman, "Estrangement and Connection: Walter Pater, Benjamin Jowett, and William M. Hardinge" (1–20).

7. Richard Dellamora, *Masculine Desire: The Sexual Politics of Victorian Aestheticism* (Chapel Hill: University of North Carolina Press, 1990).

8. Wilde understood what Pater was after, referring to the passage as that "in which Botticelli's strange conception of the Virgin is so strangely set forth." Wilde, "Mr. Pater's *Appreciations*," *The Complete Works of Oscar Wilde*, introd. Padraic Colum (New York: Doubleday, 1923), 12:478.

9. Walter Pater, *The Renaissance*, ed. Adam Phillips (Oxford: Oxford University Press, 1986 [1873]), 75–76.

10. Paglia reads what she calls Leonardo's "suffocating doubling" here as "allegorical repletion" and claims that "this is no celebration of female power. . . . Leonardo finds the condition of male servitude intolerable." Camille Paglia, *Sexual Personae: Art and Decadence from Nefertiti to Emily Dickinson* (New York: Vintage, 1991 [1990]), 157. She also claims that "doubled female faces always signify an incestuous collapsing of identities, a chthonian undertow" (493). While I would not claim that doubled female faces always signify Sapphic intimacy, that seems to me one possibility in such an image. Since the boy children in Leonardo's painting appear loving and loved, they do not suggest "male servitude" to me.

11. In the cartoon, now in the National Gallery, London, Christ is playing with the child St. John. The painting is in the Louvre. In the context of my overall argument, its extremely high position in the Western art canon is important.

12. Reprinted in Lillian Faderman, *Chloe Plus Olivia* (New York: Penguin, 1994), 303–62.

13. Paglia wonders if Pater's vampiric Mona Lisa is "a lesbian adventuress diving into genital shadows for a slippery female pearl?" but claims that she is "mother nature as perceptual oppression." Paglia, *Sexual Personae*, 488.

14. Walter Pater, *Greek Studies: A Series of Essays*, ed. Charles L. Shadwell (New York: Macmillan, 1901 [1894]), 80–156.

15. Pater, "A Study of Dionysus: The Spiritual Form of Fire and Dew," ibid., 1–48, 38.

16. Dellamora, *Masculine Desire*, 170.

17. Victoria Glendinning, *Vita: The Life of Vita Sackville-West* (New York: Knopf, 1983), 180.

18. Judy Grahn, *Another Mother Tongue: Gay Words, Gay Worlds* (Boston: Beacon, 1990 [1984]), esp. 33–35, and Christine Downing, *Myths and Mysteries of Same-Sex Love* (New York: Continuum, 1990), esp. 201–4.

19. Pater, *The Renaissance*, 148.

20. Gerald Monsman, *Pater's Portraits: Mythic Pattern in the Fiction of Walter Pater* (Baltimore: Johns Hopkins University Press, 1967), points out that the gem, the flower, and the sea shell are "three of Pater's favorite objects of beauty" (215). All three are clitoral/vulval images, associated with Mary worship.

21. Virginia Woolf, *Mrs Dalloway* (London: Granada, 1976 [1925]), 164.

22. Virginia Woolf, *Orlando* (London: Granada, 1977 [1928]), 180.

23. All citations from J. G. Links's edition. John Ruskin, *The Stones of Venice* (London: Collins, 1960).

24. John Addington Symonds, *Studies of the Greek Poets*, 1st ser. (London: Smith, Elder, 1877), 1:117.

25. Havelock Ellis and John Addington Symonds, *Sexual Inversion* (London: Wilson and Macmillan, 1897; repr. New York: Arno, 1975).

26. If the *New York Times* article cited by Marjorie Garber, *Vested Interests: Cross-Dressing and Cultural Anxiety* (New York: Routledge, 1992), 1, is correct, and blue was the color for girls and pink for boys before World War I, then Symonds may be complicating his ideal of manliness. Nicola Beauman, *E. M. Forster: A Biography* (New York: Knopf, 1994), reads blue in Symonds "as a symbol of sexual passion and freedom" (122), a connotation borrowed by Forster in his use of blue. The color also had spiritual connotations, being Mary's color.

27. John Addington Symonds, *In the Key of Blue and Other Essays* (New York: Arno, 1970 [1892]), 91.

28. In "The Dantesque and Platonic Ideals of Love" Symonds takes the conventional view that "the worship of the maiden mother of Christ" fueled medieval cults of chivalrous heterosexual love.

29. Information and later quotes from Solomon's contemporaries are drawn from Simon Reynolds, *The Vision of Simeon Solomon* (Stroud: Catalpa, 1984). All the paintings I mention are reproduced in this volume, which also contains a reprint of "A Vision of Love Revealed in Sleep." All my references to the latter work are to this edition.

30. Simon Reynolds opens his study of Solomon with the famous peroration from the conclusion ("To burn always . . . the love of art for art's sake, has most") and an account of the lifelong friendship between the two men. Pater restored the conclusion in later editions.

31. Such is the force today of the assumption that Victorian male and female homoeroticism were unconnected that Emmanuel Cooper, in his account of Solomon's work, mentions only the representations of the former and not of the latter. Cooper, *The Sexual Perspective: Homosexuality and Art in the Last One Hundred Years in the West* (London: Routledge, 198), 65–70. Dellamora, *Masculine Desire*, reproduces Solomon's "Sappho and Erinna in the Garden Mytilene" but restricts his exegesis to Solomon's representations of male-male love.

32. Wilde, letter to Ralph Payne, February 12, 1894, in Rupert Hart-Davis, ed., *Selected Letters of Oscar Wilde* (Oxford: Oxford University Press, 1979), 116.

33. This passage is especially poignant, and almost as prophetic as the end of Shelley's *Adonais* when read in the light of Solomon's downfall two years later. After the *Vision* was published, his family repudiated him and after his arrest former friends like Swinburne denounced him in terms equally hysterical with homophobia and anti-Semitism: "Let us . . . give thanks that we are not as this Israelite" (82) and again "I do think a man is bound to consider the consequence to all his friends . . . of allowing his name to be mixed up with that of a—let us say, a Platonist, the term is at once accurate as a definition and unobjectionable as an euphemism" (84–5). Rossetti referred to Solomon's "vilest proclivities" (82) and Gosse to "his notorious vices" (86). Pater was one of the few friends who maintained contact with him. Solomon remained unrepentant, continued to paint, apparently reveled in shocking his respectable friends with his life as an alcoholic tramp in the underworld, and flirted with Catholicism, thus further alienating his family. He was admitted into a lunatic asylum for a while, although perfectly sane, and spent his last years in the workhouse where he died.

34. Guy Willoughby, *Art and Christhood: The Aesthetics of Oscar Wilde* (London: Associated University Presses, 1993), does examine the poems but performs the remarkable feat of never mentioning Mary. The book is a good example of what I have called Protestant bias in literary criticism.

35. Oscar Wilde, *Complete Works of Oscar Wilde*, introd. Vyvyan Holland (London: Collins, 1966), 732.

36. The displacement of Christ crucified by Christ as child, and thus of god's forgiveness by human love and forgiveness, is evident in Blake's poems. Shelley often commented on the unfortunate glorification of bloodshed in Christian iconography, for example:

> There was a J[esus] C[hrist] Crucified by the same [Guido], very fine. One gets tired indeed whatever may be the conception & execution of it of seeing that monotonous & agonized form forever exhibited in one prescriptive attitude of torture—but the Maddalena clinging to the cross with the look of passive & gentle despair . . . & the figure of St. John, with his looks uplifted in passionate compassion . . . of the contemplation of this one never would be weary.

Percy Bysshe Shelley, letter to T. L. Peacock, from Italy, November 9, 1818, in Frederick L. Jones, ed., *The Letters of Percy Bysshe Shelley* (Oxford: Oxford University Press, 1964), 2:50.

37. Wilde, February 28, 1895, *Selected Letters*, 129.

38. Alfred Douglas, "Two Loves," in Stephen Coote, ed., *The Penguin Book of Homosexual Verse* (Harmondsworth: Penguin, 1983), 264.

39. Susan Morgan, *In the Meantime: Character and Perception in Jane Austen's Fiction* (Chicago: University of Chicago Press, 1980).

4. Anarchist Feminism and the Homoerotic: Wilde, Carpenter, Shelley

1. One of the earliest full-scale considerations of Wilde's anarchist thought as an important intellectual influence on his society is George Woodcock, *Oscar Wilde: The Double Image* (Montreal: Black Rose, 1989 [1949]).

2. Linda Dowling, "The Decadent and the New Woman in the 1890s," *Nineteenth-Century Fiction* (1979), 33(4):435–53. Richard Dellamora, *Masculine Desire: The Sexual Politics of Victorian Aestheticism* (Chapel Hill: University of North Carolina Press, 1990), argues persuasively for the radical and feminist dimensions of male-male desire in Aestheticist discourse.

3. Teresa de Lauretis, *The Practice of Love: Lesbian Sexuality and Perverse Desire* (Bloomington: Indiana University Press, 1994), 193.

4. The participation of heterosexual men such as J. S. Mill is relatively more acknowledged whereas the only homosexual man whose participation is recognized is probably Edward Carpenter.

5. Most studies of lesbian images in nineteenth-century literature assume that such images are exoticized in a misogynist way by so-called Decadent male writers (see, for example, Lillian Faderman's preface to *Chloe Plus Olivia: An Anthology of Lesbian Literature from the Seventeenth Century to the Present* (New York: Penguin, 1994). While not denying such exoticization in the writings of some male writers such as Baudelaire and Symonds, I hope to demonstrate very different strategies in writings by other male homosexual writers.

6. Oscar Wilde, letter to Wemyss Reid, April 1887, in Rupert Hart-Davis, ed., *Selected Letters of Oscar Wilde* (Oxford: Oxford University Press, 1979), 67–69.

7. Janice Raymond notes that it was in convents that medieval women practiced the arts of weaving and embroidery and brought the art of design to perfection. Raymond, *A Passion for Friends* (Boston: Beacon, 1986), 84. Wilde, with his deep interest in design, is here acknowledging women ancestors.

8. He proposed to have articles on "the attitude of Universities towards women from the earliest times down to the present—a subject never fully treated of." Wilde, *Selected Letters*, 69.

9. See the Sunflower edition of *The Works of Oscar Wilde: Essays, Criticisms and Reviews*, introd. Richard Le Gallienne (New York: Lamb, 1909), 12:240.

10. Also, the catalogues of jewels, perfumes, and tapestries write female erotic images into history.

11. Leigh Hunt, *Men, Women, and Books* (New York: Harper, 1847), 2:95–124.

12. Reviewing *Darwinism and Politics*, a book by Mr. David Ritchie, an Oxonian, on the position and future of women in the modern state, Wilde agrees with the author's contention that the ethics of the family should not be separated from the ethics of the state, in the sense that all members should be equally educated and benefited. Wilde sums up in his own words:

The family ideal of the State may be difficult of attainment, but as an ideal it is better than the policeman theory. It would mean the moralisation of politics. The cultivation of separate sorts of virtues and separate ideals of duty in men and women has led to the whole social fabric being weaker and unhealthier than it need be.

Wilde, *The Works of Oscar Wilde,* 150.

13. Josephine Kamm, *How Different From Us: Miss Buss and Miss Beale* (London: Bodley Head, 1958), 171–72.

14. *Long Ago* was the title Michael Field chose for their 1889 collection of recreations of Sappho's lyrics.

15. He had worked with her in various organizations and they participated in several demonstrations together. They were among those who led the huge 1908 suffrage procession at Manchester.

16. Edward Carpenter, *My Days and Dreams* (London: George Allen and Unwin, 1916). Shelley is an example of a writer canonized more by popular acclaim than by academic approval.

17. Leslie Stephen, "Godwin and Shelley," in *Hours in a Library* (London: Smith, Elder, 1892), 3:94.

18. G. L. Dickinson, who wrote that the Shakespeare of the *Sonnets* and the Plato of *Phaedrus* and *Symposium* were the "only two people who have given expression to the experiences which to me are intense and profound" (in a love letter), was also enamored of Shelley. His poem "At Shelley's Grave" indicates that what he feels in common with the poet is not "wisdom" or "power" but "the better part, / A share of thine abundant love" (86). See Dennis Proctor, ed., *The Autobiography of Goldsworthy Lowes Dickinson* (London: Duckworth, 1973), 111.

19. John Addington Symonds, *Shelley* (New York: Harper, 1879), 10.

20. Before reading Barnefield's book I intended to undertake such a reading of Shelley's life and work as part of the present study. Since Barnefield has done it better than I can, I sum up his reading here.

21. The Cambridge edition, Percy Bysshe Shelley, *The Poetical Works of Shelley,* ed. Newell F. Ford (Boston: Houghton Mifflin, 1975).

22. The count accuses Lucretia in 2.i of harboring this thought and passing it on to the children. Lucretia denies it and he calls her a liar.

23. Stuart M. Sperry, "The Ethical Politics of Shelley's *The Cenci,*" *Studies in Romanticism* (1986), 25(3):411–28, is typical in ignoring Lucretia completely and focusing on the ethical problem of whether Beatrice was right or wrong in planning the murder, a plan he attributes solely to her. He concludes, like Stephen C. Behrendt, *Shelley and his Audiences* (Lincoln: University of Nebraska Press, 1989), and Robert F. Whitman, "Beatrice's 'Pernicious Mistake' in *The Cenci,*" *PMLA* (1959), vol. 74, that "she was wrong" (253). None of the male critics arriving at this "ethical" conclusion indicate whether she would have been "right" to continue getting raped.

5. The Search for a "Likeness": Shakespeare to Michael Field

1. *Plato: Phaedrus,* trans. Walter Hamilton (Harmondsworth: Penguin, 1973), 56–57.

2. John Milton, *Paradise Lost,* ed. Scott Elledge (New York: Norton, 1975).

3. Keats was perhaps the most conscious of the contrary pull between these two ancestors, when he described himself as abandoning his Miltonic strivings and devoting himself to Shakespearean negative capability.

4. William Shakespeare, *The Riverside Shakespeare*, ed. G. Blakemore Evans (Boston: Houghton Mifflin, 1974). All numbers in parentheses refer to sonnet numbers, not to page numbers.

5. I follow Bruce Smith, *Homosexual Desire in Shakespeare's England: A Cultural Poetics* (Chicago: University of Chicago Press, 1991), in reading the *Sonnets* as articulating a confessional homoerotic poetics of the beloved as what Smith terms a "secret sharer." Any such reading must inevitably be indebted to Joseph Pequigney's brilliant exegesis of the *Sonnets* in *Such Is My Love* (Chicago: University of Chicago Press, 1985).

6. This reading of 130 was developed in conversation with Leela Gandhi.

7. I differ here from Eve Sedgwick's view that male bonding in the sonnets occurs through the woman. See *Between Men: English Literature and Male Homosocial Desire* (New York: Columbia University Press, 1985), 28–48.

8. Lord Byron, *The Poetical Works of Lord Byron* (Philadelphia: Jas. B. Smith, 1855), 184, 3:6.

9. Jane Austen, January 29, 1813, *Jane Austen's Letters*, ed. R. W. Chapman (Oxford: Oxford University Press, 1979), 297. A metaphor she often repeated, for example, of *Sense and Sensibility* she wrote to Cassandra "I am never too busy to think of [it]. I can no more forget it than a mother can forget her suckling child." Quoted in John Halperin, *The Life of Jane Austen* (Sussex: Harvester, 1984), 197. See also 287.

10. Austen's frequent comments on the effects of childbearing on women show that she was vividly aware of the dangers involved: "I believe I never told you that Mrs. Coulthard and Anne, late of Manydown, are both dead, and both died in childbed. We have not regaled Mary with this news." Austen, letter to Cassandra, November 17, 1798, *Jane Austen's Letters*, 29. And, again, "Poor Animal, she will be worn out before she is thirty.—I am very sorry for her.—Mrs Clement too is in that way again, I am quite tired of so many Children—Mrs Benn has a 13th." Letter to Fanny Knight, March 23, 1817, ibid., 488. In a more caustic vein: "Mrs Hall, of Sherborne, was brought to bed yesterday of a dead child, some weeks before she expected, owing to a fright. I suppose she happened unawares to look at her husband." Letter to Cassandra, October 27, 1798, ibid., 24.

11. Jan Fergus, *Jane Austen and the Didactic Novel* (London: Macmillan, 1983), argues that "Emma is a comedy more of intimacy than of judgment" (134).

12. As Austen put it, writing to her niece and friend Fanny Knight: "Mr. J.W. frightens me. He will have you. . . . I only do not like you shd marry anybody. And yet I do wish you to marry very much, because I know you will never be happy till you are; but the loss of a Fanny Knight will never be made up to me; My 'affec:Neice F.C. Wildman' will be but a poor substitute." Austen, February 20, 1817, *Jane Austen's Letters*, 478.

13. All references are to Jane Austen, *Emma*, ed. Ronald Blythe (Harmondsworth: Penguin, 1966).

14. Ruth Perry, "Interrupted Friendships in Jane Austen's *Emma*," *Tulsa Studies in Women's Literature* (1986), 5(2):185–202, in an argument that privileges equality over intimacy in friendship, sees the Jane-Emma friendship, blocked by the plot, as the desirable one, since the relationship with Mrs. Weston is unequal. Bruce Stovel, "Emma's Search for a True Friend," *Persuasions* (1991), 13:58–68, argues in unabashed heterosexist terms that Mr. Knightley is from the start the only "true friend" possible for Emma and the novel is "emotionally satisfactory" because it presents her, like most women, moving away from having a best friend in a woman to "finding that friend in her husband" (67). Jacqueline Reid-Walsh, "Governess or Governor? The Mentor-Pupil Relation in *Emma*," *Persuasions* (1991), 13:108–117, makes a more sophisticated argument for the way Mr. Knightley and Mrs. Weston learn from each other as Emma learns from both.

15. James Edward Austen-Leigh, *Memoir of Jane Austen* (Oxford: Clarendon, 1926 [1871]), 16.

16. Quoted in George Holbert Tucker, "Jane Austen's Family," in David J. Grey, ed., *The Jane Austen Handbook* (London: Athlone, 1986), 149. All their lives they shared a bedroom even when extra rooms were available.

17. Austen, letter to Cassandra, September 8, 1816, *Jane Austen's Letters*, 464.

18. Jane Austen, *Catharine and Other Writings*, ed. Margaret Anne Doody and Douglas Murray (Oxford: Oxford University, 1993), 44.

19. Edmund Wilson, "A Long Talk about Jane Austen," *New Yorker*, October 13, 1940, may have been the first to note Emma's infatuations with women. Marvin Mudrick, *Jane Austen: Irony as Defense and Discovery* (New Jersey: Princeton University Press, 1952), argues that Emma's preference for women over men and her falling in love with Harriet (203) are evidence of her being a calculating egotistic bully and a cold snob. Perry, "Interrupted Friendships," 197–98, notes in passing that "certain elements of the action call attention to the ways in which compulsory heterosexuality disrupts and distorts the relationships between women." Most commentary today continues to focus on the heterosexual plot. For instance, Laura G. Mooneyham, *Romance, Language, and Education in Jane Austen's Novels* (London: Macmillan, 1988), is typical in reading the central conflict in each novel as between man and woman. She reads *Sense and Sensibility* as a failure because the main relationship is between two women and Emma's growth from "emotional coldness" (108) into an acceptance of marriage as "particularly poignant" in view of Austen's own situation at the time as a "confirmed aunt with no prospect of children of her own" (112).

20. Jocelyn Harris, *Jane Austen's Art of Memory* (Cambridge: Cambridge University Press, 1989), points out that all the characters fantasize wrongly about others. Mr. Knightley tries to shape Martin's life as Emma does Harriet's.

21. Quoted in David Lodge, ed., *Emma: A Casebook* (London: Aurora, 1970), 60.

22. Austen, November 18, 1814, *Jane Austen's Letters*, 409.

23. I differ here from Perry, who comments on "the double estrangement of Emma from Mrs Weston when the latter has a baby girl to engross her care." "Interrupted Friendships," 189.

24. Mr. Knightley's shift to Emma's home spares her the uprooting that heroines like Catherine Earnshaw must undergo. Austen almost always empowers her heroines by marriages to brother surrogates, thus confirming their position as daughters and legitimate heirs to the house rather than aliens entering it on sufferance as daughters-in-law.

25. In a similar situation, tragically conceived, when Maggie Tulliver refuses the Stephen-Maggie-Lucy or the Stephen-Maggie-Philip triangles that will separate her from her friends and compensate her with marriage, a girl baby is born and is named by its parents for her. The baby is Bob Jakin's, and he places it in Maggie's arms. To name a child for someone is to wish that it should become like her. This gesture is made at a moment when Maggie is in social disgrace and no conventional parent would want a daughter to take her for a model. Not the biological mother of a child, and having refused biological motherhood, Maggie, like St. Anne, holds, as it were, the Maggie of the future, who may live in freer circumstances, and the imagery that surrounds the moment suggests this powerfully: " 'Eh, Miss, how good the little un is wi' you! It's like as if it knowed you: it partly does, I'll be bound—like the birds know the mornin.' " The image of the birds, who sense the morning before it is visible and begin to sing, suggests the dawn of a new day for daughters of such parents as Bob who are able to recognize in Maggie's unconventional mind the seeds of the future.

26. Michael Williams, *Jane Austen: Six Novels and Their Methods* (London: Macmillan, 1986), 117.

27. Austen, letter to Fanny Knight, March 23, 1817, *Jane Austen's Letters*, 29, declared that Fielding's virtuous male-oriented heroines were "pictures of perfection" that made her "sick and wicked." She was an admirer of Richardson's Clarissa, whose devoted love for her friend Anna frames the story of her disastrous heterosexual romance. Emma sees Mrs. Weston as perfect, and Mr. Weston returns the compliment when he says that M and A (Emma) constitute perfection. Implicitly, Austen congratulates herself here on her portrait of Emma. The word "perfect" seems encoded through the nineteenth century to suggest the wholeness of love between women. Woolf, *A Room of One's Own* (New York: Harcourt Brace, 1929), 86, remarked that "all the great women of fiction were, until Jane Austen's day . . . seen only in relation to the other sex." Since *Emma* is that "new thing in English literature" on which Woolf remarked, wherein a woman likes a woman, Austen's satisfaction is not misplaced.

28. Austen, letter to Fanny Knight, February 20, 1817, *Jane Austen's Letters*, 478–79.

29. Austen, *Catharine*, 244–45.

30. Ibid., 238–39.

31. Virginia Woolf, April 15, 1931, *The Letters of Virginia Woolf*, ed. Nigel Nicolson and Joanne Trautmann (London: Hogarth, 1975–80), 4:313.

32. Mary Gordon, *Chase of the Wild Goose* (New York: Arno Press, 1975 [1936]), 273.

33. Eleanor Butler, November 20, 1785, Elizabeth Mavor, ed., *A Year with the Ladies of Llangollen* (Harmondsworth: Penguin, 1984), 205. All references are to journal entries written by Butler, unless otherwise indicated. Jane Austen's will left everything she had to "my dearest sister Cassandra Elizabeth" and appointed her executrix. *Jane Austen's Letters*, 504. Halperin, *The Life of Jane Austen*, 343–44, points out that it was unusual for a woman to act as executrix and that Austen departed from tradition in not naming a brother.

34. Byrne R. S. Fone, "This Other Eden: Arcadia and the Homosexual Imagination," in Stuart Kellogg, ed., *Essays on Gay Literature* (New York: Harrington Park, 1985), stresses the classical roots of the idea of the garden as a place of seclusion and escape where homosexual lovers may transform their outcast status into that of spiritual outsiders. He writes only of men; while drawing on this common tradition, the Ladies of Llangollen also rewrite the Judeo-Christian originary myth, suggesting that the perfection of innocent eroticism is to be found between two women.

35. Mrs. G. H. Bell, ed., *The Hamwood Papers of the Ladies of Llangollen* (London: Macmillan, 1930), 42.

36. See Lillian Faderman, *Chloe Plus Olivia* (New York: Penguin, 1994), 37–43. In a poem, "To Miss Ponsonby" (43), Anna Seward describes the ladies as leading "the life of angels in an Eden."

37. Anna Seward to Sarah Ponsonby, June 19, 1798, 120; October 30, 1797, 196, Mavor, *A Year with the Ladies*.

38. For an exegesis of the play along these lines, see my " 'Shall We Part, Sweet Girl?' The Role of Celia in *As You Like It*," *Yearly Review* (1990), no. 4, pp. 43–55.

39. Sarah Ponsonby to Anna Seward, February 19, 1797, Mavor, *A Year with the Ladies*, 52.

40. May 28, 1786, ibid., 90.

41. Ibid., 116.

42. Gordon, *Chase of Wild Goose*, 156. Gordon stresses these constructions of ancestry and inserts herself into them in an appendix where she visits Plas Newydd and has a long conversation with the ladies' ghosts.

43. Ibid., 31, 73, 126, 166.

44. Bell, *The Hamwood Papers*, 304.

45. Sarah Ponsonby to Mrs. Parker, December 18, 1818, Mavor, *A Year with the Ladies*, 231; Eleanor Butler uses the same phrase, for example, in journal entries August 27, 1807, 161, and May 26, 1799, 103, idem.

46. April 11, 1785, ibid., 71–72.

47. July 30, 1790, Bell, *The Hamwood Papers*, 257–58.

48. Mavor, *A Year with the Ladies*, 172. This uninhibited lady was the sister of Thomas Bowdler, who immortalized his name by expurgating Shakespeare.

49. Letter to Mrs. Mathews, September 4, 1820, ibid., 178.

50. Sarah had encountered one sort of male violence when, as a young girl, she had been pursued by her aunt's husband, Sir William Fownes. Unwilling to hurt her invalid aunt by informing her of this ("I would rather die than wound Lady Betty's heart," she wrote), she suffered in silence, appealing for help to Mrs. Goddard and to Eleanor. Before leaving Woodstock, she denounced Sir William in Mrs. Goddard's presence, refused monetary assistance from him, and declared that "she would live and die with Miss Butler." Gordon, *Chase of Wild Goose*, 276–77.

51. December 11 and 12, 1788, Mavor, *A Year with the Ladies*, 222–24.

52. January 22, 1788, ibid., 26.

53. February 4, 1790, ibid., 46.

54. Ibid., 231.

55. "To the Lady E.B. and the Hon. Miss P.," in Thomas Hutchinson, ed., *Poetical Works* (London: Henry Frowde, 1906), 272.

56. Faderman, *Chloe Plus Olivia*, 34.

57. John Boswell, *Same-Sex Unions in Pre-Modern Europe* (New York: Villard, 1994), 74.

58. Ibid., 74n106.

59. Ibid., 74–75n108.

60. Reprinted in Bernard Grebanier, *The Uninhibited Byron: An Account of His Sexual Confusion* (New York: Crown, 1970), appendix 327.

61. I follow Chris White, " 'Poets and Lovers Evermore': The Poetry and Journals of Michael Field," in Joseph Bristow, ed., *Sexual Sameness: Textual Differences in Lesbian and Gay Writing* (London: Routledge, 1992), 26–43, in reading the two women as lovers, rather than Lillian Faderman, *Surpassing the Love of Men: Romantic Friendship and Love Between Women from the Renaissance to the Present* (London: Women's Press, 1981), who reads them as romantic friends (although in *Chloe Plus Olivia* she is more open to the possibility of their having been lovers). The evidence for erotic feeling between the two women seems to me even stronger than White allows.

62. November 23, 1884, T. and D. C. Sturge Moore, eds., *Works and Days: From the Journal of Michael Field* (London: John Murray, 1933), 6–7.

63. This may be the reason why, like Emily Brontë, they "belong altogether outside the tradition of Victorian women's verse" (204) constructed by Angela Leighton, *Victorian Women Poets: Writing Against the Heart* (Charlottseville: University Press of Virginia, 1992). I agree with Leighton's emphasis on Michael Field's active assumption of the role of "lover," which I interpret as central to lesbian self-construction. I differ from her view that they lacked "socio-political commitment" (204), since I see them as active members of Aestheticist circles that she reads as apolitical and masculinist (217–18) and I as anarchist, feminist, and proto-gay/lesbian.

64. Moore, *Works and Days*, 276, entry by Edith.

65. May 29, 1884, ibid., 3.

66. May 31, 1884, ibid., 5.

67. 1888, ibid., 59.

68. Mary Sturgeon, *Michael Field* (New York: Macmillan, 1922), 37. Much of my information is drawn from Sturgeon's pioneering book.

69. June 16, 1885, Moore, *Works and Days*.

70. *Underneath the Bough: A Book of Verses* (London: George Bell, 1893), 68–69.

71. Ibid., 77–78.

72. Sturgeon, *Michael Field*, 47.

73. Moore, *Works and Days*, 193.

74. *Underneath the Bough*, 67–8.

75. Letter to Robert Browning, November 23, 1884, Moore, *Works and Days*, 6.

76. Ibid., 127.

77. *Underneath the Bough*, 72–74.

78. As White, "Poets and Lovers," 31, points out, in Michael Field's formulation "virginity is not sterile . . . it . . . . embraces . . . an all-women community" and "includes fellowship and equality with men."

79. Michael Field, *Wild Honey from Various Thyme* (London: T. Fisher Unwin, 1908), 168.

80. *Underneath the Bough*, 71.

81. Ibid., 67.

82. Ibid., 66–67.

83. Ibid., 80–82.

84. Ibid., 78–79.

85. Moore, *Works and Days*, 50.

86. Ibid., 56.

87. Ibid., 47.

88. Sturgeon, *Michael Field*, 85.

89. Leighton's comment, *Victorian Women Poets*, 204, "It is at once a strength and a limitation of Michael Field's poetry that 'the cost and pain' of women's experience, with all its forbidden fruits and sexual falls, is hardly ever counted," assumes that lesbian experience involves no cost or pain.

90. Field, *Wild Honey*, 28. Further references to page numbers from this volume will appear parenthetically in text.

91. "Fading" in Moore, *Works and Days*, 330.

92. Moore, *Works and Days*, 323–24. Edenic dual solitude was crucial to Michael Field's view of their life as it was to the Ladies of Llangollen's view of theirs.

93. Ibid., 324. Clitoral imagery (buds, gems, seeds) is all-pervasive in Field's writings.

94. Letter of December 30, 1877, Moore, *Works and Days*, 158.

95. Letter of April 15, 1877, Moore, *Works and Days*, 154.

96. Ibid., 118–119.

97. This first conversation took place on June 21, 1890. Ibid., 135–38, entry by Katherine.

98. Ibid., 138.

99. Charles Ricketts, *Self-Portrait Taken from the Letters and Journals of Charles Ricketts, R.A.*, collected T. Sturge Moore, ed. Cecil Lewis (London: Peter Davies, 1939), 49–50. Ricketts wrote a passionate defense of Wilde as a man and an artist, *Oscar Wilde: Recollections by Jean Paul Raymond and Charles Ricketts* (Bloomsbury: Nonesuch, 1932). Raymond was an invented figure. When Wilde was released from prison,

Ricketts sent him a hundred pounds, which "Robbie Ross took good care was returned, as he knew the sender could ill afford to spare it." *Self Portrait*, 106, note.

100. Michael Field papers, British Library, ADD. Mss. 46789, vol. 14, 1900, f 162, Nov. 30, under clipping announcing the death of Wilde. Edith also records the withering effect of the news on Michael and how, in conversations with Ricketts and other common friends, they shrank from the mention of Oscar's death, yet could not avoid it, and mitigated grief by recounting his own fables about joy and sorrow.

101. Ricketts was sixteen when he met Shannon, then nineteen. They lived together all their life, sharing everything. That they saw their partnership as a marriage is indicated by Ricketts writing to Gordon Bottomley on October 2, 1916, that the day was his fiftieth birthday and the thirty-fourth anniversary of his first meeting with Shannon. Ricketts, *Self-Portrait*, 266–67.

102. J. G. Paul Delaney, ed., *Some Letters from Charles Ricketts and Charles Shannon to "Michael Field" (1894–1902)* (Edinburgh: Tragara, 1979), 5–6.

103. Letter dated late 1894, ibid., 9.

104. Charles Ricketts, *Michael Field*, ed. J. G. Paul Delaney (Edinburgh: Tragara, 1976), 4.

105. Delaney's introduction, ibid., v. Edith's comparison of Shannon to a Della Francesca angel and Ricketts to Christ is also interesting, suggesting the homoeroticization of the Christ-angel relationship in Renaissance paintings (iii).

106. Ibid., 12.

107. Ricketts records in his journal on Nov. 3, 1905, his shock at a "tragedy" reported in the paper where "two women in love" correspond with each other "in cipher with reference to poems by Dowson and Arthur Symons." One of the women, Dora, is dying of consumption; when her friend receives a message from relatives "Dora asleep" she understands her to have died and commits suicide, whereupon Dora actually dies. The woman who committed suicide was the wife of a blind parson arrested for sodomy. In her suicide note she wrote to him: "You are the only man I could love, the others disgust me!" Ricketts, *Self-Portrait*, 125–26.

108. Of course, this sympathy was not restricted to the homosexual community. Ricketts, May 29, 1914 journal entry, *Self-Portrait*, 195, reports a conversation with Yeats: "Yeats spoke with great intelligence of the British public during its quite senseless bursts of revengeful hypocrisy and morality such as it displayed in the Parnell case, the Wilde case. . . . The rage against Wilde was also complicated by the Britisher's jealousy of art and the artist."

109. Journal entry January 8, 1896, ibid., 12.

110. Michael Field, *Dedicated: An Early Work of Michael Field* (London: George Bell, 1914), 28–34. Katherine published this collection of Edith's early poems after Edith's death.

111. Ibid., 240.

112. Ibid., 260.

113. "Saint Sebastian—Correggio, The Dresden Gallery" in Michael Field, *Sight and Song* (London: Elkin Mathews and John Lane, 1892), 32–33.

114. It is important, in this context, to note that the support was mutual. When *The Well of Loneliness* was banned Ricketts, *Self-Portrait*, 405–6, wrote a letter of protest to the *Observer*, invoking Milton against censorship and declaring that "literature . . . has saved us in the past from witch-burnings, and perhaps over-frequent and inhuman hangings." He kept press clippings of the trial and sent them to his friends, describing the book as "a very sincere, tragic . . . study of a woman who does not like men," which " could be given to a girl of fourteen to read" (408).

115. Ibid., 69–74.

116. Vernon Lee, *Renaissance Fancies and Studies* (London: Smith, Elder, 1896), 237.

117. Charles Ricketts, *Some Letters*, 6.

118. Ibid., 11, letter quoted in endnote.

119. Sturgeon, *Michael Field*, 94. Leighton, *Victorian Women Poets*, 223, argues that faith turns their poetry "towards . . . flaccid and flowery decadence."

120. Michael Field, *Mystic Trees* (London: Eveleigh Nash, 1913), 51.

121. Michael Field, *Poems of Adoration* (London: Sands, 1912), 25.

122. Ibid., 23–24.

123. Ibid., 34–35.

124. Field, *Mystic Trees*, 124.

125. Ibid., 36.

126. Ibid., 92.

127. Ibid., 139. Given their research on Sappho and familiarity with classical sources, also perhaps an echo of Sappho as nightingale.

128. William Blake, "Milton," in Geoffrey Keynes, ed., *The Complete Writings of William Blake* (London: Oxford University Press, 1966), 117–18.

129. Ibid., 147.

6. "Sapphic Virgins": Mythmaking Around Love Between Women in Meredith, Forster, Hope Mirrlees

1. "Love's Coming of Age," extracted in Edward Carpenter, *Edward Carpenter: Selected Writings*, introd. Noel Greig (London: GMP, 1984), 1:103.

2. The centrality of this conflict to Meredith's fiction, which is absent from the "source" story of Lady Caroline Norton, renders the latter, in my view, of less than crucial importance. Janet Horowitz Murray, *Courtship and the English Novel: Feminist Readings in the Fiction of George Meredith* (New York: Garland, 1987), reads the intimacy of the two women as "primary" and as evidence of Meredith's "feminism" (170) and notes that Diana's distance from Emma, entailed by Sir Lukin's conduct, is "the measure of her distance from herself" (140), but does not draw out the erotic implications of the relationship or place its construction in a literary tradition. Despite Murray's persuasive reading, such is the power of heterosexism even within feminism that Nikki Lee Manor in her paper "Mythmaking in Meredith's *Diana of the Crossways*," presented at the 1994 MLA convention, did not even mention Emma.

3. It figures in more than one narrative of love between women, not just in Austen but in the 1777 anonymous narrative poem *Danebury*, where Emma risks her life to save that of her beloved "kindred soul," Elfrida, by sucking the poison out of the latter's wound. See Stephen Coote, ed., *The Penguin Book of Homosexual Verse* (Harmondsworth: Penguin, 1983), 185–92.

4. Murray, *Courtship and the English Novel*, 169, thinks Emma and Diana "too concerned with 'Friendship' as a religion. This sort of exaggerated utterance seems to me to be more characteristic of male friendships than of friendship between women." The evidence collected by Lillian Faderman in *Surpassing the Love of Men* (London: Women's Press, 1981) suggests otherwise; Meredith is one of the few male writers to represent at length the kind of language used by such women as Anna Seward.

5. John Boswell, *Same-Sex Unions in Pre-Modern Europe* (New York: Villard, 1994), remarks that the ritual of drinking from a common cup, present both in heterosexual marriage ceremonies and in ceremonies of same-sex union, was "not originally eucharistic, but a survival of . . . pagan chalice-based matrimonial rituals" (203–4). Emma's phrase "grandly historic" is singularly apposite.

6. This point is made by Jan B. Gordon, *"Diana of the Crossways*: Internal History and the Brainstuff of Fiction," in Ian Fletcher, ed., *Meredith Now: Some Critical Essays* (London: Routledge, 1971), 246–64.

7. That the idea persists in different forms is suggested by the lesbian singer Melissa Etheridge's remark: "I heard that in the hierarchy of reincarnation the lowest form is a heterosexual man. Then as you go up the ladder, the highest reincarnation form is a lesbian." Etheridge, *Advocate*, January 24, 1995, 14. Is it from such a reading of the image that the early American lesbian magazine the *Ladder* derived its name?

8. Forster always acknowledged Jane Austen, George Meredith, and Samuel Butler as shaping influences on his work. See Nicola Beauman, *E. M. Forster: A Biography* (New York: Routledge, 1992), 168.

9. Shelley, *The Poetical Works of Shelley*, ed. Newell F. Ford (Boston: Houghton Mifflin, 1975), 136–51. I am grateful to Shobhana Bhattacharjee for drawing my attention to this poem.

10. E. M. Forster, *Howards End*, ed. Oliver Stallybrass (London: Edward Arnold, 1973 [1910]), 71.

11. Jeane N. Olson, "E. M. Forster's Prophetic Vision of the Modern Family in *Howards End*," *Texas Studies in Language and Literature*, 35:3, 347–62, offers a heterosexually biased feminist reading, arguing that "Margaret's vision is . . . to become an equal partner in the marriage," a "matriarch" (357–58), who has learnt from Mrs. Wilcox, the "mother figure" she needed.

12. Elizabeth Langland, "Gesturing Toward an Open Space: Gender, Form, and Language in E. M. Forster's *Howards End*," in Laura Claridge and Elizabeth Langland, eds., *Out of Bounds: Male Writers and Gender(ed) Criticism* (Amherst: University of Massachusets Press, 1990), points out the importance of the Margaret-Helen relationship and the positive reaction of contemporary reviewers, some of whom thought the author must be a woman writing under a male pseudonym. But she sees Margaret as dismantling the binary opposites of masculine represented by Henry Wilcox and feminine represented by Helen and does not examine the Margaret-Ruth Wilcox relationship.

13. "The Poetry of Michelangelo" in Adam Phillips, ed., *The Renaissance* (Oxford: Oxford University Press, 1986 [1873]), 52.

14. "Leonardo da Vinci," Phillips, *The Renaissance*, 80.

15. John Boswell, *The Kindness of Strangers: The Abandonment of Children in Western Europe from Late Antiquity to the Renaissance* (New York: Vintage, 1990 [1988]), 28–29.

16. Neil Heims, "Forster's *Howards End*," *The Explicator*, 42:1, 39–41, points out Forster's quote from *Adonais* in this passage, "the white radiance" of "a more inward light" casting into shade the Wilcox colors.

17. The first legal judgment in England since the Reformation on the validity of gifts to Roman Catholic convents was passed in 1871 in the case of Cox vs. Manners when the husband of Mrs. Frances Manners challenged his wife's decision to will parts of her estate to two convents and the court upheld her right to do so. See Walter L. Arnstein, *Protestant versus Catholic in Mid-Victorian England* (Columbia: University of Missouri Press, 1982), 162.

18. John Fletcher, "Forster's Self-Erasure: *Maurice* and the Scene of Masculine Love," in Joseph Bristow, ed., *Sexual Sameness: Textual Differences in Lesbian and Gay Writing* (London: Routledge, 1992), 64–90.

19. Lionel Trilling, *E. M. Forster: A Study* (London: Hogarth, 1951), is one of the few critics to acknowledge this, but disapproves: "It is not entirely a happy picture . . . the male is too thoroughly gelded" (116).

20. Margaret addresses both Helen and Mr. Wilcox as "darling."

21. Virginia Woolf, September 24, 1919, in Nigel Nicolson and Joanne Trautmann, eds., *The Letters of Virginia Woolf* (London: Hogarth, 1975–80), 2:391. The novel appears to have been entirely neglected since then.

22. "Madeleine," *Times Literary Supplement*, October 9, 1919, in Andrew McNeillie, ed., *The Essays of Virginia Woolf* (London: Hogarth, 1988), 3:108–9.

23. Hope Mirrlees, *Madeleine: One of Love's Jansenists* (London: W. Collins, 1919), 76.

24. Madeleine de Scudéry (1607–1701), sister of Georges de Scudéry, never married, lived with her brother, and wrote novels that are landmarks in the history of the French novel. Several are romans à clef. In one of these, *Le Grand Cyrus*, she is named Sappho, and this became her pseudonym. She was a member of the first Parisian salon at the Hotel de Rambouillet, house of Catherine de Vivonne Rambouillet.

25. Jansenism was a Calvinized form of Catholicism that suggested salvation was predestined for those elected by god. It serves as a metaphor here for a homoerotically inclined intellectual elite's perception of its own "difference" as superiority.

26. Queen Christina of Sweden, who lived openly as a lesbian, met and corresponded with Madeleine de Scudéry.

27. That these lesbian tropes had become well-formulated enough by the early twentieth century to be parodied is evident in the writings of Ronald Firbank. The tropes that make an appearance in his 1916 novel *Inclinations* include the older and the younger woman, women writing the biographies of women, the Vampire, and the exchange of blood, images of oysters, porpoises, the wild goose, the moon, shadows, gems—especially pearls, violets—and the parting of leaves to find a rosy bud, Greece and the Greeks, Sappho, the Virgin Mary, the use of male names for women, and the older woman and younger man as rivals for the younger woman's love.

28. Evelyn Underhill, *Mysticism* (New York: New American Library, 1974 [1910]), 44.

29. Dennis Proctor, ed., *The Autobiography of Goldsworthy Lowes Dickinson* (London: Duckworth, 1973), 249–52.

7. Biography as Homoerotic Fiction: Freud, Pater, and Woolf

1. Leslie Stephen, "National Biography," *Studies of a Biographer* (London: Duckworth, 1898), 1:1–36.

2. Thomas Carlyle, "The Hero as Poet," *On Heroes and Hero-Worship* (London: Oxford University Press, 1959 [1841]), 61.

3. Ibid., 142.

4. Michel Foucault, *The History of Sexuality*, trans. Robert Hurley (New York: Vintage Books, 1990), 1:101.

5. Sharon Bassett, "Pater and Freud on Leonardo da Vinci: Two Views of the Hero of Art," *Literature and Psychology* (1973), 23:21–26, reads the two essays as similar in their approach to the artist but discusses them without mentioning homosexuality.

6. Sigmund Freud, *Leonardo da Vinci: A Study in Psychosexuality*, trans. A. A. Brill (New York: Random House, 1947), 28.

7. As David Garrett pointed out in a term paper written for me at Cornell, the original quote is mistranslated by Freud; properly translated it reads: "Nothing can be loved if not first considered"—the Italian *cognition* implies consideration, but not to an extreme degree. Also, that love springs from knowledge was a commonplace in Italian Renaissance thought.

8. Freud's analysis of Leonardo's sexuality depends crucially on his assumption, without any evidence, that Caterina "enjoyed" heterosexual love, never got any more

of it after her relationship with Leonardo's father, and therefore transferred her "ungratified" desires to her infant son. *Leonardo da Vinci*, 95.

9. As Louise DeSalvo argues:

> Setting themselves up as superior to the experience described on the page . . . many contemporary literary critics, while thinking themselves radical, protect themselves from feeling the pain of the uttered word. . . . These critics pull out their heavy artillery, the "in" literary critical terminology, and they aim it at the page. . . . The effect of using this homogenized language . . . suggests that one work of literature is very much like another. . . . I believe much of contemporary literary critical discourse is an act that is hostile to the work, rather than in sympathy with it, an act that tries to tear down and destroy what the author has very carefully constructed. . . . Contemporary critical discourse . . . struts and postures . . . and asserts power over the work. . . . It commits a violation."

"Virginia Woolf: Incest Survivor" in Mark Hussey and Vara Neverow-Turk, eds., *Virginia Woolf Miscellanies* (New York: Pace University Press, 1992), 165–66.

10. H.D., *Notes on Thought and Vision* (written 1919; San Francisco: City Lights, 1982), 26.

11. I do not wish to discount the radicalism of Freud's essay in its time. To a contemporary reader it very likely was empowering in its suggestion that genius may draw on homosexual feeling. Freud played a crucial role in helping some women such as H.D. accept their bisexuality. Her wonderful poem to him uses coded images of "volcanic desire / anemones like embers / and purple fire / of violets" to distinguish between vaginal and clitoral eroticism, and concludes that she "had two loves separate; / God who loves all mountains, / alone knew why / and understood / and told the old man / to explain / the impossible / which he did." H.D., *Collected Poems: 1912–1944*, ed. Louis L. Martz (New York: New Directions, 1983), 453.

12. Sheila Jeffreys, *The Spinster and Her Enemies: Feminism and Sexuality, 1880–1930* (London: Pandora, 1985), demonstrates how the ideology of the sexual revolution imposed compulsory heterosexuality on women in new ways in the twentieth century and was used as a weapon against unmarried and lesbian feminists.

13. Barbara Fassler, "Theories of Homosexuality as Sources of Bloomsbury's Androgyny," *Signs* (1979), 5:249.

14. Noel Annan points out that "for fifty years he was never not hopelessly in love with another person" (6) and that "long familiarity with personal anguish" (8) constantly fueled his political work for disadvantaged groups. "Foreword" in Dennis Proctor, ed., *The Autobiography of G. Lowes Dickinson and Other Unpublished Writings* (London: Duckworth, 1973).

15. Quoted in George Spater and Ian Parsons, *A Marriage of True Minds: An Intimate Portrait of Leonard and Virginia Woolf* (London: Hogarth, 1977), 59.

16. Virginia Woolf, October 7, 1924, in Anne Olivier Bell, ed., *The Diary of Virginia Woolf* (London: Hogarth, 1977–82), 2:317.

17. Lytton Strachey, November 8, 1912, in Leonard Woolf and James Strachey, eds., *Virginia Woolf and Lytton Strachey: Letters* (London: Hogarth, 1956), 42.

18. Woolf, December 12, 1917, *The Diary*, 1:89.

19. Woolf, to Jacques Raverat, January 24, 1924, in Nigel Nicolson and Joanne Trautmann, eds., *The Letters of Virginia Woolf* (London: Hogarth, 1975–80), 3:155.

20. Woolf, to Molly MacCarthy, March 1912, *The Letters*, 1:492.

21. Woolf, May 12, 1923, *The Diary*, 2:243.

22. Woolf, January 24, 1924, *The Letters*, 3:155; November 18, 1924, *The Diary*, 2:322.

23. Woolf, to Vita Sackville-West, March 16, 1926, *The Letters*, 3:247.

24. Woolf, to Ethel Smyth, August 15, 1930, ibid. 4:200.

25. Carolyn G. Heilbrun, *Toward Androgyny: Aspects of Male and Female in Literature* (London: Victor Gollancz, 1973), 153.

26. Woolf, June 11, 1922, *The Diary*, 2:177–78.

27. Woolf, to Lytton Strachey, October 22, 1915, *The Letters*, 2:67.

28. Woolf, April 14, 1927, ibid., 3:362; May 22, 1927, ibid., 3:381.

29. Woolf, to Ethel Smyth, July 29, 1934, ibid., 5:319.

30. Woolf, to Ethel Smyth, August 7 and 8, 1932, ibid., 5:85.

31. Woolf, October 17, 1921, ibid., 2:485.

32. Virginia Woolf and E. M. Forster, *Nation*, September 8, 1928.

33. Woolf, January 24, 1924, *The Letters*, 3:155–56.

34. Recent Woolf scholarship has amply and brilliantly demonstrated the lesbian dimensions of Woolf's fictions. In accordance with the project of this book, I examine a less-explored area, that of alliances between lesbians and gay men in her writings. It has often been assumed that she was homophobic and Forster misogynist and lesbophobic. While not attempting to deny the inevitable existence of misogyny and homophobia in the mentality of everyone living in a misogynist homophobic society, I see both writers as engaged in a continual struggle with these prejudices in themselves and in each other.

35. Virginia Woolf, *The Voyage Out* (London: Granada, 1978 [1915]), 269.

36. Ian Young, "The Flower Beneath the Foot: A Short History of the Gay Novel" in Ian Young, ed., *The Male Homosexual In Literature: A Bibliography* (London: Scarecrow, 1982), 244.

37. Virginia Woolf, *Jacob's Room* (London: Granada, 1978 [1922]), 73.

38. Virginia Woolf, *To the Lighthouse* (Harmondsworth: Penguin, 1964 [1927]), 23.

39. Virginia Woolf, *A Room of One's Own* (London: Collins, 1977 [1929]), 88.

40. Sir Leslie Stephen and Sir Sydney Lee, eds., *The Dictionary of National Biography* (Oxford: Oxford University Press, 1921–22; 1959–60 [1917]), 1:1044.

41. Lord Byron, *Lord Byron's Correspondence, Chiefly with Lady Melbourne, Mr Hobhouse, The Hon. Douglas Kinnaird and P.B.Shelley*, ed. John Murray (London: John Murray, 1922). See Woolf, February 18, 1922, *The Diary*, 2:168, "the sight of the new Byron letters just come from Mudie's," and the editorial footnote.

42. Lord Byron, *The Life, Letters, and Journals of Lord Byron*, ed. Thomas Moore (vol. 1, January 1830; vol. 2, December 1830; repr. London: John Murray, 1932). See Brenda R. Silver, *Virginia Woolf's Reading Notebooks* (Princeton: Princeton University Press, 1983), 113, for the reference to Woolf's note in the Holograph Reading Notes, vol. 20 at the Berg.

43. Byron, letter 19, to Mr. Murray, *The Life of Byron*, 60.

44. Byron, fragment of a letter to Bankes, circa March 1807, ibid., 42.

45. Byron, letter 109, to Bankes, ibid., 173.

46. Byron, letter 356, to Bankes, February 19, 1820, ibid., 435.

47. Details from Neill Bartlett, *Who Was That Man: A Present for Mr. Oscar Wilde* (London: Serpent's Tail, 1988), 58–59; and Louis Crompton, *Byron and Greek Love* (Berkeley: University of California Press, 1985).

48. In this story a prosperous elderly widower has an encounter with a young milkman; the latter, when arrested, goes to prison without betraying the former, who, when he later learns of this, notes the youth's name, Arthur Snatchfold, as that of "his lover, yes, his lover."

49. "Clive on the bench will continue to sentence Alec in the dock. Maurice may get off." Forster, September 1960, *Maurice* (written 1917; Harmondsworth: Penguin, 1972), 222.

50. There is also a "William Banks" (1820–1872) in the *Dictionary*. He was famous for his manuals on walks in Yorkshire. Interestingly, Woolf also gave the name *William* to the homosexual Dodge in *Between the Acts*. Dodge reveals his first name to the two women who befriend him; toward the end of *To the Lighthouse*, Lily, after a lifetime's friendship with Bankes, thinks of him as "William," as did Mrs. Ramsay. *William* was also the name of the most famous chosen ancestor of English nineteenth-century homosexual writers, the Shakespeare of the *Sonnets*.

51. Eileen Barrett makes the delightful suggestion that the private flower refused to Bankes by Cam recalls Private Flower! Barrett, in correspondence, 1994.

52. Thus, Woolf, May 17, 1925, *The Diary*, 3:22, "the only judgment on Mrs D. I await with trepidation (but thats too strong) is Morgan's. He will say something enlightening," and May 20, 1925, *The Diary*, 3:24, "Well, Morgan admires. This is a weight off my mind. . . . kissed my hand and on going said he was awfully pleased." She declared herself more invigorated by Lytton's dislike of *Mrs. Dalloway* than by the praise of Clive and others. June 18, 1925, *The Diary*, 3:32.

53. Woolf, October 28, 1919, *The Letters*, 2:394 (in the context of *Night and Day*).

54. Woolf, August 31, 1928, *Diary*, 3:193. On this occasion, Forster acknowledged "he thought Sapphism disgusting: partly from convention, partly because he disliked that women should be independent of men." That he realized this feeling was not rational, and did not make it his political stance, is clear from the fact that a month later, he wrote the letter with Woolf, protesting the banning of *The Well*.

55. Woolf, November 27, 1925, *Diary*, 3:48.

56. That waiting hopelessly for a brief moment of mutuality constituted the experience of many homosexuals in a heterosexist society is suggested by this poignant 1923 journal entry by G. L. Dickinson when on holiday with his beloved, Peter Savary:

Shall I see him tonight? Will he come to me and kiss me? . . . But night came . . . and he did not come, and in torture I drugged myself to sleep. . . . He is in bed and needs his sleep . . . and I, as always, wait, wait, wait, the same at 60 as at 25. Do we never learn and never change?

Proctor, *Autobiography of Dickinson*, 130. Dorothy Strachey, Lytton's sister, recorded in her autobiographical lesbian novel *Olivia* (1949) the same kind of anguish, when, as a girl, she waited in bed for her adored schoolmistress to give her a goodnight kiss.

57. The kind of highly successful war poetry in which a man mourned the loss of male soldier-lovers was perhaps most famously exemplified in the verse of Siegfried Sassoon, Forster's and Woolf's young friend.

58. *Mary* is also Stephen Gordon's second name, and the first name of her beloved.

59. Suggestion made by Eileen Barrett, in correspondence, 1994.

8. The Wilde-ness of Woolf: Evading and Embracing Death in Orlando and The Waves

1. Perry Meisel, *The Absent Father: Virginia Woolf and Walter Pater* (New Haven: Yale University Press, 1980), 45. The point was also made by J. E. Chamberlin, *Ripe was the Drowsy Hour: The Age of Oscar Wilde* (New York: Seabury, 1977), 205n39.

2. The neglect has carried over into many critical appraisals of Woolf, for example, Janus M. Paul, *The Victorian Heritage of Virginia Woolf* (Norman, Okla.: Pilgrim, 1987), does not mention Pater and mentions Wilde only once, to say that the "liberating force" (10) of his aestheticism never reached Virginia Stephen. S. P. Rosenbaum, *Victorian Bloomsbury* (New York: St. Martin's, 1987), makes more of the Pater-Wilde influence, but argues that Bloomsbury "aesthetics developed out of puritan, utilitarian Cambridge rather than Anglo-Roman Catholic Idealist Oxford" (30).

3. Wyndham Lewis, *Men Without Art* (London: Cassell, 1934), 170–71.

4. Perry Meisel, *The Absent Father*, xiii.

5. Ibid., 34.

6. Richard Ellmann, *Oscar Wilde* (London: Penguin, 1988 [1987]), 95.

7. See Mary Hyde, ed., *Bernard Shaw and Alfred Douglas: A Correspondence* (London: John Murray, 1982), 114.

8. Ellmann, *Oscar Wilde*, 188.

9. Louise Bernikow, *Among Women* (New York: Harmony, 1980), 127.

10. Jeffrey Meyers, *Katherine Mansfield: A Biography* (New York: New Directions, 1980 [1978]), 25.

11. J. K. Johnstone, *The Bloomsbury Group* (London: Secker and Warburg, 1954), 356.

12. E. M. Forster, *Two Cheers for Democracy* (Harmondsworth: Penguin, 1965 [1951]), 96.

13. Julian Thoby Stephen, "Euphrosyne," *Cambridge Review*, October 19, 1905, 27, quoted in S. P. Rosenbaum, "The First Book of Bloomsbury," *Twentieth Century Literature* (1984), 30:399.

14. *The Jessamy Brides: The Friendship of Virginia Woolf and V. Sackville-West* (University Park: Pennsylvania State University Press, 1973). The desire to read the relationship as inflected by Woolf's supposed infantile desire for a mother substitute unfortunately remains strong, especially in the writings of psychoanalytic critics.

15. Sherron E. Knopp, " 'If I Saw You Would You Kiss Me?': Sapphism and the Subversiveness of Virginia Woolf's *Orlando* ," *PMLA* (1988), 24–34.

16. Madeline Moore, *The Short Season Between Two Silences: The Mystical and the Political in the Novels of Virginia Woolf* (Boston: George Allen and Unwin, 1984), 95.

17. *Vita and Virginia: The Work and Friendship of V. Sackville-West and Virginia Woolf* (Oxford: Clarendon, 1993), 34.

18. Virginia Woolf, "Professions for Women," in Leonard Woolf, ed., *Collected Essays* (London: Hogarth, 1966), 2:288.

19. Kari Elise Lokke, "*Orlando* and Incandescence: Virginia Woolf's Comic Sublime," *Modern Fiction Studies* (1992), 38:235–52, is one of the few critics to notice this omission. Accepting the "male sublime versus female beautiful" version of Romantic poetics that I have contested in chapter 3, she reads *Orlando* as creating a comic sublime. Although, in a footnote, she agrees with Knopp that *Orlando* is "a lesbian novel," this perception is not woven into her reading of it.

20. Theophile Gautier, *Mademoiselle de Maupin* (1836), trans. Joanna Richardson (Harmondsworth: Penguin, 1981), 216.

21. See Emily Jensen, "Clarissa Dalloway's Respectable Suicide" in Jane Marcus, ed., *Virginia Woolf: A Feminist Slant* (Lincoln: University of Nebraska Press, 1984), 162–79.

22. Virginia Woolf, May 12, 1923, *The Diary of Virginia Woolf*, ed. Anne Olivier Bell (London: Hogarth, 1977–82), 2:243.

23. Woolf, December 21, 1925, *The Diary*, 3:52.

24. G. E. Moore, *Principia Ethica* (Cambridge: Cambridge University Press, 1922 [1903]), 203.

25. Virginia Woolf, to Ethel Smyth, December 11, 1932, *The Letters of Virginia Woolf*, ed. Nigel Nicolson and Joanne Trautmann, 6 vols. (London: Hogarth, 1975–80), 5:135.

26. Woolf, to Clive Bell, January 23, 1924, ibid., 3:85.

27. Woolf, to Molly MacCarthy, October 2, 1924, ibid., 3:135.

28. Woolf, to Jacques Raverat, December 26, 1924, ibid., 3:150.

29. Woolf, June 30, 1927, *The Diary*, 3:142. For an analysis of the homoeroticism in the work of eminent Victorian painter Lord Frederick Leighton and of his own homoerotic relationships, see Emmanuel Cooper, *The Sexual Perspective: Homosexuality and Art in the Last 100 Years in the West* (London: Routledge, 1986), 25–28. Leighton's painting of Sappho, entitled "The Tragic Poetess," shows her as a majestic middle-aged figure sitting alone in a chair by the sea, her lyre beside her.

30. Oscar Wilde, *The Complete Works of Oscar Wilde*, introd. Vyvyan Holland (London: Collins, 1948), 19.

31. Woolf, October 13, 1927, *Letters*, 3:431. "Campbell" was Vita's new lover, Mary Campbell.

32. Woolf, October 9, 1927, *Letters*, 3:428–29.

33. Virginia Woolf, *Orlando* (London: Granada, 1977 [1928]), 180.

34. "The Soul of Man Under Socialism," *Complete Works* 1103–04.

35. The ease with which Sally Potter's film version of *Orlando* was able to "straighten" out its content, visibilizing heterosexuality and glossing over lesbianism, suggests this. It would be near impossible to similarly distort *Maurice* or *The Well*.

36. "Theories of Homosexuality as Sources of Bloomsbury's Androgyny," *Signs* (1979), 5:245.

37. In Stephen Coote, ed., *The Penguin Book of Homosexual Verse* (Harmondsworth: Penguin, 1983), 262. Coote also includes the same passage from *The Land* that is quoted in *Orlando*. See pp. 304–5.

38. The smuggling act is repeated by Woolf, who presents photographs of the aristocrat Vita, clad in shabby tweed skirts, surrounded by dogs in her garden, a nature-loving, eccentric, but respectable English writer. One may contrast the cross-dressed photographs of Radclyffe Hall, the defiantly "different" images of lesbians in Romaine Brooks's portraits, or the pictures of Wilde and Solomon in Eastern dress.

39. "Fritillaries," excerpted from *The Land*, in V. Sackville-West, *Selected Poems* (London: Hogarth, 1941), 59–60.

40. Karen R. Lawrence, "Orlando's Voyage Out," *Modern Fiction Studies* (1992), 38:253–75, shows that Orlando's running from the gipsies back to England may be in part a domesticating gesture; in her consideration of the orientalization of desire, she omits the significance of the Egyptian references in Vita's poem.

41. For Woolf's reading of Shelley as risk-taking outsider, see her essay "Not One of Us," *Collected Essays by Virginia Woolf* (London: Hogarth, 1967), 4:20–26.

42. Mark Hussey, "Refractions of Desire; The Early Fiction of Virginia and Leonard Woolf," *Modern Fiction Studies* (1992), 38:127–46, offers a brilliant reading of Sapphic attraction and resistance to heterosexual marriage in Woolf's first two novels; quoting Vanessa's letters, where she calls the young Virginia a "Sapphist" in danger of contracting marriage to a lady, Hussey demonstrates that Virginia accepted Leonard's proposal, although troubled by her lack of feeling for him and "checked her homo-eroticism by entering a heterosexual relationship" (144).

43. September 16, 1929, Louise A. DeSalvo and Mitchell Leaska, eds., *The Letters of Vita Sackville-West to Virginia Woolf* (New York: Quill, 1984), 350.

44. Woolf, November 17, 1931, *The Diary*, 4:54.

45. Sackville-West, *The Letters of Vita Sackville-West*, 444n.

46. Woolf, March 11, 1935, *The Diary*, 4:287.

47. Woolf, January 24, 1933, *The Letters*, 5:152.

48. Woolf, November 19, 1926, ibid., 5:302.

49. *The Romantic Genesis of the Modern Novel* (Pittsburgh: University of Pittsburgh Press, 1979), 225.

50. Woolf, January 18, 1932, *The Letters*, 5:7.

51. Woolf, January 20, 1931, *The Diary*, 4:6.

52. Virginia Woolf, *The Waves* (London: Granada, 1977 [1931]), 12.

53. Michael Holroyd, ed., *Lytton Strachey by Himself: A Self-Portrait* (London: Heinemann, 1971), 82.

54. After Sybil's death, Dorian, defending himself to Basil, also echoes this sonnet: "Don't leave me, Basil, and don't quarrel with me. I am what I am" (91).

55. Woolf, footnote quoting letter to Virginia Woolf, October 23, 1931, *The Letters*, 4:395.

56. Schlack, *Continuing Presences: Virginia Woolf's Use of Literary Allusion* (University Park: Pennsylvania State University Press, 1979), 107, 118. Schlack dismisses Rhoda in passing as a "failure" with Shelleyan "longings" (110). She is much more sympathetic in her exegesis of Clarissa Dalloway's and Septimus Smith's repressed homoerotic inclinations; clearly, it is Neville's open avowal and enactment of his, which offends.

57. Woolf, February 18, 1927, *The Letters*, 3:332. For the significance of the color purple in gay culture, see Judy Grahn, *Another Mother Tongue: Gay Words, Gay Worlds* (Boston: Beacon, 1990 [1984]), 3–17.

58. This poem is addressed by an ungendered "I" to an ungendered "you," is built around images associated with Sapphic love: dream, stars, stream, flower, window, nightingale—and is pervaded by the epithet "sweet."

59. Carolyn G. Heilbrun, "Introduction," *Mrs. Stevens Hears the Mermaids Singing* (New York: Norton, 1975 [1965]), xviii.

60. Virginia Woolf, *Mrs. Dalloway* (London: Granada, 1976 [1925]), 277–78.

61. Both the *Ramayana* and the *Mahabharata* close with the leading figures consciously renouncing life and choosing to end it. In the case of Sita her return to the earth from which she was born is a protest against her husband's injustice; in the case of the Pandavas and Draupadi, and the elders in both texts, retreat into the forest and voluntary death is undertaken merely from a sense that this is the appropriate way to end life.

9. Dogs, Phoenixes, and Other Beasts: Nonhuman Creatures in Homoerotic Texts

1. May Sarton, *Mrs. Stevens Hears the Mermaids Singing* (New York: Norton, 1965), conflates the idea of the artist and the lesbian when she writes of "we women who have chosen to be something more and something less than women" (156), explicitly arguing, without citing Plato, that art takes the place of the child for such women.

2. Virginia Woolf, July 23, 1927, *The Letters of Virginia Woolf*, ed. Nigel Nicolson and Joanne Trautmann, 6 vols. (London: Hogarth, 1975–80), 3:401.

3. Keith Thomas, *Man and the Natural World: A History of the Modern Sensibility* (New York: Pantheon, 1983).

4. See Raymond Schwab, *The Oriental Renaissance: Europe's Rediscovery of India and the East, 1680–1880* (1950; Eng. trans. New York: Columbia University Press, 1984); and John Drew, *India and the Romantic Imagination* (Delhi: Oxford University Press, 1987).

5. William Wordsworth, "Hart-Leap Well," *The Poetical Works of William Wordsworth*, ed. Thomas Hutchinson (London: Henry Froude, 1906), 203.

6. William Cowper, "The Task," *The Poetical Works of William Cowper*, ed. J. M. Ross (Edinburgh, n.d.), 138.

7. Percy Bysshe Shelley, "The Daemon of the World," in *The Poetical Works of Shelley*, ed. Newell F. Ford (Boston: Houghton Mifflin, 1975), 432. See my essay "Lamb Unslain: Shelley's Demystification of Animal Symbolism," *Yearly Review* (1992), 6:13–24.

8. Nineteenth-century supporters of women's rights generally supported anti-vivisection and anticruelty to animals movements; British supporters of the Gandhi-led anticolonial movement were often also vegetarians and feminists. An example is Henry Salt, friend of Edward Carpenter and of M. K. Gandhi. Married to a lesbian, he was a socialist, active in the vegetarian society, and was one of the earliest critics to read Shelley as a poet of ideas, stressing his politics over his life history. See Henry S. Salt, *Shelley's Principles: Has Time Refuted or Confirmed Them?* (London, n.d.).

9. Michael Field, *Dedicated: An Early Work of Michael Field* (London: George Bell, 1914), 47.

10. Woolf, March 20, 1929, *The Letters*, 4:34. Woolf's awareness of what two women "must not do" was sharpened at this moment by the 1928 publication of *The Well of Loneliness* and its subsequent prosecution.

11. Woolf, July 2, 1935, ibid., 5:409.

12. Woolf, July 31, 1932, ibid., 5:83.

13. Woolf, October 10, 1919, ibid., 2:394.

14. Lytton Strachey, *Ermyntrude and Esmeralda*, introd. Michael Holroyd (New York: Stein and Day, 1969).

15. Woolf, June 2, 1935, *The Letters*, 5:396.

16. Virginia Woolf, "Gipsy, the Mongrel," in *The Complete Shorter Fiction of Virginia Woolf*, ed. Susan Dick (London: Hogarth, 1985), 274. Note, once again, the association of unconventional eroticism with the "Egyptian" (from which the word *gypsy* derives).

17. Woolf, March 23, 1927, *The Letters*, 3:352.

18. Woolf, April 13, 1926, ibid., 3:253.

19. Woolf, November 1925, ibid., 3:220.

20. Woolf, May 22, 1927, ibid., 3:382.

21. Woolf, July? 1908, *The Letters*, 1:338.

22. Woolf, January 1, 1907, ibid., 1:276. Since Virginia had been in love with both Violet and Kitty, part of the joke is that her threatened lecture will make them fall into each other's arms.

23. Woolf, ibid., 6:492–93. One reason for its neglect may be the lingering taboo on homosexual incestuous feeling that Richard Hall points out in "Henry James: Interpreting an Obsessive Memory" in Stuart Kellogg, ed., *Essays on Gay Literature* (New York: Harrington Park, 1985), 83–98.

24. Jane Austen, *Catharine and Other Writings*, ed. Margaret Anne Doody and Douglas Murray (Oxford: Oxford University Press, 1993), 41.

25. Woolf, August 14, 1908, *The Letters*, 1:355.

26. Woolf, December 19, 1935, ibid., 5:160–61.

27. Woolf, June 20, 1928, *The Diary*, 3:186.

28. Woolf, ibid., 4:28.

29. Virginia Woolf, February 16, 1930, *The Diary of Virginia Woolf*, ed. Anne Olivier Bell (London: Hogarth, 1977–82), 3:287.

30. This possibility was first suggested in passing by M. C. Bradbrook, "Getting Gloomsbury's Goat," a review of *The Letters of Vita Sackville-West to Virginia Woolf* in the *Guardian*, November 8, 1984, and followed up in slightly more detail by Françoise Defromont, *Virginia Woolf: Vers la maison de lumiere* (Paris: Des Femmes, 1985).

31. Virginia Woolf, *Flush* (Harmondsworth: Penguin, 1977 [1933]), 20.

32. Vita Sackville-West, September 21, 1937, in Louise A. DeSalvo and Mitchell Leaska, eds., *The Letters of Vita Sackville-West to Virginia Woolf* (New York: Quill, 1985), 402.

33. Nigel Nicolson, *Portrait of a Marriage* (New York: Bantam, 1974 [1973]), 222.

34. Woolf, November 6, 1930, *The Letters*, 4:248; February 16, 1927, ibid., 3:331.

35. Woolf, January 9, 1926, ibid., 3:228.

36. Sackville-West, January 21, 1926, *The Letters of Vita Sackville-West*, 89.

37. Woolf, January 31, 1926, *The Letters*, 3:237.

38. Virginia Woolf, *A Haunted House and Other Short Stories* (London: Granada, 1982 [1944]), 109.

39. Woolf, November 22, 1933, *The Letters*, 5:251.

40. Woolf, ibid., 3:468.

41. Woolf, February 2, 1927, ibid., 3:321.

42. Woolf, April 13, 1934, ibid., 5:291.

43. Woolf, ibid., 4:362.

44. Woolf, August 4, 1931, ibid., 4:365.

45. Woolf, May 8, 1932, *The Letters*, 5:61. In a brief notice in the *Nation and Athenaeum*, February 6, 1926, of Elizabeth Villiers's *Queen Alexandra the Well-Beloved*, Woolf describes the queen as "exquisitely pretty" and "completely dumb" and notes that the book tells the reader little about her. The queen's Victorian "reserve" suggests that "perhaps her most valuable contribution to her age was that she raised the standard of comfort for dogs." Virginia Woolf, *The Essays of Virginia Woolf*, ed. Andrew McNeillie (London: Hogarth, 1994), 4:336–37. Woolf underestimated Alexandra, whose patronage had revived Miss Buss's schools for poor girls at a time of severe financial crisis in 1871. See Josephine Kamm, *How Different from Us: Miss Buss and Miss Beale* (London: Bodley Head, 1958), 109–10.

46. Richard Ellmann, *Oscar Wilde* (London: Penguin, 1987), 253–54.

47. Virginia Woolf, *Mrs. Dalloway* (London: Granada, 1976 [1925]), 61–62.

48. There may be an echo of Housman's bitter critique of compulsory heterosexuality in Victorian England: "The laws of God, the laws of man / They may keep who will and can."

49. Vita Sackville-West, *Seducers in Ecuador* (London: Hogarth, 1924), 9–10.

50. Vita Sackville-West, *Heritage* (London: W. Collins, 1919), 21.

51. Vita Sackville-West, *The Garden* (London: Michael Joseph, 1946), 24.

52. Nicolson, *Portrait of a Marriage*, 221–22.

53. For a recent parallel to the rivalry between a male lover and an animal for a woman's affections, see Vikram Seth, *The Golden Gate* (Delhi: Oxford University Press, 1986), where the heroine's cat's determined efforts to worst her male lover actually pay off. Elizabeth Dorati's cat Charlemagne (whose impressive ancestry is narrated, like Flush's, in heroic vein) "conceals an ever-green-tongued flame / Of jealousy" for her lover, John, and proceeds to plague him in various ways. Liz resists John's demand that she get rid of Charlemagne. This makes him feel she loves the cat more than him. The conflict begins their drift apart, which ends in a split.

54. Woolf, "Geraldine and Jane," in Leonard Woolf, ed., *Collected Essays by Virginia Woolf*, 4 vols. (London: Hogarth, 1967), 4:36.

55. Woolf, April 15, 1933, *The Letters*, 5:177.

56. Woolf, *The Diary*, 4:287.

57. Michael Field, *Whym Chow: Flame of Love* (London: Eragny, 1914), 14, 20, 21.

58. Katherine Mansfield, *The Scrapbook of Katherine Mansfield*, ed. J. Middleton Murry (London: Constable, 1939), 121–22.

59. In an untitled poem beginning "The greater cats with golden eyes / Stare out between the bars" (a poem Yeats praised), Sackville-West contrasts the unthinking passion of the cats with human love aware of its own mortality and transience. The poem ends with a desire for catlike fidelity: "as the Polar star in me / Is fixed my constant heart on thee. / Ah, may I stay forever blind / With lions, tigers, leopards, and their kind." Vita Sackville-West, *Selected Poems* (London: Hogarth, 1941), 50–51.

60. Perhaps they were more familiar with the use of the image in their social circle—compare Wilde's reference to his dinners with young men of the underworld as "feasting with panthers" and Pater's description of his pupils at Oxford as "like playful young tigers, that have been fed"! Linda Dowling, *Hellenism and Homosexuality in Victorian Oxford* (Ithaca: Cornell University Press, 1993), 101.

61. Michael Field, *A Selection from the Poems of Michael Field*, ed T. Sturge Moore (London: Poetry Bookshop, 1923), 47.

62. Again, Firbank's parodies provide a clue. In his *Concerning the Eccentricities of Cardinal Pirelli* (1926), in *The Complete Ronald Firbank*, preface by Anthony Powell (London: Gerald Duckworth, 1961), a homosexual Catholic cardinal presides over the baptism of a duquesa's beloved male dog, the adoption of a female dog by a lesbian community in a women's college, and a funeral mass for the duquesa's female spaniel. Dogs here are transparent symbols for homoerotically inclined people seeking refuge in the Catholic church.

63. Radclyffe Hall, *The Well of Loneliness* (London: Virago, 1982 [1928]), 56.

64. Woolf, *The Letters*, 3:556. See Jane Marcus's brilliant reading of *A Room of One's Own* as in dialogue with *The Well*: "Sapphistory: The Woolf and the Well," in Karla Jay and Joanne Glasgow, eds., *Lesbian Texts and Contexts: Radical Revisions* (New York: New York University Press, 1990), 164–79.

65. Vita Sackville-West, *The Easter Party* (London: Michael Joseph, 1953), 166.

66. See Victoria Glendinning, *Vita: The Life of V. Sackville-West* (New York: Knopf, 1983), 328.

67. J. R. Ackerley, July 15, 1954, in Neville Braybrooke, ed., *The Letters of J. R. Ackerley* (London: Gerald Duckworth, 1975), 102.

68. I read these poets as inheritors of the literary traditions embedded in the language they write. The recent tendency to classify writers by nationality, or as "third world" or "postcolonial," leads to what I consider racist placements; thus Namjoshi's and Seth's writings, along with English literary criticism published in South Asia, are classified in the South Asian rather than the English literature sections of many U.S. libraries. The result is that most American students of English literature have never heard of these excellent poets. Conversely, and contradictorily, American writers' texts on South Asia are classified by subject, not by writer's nationality, that is, in the South Asian, not the American studies, section.

69. Suniti Namjoshi, preface to "The Jackass and the Lady," *Because of India: Selected Poems and Fables* (London: Onlywomen, 1989), 29.

70. Suniti Namjoshi, *The Blue Donkey Fables* (New Delhi: Penguin, 1989), 70.

71. Suniti Namjoshi, *Saint Suniti and the Dragon and Other Fables* (London: Virago, 1994), 86.

72. Namjoshi, *The Blue Donkey Fables*, 33–35.

73. Vikram Seth, *Beastly Tales from Here and There* (New Delhi: Penguin India, 1991).

74. Namjoshi, *The Blue Donkey Fables*, 62.

75. Carol Falvo Heffernan, *The Phoenix and the Fountain: Images of Woman and Eternity in Lactantius's Carmen de Ave Phoenice an Old English Phoenix* (Newark: University of Delaware Press, 1988), 111.

76. Ibid., 107.

77. It occurred in hostile narratives too, as in Robert Holloway's pamphlet *The Phoenix of Sodom or the Vere Street Coterie* (London, 1813).

78. William Shakespeare, *The Riverside Shakespeare*, ed. G. Blakemore Evans (Boston: Houghton Mifflin, 1974), 1797–98.

79. Oscar Wilde, *The Complete Works of Oscar Wilde*, introd. Vyvyan Holland (London: Collins, 1948), 776.

80. Ibid., 857.

Index

Between Men ~ Between Women
Lesbian and Gay Studies
Lillian Faderman and Larry Gross, Editors

Edward Alwood, *Straight News: Gays, Lesbians, and the News Media*
Corinne E. Blackmer and Patricia Juliana Smith, editors, *En Travesti: Women, Gender Subversion, Opera*
Alan Bray, *Homosexuality in Renaissance England*
Joseph Bristow, *Effeminate England: Homoerotic Writing After 1885*
Claudia Card, *Lesbian Choices*
Joseph Carrier, *De Los Otros: Intimacy and Homosexuality Among Mexican Men*
John Clum, *Acting Gay: Male Homosexuality in Modern Drama*
Gary David Comstock, *Violence Against Lesbians and Gay Men*
Laura Doan, editor, *The Lesbian Postmodern*
Allen Ellenzweig, *The Homoerotic Photograph: Male Images from Durieu/Delacroix to Mapplethorpe*
Lillian Faderman, *Odd Girls and Twilight Lovers: A History of Lesbian Life in Twentieth-Century America*
Linda D. Garnets and Douglas C. Kimmel, editors, *Psychological Perspectives on Lesbian and Gay Male Experiences*
Richard D. Mohr, *Gays/Justice: A Study of Ethics, Society, and Law*
Sally Munt, editor, *New Lesbian Criticism: Literary and Cultural Readings*
Timothy F. Murphy and Suzanne Poirier, editors, *Writing AIDS: Gay Literature, Language, and Analysis*
Noreen O'Connor and Joanna Ryan, *Wild Desires and Mistaken Identities: Lesbianism and Psychoanalysis*
Don Paulson with Roger Simpson, *An Evening in the Garden of Allah: A Gay Cabaret in Seattle*
Judith Roof, *Come As You Are: Sexuality and Narrative*
Judith Roof, *A Lure of Knowledge: Lesbian Sexuality and Theory*
Claudia Schoppmann, *Days of Masquerade: Life Stories of Lesbians During the Third Reich*
Alan Sinfield, *The Wilde Century: Effeminacy, Oscar Wilde, and the Queer Moment*
Chris Straayer, *Deviant Eyes, Deviant Bodies: Sexual Re-Orientations in Film and Video*
Kath Weston, *Families We Choose: Lesbians, Gays, Kinship*
Carter Wilson, *Hidden in the Blood: A Personal Investigation of AIDS in the Yucatán*

Designer: Euangkham Chuaviriya
Text: Weiss
Compositor: Columbia University Press
Printer: BookCrafters
Binder: BookCrafters